Population –
the complex reality

Population –
the complex reality

A report of the Population Summit
of the world's scientific academies

Edited by Sir Francis Graham-Smith, F.R.S.

North American Press
a division of Fulcrum Publishing

British Library Cataloguing in Publication Data

A CIP catalogue record for this book is available from the British Library.
ISBN 0-85403-484-6 (U.K.)

Library of Congress Cataloging-in-Publication Data

Population Summit (1993: New Delhi, India)
    Population, the complex reality: a report of the Population Summit of the world's scientific academies.
           p.   cm.
    Includes index.
    ISBN 1-55591-926-X (U.S.)
    I. Population—Congresses.   2. Population forecasting—Congresses.   3. Population—Environmental aspects—Congresses.   I. Title.
    HB849.P688   1993
    304.6—dc20   94-14992
                                                                            CIP

Typeset in 10pt on 12½pt New Baskerville
Printed in the United Kingdom by the University Press, Cambridge

10 9 8 7 6 5 4 3 2 1

Published outside North and South America by The Royal Society, 6 Carlton House Terrace, London SW1Y 5AG, UK

Published in North and South America by North American Press (a division of Fulcrum Publishing), 350 Indiana Street, Suite 350, Golden, Colorado 80401-5093, USA

Contents

SESSION 1: THE COMPLEX REALITY

SESSION 2: LINKAGES BETWEEN POPULATION, NATURAL RESOURCES AND THE ENVIRONMENT

SESSION 3: DEMOGRAPHIC TRANSITION IN A GENDER PERSPECTIVE

SESSION 4: FAMILY PLANNING AND REPRODUCTIVE HEALTH

SESSION 5: THE FUTURE

List of principal contributors

Ms Srilatha Batliwala
DAWN (Development Alternatives
    with Women for a New Era)
India

Professor Sir Hermann Bondi
Churchill College
Cambridge

Dr M. Buvinić
International Center for Research
    on Women
U.S.A.

Professor Michael J. Chadwick
Stockholm Environment Institute
Sweden

Professor John Cleland
London School of Hygiene and
    Tropical Medicine
U.K.

Professor Partha Dasgupta
University of Cambridge
U.K.

Dr Soledad Díaz
Instituto Chileno de Medicina
    Reproductiva
Chile

Professor Malin Falkenmark
Swedish Natural Science Research
    Council
Sweden

Professor Mahmoud F. Fathalla
The Rockefeller Foundation
Egypt

Dr Kerstin Hagenfeldt
Department of Obstetrics and
    Gynaecology
Karolinska Hospital
Sweden

Dr Nathan Keyfitz
International Institute for
    Applied Systems Analysis
Austria

Professor Dr Lydia Makhubu
University of Swaziland
Swaziland

Dr Jane Menken
Population Studies Center
University of Pennsylvania
U.S.A.

Dr Norman Myers
Consultant in Environment and
    Development
U.K.

Professor H.W.O. Okoth-Ogendo
Centre for African Family Studies
Kenya

Dr Samuel H. Preston
Population Studies Center
University of Pennsylvania
U.S.A.

Dr Zhao Quiguo
Institute of Soil Science
China

Professor V. Ramalingaswami
All India Institute of Medical Sciences
India

Dr Nafis Sadik
United Nations Population Fund

Dr Fred Sai
International Planned Parenthood
    Federation
Ghana

Professor Gita Sen
Institute of Management
India

Professor Roger V. Short
Monash University
Australia

Professor K. Srinivasan
Population Center
University of North Carolina
U.S.A.

Professor G.P. Talwar
National Institute of Immunology
India

Sir Crispin Tickell
Green College Oxford
U.K.

Acknowledgements

The co-sponsoring academies thank the Indian National Science Academy for its help in hosting the Summit and wish to acknowledge the generous donations from the following organizations which made the Summit possible:

Cookson Group plc
Ford Foundation
Henry Moore Foundation
Hungarian Academy of Sciences
MacArthur Foundation
Mitchell Energy and Development Corporation
Packard Foundation
Rockefeller Foundation
Royal Netherlands Academy of Arts and Sciences ·
RTZ Limited
Shell International Petroleum Company Limited
Swedish International Development Authority
The Wellcome Trust

'The Family Group' sculpture reproduced on the cover of this book is by kind permission of the Henry Moore Foundation. © Henry Moore Foundation.

Introduction
by Sir Francis Graham-Smith, Physical Secretary, The Royal Society

The New Delhi Summit was convened to explore the complex and interrelated issues of population growth, resource consumption, socioeconomic development, and environmental protection. The 25 papers presented at the Summit and published in this volume were grouped under the headings of The Complex Reality; Linkages between Population, Natural Resources and the Environment; Demographic Transition in a Gender Perspective; Family Planning and Reproductive Health; and The Future. The Joint Statement, which was formally agreed at the Summit, had already been circulated to academies worldwide, and the final text reproduced in the volume is the product of numerous edited comments. Most academies endorsed without reservation: the statement by the French Académie des Sciences (p. 385) well represents these responses. A common theme of the supporting remarks was the fact that the Statement originated from a broad range of scholarly, scientific organizations, and in no way reflected any particular social, religious, humanitarian or political viewpoint.

Many academies, while endorsing the text, indicated that in their view there were aspects that might have received more emphasis. In particular, these included greater international assistance in development programmes; geographical imbalances in populations including underpopulation of certain areas, migration, urbanization; the impact of AIDS; problems posed by rapidly ageing populations and the need for healthcare and insurance provisions; food production and distribution; the socio-ethical questions raised by family planning; the need for different mixtures of family planning policies for different areas; technology transfer; and the relation between education and economic development. Many more points were raised and were incorporated into the Summit Statement with due regard for consistency, brevity and impact. Inevitably the final document could not hope to do justice to all the issues that individual academies felt were important. However, we believe that the consensus represented is the pre-eminent achievement of this Statement. A list of those academies that sent in written comments is given on p. 393.

There were, none the less, some academies which, while acknowledging the importance of the subject, felt that such international issues were outside their competence, and declined the invitation to sign. Two others, the Pontifical Academy of Sciences and the African Academy of Sciences, submitted their own statements which are reproduced on pages 387 and 391 respectively.

The 25 papers published here reflect a truly multifaceted and complex situation, in which the only common theme is the pressure of a rapidly increasing world population. It is all the more remarkable that no fewer than 60 of the world's academies have joined in signing the Statement, which is set out in full on p. 377.

A summary of the Statement follows on p. 17. This is followed by the papers, and the full Statement, with the comments by the French Académie des Sciences and the statements by the Pontifical Academy of Sciences and the African Academy of Sciences.

1

Message
from P. V. Narasimha Rao, the Indian Prime Minister

India is privileged to play host to the Population Summit of the World's Scientific Academies in New Delhi this week. It is entirely fitting that this meeting begins on United Nations Day, which is enshrined in the calendar of man as a recognition of his resolve to address global challenges and issues in global partnership and harmony. The extraordinarily wide spectrum of issues related to population has stimulated the minds, energies and efforts of governments and peoples for several years now. There is a collective recognition of the truth that the right to a life of quality and fulfilment is one that it is within our means and responsibility to ensure to those who shall inherit the planet we tenant. The particular contribution of the scientific community in this regard is vital because it is through innovation and discovery that the task of persuasion and education is lightened and made more direct and purposeful. To all the distinguished participants gathered here this week, I extend warm greetings and my sense of assurance that your deliberations will invigorate still further the sense of mission with which your calling is so intimately imbued.

Welcome
by Sir Michael Atiyah, President, The Royal Society of London

On behalf of the sponsoring academies, I welcome you all to this Population Summit of Scientific Academies. We are delighted that so many of you from all parts of the world have agreed to attend. It is an indication of the unique nature of this meeting and the importance of the topic we are addressing. Never before have the scientific academies of the world met collectively on such a scale for such a purpose. We are now used to political, economic or financial summits, organized by governmental or international bodies, but a summit of scientists is a novelty.

The reason for taking this step is the increasing recognition that scientists have, because of their expertise, a duty and responsibility to inform and advise people and governments. Most of the problems we face are ultimately consequences of the progress of science, so we must acknowledge a collective responsibility. Fortunately, science also opens up possibilities of alleviating our problems, and we must see that these are pursued.

In all this scientists have a dual role. We must pursue scientific investigation and research which will increase our understanding and provide us with new tools. Equally, we have to encourage the application of present day knowledge, incomplete though it may be, to tackle contemporary problems. We cannot postpone action on grounds of ignorance. Understanding and action have to develop hand in hand.

A meeting of scientists has several advantages over a meeting of political leaders. First, at a technical level, we are better acquainted with the scientific issues: after all, that is our job. Second, we are free of political pressures and the need to consider extraneous factors (money, influence, competition). For these reasons I hope this meeting will be relatively smooth, objective and not too controversial, enabling us to overcome cultural and national differences.

Of course, the reason that we scientists, unlike the politicians, can be so amicable is that we have no direct power. All we can do is to provide information, argue our case and try to influence events. Our hope is that, acting collectively, we have more chance of being heard.

We all know that the population problem is intimately linked with environmental problems and with the rate of economic development. At the Earth Summit in Rio in 1992 the main focus was on the environment, and this was an important first step for the world community. Many of us feel, however, that, for various reasons, population was inadequately dealt with. The number of people on this planet, now and in the future, will have a fundamental effect on everything else.

One purpose of this meeting is therefore to bring population problems back into the limelight by showing the importance attached to it by the world scientific community. We hope to exchange views and experience from a wide variety of countries, to stimulate further thought and to encourage action. One thing should I feel be emphasized. Although the growth of world population poses daunting problems, they are not insuperable. Experience in different countries shows that dramatic improvements can be achieved, provided the will and resources are there. The message that we should be sending out therefore is not one of unmitigated gloom or despondency. Rather, it should be one of restrained hope; not, of course, to be confused with complacency. The problems are serious, and urgent action is needed.

This brings us back to the arena of political decision, where scientific knowledge and advice will be confronted by social and financial realities. In particular, the views and conclusions of our meeting here must be presented to the International Conference on Population and Development in Cairo next year. We are not here just out of academic curiosity. We hope that our collective views will influence subsequent action and for this we will have to work through political and governmental channels. I am very glad that Dr Nafis Sadik is here with us and I am sure she will have more to say in this direction.

Finally, let me thank all those who have assisted in the preparation of this meeting. First of all, Professor Tandon, I would like to thank the Indian National Science Academy for having invited us to hold the meeting here in New Delhi. It is appropriate that we should be holding this conference in a part of the world where population growth is still of major concern. But there are other reasons why India is a suitable host. Your first Prime Minister Jawaharlal Nehru was a trained scientist and a firm believer that science had to be put to the benefit of society. He encouraged science in this country and would, I am sure, have strongly approved of this meeting being held in Delhi.

We are very grateful for the interest and support of the Indian Government, evidenced by the presence for this opening of the Minister for Science and Technology, and the kind invitation which the President of India has extended to the conference participants tomorrow.

On the organizational side, much hard work has been done by the staff and Officers of several of our academies, and we are grateful to all our speakers who are presenting papers at the conference. Financial assistance has been provided from many sources but I should express our particular thanks for major donations from the Ford Foundation, the MacArthur Foundation, the Packard Foundation, the Rockefeller Foundation, Shell International Petroleum Company Limited, the Swedish International Development Authority and The Wellcome Trust.

Tomorrow we start our real business. I hope you will find the presentations informative and that you will take an active part in the discussions. It is important that we get the views from all parts of the world. After the science summit is over I hope that we can continue to get our message across, both through international meetings such as the Cairo conference and also, at the national level, through more direct channels. We all have a part to play.

Welcome
by Dr Nafis Sadik

CURRENT AND PROJECTED SITUATION

The exercise of free and informed choice in the size and spacing of the family is a human right; but it is also a demographic necessity. The latest United Nations projections indicate a world population of 8.5 billion by the year 2025 and 10 billion by 2050. Annual additions to world population in the next decade will average 93 million, the highest in history. Around 90% of this growth is concentrated in the developing world and this percentage is edging ever upwards. Over half of all growth will be in Africa and South Asia alone.

These projections represent an optimistic scenario, based on continued increases in contraceptive growth. Growth could readily be much higher, reaching 12.5 billion in the year 2050, and 28 billion a century later. The difference between the medium and the high projection in 2050 is 2.5 billion—equal to the whole of the world's population in 1950.

After the year 2000, the high and medium projections diverge more and more sharply. That means we must act now. Fertility must fall in this decade, if growth rates are to fall in the decade following.

Besides the great concern with population growth that all of us share, there are other demographic changes under way which should also merit our attention.

One of these is migration. Each year around the developing world, tens of millions of rural people gravitate towards urban areas. Latin America is already as urbanized as the developed world, at least in the demographic sense, and by the year 2015 the developing countries as a whole will be more than 50% urban, their cities being home to a projected 3.1 billion people. Compared with their present population of around 1.5 billion, urban expansion is exploding and far outpacing the ability to provide the needed physical and social infrastructure.

The differentials between incomes in North and South and the long-term problems of development and environmental degradation in developing countries are also contributing to a massive build-up of pressure to migrate across national borders.

The greatest pressures will not necessarily come from the poorest countries, or those with the most rapid population growth. Emigration appeals to the energetic and the educated, and to those with some marketable skills. There are, nevertheless, disturbing trends which indicate that demographic 'push factors' may be playing a growing role in fuelling population movements.

Another aspect of the current situation that must be highlighted is the link between population and poverty. The highest rates of population growth are among poor people and poor countries. The means of slowing rapid population growth – education, health and family planning services – are best delivered as part of a total anti-poverty programme. Poverty and population problems are linked so closely that their solutions must also go hand in hand.

The common belief that family planning programmes will not work in poor communities is completely wrong.

The evidence is that where service quality is good, poor families – especially women – will take advantage of family planning programmes. But the quality of services for the poor is usually not good, if it exists at all.

Another linkage much discussed since the Rio Conference is that between population and the environment. Yet, despite considerable work over the past few years, the precise nature of the relationship is still elusive. The poor are sometimes unfairly blamed for a large share of environmental damage. Because the poorest groups have by definition least access to resources, they have individually the least power to damage the environment. However, they have an effect in two main ways: first, because they exploit the commons: wood, water, land and wild species; second, because they exist in such large numbers and concentrations, for example in squatter settlements and on fragile land such as desert fringes or upland areas.

Thus without blaming the poor for their poverty, it is possible to say that poverty and numbers together have a profound and damaging effect on the environment in developing countries.

LESSONS LEARNED

Despite the sobering problems connected to population, some of which I have just highlighted, the lessons we have learned over the past 25 years of experience with population programmes in a wide variety of settings in the developing world should instil us with a sense of cautious optimism rather than unmitigated pessimism. I would like to review with you now some of these lessons.

A major lesson, and one that was not at all obvious at the start of the 1980s, is that population programmes can succeed, sometimes spectacularly, to a large extent independently of the level of socio-economic development. Although balanced development reaching all sectors of society is in the long run the only real kind of development that will endure, lower fertility need not wait for other aspects of development to be in place first. Lower fertility and lower population growth can come first and can even support and facilitate the other aspects of development such as progress in health, education, poverty alleviation and the economy.

Most developing countries have made notable progress in adopting and implementing population policies and programmes. Indeed, several countries have been highly successful in drastically slowing population growth. Examples can be drawn from around the world: Colombia, Fiji, Indonesia, the Republic of Korea, Mauritius, Mexico, Sri Lanka, Thailand and Tunisia. And fertility declines are now evident in many more countries, including Botswana, Cape Verde, Egypt, Bangladesh, Kenya and Zimbabwe.

Overall, the achievements of population programmes in developing countries have been truly impressive. Since the early 1960s, contraceptive use has gone up from around 10% of couples in reproductive ages to more than 50% today. And over the same period, the number of births per woman dropped from over six to 3.7, almost half the fertility of just one generation ago.

Among the ingredients needed for success, political commitment has proved to be the main factor influencing the strength of any population programme. Not only is such commitment essential for the appropriate allocation of resources towards population programmes, but it is also the precondition for change in favour of smaller family-size ideals.

Successful family planning programmes do not start with technology, they start with an idea. The idea is that each individual can make a choice about family size; and that it is a necessary part of everyday life. It must be based on full information about the services available, and counselling if necessary to assist in making it. It must be completely voluntary, not mere acquiescence to the wishes of a service provider. Once the choice is made, there must be adequate provision for follow-up and further counselling if necessary. At all points the client must be treated with respect.

This approach rules out the practice of setting quotas or targets for family planning programmes. Programmes driven by the need to meet targets will inevitably be led to skimp on human contact between provider and acceptor, to take less time with clients, to regard acceptance as the end of the process rather than the beginning.

The choice-based approach also rules out single-method programmes of family planning. Contraceptive needs change with age, family status and parity. Women have different needs from men. To reach the whole population with family planning services means supplying the needs of the whole population.

There is no substitute for this approach. I cannot say too strongly, that if we do not meet the family planning needs of individual women – and men – in what remains of this century, then we have no hope of meeting the world's development needs in the next century.

Abandoning quotas and broadening choice does not imply relaxing commitment to family planning. In fact, a choice-based approach demands more of everyone concerned, if it is to be effective. Such services are more expensive and more difficult to organize, supply, staff and administer than programmes where the options are limited. But in the long run, the investment will be repaid many times over in a population which accepts family planning as the norm, and does not require to be re-motivated in every succeeding generation.

In many societies, women are trapped in a web of tradition that determines their worth solely in terms of their reproductive role. Prevailing cultural patterns prevent women from developing a sense of self esteem, and customary practices make girls second-class citizens within their own households. For too many women, choice and opportunity are largely unknown experiences.

There is no question that the conventional prescriptions for development have not worked, especially for women. A cornerstone of new development thinking is the full integration of women into the mainstream of development and concern for progress in all aspects of their lives — health, education, employment, nutrition, legal and political rights. In traditional development thinking, investment in social development was seen as a luxury, a fruit of economic success. But we now know that the opposite is true: the basis of economic progress is a healthy, socially stable and slow-growing population. Instead of being the fruit of development, social programmes, especially those addressing the status of women, are at its very foundation.

If women are to realize their full potential in their productive and community roles, they must be guaranteed their reproductive rights and must be able to manage their reproductive role. The ability to decide freely and in an informed manner the number and spacing of one's children is the first step in enabling women to exercise choices in other areas. When a woman realizes that she can make decisions regarding her reproductive function, this experience of autonomy spreads to other aspects of her life. It is a first, essential step on the road to empowerment and to making contributions to the real development of her society.

In recent years, quality has emerged as a very important issue in family planning programmes. Empirical evidence shows that improvements in quality encourage acceptance and continuous contraceptive use.

Quality means that services take into account the needs and preferences of users, especially women. Women want clinics that are easily accessible. They want to be treated with respect and dignity in an environment of privacy and confidentiality. They want a wide range of safe, effective and affordable contraceptives. They want information and guidance that will allay their doubts and help them to make an informed choice. And they want a facility with a wide variety of services, so that as many of their needs as possible can be met in one place.

Success in family planning also means redefining many long-held attitudes, especially towards women. Women are at the centre of the development process. If we are to achieve sustainable development they will have to become both the architects and the beneficiaries of policies and programmes.

An important step is increasing investment in education. Education breeds confidence and encourages a woman's belief that she is in control of her life. It is a key factor in family planning acceptance and reducing fertility and infant mortality rates. Educated women can explore their options such as careers before or instead of marriage.

WHAT CAN BE DONE THIS DECADE

These then are some of the most important lessons that we have learned about what works and how to go about implementing population policies. Much can be achieved now, in the six remaining years of this millennium and beyond, to obtain the sort of demographic future that will contribute to the goal of sustained economic growth and sustainable development.

The international community, in 1989, adopted the U.N.'s medium projection as the target for the year 2000. The central requirement for meeting this target is a rise in contraceptive prevalence in developing countries, from 387 million to 567 million couples by the end of the century — a 50% increase over 1990. It means reaching over a billion couples with family planning services in the course of the decade. Even then, contraceptive prevalence will have risen only from 50% to around 60%, but we will be on the right track.

This seems an ambitious target, and it is. But it is well within our power. The first step will be to meet existing demand for family planning. Almost 400 million couples in developing countries do not have access to modern family planning services. A large proportion of them would like to delay or space their pregnancies, or stop having children altogether. At least 120 million would use family planning now if services were available. Reaching only this group of motivated couples would go a long way towards meeting the international target for the year 2000.

Besides increasing family planning services, there are actions aimed at empowering women that should be made a priority: improving health, education and opportunities for work for women; removing customary and legal barriers to women's full participation and equal treatment in the areas of marriage, property ownership and inheritance, politics, religion and the work place; and there are unstated but nevertheless real barriers in the form of different standards in respect of sexual behaviour as between men and women. All of these issues need full and open discussion in the widest possible context.

For adolescents, the immediate agenda must include winning better legal protection for young girls and unmarried women; a great improvement in the reproductive health and counselling services available to young women; the commitment of parents, teachers and community leaders; above all a change in the attitudes and practices of men.

It has always been an article of faith at UNFPA that policies are made by governments for the benefit of their populations, and with the intention of securing their full participation. How should governments respond in population matters? And how should agencies working with developing countries proceed?

In the first place, it is no longer sufficient for a government to draw up population policy only in broad and general terms. To be effective, policies must be sectoralized and adapted to local variations of circumstances and needs. This may imply a greater use of local government and NGO structures, and more involvement with NGOs and the private sector.

Progress in making and carrying out policy has been uneven. Many Asian countries have a record of success. On the other hand, parts of south Asia and some countries like the Philippines are relatively experienced in population programming, but have made little headway. Policy making is now moving at a much faster pace in Latin America and Africa, but both regions show a wide variety of experience and attitude.

We should also be prepared to work more closely with the private sector. As the demand for family planning services grows in the more successful developing countries, the growing private sector can be relied on to provide an increasing share of non-medical services and information.

In striving to meet the demands for policies to adequately deal with the challenges posed by demographic change, efforts are needed to assist governments to be fully aware of the demographic situation in their countries and of the ways in which population interacts with social and economic development. UNFPA, perceived as a neutral party in an area where emotionalism is an only too ready reflex, has always promoted policy dialogue and sought to encourage a better understanding of the need by governments to fully integrate population in all development planning. The ICPD, about which I shall talk more fully in just a moment, is, in a way, another albeit transcendental example of this policy role which UNFPA feels to be so important.

THE CHALLENGES AHEAD

Today, there is an international consensus on what we should do to confront the population challenge. In Amsterdam in 1989, at the International Forum on Population in the Twenty-First Century, leaders and policy makers from 79 nations agreed on population goals for the remainder of this century. Chief among them was, as I mentioned, holding population growth to the level of the United Nations medium projections for the year 2000.

These goals are realistic. But resources for population activities in developing countries lag far behind the actual needs. To reach global targets and to give all couples access to family planning would require a doubling of annual expenditures for population programmes, from currently $4.5 billion to $9–11 billion annually by the year 2000. The governments of developing countries now finance at least three-quarters of the cost of those programmes. On the other hand, international population assistance has hardly increased at all in real terms over the past two decades, barely keeping up with the growth of couples of reproductive ages.

International development funds are tight and the prospects for their rising dramatically through the year 2000 are slight. In these circumstances, some realignment of how these funds are shared out must be accomplished. The latest data available show that less than 1.5% of ODA funding goes towards population programmes. We have long advocated that the share for population activities must be raised to 4%. With this small change in proportion the extra billions of dollars needed would materialize and the goals I have alluded to would be able to be realized.

As we have said so often, success in balancing population growth with growth in other areas means that we need to find an integrated approach to development and one, in particular, which gives sufficient importance to human resource development. For this reason, besides increasing international assistance to population it is equally vital to increase the priority of other social sectors such as education and health. In our view, at least 20% of total international assistance should be earmarked for social-sector programmes.

Speaking for the United Nations Population fund, I can say that requests for assistance from all regions have mounted to a level that can no longer be met by our organization. We estimate that the demand for UNFPA support already exceeds our resources by $500 million. And many countries – particularly in sub-Saharan Africa – wish to expand their current population programmes. Unfortunately, we simply lack the resources to provide assistance to the extent required around the world.

We have every incentive to spur our determination. Universal access to a wide range of safe, affordable and effective family planning choices would bring more benefits to more people at less cost than any other single technology currently available to the human race.

The demand is there. We know what to do. Now the main challenge for the population community is to raise resources to the level where demand can be met. The last decade of the 20th century offers a real possibility of achieving integrated goals in the areas of population, environment and socio-economic development.

Inaugural Address
by the Honourable Shri P.R. Kumaramangalam,
Indian Minister of State for Science and Technology
& Parliamentary Affairs

I consider it a great privilege to be here with you on this momentous occasion, when representatives of over 50 scientific academies have gathered together to discuss one of the most crucial issues of our time, which has a direct bearing on the health and happiness of those inhabiting this world today and even more so for the generations to come. For us in India, it is an auspicious day - the country is celebrating the festival of Dussehra which symbolises the victory of good over evil.

First of all, I would like to join Professor Joshi in warmly welcoming you to India. It is no doubt a rare privilege for us and especially for the Indian National Science Academy to play a host for this unique meeting. I am delighted that you accepted the invitation of the Indian National Science Academy to hold this conference in Delhi. I sincerely hope that your stay will be pleasant and your deliberations fruitful.

It took thousands of years for the human population to reach one billion mark in 1830 – but only 100 years for the second billion, 30 years for the third, and the last billion in just about 12 years. The world population has already crossed the 5.5 billion mark. The spectre of this continued growth looms large on the horizon. Demographers have made estimates varying from 10 to 15 billion people during the life time of those who are already born. A large percentage of this increase would no doubt take place in countries which are already over-burdened with the problem of overpopulation.

We in India are deeply concerned about our rapidly increasing population. Between 1891 and 1921, we had an addition of only 12 million. In the next 30 years (1921–51) 109 millions were added. Notwithstanding our efforts to control this exponential rise, in 20 years (between 1971–91), 12 million more were added. Based on current trends, a 1988 UN study has predicted India's population to be 1043 million in 2000 AD and 1513 million in 2025 AD. We all know that increasing population is not just a matter of counting more heads. The country has to provide for their food, education, health, housing, employment and recreation.

The Earth and its resources are finite. Human ingenuity and efforts have their own limits to fulfil the needs of these increasing numbers. Our developmental efforts since Independence have, no doubt, resulted in impressive gains on most fronts. We have achieve near self-sufficiency for food, the infant and maternal mortality rate continues to come down, the literacy rate has shown progressive improvement, the life expectancy at birth has nearly doubled, the percentage of people living below the poverty line has diminished. Yet a critical look at the current scenario leaves very little cause for complacency. Notwithstanding the vast increase in our GNP/GDP, we continue to rank 123rd among 160 countries of the world on the basis of measures for quality of life as per

United Nations Human Development Report 1990. This, no doubt, is primarily due to ever increasing numbers.

It is somewhat of an irony that a country which became conscious of the problem of rising population nearly 60 year ago, even today continues to grapple with its complexities. This in itself may have a lesson for others, which I will come to a little later. Many may not know that the first birth control clinic was opened in India in 1921 by Dr R.D. Karve, the same year as Marie Stopes opened her clinic in the UK. Even more revealing is the fact that the leaders of our independence movement, as early as 1930s, were concerned about this issue. The National Planning Committee of the Indian National Congress under the Chairmanship of Pandit Jawaharlal Nehru in 1935 supported the establishment of birth control clinics in various states of India. Subash Chandra Bose in his Presidential Address to Indian National Congress at Tripura, in 1939 stated, 'with regard to the long period programme of a free India, the first problem to tackle is that of our increasing population... I would urge that the public attention be drawn to this question'. It is worth pointing out that population of undivided India at that time was approximately 315 million and an average growth rate of only 1.34. The population sub-committee of the Indian National Congress under the Convenership of Dr Radhakomal Mukherjee, an outstanding social scientist, in its report submitted already in May 1940, recommended a comprehensive approach to family planning taking into consideration socio-cultural-economic and health issues. Based on this recommendation, the Planning Committee resolved, 'while measures for improvement of the quality of population and limiting excessive population pressure are necessary, the basic solution of the present disparity between population and standard of living lies in the economic progress of the country on a comprehensive and planned basis'. How true are these facts even today!

Soon after Independence, in 1951 the then Prime Minister and Chairman of the newly established Planning Commission initiated the first state-sponsored population control programme as a part of the country's first Five Year Plan (1951–56). Thus India became the first country in the world to give official recognition and implementation of family planning activities. Ever since it has remained as an increasingly important agenda of our Plans as is obvious from the rising plan allocations for these programmes. From a meagre budget of Rs 6.5 million in the First Plan, it was raised to Rs 13 870 million in the Sixth Plan and Rs 32 560 million in the Seventh. The allocation for the Eighth Plan are Rs 65 000 million.

One may ask why then our population has increased to the present level, why our population growth rate continues to be around 2%? Answers to these questions are not only of importance for our future plans and programmes but may be equally important for other countries in the world who are grappling with the problem of growing population.

Before I proceed further, let me first state that not all our efforts have gone in vain. The national fertility rate has gone down from 5.97 in 1950–55 period to 4.2 in 1980s and 3.9 at present. The couple protection rate (CPR) has gone from 10.4% in 1970 to 43.5% in 1992. Even more significant is the fact that in some of the states in India, beginning with Kerala and now including Tamil Nadu, Maharashtra, Karnataka, Punjab and Goa, have already attained or are very near approaching the targets set out a decade ago. It has been estimated that as a result of our programmes 130 million births have been prevented, nearly 100 million during the past decade. Thus there is real hope that if we persist with our programmes, learning from our past failures, modifying these in the light of our experience and observations, taking lessons from those who have done better than us we may achieve the coveted target of Net Reproduction Rate of unity sooner than some sceptics are predicting.

Our experience over the years clearly indicates that population control is just not a matter of number, name or provision of contraceptives, or even establishment of family planning clinics. It is a complex issue which must take into account socio-economic, cultural and religious issues on one hand, and provision of affordable, easily available health care services especially in respect to reproductive, maternal and child health. Another vital parameter appears to be female literacy and status of women in the society. Our current programmes thus consist of a comprehensive strategy of poverty eradication, elimination of illiteracy, universal immunization, nutritional supplementation for the vulnerable groups, dissemination of health and family welfare-related educational material in addition to provision of primary health care for all. At the same time efforts are being made to strengthen our research efforts in the field of reproductive biology and fertility control. Probably you are aware that our scientists have already developed a non-steroidal weekly oral pill (Centchroman), which is as good, if not better, than most other available pills. After very prolonged research efforts it was released in the market one and a half years ago. In extensive clinical trials, it has proved to be effective without any side effects. Currently more than 30 000 women are using it.

Intensive work is also going on in the field of immunological approaches to fertility control. A vaccine (about which you will hear more during the conference) has already completed Phase II clinical trial. Work is going on in several laboratories to develop a male contraceptive vaccine, novel anti-implantation compounds, and plant-derived contraceptive creams, etc.

We are conscious that in today's world such complex issues cannot and should not be viewed just from national perspectives. As you all know there are many interactive issues, which directly or indirectly influence and are in turn influenced by what prevails across the national geographical boundaries.

The world today is really a global village, more interdependent than ever before. Rising population in one region, increasing consumption in the other, deforestation in one and industrial pollution in the other have consequences for everyone globally. It is now generally accepted that besides everything else there is a link between income and fertility, with fertility lower in higher income regions. There are no doubt exceptions to this rule. However, an equitable world economic order is indispensable for attaining global population stabilization. There is, of course, an intimate connection between economic activity, population growth and environment. Since we have had a major UN Conference on Environment & Development, I would not like to talk anything more about it here. Besides other factors mentioned above which are within the scope of national efforts, in today's world, these economic factors have global implications. Any international steps that may directly or indirectly adversely affect the economy of an already-poor country are likely to have a negative effect on population control.

There is another area where global efforts are equally important and which is of even greater significance for the participants of this 'Summit': this relates to science and technology efforts. Although fertility control research may not have the same priority for countries with advanced know-how, facilities and talents, their commitment to this area is vital. You in your capacity as leaders of the scientific community could contribute a great deal in this respect. Increased efforts for research, both basic and applied, man-power training, free and regular exchange of information and mechanisms for quick transfer of technology require international co-operation. Scientific academies are the ideal institutions to encourage such activities. It is, therefore, very timely that the scientific academies of the world decided to hold this conference to assess critically the current scenario and evolve suitable plans for future action.

I wish your conference every success and look forward to your final recommendations.

Summary of Population Statement signed by 60 Academies

*Let 1994 be remembered as the year when the people of the world
decided to act together for the benefit of future generations.*

The academies of the world call upon the governments and international decision-makers, especially those at the 1994 UN International Conference on Population and Development, to take incisive action now and adopt an integrated policy on population and sustainable development on a global scale.

The problem

The world is undergoing an unprecedented population expansion. Within the span of a single lifetime, world population has more than doubled to 5.5 billion, and even the most optimistic scenarios of lower birth rates lead to a peak of 7.8 billion people in the middle of the next century. In the last decade, food production from both land and sea declined relative to world population growth.

The relationships between human population, economic development, and natural environment are complex and not fully understood. Nonetheless, there is no doubt that the threat to the ecosystem is linked to population size and resource use. Increasing greenhouse gas emissions, ozone depletion and acid rain, loss of biodiversity, deforestation and loss of topsoil, shortages of water, food and fuel indicate how the natural systems are being pushed ever closer to their limits.

The developed world, containing less than a quarter of the world population, accounts for 85% of the gross world production and the majority of mineral and fossil-fuel consumption. Both rich and poor countries add to environmental damage through industrial activity, inappropriate agricultural practices, population concentration, and inadequate and inattentive environmental concern. Yet development is a legitimate expectation of less developed and transitional countries.

The solutions

Our common goal is the improvement of the quality of life for all, both now and for succeeding generations. By this we mean social, economic, and personal well-being while preserving fundamental human rights and the ability to live harmoniously in a protected environment. To deal with the social, economic, and environmental problems, we must achieve zero population growth within the lifetime of our children.

These goals are achievable given time, political will, intelligent use of science and technology, and human ingenuity. But only if appropriate policy decisions are taken now to bring about the requisite social change.

How do we go about this task?

We need:
- equal opportunities for women and men in sexual, social, and economic life so they can make individual choices about family size;

- universal access to convenient family planning and health services, and a wide variety of safe and affordable contraceptive options;
- encouragement of voluntary approaches to family planning and elimination of unsafe and coercive practices;
- clean water, sanitation, broad primary health care and education;
- appropriate governmental policies that recognize longer-term environmental responsibilities;
- more efficiency and less environmentally damaging practices in the developed world, through a new ethic that eschews wasteful consumption;
- pricing, taxing and regulatory policies that take into account environmental costs, thereby influencing consumption behavior;
- the industrialized world to assist the developing world in combating global and local environmental problems;
- promotion of the concept of "technology for environment;"
- incorporation by governments of environmental goals in legislation, economic planning, and priority setting, and incentives for organizations and individuals to operate in environmentally benign ways;
- collective action by all countries.

Natural and social scientists, engineers, and health professionals have their part to play in developing better understanding of the problems, options, and solutions, especially regarding:

- cultural, social, economic, religious, educational, and political factors affecting reproductive behavior, family size, and family planning;
- impediments to human development, especially social inequalities, ethnic, class, and gender biases;
- global and local environmental change, its causes (social, industrial, demographic and political) and policies for its mitigation;
- improving education and human resource development with special attention to women;
- family planning programs, new contraceptive options, and primary health care;
- transitions to less energy– and material–consumptive economies;
- building indigenous capacity in developing countries in the natural sciences, engineering, medicine, social sciences, management, and interdisciplinary studies;
- technologies and strategies for sustainable development;
- networks, treaties, and conventions that protect the global commons;
- world-wide exchanges of scientists in education, training, and research.

Introduction to Session 1:

THE COMPLEX REALITY

by P.N. Tandon, Spokesperson for the Summit
and President, Indian National Science Academy, 1991–92

The first presentation of the Population Summit was that by Professor Lindahl Kiessling and Dr Keyfitz, who pointed out that demographic change is taking place at several speeds in different regions of the world. However, the overall rate of increase continues to be 1.7% per year. They warned that it is not realistic to assume that 'the present North–South division of consumption and pollution can prevail if we are to achieve sustainable development'. While there was an urgent need for population stabilization along with resource development in the developing world, there was simultaneous necessity for curbing the excessive consumption pattern in the developed world.

Professor Okoth-Ogendo provided the African perspective on 'Population and Natural Resource Use'. Without appropriate technologies for sustainable development, population has become an essential component in resource generation. This dictates the necessity of capacity building in science and technology to harness endogenous resources as a prerequisite for population stabilization.

Dr Jane Menken discussed the demographic–economic relationship and development, and found the linkages between population and the economy to be complex, difficult to elucidate, in many cases context specific and worthy of careful scientific research. Echoing the views of Dr Sadik, she pointed out that population growth has not invariably prevented development, nor has reduction in population been a panacea for development. Several examples of lowering of fertility and population growth rates preceding developmental advances, like Kerala and Tamil Nadu in India (Srinivasan), Bangladesh, and Indonesia (Cleland) were referred to by others also. Nevertheless, it was generally agreed that in the long run poverty alleviation and development are essential for population control.

Professor Ramalingaswami's presentation analysed the two-way interrelationship between health and population: 'each can be a determinent as well as a consequence of the other.' He highlighted the substantial health hazards of high fertility to the individual, the family and the community. Too early, too many and too frequent pregnancies have an adverse effect on infant and mother survival. It was important to prevent young girls from becoming mothers before they are physically, emotionally and socially able to face motherhood with responsibility.

1/1

The World Population Debate: Urgency of the Problem

Nathan Keyfitz and Kerstin Lindahl-Kiessling

ABSTRACT

The international population debate has been thoroughly researched and repeatedly reviewed from the economic and ecological viewpoints (Keyfitz 1991; Harrison 1992). So has the social science perspective on the population–development issues (Greenhalgh 1990; Hombergh 1993), but usually in a different context, which may be the reason why we still lack a clear understanding of the pertinent linkages between social (human driven) factors and the environmental factors and forces involved (Keyfitz 1993). What we lack most of all are reliable conclusions, followed by the actions to implement these conclusions. We assume that the most relevant task for science is to deepen the understanding of the basic conditions that originate from the fact that the natural environment is our life-support system and also the prerequisite for development (Brundtland 1987). What we present herein are efforts to illustrate, from different perspectives, and disentangle the population–environment–development complex and, thus, encourage the necessary scientific and political actions.

1. A SKETCH OF POPULATION HISTORY [1][†]

10,000 B.C. With a human population of only 6 millions, the danger of extinction of the human race was ever present. Life expectancy was 20 years; birth rate was only 0.008% higher than death rate. If deaths were 40 per thousand, births must have been 40.08 per thousand. Births falling to 39.00 per thousand, say, would have led to rapid extinction. It took 8000 years for the population to double. The continuance of the human race depended on the very highest possible birth rate and some of the culture elements that favour reproduction dating back to that period survive still.

With 6 000 000 members of the human race the world was in effect full. Says Massimo Livi-Bacci: 'The system of hunting and gathering could not have allowed the survival of more than several million people'[2] and at the same time, say Irven Devore and Richard Lee, 'The hunting way of life has been the most successful and persistent adaptation man has ever achieved.' Lee and Devore (1968) compare hunting favourably with the agricultural and industrial phases of history that followed. The more we have advanced, is the implication of their account, the more change we have made in the ecosphere, and the more unintentional degradation has occurred.

0 A.D. Population had grown to 250 millions by the beginning of the Christian Era. The population increase was due to improved mortality; life expectancy had risen, though only to 22 years, but that enabled more people to live

† Numbers in this form refer to notes at the end of the text.

through the years of reproduction. The birth rate was still only 0.037% higher than the death rate and doubling time had now diminished to 1900 years. Effective weaponry, developed for hunting and war, gave almost complete protection against wild animals, but deaths from disease increased with the size of human settlements and with people living closer together (McNeill 1976).

Rome needed men for its legions that expanded the boundaries of the Empire and then defended them, and it needed women to bear the men. Cicero was among the most eloquent of many who called for more births (Cicero circa 44 BC).[3] With the collapse of the Empire and the dominance of Christian doctrine in Europe, the writers supporting the imperial power of Rome gave way to writers making holiness the purpose of life. The populationist view disappeared for more than a thousand years, until it came back strongly after the Middle Ages in mercantilist times.

To many writers of that period, man was a breeder and worker for the state, a tool whose sole function was to make the state strong, the strength of the state turning ultimately on how many such tools it had at its disposal (Spengler 1942). 'One should never fear there being too many subjects or too many citizens,' wrote Jean Bodin (1577), 'seeing that there is no wealth or strength but in men (sic).'

1750 A.D.   World population was 771 million as the mercantilist period was coming to an end. Life expectancy was now 27 years. Rate of increase had increased, but doubling time over the preceding period was still over 1000 years.

Livi-Bacci again stresses the relation between human numbers and the means of subsistence. He says for the 18th century that 'The European system of agriculture could not have allowed the survival of many more than the hundred million inhabitants who lived on the continent prior to the Industrial Revolution.'[4] East Asian agriculture, centred on irrigated rice, was more land-intensive, and showed especially rapid increase in the 11th century, when faster-growing varieties for such cultivation were introduced, and in the 18th century when American crops, especially corn, peanuts and potatoes, were introduced (Ho 1959).

Thomas Robert Malthus is the best known writer on population, cited more by his critics than by his friends and by both more cited than read. In the *First Essay*[5] he is unqualified on the harm of population growth and the misery to which it inexorably gives rise: 'The power of population is indefinitely greater than the power in the earth to produce subsistence for man…This implies a strong and constantly operating check on population from the difficulty of subsistence.' His text, written with a young man's verve, leaves few qualifications that could blur his meaning: either people practice continence, restrain their sexual impulses, or they breed themselves into starvation. Nor did he seem to have much confidence in people practising the needed restraint and, as a 19th century cleric, he strongly disapproved of contraception. This is the box of permanent hardship in which the early Malthus placed mankind (Malthus 1967).

Nevertheless, like other young people, Malthus grew up. He wrote some six subsequent editions that really were quite separate books with little overlap with the First Edition. The fact that he called them 'Editions' rather than giving them new titles, suggests that he wanted the first book with its unqualified stand to be forgotten. Ordinarily one does not read the first edition of a book when the seventh has appeared. However, if he wanted readers to forget the first edition, he had no luck. Unfortunately for him, it is the Malthus that wrote the first edition that has been in the public eye for nearly two centuries.

The later editions were no longer pure biology, assimilating man to the animal, but were a genuine and important contribution to social science. They stressed cultural control of the animal within each of us, as fortified by education and social betterment. People are like animals in that they still have the sexual urge, but they do not blindly exercise it, they do not wait to be hit by the positive check of mortality; they anticipate crises with the exercise of reason. This self-control he called the preventive check on population, and people are more capable of applying it in the degree that they become better off and especially as they become educated.

The change of position, amounting to a complete reversal, was based on the large amount of data in the later editions, data completely absent from the first. Malthus in effect spent his mature life travelling and collecting statistics on what people throughout Europe were doing about population. Thus, for the Canton of Berne, Malthus found that, 'The proportion of unmarried persons, including widows and widowers, is above half of the adults...strong proof of the powerful operation of the preventive check)[6] and, in Savoy, people...were perfectly aware of the evils which they should probably bring on themselves by marrying before they could have a tolerable prospect of being able to maintain a family,[7] while, in England, evidence shows...that the preventive check to population operates with considerable force throughout all the classes of the community.'[8]

Malthus gives page after page of data showing that people do not breed themselves into poverty, at least once they have attained a certain level of education and income. He was virtually alone in his time in recommending education for the poor; his opponent Godwin (1793) thought education too dangerous.

In these respects, modern thought as well as modern policies to provide population aid to the less-developed countries (LDCs) have followed Malthus exactly: we know that we will not solve the population problem by leaving people to breed and starve; the effective as well as the humane way is education, especially to promote education for women, and so help to create gender equality and encourage poor populations to develop socially and economically, to eradicate poverty.

The one constant in Malthus through all of the seven editions was the assertion that population had a tendency to outgrow the means of subsistence. Alfred Sauvy says that once the welfare of people came to be the main consideration, rather than the power and wealth of kings, Malthus—or someone of a different name saying the same thing—became inevitable (Sauvy 1956). Once the total had passed the billion mark it became clear that more people would lead worse lives. The difference between the early Malthus and the later is whether something could be done about it; the first Malthus seemed to think that the growth and misery were inevitable, while the later Malthus saw that people were doing something about it in virtually every country he visited.

1950 A.D.   The modern acceleration of population was well under way by the 20th century, and the number of humanity had grown to 2530 million (2.5 billion). Life expectancy was 35 years, and over the previous two centuries doubling time was down to 116 years.

For the 150 years from the time of Malthus to the middle of the 20th century, the dominant view in economics was that populations were large enough. John Stuart Mill speaks for the 19th century mainstream: 'The niggardliness of nature, not the injustice of society, is the cause of the penalty attached to overpopulation…It is vain to say that all mouths which the increase of mankind brings into existence bring with them hands. The new mouths require as much food as the old ones, and the hands do not produce as much.'[9]

1990 A.D.   Now the population is 5292 million, or pushing towards the 6 billion expected well before the end of the century. Life expectancy is 55 years, in some countries nearing 80 years. The population has more than doubled since 1950, that is, in 40 years.

For various reasons, some of them, one suspects, outside science, economics has tended to repudiate its 19th century ancestors. The revisionist view is that population is only one of a number of problems, some of them more urgent than the growth of population (Hodgson 1988). Past history has seen alternation between 'too few people' and 'too many people', but there has been no alternation in growth. The march of population numbers has been consistently upward.

Our population today is five times as large as when Malthus wrote, while the capacity of nature for sustaining it is lowered by desertification and other damage to the ecosphere, yet many choose to downgrade the problem, relying on technology to save us. The irony is that while economists write that technology will solve all problems, the scientists who create the technology are sceptical.

    … it is not prudent to rely on science alone to solve problems created by rapid
    population growth, wasteful resource consumption and harmful human practices.[10]

With that phrase, we close this much too brief history of population growth, and the varied theories that have interpreted that growth from ancient Rome to the present.

2. INTRODUCING THE CHANGING PERSPECTIVES ON THE POPULATION ISSUES

2.1 The Malthusian trap

The population debate in the past has often been a question of numbers only. Too many or too few, depending on the context. However, already Malthus, as we have seen, understood that it is more than numbers. Reviews of the population debate often start by repudiating Malthus and his original statement that 'population, when unchecked, increases in a geometrical ratio. Subsistence increases in an arithmetical ratio—'. The interpretation has been that Malthus anticipated that human populations will outgrow food supplies. With a different reading frame we may say that the part of Malthus' hypothesis that has been superseded over the centuries is not his conclusion that there are limits to the growth of human population, but his belief of mature age that the foresight of mankind would ensure that resources would tend to balance population growth by means of a preventive check on fertility, based on marriage practices. In spite of the present occurrence and acceptance of more attractive regulative methods—Malthus would accept only sexual restraint—these are available to only a fraction of the world's population. As for the 'positive check' of Malthus, that is, decreased growth rate through mortality changes, it is also obvious that at present it is not a general shortage of world food and medical supplies that determines now existing starvation and untimely death, but their unequal distribution.

In Malthus' static vision of human achievements, food production was, as we have seen, a limiting factor for population growth. We now know that these limits are of a much more complicated nature and intimately connected with our lifestyles and our understanding of the very basis for life on earth, the ecological framework.

2.2 Population growth versus economic development

In the 1960s and 70s, the population debate was centred around the relation between population growth and economic development (Kelley 1973; Johnson & Lee 1978). The pertinent question was considered to be: are many children an asset or a hindrance for economic development? The more investigations and case studies put forward, the more difficult it seemed to answer this question; the answer depends on so many factors, some of which may be quantifiable, others not. The question has to be asked specifically for different regions of the world or narrowed down by so many qualifications as to lose interest (Keyfitz 1993b). It is no longer asserted, except by a few eccentrics (Simon 1981), that there are generally applicable causal correlations between population growth and economic development. Furthermore, the classical pattern of transition is maybe a thing of the past: 'We are witnessing a demographic diversification in the third world.The simple two-speed pattern of population growth of twenty years ago is being superseded by one that is increasingly varied. All the signs are pointing to a world where demographic change takes place at several speeds—and looking into it more closely, it is obvious that those countries which are quickest in accomplishing the demographic transition are the ones which are in best position in terms of international competition' (Tabah 1992).

2.3 Sustainable development

During the 1980s, environmental issues provided the population debate with a new dimension, the concept of sustainable development (Brundtland 1987). The central dogma of this concept, that there are limitations imposed by the state of technology and social organisation on the environment's ability to meet present and future human needs, soon pervaded the population debate. No doubt the new perspectives were a great inspiration all over the world, but they also awoke criticism because of the emphasis on economic growth being a prerequisite for sustainability (Adams 1990; Arizpe 1991).

The most important components of sustainable development, equitable distribution of the determinants of human well-being and health, were shown to be contingent upon the protection of the environment. Thus, the limits of the capability of biological systems to accommodate the multitude of human activities became the crucial question (World Women's Congress for a Healthy Planet 1991)[11]. Without doubt, there are finite limits, but have we already surpassed these limits or do we still have time to adjust? The only answer at present is that, in coming decades, unavoidable increases in population will take us into unknown territory. There is great uncertainty about the ability of the biosphere to accommodate our present use of both renewable and nonrenewable resources. What will happen when 10 billion people try to exercise their indisputable right to live like the rich 1.1 billion, present high consumers and high polluters (Royal Swedish Academy 1991)?[12]

2.4 Micro-perspectives

This last question has opened a new point of entry into the modern population debate, that takes us back to the predictions of Alfred Sauvy (1956). Firstly, it is, in the long term, not realistic to assume that the present North–South division of consumption and pollution can prevail if we are to achieve sustainable development. The aim must be equal access to the earth's resources and equal responsibility for their preservation. Secondly, the quest for an increased wellbeing for everyone is not compatible with a perpetual population growth. Emphasis has therefore been laid on individual autonomy and the mediating role of human behaviour and institutions for the interaction between population growth and development. In keeping with this view, it has now become broadly acknowledged that the family planning debate—in this context being the operative extension of the population debate—must be based on the individual's situation, especially that of women. From the gender perspective the dominating feature is the micro-level, that is quality of life, the options people have and the rights and responsibilities of the individual (Moghadan 1990, 1993).

Undoubtedly, equality and gender-based analyses have gained impetus through suspicion and fear of a hidden agenda in the classical population debate of the rich world. Advocacy for fertility control, family planning, has been seen as an imposition of western values on other cultures. Therefore, egalitarian and gender issues will constitute a first priority for population activities in the 1990s. Fertility control will evolve into concern for sexual and reproductive health (International Symposium 1993).[13]

However, there is a risk that the rich world, intimidated by economic recession, will curb its willingness to change lifestyles and attitudes and at the same time deprive the poor world of the means of help to self-help. Reluctance to risk the opposition of the Roman Catholic Church may restrict the funding of legal and voluntary abortion and contraception programmes. Our responses to the problems involved will determine to what extent we will succeed in keeping human activeness within ecological limits. In this lies the urgency—what is the answer of today's scientists to this challenge?

3. EFFECTS OF DEVELOPMENT
3.1 From high to low birth and death rates

About half a century ago, demographers noted the historical decline of fertility in Europe and America, and remarked on the curious fact that simultaneous with the decline in fertility came an acceleration of population growth (Notestein 1945; Davis 1945). In Europe and elsewhere, the decrease in fertility in many countries in the latter half of the19th century seemed to bring about an increase in population growth. Kingsley Davis eloquently describes the phenomenon:

> Viewed in the long-run perspective, the growth of the earth's population has been like a long, thin powder fuse that burns slowly and haltingly until it finally reaches the charge and then explodes. The first real burst of world population growth

came with the latest stage in cultural progress—the Industrial Revolution.

At the time Davis wrote this, it was anticipated that the world population would rise to somewhere between 3 and 4 billion by the year 2000. In fact it passed the 3 billion point before 1960, and will have reached 6 billion before the year 2000. Although Davis could not know that the increase would be so great, he does provide a framework within which it can be interpreted:

> The techniques of reducing death rates (medical science, sanitary engineering, agricultural improvement, and better transport) were imported for both humanitarian and economic reasons, and proved one of the most acceptable features of European culture…Fertility, however, was not correspondingly reduced.

A result of this can be seen in the difference in population growth that has taken place in the world between the peoples of the industrial countries and those of the third world. Current United Nations' estimates and projections document this fact. Of the 139 million births anticipated for 2020, some 119 will be in the LDCs (UNFPA 1992). Davis goes on to show the European response to rapid rates of increase:

> The European peasants' response to sustained natural increase clearly reflected a social structure that held married couples responsible for their children. This feature—along with its corollary, postponement of marriage for those incapable of supporting children—was part of the independence and separateness accorded the nuclear family, as opposed to the joint household, in west European society. As such, it went back to medieval and post-medieval times, and it tended to yield a later age at marriage than is found in most joint household systems.

Davis suggested that response to high rates of increase will come in a number of ways, including birth control, abortion, emigration, all of them contributing to the lowering of effective growth rates. This multiphasic response is now found in the industrialised countries and in some parts of the third world. However, this type of response, which could be said to come close to solving the world's numerical population problem, is not likely to become universal until the elimination of poverty has reached a much more successful stage.

3.2 Why next year is not so good: every year makes it harder

To see why solutions to the population question have been considered so urgent, observe the diagram (Figure 1). This is a somewhat stylised representation of the demographic transition from high birth and death rates to low rates, from stability under traditional conditions of fertility and mortality to stability under modern conditions. Divided into three parts, this diagram shows in the left part the traditional stability of high birth and death rates just starting to be unsettled by decline in the death rate, while the birth rate is constant or even slowly rising; in the centre part the difference between birth and death rates reaches its highest point; this difference is the rate of increase, that has been as high as 2% per year. The right-hand part shows the birth rate falling to come into line with the death rate. It is the middle interval in which the world as a whole, heavily weighted by the LDCs, is now located. The birth rate has started its decline, but is still high enough that the rate of increase is 1.7% per year. Thus, the population will double in 47 years.

Through history, it has taken hundreds or even thousands of years for a doubling to occur. It can be shown that the total expansion of the world population during this transition will be equal to the area between the solid curve in the diagram, representing the death rate and the dotted curve above it for the birth rate. If this area is increased by a lag of even one year in the fall of births the result will be an extra growth of 1.7%, about 60 million people, that would not otherwise have taken place. As long as this growth continues, an increment equal to the population of France will be added every year.

Correlation of economic with population growth rates:

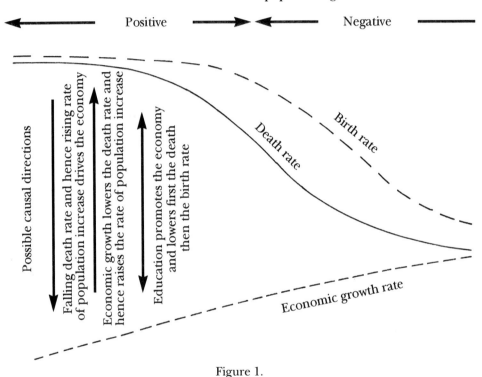

Figure 1.

3.2 Lifestyles and the ecosphere

It has been objected that insofar as the 60 million increment will be mostly poor peasants or equally poor inhabitants of the slums of third world cities, they will add very little to the burden on the ecosphere. This is true if one looks at the way poor people have lived in the past, but the goal must be to make them a part of the development process. We will have then not 60 million poor people, but 60 million middle-class citizens. What these 60 million will represent for the future of the ecosphere depends on whether they live as meagrely as at present, whether they insist on living according to what are now the middle-class standards of the developed countries, or if new, alternative lifestyles take precedence. It is, however, an undeniable fact that the immediate future of the ecosphere will mainly depend on to what extent people in the developed world have succeeded in changing *their* overall pattern of life. Says Egerö (1991):

Given the exceedingly high per capita consumption in the industrialised states, with its environmental impact, the industrialised world certainly is endowed with population problems no less important to tackle than those of the poor countries in the South.

Since it has not been implied that the poor countries will, in fact, remain poor and we have no final proof so far that rich countries will drastically amend their lifestyles, then we must regard the increase in population as an additional number of prospectively rich people.

That is what makes the urgency of the ecological problems, created by human dominance: the combination of 1.7% population increase per year with 2, 3 or 4% increase of polluting, resource-demanding consumption per person.

3.3 Is family planning a solution?

For a very long time the slogan 'development is the best contraceptive' has been used, honestly and maybe also as an excuse for inaction. Is it really valid? If so, could we not casually wait for the problem to be solved in the natural course of development, as some groups suggest? Others have objected to this suggestion, however, because for one thing the burden of too many people may slow down and even prevent development in some areas (Keyfitz 1991d). With our present knowledge, it is difficult to prove such direct effects—the interlinkages are too multifactorial and far too complex, but in any case we have to remember that the development process is naturally slow. Development has been officially proclaimed many times, but has grown less rapidly than initially promulgated. The results of efforts made to date, to find solutions to the problems, constitute examples of the difficulties involved.

On the other hand, the availability of equipment and information on contraceptives is obviously *not* the whole answer. Investigations prove without doubt that most family planning programmes influence the birth rate only as they go along with socioeconomic development, as was the case earlier in Europe. The one book-length study on the subject (Hernandez 1984) credited family planning with 3–10% of the observed fertility decline in LDC (Demeny 1992). Mauldin and Ross (1991) reported a figure above 40%, but their investigation has been heavily criticised (Postel 1992). For many people, family planning may be of marginal interest for many reasons. It may well be in their economic interests to retain the security of many children, if they are not already part of a surge in economic development.

If family planning is unattractive because of the absence of development, and because development programs are too slow, what course should be followed? Ultimately, straining every effort simultaneously towards (i) worldwide sustainable development; and (ii) universal acceptance of the individual's reproductive rights and providing the means to execute that right, will be necessary.

Curiously enough, these completely obvious statements are challenged by some, and the way that they are challenged tells us something about the way that scientific, and indeed human, thought processes act.

In the following, we will try to illustrate this discussion, which has taken place mainly among economists and biologists.

4. VIEWS OF ECOLOGY AND OF ECONOMICS: WHAT YOU SEE DEPENDS ON THE MODEL THAT PROVIDES YOUR SPECTACLES

4.1 The classical view

Until the last two or three decades, economists agreed on some version of the assertion that without checking population, growth in per capita income was difficult or impossible: any gain in income would be swallowed by the increase in population — the famous Malthusian trap. If there is one noncontroversial proposition in the whole of social science, this formulation of the population problem was it (Notestein 1975; Higgins 1979). Beyond social sciences, biologists presented their own analogous proposition: any species that grows beyond the number sustainably supportable by its environment is a pest and will sooner or later suffer a collapse. The models of Volterra, Lotka, and others have shown how this follows from the lags built into biological systems (Ehrlich 1968).

4.2 'One mouth, two hands'

Unanimity is now at an end. A new and sophisticated generation has come on the scene and has proclaimed that the Malthusian formulation, on which Darwin built his theory of evolution, is too simple. Ingenious arguments have been put forward that prior to World War II would have seemed bizarre; e.g. the statement that population growth and increased density modifies institutions in the direction of private property, and the benefits of this are such as to offset harmful direct effects of increased population density. With every new mouth to feed there are two hands to increase production, is the slogan. This is exactly the opposite view to that stated by John Stuart Mill, who coined the expression (cited above).

These arguments may, however, be seen as offshoots of an interesting theoretical tradition of economic history,[14] best represented by Ester Boserup, who has had an enormous significance for the recognition of women's role in economic development (1965, 1970, 1981).[15] Essentially, her theory holds that intensified land use and increased productivity is labour-demanding and therefore to be seen as the outcome of necessity. Population increase has, under certain circumstances, historically provided an impetus to intensification, thus paving the way for surplus generation and the growth of production in other sectors than agriculture. An example of this trend is the growth of labour-intensive irrigated rice cultivation in Asia (Mahtab & Karim 1992).

This trend is by and large absent in sub-Saharan Africa. Why? Historical research has pointed at the effects of colonial policies aimed at preventing the threat to European agriculture from enterprising African peasant farmers. Others, among them Pingali and Binswanger (1988) emphasise the paradoxical aspect of relative underpopulation and labour shortage in rural economies jointly with rapid population increase, and the structural obstacles to agricultural growth in low density areas with poor infrastructure and adult outmigration. A recent report from Kenya (Tiffen 1993), to take just one example, demonstrates the multidimensionality of the question. Her investigation shows that labour-intensive new agricultural methods have increased productivity during 1980 to 1990 faster than consumption dependent on population growth, thus outweighing the increased population pressure.

These observations confirm the futility of searching for a single answer to the sometimes extremely heated debate centred around the question: is it better to have more people or fewer? We argue that the problem is badly posed when stated in this way. The answer depends critically on how many people there are to begin with, and under what conditions the advantages of more people outweigh the disadvantages. When a large fertile territory contains only few people, it would be an advantage to increase the numbers; among other things, for the broader division of labour that would be possible.

On the other hand, where the climate and/or soil conditions prevent intensification of agriculture and where there are so many people that the number of landless labourers increases, and there is no capital for industry that can employ them, the disadvantages of more people become obvious, from both the economic and ecological perspectives.

4.3 Limited resources

The crucial question then, mostly among biologists, has been the cutoff point — the point at which more people become a drawback. It has been argued that from an ecological point of view, the population density above which more people are a drawback is relatively low. Renewable resources, e.g. firewood, soils, fresh water, fisheries, are a clear illustration of the negative effects of population growth which have reached the drawback phase (World Resources 1992–93).[16] If exploited up to their annual harvestable increase these resources will last forever; beyond that they will be exhausted surprisingly quickly (Keyfitz 1991c).

Another resource that is of the same renewable character is the capacity of the ecosphere to absorb emissions of sulphur and its compounds, carbon dioxide, methane,and many other types of gaseous, liquid, and solid waste produced by industry and the consumption patterns of the developed countries. This renewable resource, the absorptive capacity of the biosphere, appears to be the most critical of all. One of the major problems involved is the estimation of the resilience of the natural systems, especially as phenomena of discontinuity are likely to appear (Holling 1986).

When we proceed from conditions under which the income that nature provides is consumed, to conditions under which we consume the capital, then all the rules change. The discontinuity is mathematically similar to the situation where the individual with a fixed yearly income from capital begins to spend more than this income each year. The atmospheric pollution is a good illustration of this dilemma so it will be discussed below in some detail.

4.4 UNCED and the climate convention

The question of how much the atmospheric concentration of greenhouse gases, particularly carbon dioxide, could increase before disastrous changes of the climate would develop, was one of the main issues at the United Nations Conference on Environment and Development 1992 (UNCED). The Climate Convention adopted clearly recognises that the ongoing increase of the greenhouse gases in the atmosphere must be stopped, although there was no agreement on what levels must not be exceeded, nor were any compelling agreements reached on preventive actions. The concerted efforts by the scientific community undoubtedly played a decisive role in providing a sound basis for the political negotiations. As a matter of fact, few key scientists disagree with the concluding statements as formulated in the assessment reports. The role of the biosphere as well as its sensitivity to likely forthcoming changes of the global environment is, however, in many regards unclear.

The Climate Convention accepts that developing countries for the time being may increase their emission of greenhouse gases into the atmosphere. This implies, on the other hand, that the industrialised countries must reduce their emission by at least 60%, some by as much as 80%, if stabilisation of atmospheric concentrations is aimed for as well as equity between the countries of the world (in terms of per capita emission). Since this necessarily requires much more effective use of energy and also far-reaching changes of the energy supply systems of all countries, a programme for preventing a major climate change requires sustained actions for several decades to half a century if a smooth transition is to be achieved. Obviously, the sooner such changes are initiated the less drastic are the measures that will be required.

Scenarios of likely future emissions of greenhouse gases are, of course, dependent on the expected increase of the world population. There is, however, no simple and straightforward relationship. The amount of energy being used by people very much depends on their economic status. Even though it is true that the emission of carbon dioxide per person is about 30 times larger in the United States than in India, it should also be recognised that the rich people in an industrialised as well as a developing country may well make use of ten times as much energy as the poor people in that same country and also contribute correspondingly much more to the emissions of greenhouse gases. Future emissions will therefore be dependent on the population increase *and* economical progress in developing countries, which is conducive to increasing emissions, and on the rate of technological development, particularly with regard to the employment of new non-emitting energy sources worldwide (Bolin 1993).

Economists appear wary about trusting to substitutes in this context, but tend to say that we ought to wait until scientists have more precise information and, in the meantime, promote growth as usual. Biologists, however, are not so complacent; they see our present mode of development as performing experiments on a massive scale without regard for the ultimate consequences.

If Malthus underestimated the power of science, we now tend to overestimate what science can achieve (Brooks 1992). No doubt the effects on the ecological systems can be influenced by human choice in interplay with human inventiveness, but our knowledge about ecological systems is far from complete and we may, by ignoring this lack of knowledge, inadvertently damage the economy's life support system beyond its ability to repair itself. To prevent *potential* environmental disasters in the future, the precautionary principle of erring on the side of caution should be applied.

This insight may be the most valuable new contribution at UNCED. The precautionary principle has been advocated by both sides and finally has come to be adopted, at least verbally, by the world's politicians at UNCED, where it was stated in the Rio Declaration, Principle 15:

> In order to protect the environment, the precautionary approach shall be widely applied by States according to their capabilities. Where there are threats of serious or irreversible damage, lack of full scientific certainty shall not be used as a reason

for postponing cost-effective measures to prevent environmental degradation.

4.5 Economists versus biologists: substitution

Returning to the 19th century economists, who saw population growth as forcing down the standard of living: focus was on the nonrenewable resources—copper, coal, and the other minerals—that were only available in fixed quantities, but since then our success in identifying new sources and contriving substitutes has been so great that this threat appears no longer convincing (excepting perhaps a few elements like phosphorus).

Again for the 19th century, the three factors of production were land, labour and capital. Land, which included the nonrenewable minerals, has now been dismissed as a limiting factor because land suitable for agricultural production is considered to be exploitable ever more intensively—or at least so the optimists argue. The biologists counter this argument with the fact that loss of biodiversity, water scarcity, climate restraints and land fertility constitute finite limits to growth.

Capital is now assigned less importance than it was in the 19th century. Developed countries, of course, have access to capital. In substance, the most sophisticated economic argument is that when physical capital is lacking one can generate it—the most important element is human capital, i.e. skilled labour.[17]

Once both land and capital are dismissed as factors of production then, in theory, the remaining factor, labour, can be indefinitely multiplied. The essentials for consumption that will sustain the increase of population will be produced under the impulse of the market. To those among whom are biologists, who still see the natural environment, including land, as essential for production, and its exploitation as requiring material capital, this argument for growth is totally lacking in credibility.

To complete this contrast between the two points of view, economists argue that change and substitution are lacking in the biologists' perspective. They point out that as soon as the forests in England disappeared in the 18th century coal was substituted; that in fact the disappearance of the forests brought a more concentrated and hence superior fuel, coal, into use. When coal emissions were discovered to pollute and blacken the 19th century cities, oil came into use, followed by gas, and then nuclear fission. These are indeed responses to various kinds of ecological change, and show the flexibility of our economy, but to assume that a saving change will be available for every crisis that will ever arise is at best saintly trust in human ingenuity, at worst foolish optimism. Maybe the incompatibility between economists' and biologists' views is a question of scientific framework, obtained during education within each discipline: biologists think in terms of centuries, irreversibility and limits which cannot be accommodated in the economist's paradigm (Keyfitz 1993a). A remedy for this lack of cross-disciplinary understanding must be a major entry on any science agenda.

4.6 Can statistics provide an objective answer?

Statistical data have frequently been used to discriminate between the economic view that increased population does no harm, is even a benefit; and the ecological view that there are sharp limits to the advantage of more people, limits that have already been reached.

One would hope that the data could discriminate between two such sharply contrasting points of view but, unfortunately, that is not the case. During the first phase of the transition (Figure 1), income rises and so, because deaths fall, does the rate of population increase. A cross-sectional correlation between income and rate of increase of population in a number of countries in the left third of the diagram would thus show that it is positive—those countries that have the highest economic growth rate have also the highest rate of population increase.

Economists have actually used the cross-sectional correlation that exists in the early phase of the demographic transition as evidence that the increase in population *causes* the economic growth. To a demographer or a biologist it is equally clear that what drives the correlation is the increase of income that permits better diet, better medicine, and so lowers the death rate which in turn, and through simple arithmetic, raises the rate of population increase. All one can do in this situation is use one's best judgment: no rigorous scientific discrimination is possible between the two interpretations of the positive correlation.

4.7 Conclusion

To sum up what the diagram (Figure 1) can teach us: initially, the economic value of more people increases faster than the negative effects on the environment, and inevitably leads to a higher density. Thus, the whole range of population increase can be divided into three parts: at low densities, the ecologist and the economist will agree that more people are desirable, or at worst will do no harm; at middle densities, there is room for disagreement, with the ecologist against and the economist in favor of further growth; at higher densities, agreement is possible again: once we are standing elbow to elbow not only economists and ecologists, but the whole human race, will concede that more people are a drawback from all points of view.

However, from a different perspective, sociologists maintain that long before this has happened the complex patterns of human relationships will overlay, alter, and modify the relation human beings have to land and natural resources. Thus, it does not make sense to talk of the earth's carrying capacity for humans in the same way as we discuss the carrying capacity for other species. The distinctive feature of human beings is adaptive behaviour which makes 'the number's game' irrelevant in their eyes. This confidence in the appropriateness in human behaviour is, however, no reason for inaction. On the contrary—the present debate is maybe part of that very adaptation process.

This proposal take us to next section, considering the interplay between humans as moral and social creatures.

5. ECOLOGY, ETHICS AND CULTURE

The culture to which the writers of this paper belong is so familiar that we do not notice it. As Sherlock Holmes noted,[18] 'The world is full of obvious things, which nobody by any chance ever observes'. People in the developed countries live in solid houses or apartments rather than in tin-roofed squatter settlements, own a car and a refrigerator, take summer and possibly winter vacations, have no more than two or three children. Consumption and economic well-being take precedence over large numbers of children.

Similar trends are evident in urban settings everywhere. In all countries, even the poorest, we see a process of convergence that is one of the most conspicuous marks of our times. We see movements towards a way of life characterised by supermarkets, homes with television and refrigerators, automobiles, a diet that includes fish or meat at least once and often twice a day, and ultimately very few children. Perhaps the absence of children enables citizens to afford the multiplicity of goods; perhaps it is the plentiful goods that distract them from having children. What can be said is that the energy consumption, even the consumption of primary food calories, of the middle-class family with one or two children is greater than the consumption of the peasant family with five or more children, and this makes for instability in traditional energy balances.

A partial adoption of western artifacts, those that control death through inoculation and antibiotics, without adoption of the corresponding means of controlling births by contraception, has a destabilising effect on traditional societies. It launches them on a growth pattern that cannot be sustained in most settings. In its most extreme form, this argument has been presented by Maurice King, who aroused a heated debate in his widely quoted article in *The Lancet* (1991) where he stated that rich countries should refrain from advocating public health policies for other communities which, unappreciated by them, worsen their sustainability so that they ultimately starve.

In a different fashion, the education that becomes widespread in the early stages of development has an unsettling effect. Once young people become literate they almost always become dissatisfied with the traditional life style (Harrison 1992).

5.1 The middle class lifestyles

The chief historical event of the past century is the expansion of the middle class, most of whom are no longer small independent entrepreneurs, but clerks, assembly line workers, managers of the local branch of McDonald's—anyone who has a good enough job to command the appurtenances with which we are familiar.

The culture of poverty was debated two or three decades ago, including the features that are common to poor people throughout the world. However, middle-class people have more in common with one another; the poor are often in the grip of their traditional practices, while people of the middle class seem to be part of the same model, whether they started out in a village of India or of Brazil, or amid the skyscrapers of Manhattan.

At the same time, there is some variation in what middle-class people regard as important components of the good life. When an Indian or a Burmese has completed his life's work and amassed what wealth he needs, he often settles down to a life of meditation and prayer; the typical western couple in retirement may choose world tours, or trips on their own continent by car and trailer. Obviously, modern travel uses more energy than does meditation, and energy use places burdens on the environment. This extreme example is not a proposal in favor of meditation, but only an example of the divergent consequences for the environment of different ways of life, all apparently satisfactory to the individual. Sustainability does not so much require physical sacrifice as a different set of values from those that now determine the middle-class style of life.

Rich (well-off) people in the past lived very differently from the way rich people live today; compare the lives of minor German aristocrats in the 18th century with their patronage of chamber music, and of the medieval knights with their interest in hunting and warfare. Our present lifestyles are definitively a recent phenomenon. It is barely a century since Thomas Edison proposed and built the first central electric plants and so gave us simple access to electricity. The introduction of the domestic electric refrigerator is as recent as the 1920s, which is also when the mass use of the automobile began.

Moral superiority of any one lifestyle over another is not the controversy, but if activity and expenditure patterns are to converge worldwide, then the resulting stress on the environment will be tolerable with the one lifestyle, disastrous with the other. The problem is who is to lead the way in introducing the changes.

5.2 Introducing a benign lifestyle

We need to clarify the nature of the choices that are being made by more than one billion people now, and that will be made by about 10 billion by the middle of the 21st century,in the event of development. Who can lead the way to a pattern of lifestyle that will tread more lightly on the biosphere?

Choices made by the people who are in a position to choose are often influenced by press reports of incident after incident, case after case, of poisoned streams resulting from driving agriculture too hard, to nuclear accidents that show the intrinsic risk associated with any kind of energy use. Today, there is a tendency among the elite in the developed countries to eat less or no meat, to bike to work. There is increasing awareness of the fact that 'development' and 'growth' are not synonymous and one can prosper without the other (Arizpe 1991). Quality of life is not just affluence.

The realisation that lifestyles must change will have a downward movement through the social and educational classes within countries. After the realisation goes down the income gradient within and between rich countries, then it will leap the gap between the more-developed countries (MDCs) and the LDCs.

This development is not our invention, but is in fact the trajectory of automobiles and contraception as they diffuse around the globe. So far, the process of imitation has been from the better-off to the poorer within the developed countries, and at some point from the developed countries to the less developed. Not only has contraception been diffused in this way, but some signs that ecological consciousness is following this pattern today is to be seen in the reduction of meat consumption in the US and elsewhere, in efforts to protect the rain forests, in the use of lighter cars, in the great number of voluntary associations dedicated to preserving the environment.[19] These phenomena are occurring among the rich and middle-class in the developed countries. Cultural change in the modern world must start with these groups, and they have a corresponding responsibility, since they belong to the 20% of humankind that utilise 75% of the earth's resources.

5.3 Youth and the south leading the way

It has become increasingly appreciated that human cultural diversity is as important as biological diversity in our search for sustainable lifestyle patterns. Grassroots movements all over the world indicate new ways to find long-term societal survival patterns through natural capital use without destructive depletion. Early examples from third world countries include the Chipko Movement, the Green Belt Movement, the Orangi Project among others (Ekins 1992).[20]

Representatives of the young and vocal environmental movements who participated in the 1992 Rio conference on environment and development (UNCED) and made themselves very visible, did not agree with northern leaders in their attempt to protect affluence, nor did they accept the blackmail-like trap of the southern leaders in their demands for cash and technology. What the nongovernmental organisations (NGOs) demanded was a fair share of the earth's common resources and help to self-help towards a sustainable society, based on participatory democracy in the use of the world's natural resources and a democratic system of checks and balances worldwide.

> We must reawaken to the reality that quality of life is based on development of human relationships, creativity, cultural and artistic expression, spirituality, reverence for the natural world and celebration of life, and is not dependent upon increased consumption of nonbasic material goods.[21]

The international debate at UNCED proved that today's environmentalists are well aware of the fact that population–environment linkages are not just an issue of numbers and carrying capacity, but a complex relationship involving distribution of resources, consumption and production patterns, cultural and power relations and all the other factors that govern birth, death and migration (Lindahl-Kiessling & Landberg 1992).[22] There is a growing understanding between these new environmentalists and the grassroots groups in the south, who also have much in common with feminist groups in their visions of a sustainable society and in the participatory methods they use.

5.4 The equity issues

Economics does not provide much advice on the distribution of income, which is to say who gets what, beyond providing indicators or criteria of distribution, which means departure from equality in sharing the fruits of progress, and then using these criteria to measure statistically the amount of dispersion. Economics does not indicate solutions. It does not, for example, say much about the dynamics that result in incomes being more egalitarian in one country than in another, and even less what amount of spread would be optimum.

One can indeed assert that if there was no inequality of income at all then the incentive to produce would disappear, and so would production. However, in the real world the amount of inequality is apparently greater than that required to provide the incentives for maximum production. Between the two opposite extremes, then, there must exist some intermediate degree of inequality at which production would be maximised, and one can hope that this optimum amount of inequality would be an amount of dispersion of income such that our sense of fairness would not be outraged.

The amount of inequality seems now to be exceeded both among countries and within many countries. Among countries, the process of development does include some market economy success stories: Singapore, Hong Kong, Taiwan, and Korea are coming along to the point where they economically already match several European countries. However, for each of those instances of success there are many cases of stagnation, where, especially in the present worldwide depression, the whole notion of development as it was preached in the 1960s and 1970s has come to seem like an illusion.

The countries where development has stalled include those where internal inequality is greatest: the Philippines and much of Latin America and Africa. This is not only dispersion of income as reported statistically, but very visible inequality as exhibited in huge estates, palatial homes, imported limousines, all set amid the huts of landless labourers.

China, on the other hand, is still poor, but its conspicuous change in health and family planning carries an important message: even in the poorest country, sharing its poverty among virtually the entire population, people will tolerate severe measures as for the common good—they can even accept such an extreme as the one-child family, to what extent on an educated participatory basis or because authorities say so, we do not know (Jacobson 1992). However, the results may most likely be attributed to an effective popular mobilisation. If the Tiananmen events in 1989 have weakened the government's ability to mount such mass mobilisation efforts, Chinese policy-makers may now rely on rapid economic growth and urbanisation to exert some influence on fertility (Laquian 1991). Other countries need not have a regime that calls itself Marxist to profit from this lesson: a basic material and social security system for almost everybody, even on a level far short of the western middle class standard, may be an incentive which counteracts the dependence on children as manpower or old age insurance (Nugent 1983).

5.5 Tolerance of inequity

The inequity that is so obvious in the world today is probably less than in imperial times, when most of the earth was divided among the great powers who used it as they pleased. The tendency was to orient the economies of the less-developed parts to service the metropolitan economies, providing raw materials to the centres and absorbing their manufactured products. In pursuing that aim, British rule effectively destroyed the textile industry of India. That period is now over, but the expected improvement has not occurred; it appears that the developed countries have found other ways of achieving the same result without imperialistic rule (George 1993).

In their attempt to develop independently, the less-developed countries borrowed heavily in the 1970s, the idea being that this would enable them to purchase the capital goods needed so that they could industrialise, pay back the loans, and be launched on their own. The result was exactly the opposite. Development did not result and cannot result as fast as required; the servicing of the loans now transmits more capital to the industrial countries than the latter provide for development in all forms (World Resources 1992–1993). What was initially given as a solution is now one of the great obstacles to further economic growth of the third world. The other obstacle is the recession in the world economy that has blocked the output for LDC goods.

The thoughtless borrowing that initiated the debt crisis can be directly related to population issues, especially to the increasing number of young people. We have to see the use of foreign funds for development, and the repayment of loans, in relation to population growth and urbanisation. In particular, the demand for employment by large, educated, urban populations has created an intensive search for new money and difficulty in repaying old debts. Even when net borrowing was at its height, the job-seekers outnumbered the jobs that could be created at their level of education. Foreign private investment is, of course, a cherished dream, but for countries with large populations there has not been enough of it.

The agricultural stagnation in the poorest countries, coupled with a drastic decline in terms of trade and rapidly increasing debt service obligations (Bangura 1989), make any argument that growth is about to resume less and less convincing. The reaction is expressed in many ways, none of them favourable to development. In some instances, people look back with nostalgia to tradition; in effect, they say if modernisation is an illusion we ought to turn to the way our ancestors lived. Fundamentalist religion is one manifestation of this, and it has become powerfully established in some countries and threatens to gain ground in others. In some places, hope is being set on partitioning countries into areas occupied by the various ethnic groups. Returning to a society made up of one's own ethnic group; turning away from the cosmopolitanism of the Enlightenment; these trends are seen today from Yugoslavia to Moldavia and at least in part can be attributed to the unacceptability of inequities. Inequity, in turn, is due in large measure to development which is too slow or has altogether stalled.

The economic crisis is also a deepening crisis of legitimacy of the state. In the worst cases there is a virtual disintegration of the national society through regional and ethnic conflict (Ghai & de Alcantara 1990). In others, *de facto* dictatorships emerge whose methods of maintaining national unity leave little scope for social and economic development. Others, perhaps military rulers, may understand a little more of the requirements for economic progress than do the fundamentalists, but still not enough.

The combination of deep economic crisis and structural adjustment packages tends to hit hard at vulnerable strata in society, worsening the situation in ways which put fertility transition aided by good family planning services further into the future. Real value of incomes has slumped, and cuts in state budgets for social services combined with cost-recovery policies have in many cases severely reduced public access to education and health (Hermele 1993; Stewart 1991). The introduction of family planning services is hampered both by increasingly weakened health service infrastructures and, in many social contexts, by people's reaction to their living conditions. When people have no assurance that they are going to make economic progress during their lifetimes and earn security for their old age, they fall back on the age-old means of protecting themselves: as large a number of children as possible. A multitude of reasons of all shades, economic, institutional, administrative, distribution of power, thus prevent the free and responsible decisions of men and women.

6. INDIVIDUAL RIGHTS VERSUS SOCIAL CONCERNS
6.1 Human rights

Decisions concerning family size are a very private matter and cannot be ruled by laws or general regulations without treading upon the human rights ratified again and again in UN declarations. As early as the Pakistan declaration of 1968, the human rights argument was used, i.e. each couple should decide how many children they want. If this formula is interpreted to imply that it is a human right to regulate one's own fertility, it becomes a very powerful argument against groups that want to fade out the use of contraceptives and abortions, and for family planning programmes. However, this is not a universally accepted interpretation.

In its ideal form, 'family planning' has been the code concept for a broad development strategy, comprising measures to achieve reproductive health, contraception, safe motherhood, child health and survival. It has, however, also been seen to cover inhumane and coercive actions with highly authoritarian connotations, promoting decisions made at the top instead of participatory programs. The human rights argument, therefore, has been used to oppose family planning.

Seen from this divergent viewpoint, the human rights argument has been considered a treacherous trap because a collision with other human rights is foreseen. In this context, freedom for men and women to regulate their own fertility would inevitably lead to overpopulation and finally to starvation. Therefore, the human rights argument is rejected with reference to Article 25 in Universal Declaration of Human Rights which states that everyone has the right to a standard of living adequate for health and well-being, not to mention environmental and other security.

The main difference between the two approaches seems to be value-based: can and will people make responsible decisions for themselves and for society given true possibilities and full responsibility, or will they use their human right to regulate their own fertility without social concern?

Science cannot give a definite answer to this question, but certainly experience from innumerable case studies favours the first interpretation. Wherever people have full reproductive choice without coercion, they have chosen to have smaller families if opportunities to regulate fertility are available. Only when families feel that their human rights are protected—the rights to education, medical care, old-age security, jobs and, above all, alleviation from poverty—will they feel that they no longer need to depend on large numbers of children for survival, and will then choose to have smaller families (Sen 1992).

6.2 Women's rights

Reproductive choice cannot exist in a non-egalitarian society. The connection between gender bias and family size has been investigated in depth by Jacobson (1992a), who writes:

> Gender bias is also the single most important cause of rapid population growth…
> Gender bias is thus a primary cause of poverty, because in its various forms it
> prevents hundreds of millions of women from obtaining the education, training,
> health services, child care, and legal status needed to *escape* from poverty. A
> necessary step in reducing births voluntarily, then, is to increase women's
> productivity and their control over resources.

The importance of gender equality is not unknown to conventional wisdom. There is an impressive array of international declarations and agreements concerning women's rights to equal status, including the Commission on the Status of Women established in 1946, to the recent 1979 Convention on the Elimination of All Forms of Discrimination against Women. The use of the new terminology *gender issues*, which has been the focus of increasing international attention in a variety of contexts, may indicate a new way of thinking which can open the arena for a more effective implementation of these long-standing principles. In this context, the empowerment of women is seen as part of equality between men and women which cannot be realised without women's full control of their own fertility. One obvious aspect is, as has been argued by Sen (1991), increasing women's status by investing in female education and increasing women's access to employment gives women better bargaining power, a clearer perception of their individuality, and increased value through higher perceived—or more visible—contributions to their family's economic position.

The population debate of the 1990s has been dominated by the microperspective with a new gender-related vocabulary. Underlying this change, despite the lack of scholarly consensus on the macro-level, a common wisdom exists, expressed in grass-root movements, that sees a balance between people, environment and natural resources as necessary condition for human happiness, prosperity and peace. This provides scope for a debate on implementation.

The point of entry for the debate is then not population growth, but development and quality of life. The approach is holistic, and considers economy, environment, health and fertility in an interactive perspective, challenging aggressive fertility control as a solution for poverty and for the global environment. This debate argues in favor of population stabilisation by choice, not coercion. Women need to be recognised as actors, decision-makers and political constituencies, not simply as providers of service and acceptors of contraceptives. However, 'it should be remembered that women are neither responsible for the crisis in the world system, nor can they be expected to resolve it' (Sen & Crown 1987).

6.3 The gender issue

Disagreement in terms of ultimate goals, between old-fashioned vertical 'population control' advocates and the advocates of the new gender approach, is not inevitable. The differences lie in the hierarchy of motives and the preferred means to achieve a balanced population, which in turn may represent different degrees of awareness more than different ethical standpoints. Harrison (1992) considers the controversy:

> In some cases the radicals may find themselves defeating their own objects. To say that population growth is 'not the problem' implies that it is not a problem. It provides ammunition for all those who wish to deny women the right to determine their own fertility. It also ignores the way in which population aggravates all those problems that are accepted as 'real' problems...But there are equal dangers in overstating the case and saying that population is *the* problem—the obsession with population above all other problems has been used (though thankfully, very rarely) to justify the use of coercion in family planning...Coercion is just as wrong as denial of the right of access to family planning.[23]

In the conventional, vertical perspective—more topdown than user's perspective—the control of fertility is discussed as a societal good, making balance between people and resources possible within prevailing gender relations. However, where women have no power, their only means to obtain status is through children, especially sons.

The gender-based analysis is centred on the individual and maintains that, as a primary goal, not because of environmental or societal concern, women have the right to control their own fertility. Broad changes in women's circumstances are required to make it possible for them to exercise their reproductive rights.[24] More and better contraceptive technology and services alone are not enough. However, the reverse is also essential:

> The ability to exercise free and informed choice regarding the number and spacing of their children is obviously an important step in enabling women to make choices in other areas, such as education and participation in life outside the home (Sadik 1993).

From the gender perspective, the complexity of the population debate is a consequence of its relation to the whole of the development debate. In fact, population is a sub-theme within development and, as such, it has continuously been framed in the context of one or the other approach to the development discourse (Sen 1992). It is in this array that one has to look for the explanation of some of the resistance against population issues becoming part of the environmental–developmental discussion at the UN conference in Rio 1992.

6.4 Rio 1992 and family planning

There was no debate on population issues at the Ministerial level at the UNCED. Population declarations in Agenda 21 and in the Rio Declaration were passed over without discussion. However, statements connected to the population debate were accepted in very many of the Agenda 21 chapters with identical wording: 'to enable women and men to fulfil their personal aspirations in terms of family size, in a way in keeping with their freedom and dignity and personally held values' (5.49), taking into account measures to 'have access to the information, education and means, as appropriate, to enable them to exercise this right in keeping with their freedom, dignity and personally held values taking into account ethical and cultural considerations.' However, the complete omission, in the separate chapter on demographic dynamics, of any specific mention of family planning, access to contraceptives or abortion is very much in evidence.

The question is, do these statements echo a debate on human rights and the empowerment of women or do they give voice to a conservative concern to preserve traditional family structures and gender roles?[25] Religious and pronatalist opposition has certainly made abortion a political taboo for most foreign aid programs, and the moral overtones of an anti-contraception and anti-abortion debate are lingering in the Agenda 21, in sharp contrast to the debate that took place among the nongovernmental organisations (NGOs) at the Rio Global Forum congress, at the opposite side of Rio. The Treaty on Population, Environment and Development accepted by this congress declares:

> Women's empowerment to control their own lives is the foundation for all action linking population, environment and development and demands women-centred, women-managed and women-controlled comprehensive reproductive health care, including pre-and postnatal care, safe and legal voluntary contraceptives and abortion facilities, sex education and information for boys and girls, and programmes that also educate men on male methods of contraception and their

parental responsibilities.

Had there been more of a gender than a feminist perspective in 'Planeta Femea' at Global Forum, someone may have added that 'men's parental responsibilities' is not sufficient; men have also to respect the health and well-being of their partners and children in all aspects of sexual behaviour (most notably disease transmission, and violence).[26]

7. THE WORLD SOCIETY AND THE PROCESS OF DIFFUSION

No doubt the most conspicuous on-going debate is not on human rights or gender bias, but on how developing countries will tackle their most urgent task: to improve their economic situation and at the same time generate the new and eco-friendly means for human activity. How will the rich part of the world fulfil its task to take the lead in this development and deliver constructive help to self-help? What are the prospects?

No amount of development assistance, no finely-tuned structural adjustment policy, will enable developing countries to resolve their problems when their resource base remains strangled by restrictive trade policies—the population and development crisis will not be resolved until this problem is addressed. The rich countries should not use their power to damage the economic prospects of poorer countries.[FN27]

7.1 Foreign aid

The industrial countries react to confusion and uncertainty with a certain foreign aid weariness, including reluctance to make further loans. Like many other debtors, the LDCs were over-optimistic in their projections of net return, and now the poorest among them need money even more than before, yet their credit rating is low.

Another factor in the declining enthusiasm for foreign aid may be a sense that environmental constraints, together with population growth, set limits on development. Given present technology and the style of life to which the whole world now aspires, the greenhouse effect and the disposal of waste are such serious problems that only a limited amount of development in the present style remains possible. Already there are 500 million automotive vehicles, operated by about one-fifth of the world population, and the effects in acid rain and terrestrial warming are ominous. Full development on the present pattern, with the resulting 2.5 billion vehicles, is inconceivable.

If world development is to be limited, then the question who *will* develop is going to dominate international politics in the short term. How much of it will Northern Americans have, how much Europeans, how much will be left for Turks, how much for Brazilians, how much for Nigerians? Such a zero-sum formulation could be based on the greenhouse effect alone, but this is reinforced by other limits.

If the total is limited, then it would take an improbable amount of altruism to provide foreign aid to the LDCs on a scale that would be decisive. Others becoming richer would still expand our markets, but would also increase global warming and waste, so reducing our possibilities. One wonders whether the currently diminished scale of nonmilitary foreign aid is due to some sense of this. In accord with the smaller hopes for development, an increasing fraction of the foreign aid from all the MDCs is called humanitarian, which is to say it is to cover current emergencies and extreme poverty, satisfying what are called basic needs, without much pretence that it will be more than a palliative for the longterm state of underdevelopment.

7.2 Rio 1992 and equity

It is against this background one has to consider the debate—or rather the lack of debate—at the United Nations Conference on Environment and Development (UNCED) on the demands that the unavoidable demographic changes will make upon international solidarity and cooperation. Principle 1 of the Rio Declaration on Environment and Development says that:

> Human beings are at the centre of concerns for sustainable development. They are entitled to a healthy and productive life in harmony with nature. Principle 3 goes on: 'The right to development must be fulfilled so as to equitably meet developmental and environmental needs of present and future generations.'

However, the Rio Declaration contains only nonlegally binding statements. The imperative documents are the Conventions on Climate Change and on Biological Diversity. The heated debates around those documents did not include concern for the drastic changes that the demographic momentum will give rise to. No time frames for the reduction of emission of greenhouse gases were stipulated. The Biodiversity Convention was not signed by a number of states, including the USA (under the Bush administration).

7.3 Where we stand

The demographic transition is the shift from high to low birth and death rates. The initial state is characterised by a superficial stability with high birth/death rates and in the ultimate state with low birth/death rates; the transition from the one to the other constitutes a period of instability that may be as short as a generation or as long as a century. Since instability takes the form of unprecedented growth, it matters a great deal over what a time-interval it stretches; one of the purposes of family planning programmes is to make possible a shortening of the time-interval at the same time increasing the well-being of mother and child.

The route of diffusion of innovations around the world has been consistent over time —always from the better-off to the poor in the developed countries, then to the better off and finally to the poor in the less developed countries. As the demographic transition moves along this route, so will changes in consumption patterns. The zero or even positive correlation between population growth and economic growth among countries has been interpreted as proof that controlling population growth does not necessarily increase development. The opposite interpretation is statistically valid as well.

In due course, the anticipated development process will result in a world society with a middle-class style of life. People will live in solid houses, suitably equipped with refrigerators, heated in winter, cooled in summer; they will drive cars; and they will save for summer holidays on another continent. Population numbers will barely be replaced; and a stationary population level will have been attained. However, the ecological cost of achieving this is such that the planet will have been seriously damaged; perhaps irretrievably. It is also highly conceivable that population increase, before stability sets in, will have been so great that it will also prevent the development that would solve the problems relating to population increase (Keyfitz 1991).

We also know that decisions on family size are not taken in governmental departments or boardrooms, but by individuals, who regard their lives from a holistic viewpoint. Population policies must take into account the total developmental perspective, which is centred on the well-being of all people, in this and future generations. This implies that gender issues, sexuality, health status, ageing, urbanisation, and societal factors such as migration, political, racial, ethnic, religious and class factors that directly affect women's and men's ability to exercise their reproductive rights must be taken into account.

7.4 What are we aiming at?

Whether human ingenuity is ultimately used to impoverish the earth or to create the means to change the fatal course of human life we do not know. We have examined the process and direction of changes in the world society and in environment issues. We have also examined what divergences are occurring between the direction in which we are now going and the target of our ambition. We discuss what can be done to bring the two into line, i.e. to reorient both our movement and our target in directions that make them consistent with one another.

An objective breathtakingly ambitious, indeed insolent, you may say, especially considering that this paper reports no primary investigation, in a sense contains nothing new. Nevertheless, we think it is the responsibility of the New Delhi conference to draw conclusions from what is already known and to suggest actions to implement these conclusions, addressing the problems facing this and coming generations.

What we have to face is that the limits set by the environment itself may be much closer to us, as well as being much more difficult to calculate, than previously imagined. The task requires technical knowledge that we do not yet possess, as well as an increase in our social and economic knowledge about how people want to live in the future. It is obvious that the present 1.1 billion people driving automobiles and eating meat to their pleasure, plus the 4 billion living in restricted circumstances, are rapidly approaching the natural-resource limits of our planet. What will be the outcome for the 10 billion that the earth is expected to contain in the next half century? Without drastic changes in technology, and in consumption patterns and distribution of wealth, the problems will continue to increase. The damage occurring is already visible to farsighted scientists, especially to biologists, and it is to be expected that public awareness will continue to grow.

The concepts presented here are contested by many citizens in the affluent world, and especially among politicians with a mandate at risk. The political message should be the very necessity for change and limitations. Says Boulding (1991):

> Those who are concerned with the future of the planet in its totality have to ask themselves: What are the sources of power in the human species directed towards changing the future in a desirable direction? It is not enough to preach we must do this, we must do that. Such preaching is perhaps a necessary prerequisite to action, but it does not necessarily produce the action required. We do need to study very carefully, therefore, the structure of power in human race over the

future, which involves not only particular decisions but also the overall images of the world in the minds of the decision makers, and the learning process by which these images are created. And in the solution of these problems—if there is one —we will undoubtedly have to make some use of threat power—taxation, regulations and so on—and some use of economic power. But the major element unquestionably will be integrative power, based first on widespread knowledge that we all live on the same fragile planet, which we have now seen from outer space and to which we owe a common loyalty and affection. Unless this view is very widespread, legitimacy will not be granted to those frequently painful processes which may be necessary to prevent catastrophe.

The natural environment is our life-support system, and a sustainable use of the natural resources is a prerequisite for human development. We are all an inherent part of nature. For the well-being of present and future generations, concerted efforts are needed to ensure that the earth's natural resources are nurtured and protected in a sustainable manner. To achieve sustainable development, we have to learn how human beings encroach on the natural environment. An increasing awareness of what sustainability involves is needed among people in all walks of life.

What is certain is that sustainable development will involve changes in the lifestyle of people in the developed world if ecological space is to be available for sustainable development everywhere. In addition, the obvious implication of our present knowledge is that we have to realise, all of us, that the quest for an increased wellbeing for everyone is not compatible with the present perpetual population growth insofar as a healthy planet is the basis for the envisioned quality of life.

Turning ourselves specifically to the New Delhi Population Summit, we conclude that the scientific community has not only a responsibility but also a moral obligation, to continue to increase the store of knowledge, to disseminate knowledge, to sharpen the analysis, and to translate the results into politically meaningful advice and proposals. Although there will be disappointments, drawbacks and the inevitable shortcomings, the debate must continue. Business as usual is no solution.

ACKNOWLEDGEMENTS

Many of our friends have read different versions of this manuscript and we are thankful for their comments even if we have not been able to include all proposals. They gave us constructive-minded food for thought. A very special thanks goes to Bertil Egerö, whose penetrating knowledge has been an invaluable asset. Some of the contributions from Bert Bolin and Adrienne Germain are marked in the text. However, as usual the authors are responsible for all shortcomings that may be found out'later.

REFERENCES

Adams, W.M. 1990 *Green development. Environment and sustainability in the third world.* London: Routledge.

Arizpe, L., Constanza, R. & Lutz, W. 1992 Population and natural resource use. In *An agenda of science for environment and development into the 21st century* (eds. J.C.I. Dooge, G.T. Goodman, J.W.M. la Rivière, J. Marton-Lefévre, T.O'Riordan and F. Praderie). Cambridge University Press, UK: pp. 61–79.

Atiyah, M. 1992 Population growth, resource consumption and a sustainable world. A Joint Statement by the officers of the Royal Society of London and the US National Academy of Sciences. Sir Michael Atiyah, President of the Royal Society of London and Frank Press, President of the US National Academy of Sciences.

Bangura, Y. 1989 The political and social context of structural adjustment in sub-Saharan Africa. *Nytt från Nordiska Afrikainstitutet* **24**: 22–3 Uppsala.

Berkes, F. & Folke, C. 1994 Investing in cultural capital for sustainable use of natural capital. In *Investing in natural capital: why, what and how?* (eds. A.M. Jansson, M. Hammer, C. Folke and R. Constanza). Beijer Discussion Paper No.33, Royal Swedish Academy of Sciences.

Bodin, J. 1577 *La République*, Book 5, Chap. II.

Boserup, E. 1965 The conditions of agricultural growth. London: Allen & Unwin.

Boserup, E. 1981 *Population and technological change: a study of long-term trends.* Chicago: University of Chicago Press.

Boserup, E. (1970/1989) *Women's role in economic development.* London: Earthscan Publications Ltd.

Boulding, K. E. 1991. What do we want to sustain?: environmentalism and human evaluations. In *Ecological Economics* (ed. R. Constanza). New York: Columbia U. Press.

Brooks, H. 1992 Sustainability and technology. In *Science and sustainability*, pp. 27–61. Vienna: IIASA.

Brundtland, G.H. (Chair). *World commission on environment and development. Our common future.* Oxford, England: Oxford University Press.

Cicero, Marcus Tullius (circa 44 B.C.). *De re publica*, Book IV, para. 5.

Daly, H.E. & Cobb, J.B. 1990 *For the common good: redirecting the economy towards community, the environment and a sustainable future.* London: Merlin Press (first publ. 1989, Beacon Press, Boston).

Davis, K. 1945 The world demographic transition. In *World Population in Transition, the Annals*, **237**, (ed. K. Davis) pp. 1–11.

Davis, K. 1963 The theory of change and response in modern demographic history. *Population Reprint Series* **123** (from Population Association meeting, April 26, 1963).

Demeny, P. 1992 Can population policies make a difference? 'Demographers and the next world population conference' at the annual meeting of the Population Association of America, Denver, Colorado, 1992.

Dixon-Mueller, R. 1993 *Population policy and women's rights. Transforming reproductive choice.* Westport CO & London: Praeger Publishers.

Doyle, C. The Hound of the Baskervilles.

Egerö, B. 1992 No longer North and South – the new challenges of demographic-economic interrelations. In *Human responsibility and global change.* (eds. L. O. Hansson and B. Jungen). University of Göteborg, Section of Human Ecology.

Ekins, P. 1992 A new world order: grassroots movements for global change. London and New York: Routledge.

George, S. 1990 *A fate worse than debt.* (3rd ed.) England: Penguin Books.

Ghai, D. & de Alcantara, C.H. 1990 The crisis of 1980s in sub-Saharan Africa, Latin America and the Caribbean: economic impact, social change and political implications, *Dev. and Change* **21**: 389–426.

Godwin, W. 1793 Enquiry concerning political justice.

Greenhalgh, S. 1990 Toward a political economy of fertility: anthropological contributions. *Pop. Dev. Rev.* **16**, no 1: 85–106.

Harrison, P. 1992 *The third revolution: environment, population and a sustainable world.* I.B. Tauris & Co Ltd. London & New York: pp. IX–X.

Hermele, K. 1993 Mortgaging the future? The social impact of economic decline in Latin

America. A record of the 1980s. *PROP Publication Series*, Lund (forthcoming 1993).

Hernandez, D.J. 1984 *Success or failure? Family planning programs in the third world.* Westport: Greenwood Press.

Ho, Ping-ti. 1959 *Studies in the population of China, 1368–1953.* Cambridge, MA: Harvard University Press, p. 176 and *passim.*

Hodgson, D. 1988 Orthodoxy and revisionism in American demography. *Pop. Dev. Rev.* **14**: 4, 541–69.

Holling, C.S. 1986 The resilience of terrestrial ecosystems: local surprise and globalchange. In *Sustainable development of the biosphere* (eds. W. C. Clark & R. E. Munn). IIASA. Cambridge University Press, pp. 292–317.

Hombergh, van den H. 1993 *Gender, environment and development: a guide to the literature.* The Netherlands: International Books.

Jacobson, J.L. 1992a *Gender bias: roadblock to sustainable development.* Washington, DC: Worldwatch Inst.

Jacobson, J.L. 1992b China's baby budget, cited in Jacobson 1992a, p.45.

Johnson, D. G. and Lee, R. D. 1987 *Population growth and economic development: issues and evidence.* Madison: U. Wisconsin Press.

Kelley, A.C. 1973 Population growth, the dependency rate, and the pace of economic development. *Pop. Stud.* **27**, no.3, 405–414.

Keyfitz, N. 1991a From Malthus to sustainable growth. Working Paper, Vienna: IIASA.

Keyfitz, N. 1991b Population and development within the ecosphere: one view of the literature. *Population Index* **57**(1): 5–22.

Keyfitz, N. 1991c Completing the worldwide demographic transition: the relevance of past experience. *Ambio* **21**: 1, 26–30.

Keyfitz, N. 1991d Population growth can prevent the development that would slow population growth. In *Preserving the global environment: the challenge of shared leadership* (ed. J. Tuchman Mathews). pp. 39–77. New York: W.W. Norton.

Keyfitz, N. 1993a Are there ecological limits to population? *Proc. Nat. Acad. Soc.* **90**, 6895-6899.

King, M.H. 1990 Health is a sustainable state. *Lancet* **336**: 664–667.

King, M.H. 1991 An anomaly in the paradigm. The demographic trap, UNICEF'sdilemma and its opportunities. NU. *News on health care in developing countries.* ICH, Uppsala University **1**: 5–10.

Laquian, A.A. 1991 Family planning–the Chinese experience. NU, *News on health care in developing countries.* ICH, Uppsala University **2**: 91, 13–16.

Lee R.B. & Devore, I. 1968 (eds) *Man the hunter.* Chicago: Aldine.

Lindahl, K. 1993 Let's fight for the gender perspective at the ICPD. *Planned parenthood in Europe* **22**: 2, 13–15.

Lindahl-Kiessling, K. & Landberg, H. 1992 Population, natural resources and development. *Ambio* **21**: 1, 4–5.

Livi-Bacci, M. 1992 *A concise history of world population.* Oxford, UK: Basil Blackwell.

Mahtab, F.U. & Karim, Z. 1992 Population and agricultural land use: towards sustainable food production systems in Bangladesh. *Ambio* **21**: 1, 50–55.

Malthus, T.R. 1960 *On Population* (ed. G. Himmelfarb). New York: Modern Library, p.246.

Malthus, T.R. [1798] 1967 *Population: The First Essay.* With a foreword by Kenneth E. Boulding. Ann Arbor: University of Michigan Press. Chap. I.

Mauldin W.P. & Ross, J.A. 1991 Family planning programs: efforts and results. *Studies in Family Planning* **22**: 6, 350–367.

McNeill, W.H. 1976 *Plagues and peoples.* New York: Anchor Books.

Mill, J. S. 1962 *Selections from the principles of political economy.* Chicago: University of Chicago Press. Book I, Chap. XIII, p. 3.

Moghadam, V.M. 1991 *Gender, development and policy: toward equity and empowerment.* Helsinki: WIDER Publications.

Moghadam, V.M. 1993 *Gender and the development process in a changing global environment.* Helsinki: WIDER Publications.

Notestein, F. 1975 Population: The long view. In *Food for the world* (ed. T.W. Shultz). Norman Wait Harris Fund Lectures.

Nugent, J.B. & Gillaspy, R.T. 1983 Old age pensions and fertility in rural areas of less developed countries: some evidence from Mexico. *Economic Dev. and Cultural Change* **31**: 809–829.

Postel, E. 1992 The value of women, women's autonomy, population and policy trends. *Int. Conf. on Pop. and Dev.* Gaborone, 22–26 June.

Royal Swedish Academy of Sciences and The Swedish Council for Planning and Coordination of Research, 1991, Stockholm.

Sauvy, A. 1956. *Théorie generale de la population.* Paris: Presses Universitaires de France.

Sen, G. 1992 Women, poverty and population — issues for the concerned environmentalist. New York: DAWN.

Sen, G. & Grown, C. 1987 *Development, crises, and alternative visions: third world women's perspectives.* London: Earthscan. Cited in Moghadam, V.M. 1990

Simon, J. 1981 The ultimate resource. Princeton, NJ: Princeton University Press.

Spengler, J.J. 1942 *French predecessors of Malthus: a study in eighteenth century wage and population theory.* Durham, NC: Duke University Press, p. 8.

Stewart, F. 1991 The many faces of adjustment. *World Development* **19**: 2, 1847–1864.

Tabah, L. Population growth in the third world. In *Science and sustainability* (ed. N.Keyfitz). Vienna: IIASA.

World Women's Congress for a Healthy Planet 1990. New York: WEDO.

NOTES

[1]   Data from Massimo Livi-Bacci. 1992. *A Concise History of World Population.* Oxford, UK: Blackwell.

[2]   Livi-Bacci, p. xv.

[3]   Marcus Tullius Cicero. (circa 44 B.C.). *De re publica,* Book IV, para. 5.

[4]   Livi-Bacci, p. xv.

[5]   Thomas Robert Malthus. [1798] 1967. *Population: The First Essay.* With a foreword by Kenneth E. Boulding. Ann Arbor: University of Michigan Press. Chap. I.

[6]   Thomas Robert Malthus. *On Population.* Gertrude Himmelfarb, Ed. 1960. New York: Modern Library, p. 246.

[7]   *Ibid.,* p. 251.

[8]   *Ibid.,* p. 277.

[9]   John Stuart Mill. 1962 *Selections from the Principles of Political Economy.* Book 1, Chapter XIII, p. 3. Chicago: University of Chicago Press.

10   Population Growth, Resource Consumption and a Sustainable World. 1992. A Joint Statement by the officers of the Royal Society of London and the US National Academy of Sciences. Sir Michael Atiyah, President of the Royal Society of London and Frank Press, President of the US National Academy of Sciences.

11   See for example World Women's Congress for a Healthy Planet 1991. WEDO, New York, NY 10022.

12   Statement issued by the international conference on Population, Natural Resources and Development organized by The Royal Swedish Academy of Sciences and The Swedish Council for Planning and Coordination of Research, Stockholm, Sweden, 30 September–3 October 1991.

13   Declaration of The International Symposium on Contraceptive Research and development for the Year 2000 and Beyond, Mexico City, 8-10 March, 1993.

14   This view was suggested to us by Bertil Egerö.

15   Ester Boserup has adduced cases in which population growth has been a stimulant to economic development. What seems to have happened in these cases is that population pressure induced modifications of institutions in the direction of private property, an effect that is clearly not universal. Unfortunately Boserup has had followers who generalized the result with no authorization from Boserup's data or their own (Keyfitz 1991, p.11).

16   World resources, 1992–93: A guide to the global environment. Towards sustainable development. New York, Oxford: Oxford University Press 1992.

17   Population Growth and Economic Development: Policy Questions. A report from National Academy Press, Washington, DC 1986, p.40-46.

18   Conan Doyle, The Hound of the Baskervilles, Chapter 3.

19   At The Global Forum there were more than 9000 NGOs registered, from all over the world and more than 14000 delegates participating in the daily seminars, that produced around 40 treaties on different topics.

20   See UN Human Development Report 1993, chapter 5: People in Community organizations pp 84-100.

21   From Treaty on Consumption and Lifestyle at the Global Forum seminars, UNCED 1992.

22   It is, however, less clear if all fractions of the feminist movement at UNCED had got the environmentalists' message. At least a small fraction made eminently clear at all

meetings I attended that they did <u>not</u> accept the formulation by other women's organisations that "we must acknowledge that the world cannot sustain an unlimited number of people, just as women's bodies cannot sustain unlimited pregnancies" (Marge Berer, Women's Global Network for Reproductive Rights). KLK.

23 Harrison pp.IX-X.

24 Although women have claimed at all times that it must be in the woman's power to decide over her own body, still the expression 'reproductive rights' is a rather new invention and the structure is not at all ready: 'women's organisations and feminist groups have found themselves struggling to define their own agendas within the contradictions of pronatalist and antinatalist ideologies expressed by increasingly powerful networks of international organizations on both sides.' (Ruth Dixon-Mueller 1993).

25 'There are a lot of code words in this field. One of the code words that worried me most was when delegates said that issues relating to women and/or sexual and reproductive health must be put in their 'cultural framework'. This seems to mean: 'We don't want to change anything. These issues are too sensitive to even bring up in our countries.' (K. Lindahl 1993).

26 Comment by Adrienne Germain.

27 Parliamentarians for global action: May 17, 1993, New York.

Population and Natural Resource Use
H.W.O. Okoth-Ogendo

ABSTRACT

At the end of 1992, the world's population had passed the 5.4 billion mark and was growing at the rate of approximately 1.7% per annum. This has important implications for resource development and use, especially in Africa with 12% of that population and where the annual growth rate is 3.0%, the highest in any region of the world.

There are perhaps three major issues to consider in this population–natural resource interaction.

The first is the need to ensure that Africa's population is an essential component in resource generation and development. An approach that places demographic variables at the consumer end of the population–natural resource equation ignores the most important lesson of history, namely that it is to their people that nations must look for the establishment of development thresholds. Capacity building in science and technology management and the harnessing of endogenously propelled development policies and strategies are important issues for Africa to consider.

The second is the necessity to ensure that sufficient resources are available for the complex needs of the population. With an economic growth rate well below that of the rate of natural increase, Africa is in an especially vulnerable position in this respect. Without appropriate technologies of sustainable development it has become evident that this vulnerability can be the source of resource depletion and widespread environmental damage.

The third relates to the nature of the medium-term strategies needed to manage the exceptionally high rates of population growth. African countries have, in this respect, adopted a series of fertility management strategies aimed at stabilizing, if not significantly reducing, growth rates in the next 30 years. The fact that the character of Africa's population (its age structure, settlement patterns and mortality levels) remains fairly complex means that success is unlikely to be easy.

The topic that I have been asked to address is on population and natural resource use. My concern is not to make a statement about the global balance between population and natural resources, but to contribute to this whole debate about the population problem as far as it relates to the African continent.

There are three questions that need to be resolved. The first is to assess the contribution that the African population can make to the generation of natural resources. The second has to do with the general and specific impact of demographic variables on the consumptive utilization of natural resources. The third question is perhaps the one that is occupying most people's minds, and that is how to balance population size and growth with natural resource demands.

In discussing the nature of the problem it is important to understand the demographic parameters in Africa. Note has already been taken that globally, the world population growth rate is alarming. It has been indicated that it is even more alarming in Africa where it is averaging 3%, even though we know that the growth rate is beginning to fall in some countries. The explanation for that growth rate has to do with consistently high fertility rates, particularly in conditions of falling mortality. It is also the case that the rising population growth rate is not evenly distributed within most countries. Therefore when we are talking about the growth rate within the continent we must also understand that the distribution of the population varies very widely within and between countries, and therefore the problem is not similar for most countries, as I indicate later. However, recent trends, even in Africa, indicate that some of the predictions made before may not necessarily be correct, that in some cases growth rates are beginning to fall, in some cases very precipitously, and that mortality rates are also falling.

However, we also know that Africa is suffering very badly from the Aids pandemic, and therefore that the reverses that we see in the population growth rate may be compromised by other factors that are hitting the continent at this particular point.

Given that brief scenario, it is also important to point out the fragility of Africa's natural resources. It is estimated that no more than 19% of African soils may be defined as without inherent fertility limitations, as much as 55% of the soils in Africa have severe or very severe soil constraints, 33% of the continent is too dry to support rain-fed agriculture, and 6% is subject to very exceptional variations in rainfall. Consequently, the stress on the natural resources of the continent can be extremely severe, particularly if the high variations in temperature that cause accelerated decomposition of matter in much of the continent are taken into account. There is not much to talk about in terms of the distribution of minerals which are a basis for economic development, although some countries are of course extremely rich in mineral cover.

In addition to natural resources, it is important to note that the human resources in Africa remain extremely poor, with high illiteracy rates, especially among women, low technology management capacity throughout the continent, fairly high dependency ratios (especially in those countries where education is now becoming universal), and a very large working-age population that is increasing by the day because of the entry into the labour force of uneducated, and to some extent unskilled, young people, and also with little mobility within the continent as a result of a combination of cultural and institutional factors that make it impossible for many of these countries to address their own internal economic problems through migration.

The debate, therefore, that relates population to natural resources is one that must be defined very carefully. One way of defining that debate is either to state that the problem that we have on the continent is one of population size in relation to the resources available. The other, which is perhaps more sensible, is to define the problem as one of rapid population growth in relation to the generation and utilization of natural resources. If defined in the latter sense then what we must look at is how the population question affects development parameters through size and composition of the population, and also its social and kin structures. We know that population size will affect natural resource use through the creation of demand for material flows, especially as regards the consumption of energy, and the distribution of that energy, and also with respect to food requirements and the requirements of urbanization and the services that go with it. The population composition will affect the consumption patterns of that population, and therefore the availability of resources for consumption, the age and kin structures are important when assessing the resource expectation and exploitation of that population. The debate therefore is a complex one that cannot be resolved even at a meeting of scientific academies like this.

The reality therefore, as the session indicates, is a very complex one. It is complex because in the first instance for agricultural Africa and in the absence of rapid technological development the population of Africa is its primary resource. Therefore the first thing that we must try to do is to understand what the potential of that resource is. We know historically that many countries have reached their own development thresholds through the utilization of their populations, through focusing not so much on questions of size or growth but on the question of quality of that population. We have examples of many eastern countries (Japan, Korea and others) that have depended to an extremely high degree on their own population potential for development, for the creation of skilled economies, for technological absorption and adaptation, and therefore for the creation of the necessary threshold capacity for development. This is an issue that must concern us in discussing the role of population in the African continent. Technological change will assume that the availability of a population that is not only educated but is also able to absorb and utilize that technology, and therefore efficiency in the management of development resources, must assume a certain level of capacity within the African population.

But population is not simply a resource. For Africa, population has also become a constraint to development. The population effects on resources depend on the level of development for each country, the resource availability for that country, the level of technology, and the size of the population. For Africa, and in the absence of technology, we are beginning to witness tremendous effects on natural resources, particularly increased demand on those resources, which have had effects on the quality of the resources available. We have witnessed, for example, a tremendous amount of pressure in certain (not all) countries that have led to transformations in the social institutions that control resource management, for example in relation to land, in the transformation of institutions, and in the breakdown of social systems that control the location and access to these resources.

We have also witnessed what has become suboptimal utilization of land in some of the countries, leading to degradation to levels that have not been witnessed before. We have also witnessed a tremendous amount of land invasion, particularly the invasion of marginal resources by people who are displaced from their traditional land areas, and those marginal resources have usually led to the reduction of forests and woodlands. The contemporary evidence also indicates that the level of forest depletion may be as high as 6% annually, that agricultural expansion is beginning to take a toll on other land uses, particularly woodland (as I have indicated), and while total production is increasing in Africa, per capita production is in fact declining. The result of that is constant use and reuse of land, which always leads to land degradation. Although irrigation technology has been used in some countries to minimize the effects of the absence of rain, the irrigation technology is still an extremely underdeveloped process in the African continent. As has been noted, whenever population increases livestock numbers also increase, and we have also witnessed a tremendous increase in livestock numbers in several countries which also has effects on the development and availability of grassland. As a result of the expansion of agriculture into protected areas, some of these questions lead to the issue of biodiversity, an issue that has been raised at this conference and which will continue to be raised.

In discussing some of these issues it is very easy to blame population size and growth rate. We must remember that the African continent is operating within an international framework that has tremendous effects on the ability of the continent and its managers to use resources judiciously. The chronic spiral of poverty, which is a factor of the historical exploitation of the continent, remains an important issue that must be confronted at international level to understand fully what the problem of resource development in Africa is.

We also know that as a result of global climatic changes, which have resulted from abnormal concentrations of greenhouse gases in the atmosphere, the whole problem of human adaptation is one that is not only an issue for the North, but more importantly for fragile Africa, and that in itself is going to become increasingly important in understanding the ability of the African continent to confront some of the development questions that we are dealing with. We have also noted the whole issue of negative economic policies that have been imposed on African countries under the guise of structural adjustments, as a factor that is important to consider in understanding how populations are handling resource questions in the continent. Given that scenario it is important also to understand how that complex reality is being confronted in Africa. The issue is that attempts must be made, even in Africa, to stabilize population growth with resource demand.

Some of the premises that have been adopted can be summarized at two levels. The first concerns policies that deal with the stabilization of population growth. Some of these that relate to population management have concentrated, perhaps unduly, on fertility management structures. Fertility reduction strategies, which have been adopted in just about all African countries (apart from one or two where fertility is still an issue), are beginning to prove extremely successful and these relate not only to family planning, but also to the improved health status of the people, the question of the status of women, and poverty alleviation. Success has been noted in several countries. In Nigeria, for example, fertility management has led to a drop in the total fertility rate from an average of 8.1 in the period 1969–1979, to 6.7 in 1985, and as recently as one month ago we have indications that it has dropped to 5.4. That will translate into tremendous reductions in the population growth rate, which makes predictions about the high rate of population growth in that country wrong.

What that is saying is that while attempts are being made to stabilize population growth rates, it is important also that African countries must confront the development question; that it is by increased production and investment, and through sustainable development policies that will ensure that the quality of life for that population improves even as we try to control its level of growth. I am not recalling the argument of the American

Government in Mexico that development is the best contraceptive, rather that the issue of balancing resources and population growth rate must be handled both at the development part of that transect and at the population growth part of that transect.

More important, perhaps, is to stabilize resource demand not only at the national level but also at the international level, particularly through the reduction of per capita energy consumption in the North, which has a tremendous effect on the South. The North must also assist the South to adopt technologies that will use energy and resources more efficiently, and in encouraging sustainable energy options not only in Africa but on a global scale.

It is important to note that there have been several attempts at global environmental government, which might bear fruit in this particular process. We have seen the development of a whole new range of conventions relating to biodiversity, climate and desertification. Some of these international government initiatives are important and must be encouraged at that level not simply because the problem is an African one, but because the problem has global consequences. The debate is not one that can be resolved either by completely internationalizing it or by completely localizing it. For Africa there may be problems that can only be tackled and which must be understood at the level of continental relationships before they are internationalized, but what is most important is concerted effort by the global community. While that process continues we should not begin to consider that population control, as some people refer to it, is the only option available, even for Africa.

1/3

Demographic—Economic Relationships and Development
Jane Menken

ABSTRACT

This paper summarises three reports prepared by committees of the National Research Council, the principal operating agency of the US National Academy of Sciences and the National Academy of Engineering, on their services to the US government, the public, and the scientific community. In 1971, the volume *Rapid population growth: consequences and policy implications* appeared. In 1986, the Committee on Population published *Population growth and economic development: policy questions*, and in 1993, it issued *Demographic effects of economic reversals in sub-Saharan Africa*.

The first two volumes examined the effect of population growth on various aspects of development, while the third considered causation in the opposite direction, that is, the impact of a declining economy on basic population processes, namely fertility, mortality, and marriage. These reports, and related papers, find the linkages between population and the economy to be complex, difficult to elucidate, in many cases context-specific, and worthy of careful scientific research based on improved data availability. The second report finds that the impact of population growth on economic development is, in many cases, less than had previously been thought. Specifically, it reaches 'the qualitative conclusion that slower population growth would be beneficial to economic development for most developing countries' but that a 'rigorous quantitative assessment of these benefits is difficult and context-dependent'.

The third report studies recent economic conditions in seven sub-Saharan African countries and finds the deterioration of economic conditions associated with higher mortality of children and postponed marriages and first births, although not uniformly so in all countries. These studies, based on the best data available and careful analysis, indicate that relationships between population growth and economic development, while not negligible and not well understood, are complicated and vary from one setting to another.

1. INTRODUCTION

I am delighted to be discussing population and development interrelations as background information for the Population Summit of the World's Scientific Academies. I want to be certain, however, that I am not addressing this issue under false pretences. I am a demographer who specialises in fertility. My recent demographic research has focused on Bangladesh, where I collaborate with researchers at several institutions. So why am I, a non-economist, commenting on population and development? We are grappling with issues that cross disciplinary boundaries, and it seems to make sense to have a non-economist review some research in the economics field.

I observe that, far from being the 'dismal science', economics, in comparison with other fields interested in population and development, is considerably more optimistic about the effects of rapid population growth. Its optimism is, however, qualified and, for our purposes here, I believe it is important that we understand economists' findings, how they have been reached, and the qualifications they themselves add to their conclusions.

I will first give my own conclusions based on a recent close reading of major studies of the impact of population growth on development:

1. Population growth has important effects on economic development, but they are, in some cases, not as great as was thought in the past.

2. Feedback mechanisms are important—societies adapt; if this is not taken into account, we can vastly overestimate the impact of population growth in our forecasting.

3. Population growth has not prevented economic growth, although it may have reduced it.

4. The effects of population growth depend upon the situation of individual countries—for example, concern about self-sufficiency in food production is quite different for Kuwait, which has oil to trade in international markets, than for Bangladesh, where trade is far less likely to make up for internal shortages.

5. No singly-directed policy can address all the ills of societies. Reducing population growth through declining fertility is not a panacea; it will not, in and of itself, make a poor country rich. Rather, rapid population growth exacerbates problems, but it is not a root cause of many of the deterrents to economic development.

6. Reducing population growth acts both directly, on some aspects of economic development, and indirectly, by 'buying time' for root causes of development deterrents to be addressed.

7. Effects also go in the opposite direction: economic change can affect population growth and change.

To explain these conclusions, I will review three reports that have been published in the last two decades by the National Research Council (NRC) of the US National Academy of Sciences and the Academy itself; the latter two are the work of the Standing Committee on Population, which was chaired until recently by Samuel Preston, whose discussion of population and the environment is included in this volume. To the first report (National Academy of Sciences 1971) is attributed the view that rapid population growth is seriously damaging and, further, that reduction in that growth will lead to development. The second (National Research Council 1986) is widely thought to say that growth doesn't matter. I will summarise my recent close rereading of these two reports—which does not agree with either of these characterisations—and of a third report, released in mid-1993 as part of a major study of population change in sub-Saharan Africa, that looks at the reverse direction: the demographic effects of economic reversals in that region (National Research Council 1993). The 1986 report is particularly relevant to this meeting for two reasons: little that I have seen in the intervening years contradicts those findings; second, recent work confirms and goes beyond that report.

2. BACKGROUND

First, however, I wish to set the stage with some background review. 'During the 1960s and 1970s there were many assessments of the world population situation. Some were by alarmists who wrote of the "population explosion" and blamed population growth with responsibility for many, if not all the afflictions of the developing world. Others, taking a more cautious view, concluded that rapid growth, on balance, had consequences sufficiently detrimental to prospects for improving conditions in much of the world to warrant efforts to reduce fertility. Indeed this has been the primary rationale' for family planning programmes (Menken 1986).

In 1974, the United Nations sponsored an International Conference on Population in Bucharest. Although some countries urged adoption of policies aimed at slowing growth, primarily through family planning, the dictum that 'development is the best contraceptive' resulted from that conference. It was not followed by even its most fervent supporters in the developing world; instead, developing countries increasingly turned to population policy and family planning programmes aimed at reducing their fertility.

'One of the major challenges to the received wisdom on population questions came in 1981 with the publication of Julian Simon's book, *The ultimate resource*. Simon, while not opposed to the principle that individuals should be able to control the number of children they have if they so choose, [contested] the view that rapid growth had deleterious effects. He [argued] that population growth is a significant and effective long-term stimulus to economic development, exerting its influence by, among other ways, increasing the tempo of innovation' (Menken 1986). His views profoundly influenced the US Government's stance at the 1984 United Nations International Conference on Population.

Today, as we move toward the 1994 International Population Conference, the US position, like those of many other countries, is changing, with concern for human rights, status of women, maternal and child health, and the environment being discussed in meetings around the world. But my task here is not to focus on these concerns, many of which I personally share, but to review the evidence for consequences on economic development of population growth.

The 1971 US National Academy of Sciences report was an outgrowth, in part, of a study by Ansley Coale and Edgar Hoover (1958), from which much of the early scientific rationale for concluding that rapid growth is detrimental to economic development derived. They considered the effects of fertility on the growth of *per capita* income. More specifically, they identified growth of capital and the capital to worker ratio as crucial in economic change and considered two scenarios: fertility continues at a high and unchanging level; second, it falls continuously over 25 years to half its original level. Their findings: 'after 30 years, the population with lower fertility would be only 76% as large as the sustained-fertility population; the *per capita* income would be nearly 50% greater'.

In the early 1970s, 'elaborate models that predicted the effects of rising numbers of people (exemplified by *Limits to growth*: Meadows *et al.* 1971) captured the public imagination. They indicated that continued population growth was at best alarming, and more likely would have fearsome consequences for the world' (Menken 1986).

3. THE 1971 US NATIONAL ACADEMY OF SCIENCES REPORT

Against this background, the 1971 report examined many areas of life as they would be affected by increasing population. I call attention here to only two: resources and economic development. 'One of the main fears expressed in the early discussions of population growth was Malthusian, that the resource base, food included, would be outstripped by rapid increases in the numbers of people it had to support. The 1971 report was relatively optimistic on this issue, calling food "the crisis that has not materialised" and saying that technological progress offered promise of assuring the availability of resources at least to the end of the twentieth century and probably beyond so long as efficient management could be achieved and with exceptions in regions of the world where food production was not keeping pace with population growth' (Menken 1986).

Related to economic development, 'the effects of rapid growth seemed certain, in the committee's opinion to "increase the number of landless, subsistence, or disadvantaged" and to raise "administrative burdens and social costs of absorbing urban arrivals". They concluded, however, that "unprecedented and still accelerating population growth has not prevented very rapid economic advance. Population growth, though not a negligible block to development and modernisation, has also not been an overriding factor....it appears clear that rapid population growth in the less developed countries has been a decided obstacle rather than an aid to economic growth and that the more rapid the rise in numbers, the greater the deterrent effects"' (Menken 1986).

The 1971 report found that 'rapid population growth has neither prevented overall economic growth nor brought about widespread famine. However, rapid population growth has resulted in a slow growth of *per capita* incomes, *per capita* food production, and standards of living, while national economic growth rates are rapidly rising. Moreover, with current population growth rates, the present optimism about food production need not apply far into the future. An immediate and continuous decline in fertility would soon increase the welfare of individuals and households in all economies, and after 15 to 20 years could result in very substantial—and cumulatively rising—overall economic gains, particularly in the developing countries'.

Its recommendations: 'Population growth is only one of several variables that affect the quality of life...thus it would be a gross oversimplification to blame numbers of people alone for the set of problems confronting modern society'. They recommended a series of policies related to inducing fertility change, including that all people have the freedom to determine family size; that there be national population-influencing policies, to serve national objectives of economic development, public health and welfare, and environmental conservatism; and stressed the need for research.

Unfortunately, the executive summary of the report contained a paragraph that has been used to characterise the report. It claimed that developing countries could raise their *per capita* income growth by a third through a 25% drop in their fertility alone. This paragraph, long used as the economic underpinning for family planning programmes, was apparently not endorsed by the committee and may, according to some reports, have been added at the last minute by a young staff member!

4. THE 1986 NRC REPORT

Some 15 years later, early in 1986, the National Research Council released another, assuredly less pessimistic, report entitled *Population growth and economic development: policy questions.* Papers that served as background and provided the evidence for the findings were published in a separate volume (Johnson & Lee 1987). This study asked whether slower population growth, achieved by the reduction of fertility through a national family planning programme, would improve various aspects of economic level and development. It took as its framework the nine questions that are shown in Table 1. I will consider only a few of these in any detail. For each of the questions, the Committee considered the theoretical rationale for the hypothesis and the empirical evidence that was available. Historical and time-series data were taken as especially relevant, but cross-sectional comparisons of countries with differing characteristics and at differing stages of development were considered. I will report briefly on some of their findings and keep a scorecard, which is shown in full in Table 1.

Question 1. Will slower population growth increase the growth rate of per capita *income through increasing* per capita *availability of exhaustible resources?*

'Many of the early fears that population growth would lead to exhaustion of non-renewable resources did not take into account the impetus that scarcity would have for development of adaptive strategies involving alternative resources' (Menken 1986). Economists say that use of non-renewable resources is allocated through market mechanisms in which price is determined by both supply of and demand for a particular resource. If a non-renewable resource is depleted, the price will rise, either because the supply falls or the costs of extraction rise or both. But high price will then stimulate the search for substitutes and for conservation. The NRC report gives an example: Zaire, at a time when it produced more than half the world's supply of cobalt, reduced its production by 30%. Prices more than tripled—but they led to substitution of other materials so that consumption of cobalt by the US dropped by fully half.

Thus, economists appeal to what are called perfect markets, which allocate resources efficiently over time. In this situation, the number of people who have access to a resource may not change; rather, the time frame of use depends on cumulative population numbers. There may, however, be problems. Overestimation of future use can lead to unnecessary conservatism in current use. Also, changes in demand for a resource and in technology may not be well anticipated. Monopolies may depress demand by artificially raising prices and keeping them high, leading to resource conservation. Difficulties may arise in allocating shared resources, such as oil reserves under land owned by many parties. On the basis of their discussion of these issues and the evidence available, the panel that prepared the report concludes that the rate of resource depletion bears no necessary relationship to the rate of population growth. Rather, depletion depends more on level of income and, thereby, demand for goods.

Table 1 *Policy questions addressed in the 1986 US National Research Council Report,* Population growth and economic development *and brief answers*

	questions	scorecard
1.	Will slower population growth increase the growth rate of *per capita* income through increasing *per capita* availability of exhaustible resources?	No, qualified
2.	Will slower population growth increase the growth rate of *per capita* income through increasing *per capita* availability of renewable resources?	Yes, and with ramifications
3.	Will slower population growth alleviate pollution and the degradation of the natural environment?	Yes, qualified
4.	Will slower population growth lead to more capital per worker, thereby increasing per worker output and consumption?	Yes, but less than previously thought
5.	Do lower population densities lead to lower *per capita* incomes via a reduced stimulus to technological innovation and reduced exploitation of economies of scale in production and infrastructure?	No
6.	Will slower population growth increase *per capita* levels of schooling and health?	Yes, for education No, for health
7.	Will slower population growth decrease the degree in inequality in the distribution of income?	Yes, almost unqualified
8.	Will slower population growth facilitate the absorption of workers into the modern economic sector and alleviate problems of urban growth?	Yes, qualified
9.	Does a couple's fertility behaviour impose costs on society at large?	Yes, but voluntary rather than drastic measures are warranted

Thus, the economists' view is that, theoretically, the market functions through the price mechanism to allocate resources. However, perfect markets do not exist, and, especially in developing countries, 'population growth may be more directly linked to inefficient resource use in reality than in theory, although population policies appear to be a very crude instrument for dealing with inefficient markets'. However, the prescription of letting markets function efficiently without worrying about resource exhaustion is qualified. The report acknowledges the argument that slowing population growth may 'buy time' to find alternatives to a particular resource and for technological development to occur; it does, however, emphasise that scarcity is a major stimulatory factor in the search for alternatives, which, historically, has been quite successful.

Despite the caveats just discussed, the economist's faith in 'price-driven technological change' led the NRC panel to conclude: 'On balance,…we find that concern about the impact of rapid population growth on resource exhaustion has often been exaggerated, and, in any case, that the effect of changes in population growth on global resource use has been and will probably continue to be quite weak'.

Score: No, but

Question 2. Will slower population growth increase the growth rate of per capita *income through increasing* per capita *availability of renewable resources?*

Here the story is quite different. The report identifies two mechanisms that may link population growth rates and renewable resources: diminishing returns and resource depletion. 'The number of people alive at any one time [affects] the amount of a renewable resource, such as arable land, that is available to each person…Reduced availability [of some resources] lowers individual productivity (and therefore individual income). In Bangladesh, for example, there appears to be clear evidence that agricultural productivity dropped as population grew rapidly in this most densely settled rural nation' (Menken 1986). The danger of resource depletion is especially high when there is no system that governs access to and use of the resource. With free access, users pay only the cost of harvesting, which is lower than the cost if the asset value were taken into account. Two examples of resources of this type are forests to which access is unrestricted, and fishing.

Population growth could, however, provide the stimulus for innovation (for example, improved technology or institutional change) that would counter these problems. But there are dangers in relying on innovation: the resource could be completely depleted before adaptation could occur and, even if existing institutions could be 'fixed', the process could be difficult and costly, with the need to bear this cost itself a consequence of population growth. Slower population growth would ease the problem, at least in the short term.

Here I quote the final conclusion: 'Slower population growth, in some cases nationally and in others globally, is likely to lead to a reduced rate of degradation of renewable common-property resources such as air, water, and species of plants and animals. If significant amounts of land and forest resources are held in common [rather than having unlimited access] in a country, they will also tend to be degraded less rapidly. These effects are likely to be more evident in the short run—in say, a decade or two. In the long run, population growth itself might create greater incentives to develop the social and political institutions necessary for conservation. Such incentives are irrelevant, of course, if the resource has become depleted beyond the point of restoration. Moreover, changes are costly and the need to bear such costs is itself a consequence of population growth'.

Score: Yes, and with ramifications

Question 3. Will slower population growth alleviate pollution and the degradation of the natural environment?

Because this issue is discussed in detail elsewhere in this volume, I will mention only that the 1986 NRC report's answer to the question posed above is a qualified yes. The panel concluded that population growth contributes to environmental problems, but that much of the damage is because environmental resources are common property, without sufficient access controls, so they tend to be overexploited. Governments in developing countries thus far have not met the substantial fiscal and institutional requirements for controlling and repairing environmental damage. Meeting these requirements may be postponed until irreparable damage has occurred. Slower population growth allows time for institutions to protect the environment.

Score: Yes, qualified

Question 4. Will slower population growth lead to more capital per worker, thereby increasing per worker output and consumption?

'Coale and Hoover (1958) believed that higher ratios of capital to labour would lead to higher *per capita* output and, therefore, higher *per capita* income. Lower population growth would under their formulation increase the supply of capital by encouraging savings' (Menken 1986). The NRC panel agreed that slower population growth would indeed lead to more capital per worker than in a rapidly growing population. It concluded, however that research in the years between 1958 and 1986 indicated that an increase in the capital/worker ratio is only modestly related to increased productivity (in terms of *per capita* output). Thus, while this appears to be a genuine example of a positive consequence of reduced population growth, it may not be a decisive influence. This result is important because many of the early models, including the Coale–Hoover model, were based on theory that posited a strong relationship. The current estimates of the effect of population growth on capita/worker ratios would lead to far smaller effects on economic well-being.

Score: Yes, but less than previously thought

Question 5. Do lower population densities lead to lower per capita incomes via a reduced stimulus to technological innovation and reduced exploitation of economies of scale in production and infrastructure?

The panel found that any economies of scale in manufacturing that resulted from the higher population densities in cities occurred with cities of moderate size. They found no relationship between national population density and economies of scale and, because markets are international, that little stimulus to technological progress results from increased density.

The report also concludes that increased densities could lead to diminishing returns to labour in agriculture that would not be offset by the stimulative effects of increased population density.

Score: NO

Question 6. Will slower population growth increase per capita levels of schooling and health?

'Improving education and health is part of every country's development plan. Children in large families tend to have lower education and poorer health than their peers who have fewer siblings. But this association does not mean that higher fertility necessarily causes poorer health and less schooling. Rather, families may make a trade-off, choosing more children and therefore having less money to spend on each child. But where family size is not the result of deliberate choice, family planning programs that enable parents, especially the poor, to reduce the number of unwanted children, are likely to increase both the level of education and the health of children' (Menken 1986).

But data are not unambiguous. The report found that school 'enrolment was unrelated to population growth, but that faster growing populations tended to spend less per child on education. Whether education is now considered such an important goal that countries are willing to devote large portions of their national budgets to providing schooling, or whether there is simply no relationship is not known' (Menken 1986).

Here I want to mention two studies subsequent to the report. In Thailand, it was found that those families that participated in the family planning program were more likely to be able to act on their values regarding education and obtain more schooling for their children (Knodel *et al.* 1990). In Matlab, in rural Bangladesh, long a site of a well-documented maternal and child health and family programme, it was found that children who reached the age when they were eligible to start school were more likely to do so if they did not have a younger sibling. The family planning programme was directly related to increasing the likelihood of schooling (Foster & Roy 1993).

The findings on health were more clearcut. Because health programs in most developing countries favour tertiary care in urban settings, the committee concluded that these programs would not be impeded in any major way by rapid population growth.

Score: Yes for education, No for health

Question 7. Will slower population growth decrease the degree of inequality in the distribution of income?

Historical studies have shown that, in the past, when populations grew more slowly, wages tended to rise, so that the income of workers would be higher, relative to those of owners of capital. The same type of effect can follow from contemporary family planning programmes. If they help poorer people to reduce their fertility, then the supply of labour will decrease, and wages will rise, thus reducing income inequality.

The effect may be especially pronounced for women. 'In most countries, women assume most of the time, health, and energy burdens of bearing and raising children. When this burden is increased by unwanted children, there is probably a greater welfare loss for women than for men. Programmes to improve contraception are thus likely to raise the welfare of women relative to men; in most societies, such a change would promote sexual equality'.

Score: Yes, almost unqualified

Question 8. Will slower population growth facilitate the absorption of workers into the modern economic sector and alleviate problems of urban growth?

When considering issues of employment, the NRC group distinguished between the effects of urbanisation and the effects of national population growth. Urbanisation, caused by migration from rural areas to the cities, can be beneficial in that it gives more people access to the benefits of the modern sector of the economy, including the prospect of high wage employment, and better education and health facilities. But when urbanisation is very rapid, these facilities may not grow quickly enough. The conclusion of this report is that the distribution of services, with enormous favouritism shown toward the urban areas, is at least a partial cause of the problems of cities. 'A first step toward slowing excessive urban growth would involve reducing the public sector's disproportionate subsidies for urban residents and urban-based economic activities'.

There is little evidence of excessive unemployment even in rapidly growing countries. As one member of the NRC panel commented, 'the poor cannot afford to be unemployed'. The effects of rapid growth may be expected in low income and underemployment, rather than no employment at all.

Slower population growth, in and of itself, clearly will not solve these problems but may offer time to find better approaches to them.

Score: Yes, but

Question 9. Does a couple's fertility behaviour impose costs on society at large?

Does having an additional child have a negative effect on the public welfare? Does the decision by an individual couple impose costs on others in the population? The NRC committee considered this issue because the existence of what economists refer to as externalities (effects external to the decision maker) may justify public policies that influence the essentially private decisions of individual couples. While there was no universal answer, the conclusion reached was that there is likely to be a negative external effect of childbearing in most developing countries, especially those that lack social security systems and where the economies of scale that result from population density are likely to be counterbalanced by congestion costs. The report concludes that the consequences of individual childbearing decisions do provide a basis for policies directed toward family planning but 'there is no evidence to suggest that drastic financial or legal restrictions on childbearing are warranted'.

Score: Yes, but drastic measures are not warranted

5. DEMOGRAPHIC EFFECTS OF ECONOMIC REVERSALS

Finally, I want to mention the report on the demographic effects of economic reversals in sub-Saharan Africa. It stemmed from concern that economic decline in some of the region's countries over the last 15 years may have especially affected the welfare of vulnerable groups, especially children. Historical evidence from pre-industrial Europe (Lee 1990) and more recent work for Latin America (Hill & Palloni 1992) support the notion that changes in economic conditions over time are linked to mortality, marriage, and childbearing. The NRC study assesses the situation for seven countries: Botswana, Ghana, Kenya, Nigeria, Senegal, Togo, and Uganda. They were chosen for their varying socioeconomic situations and because data were available that could support this kind of analysis. The study found that economic conditions were connected to changes in child mortality, marriage, and first and second births, although not in all cases and not in all countries. These studies would not have been possible without data collection by the Demographic and Health Surveys and the former World Fertility Surveys that provided detailed information both at the individual level and by national governments.

6. CONCLUSIONS

So, to recapitulate, reports on the relationships between population growth and economic development lead me to the conclusions I described at the beginning of this paper. I want to add, vide last report, a conclusion on the need for data collection efforts that will permit the issues raised in all of these reports to be addressed — not just once, but monitored over time.

In sum, the first two reports discussed here 'take a much more balanced view of the role of population growth in impeding or promoting economic development than do the impassioned messages of some scientists and popular writers of the last 20 years' (Menken 1986). Economists seem to be saying that slowing population growth alone cannot make a poor country rich or solve all the problems. I am reminded of a comment made by my colleague at Penn, Etienne van de Walle, nearly 30 years ago. He said that development programmes would be far more effective if, out of every $20 spent, $1 went for family planning programmes. They are not a panacea for all societies' ills; but they can promote change in directions that improve people's lives.

Finally, I believe we need to appreciate that the world is complicated; we would be remiss if we failed to realize that difficult, complex questions are hard to answer.

ACKNOWLEDGMENTS

The review of the first two reports considered here draws on work undertaken when I was Director of the Seventy-first American Assembly on 'The New Population Dilemma: Issues and Choices for the United States', which took place April 17–20, 1986. I have quoted liberally and with permission from my introduction to the published volumes.

REFERENCES

Coale, A.J. & Hoover, E.M. 1958 *Population growth and economic development in low-income countries.* Princeton, NJ: Princeton University Press.

Foster, A.D. & Roy, N. 1993 The dynamics of education and fertility: evidence from a family planning experiment. Submitted.

Hill, K.H. & Palloni, A 1992. Demographic responses to economic shocks: The case of Latin America. Paper prepared for the International Union for the Scientific Study of Population, Peopling of the Americas Conference, Veracruz, Mexico, May 18–22.

Johnson, D.G. & Lee, R.L. (eds.) 1987 *Population growth and economic development.* Madison, WI: University of Wisconsin Press.

Knodel, J., Havanon, N., & Sittitrai, W. 1990. Family size and the education of children in the context of rapid fertility decline. *Pop. Dev. Rev.* **16** (1): 31–62.

Lee, R. 1990. The demographic response to economic crisis in historical and contemporary populations. *Pop. Bul. UN* 9:1–15.

Meadows, D.H., Meadows, D.L., Randers, J., & Behrens III, W.W. 1972. *The limits to growth.* New York, NY: Universe Books.

Menken, J. (ed.) 1986 World population and US policy: The choices ahead. New York, NY: W.W. Norton. Also published in limited edition as *The new population dilemma: Issues and choices for the United States.* New York, NY: The American Assembly, Columbia University, 1986.

National Academy of Sciences. 1971 *Rapid population growth: consequences and policy implications.* 2 vols. Baltimore, MD: Johns Hopkins University Press.

National Research Council. 1986 *Population growth and economic development: policy questions.*

Committee on Population. Washington, DC: National Academy Press.

National Research Council. 1993 *Demographic effects of economic reversals in sub-Saharan Africa.*
Committee on Population. Washington, DC: National Academy Press.

Simon, J.L. 1981 *The ultimate resource.* Princeton, NJ: Princeton University Press.

van de Walle, E. 1964 (Personal communication).

Population and Health
V. Ramalingaswami

ABSTRACT

The relationship of health to population is a two-way process, each being a determinant as well as a consequence of the other.

The rate of change of indicators of health is compared in developed and less developed countries and the effects on population growth are examined.

The causes of maternal and child mortality are analysed and specific issues such as adolescent childbearing are addressed. Implications for policy-making are discussed with recommendations.

1. INTRODUCTION

Human health and its relevance to population growth is one of the great themes of human history. Historical demography and evolution of health problems, although so closely linked, are often considered separately. The relationship between health and population is a two-way process; each can be a determinant as well as a consequence of the other. The pathways by which they influence each other can inform policy and intervention.

2. HISTORICAL TRENDS

A striking feature today of the world health scene is the large differences in the mortality profile of more developed, less developed and least developed countries. In the most developed countries, there is an enhanced expectation of life at birth, an important component of which is improved survival in early life, particularly from birth to the first birthday. This process began generally in the 19th century and was largely associated with the decline of infectious diseases. Three groups of factors were associated with this phenomenon: rising incomes; growth in medical technology in the form of antibiotics, vaccines and clinical technologies; and shifts in social, behavioral and cultural factors such as education, in particular female education and nutrition (WHO 1993).

Each of these groups of factors has influenced mortality decline and is increasing life expectancy in developing countries in varying degrees (WHO 1993). The role of preventive and curative technologies depends upon the degree to which a technology is established in a culture or integrated into the institutions of a society. The shift in causes of death from infections to age-related cardiovascular disease and cancer, the so-called epidemiological transition that had taken place in developed countries, is currently being enacted in many developing countries as well. These countries carry a *double burden* of the pre- and post-transitional states of health in the form of persistent infection–malnutrition complex on the one hand and rising non-communicable diseases on the other. The contribution of any particular factor to contemporary mortality declines is difficult to quantify, but is significantly influenced by recent advances in medical

71

technology, whereas historical mortality declines are attributable more to economic factors, education, nutrition and behavioral changes. Economically-induced changes do not operate independently of technologically-induced changes and their sustainability cannot be presumed.

Both developed and developing countries are subject to the uncertainties of the new plagues such as AIDS, for which there are no national boundaries and no developmental statuses as safeguards, and to the resurgence of disease earlier brought under control in many parts of the world, such as malaria, tuberculosis, visceral leishmaniasis and cholera.

3. THE SPEED OF CHANGE IN HEALTH STATUS AND POPULATION GROWTH

The differences in the speed of change in indicators of health between then and now are striking. It took 100 years for the infant mortality rate (IMR) to fall from 200 per 1000 live births to 70 per 1000 in today's industrialised countries. This reduction in developing countries in more recent times took just 35 years. The gap in IMR between the northern and the southern hemispheres fell from 130 points in 1950 to 50 points in 1985. With regard to life expectancy at birth, in the middle of the 19th century, life expectancy was broadly similar, north and south. Now it is over 76 years for the north, and in the south it rose from 40 (1950) to over 60 (1985). So far as education is concerned, the time lag of 100 years between north and south that existed in 1950 is now a lag of only 30 years. The south achieved for education, in one generation, what took the north two (Patel 1989).

Similar trends can be observed in population growth between the north and the south. The momentum of population growth gathers in the time lag between fall in mortality rates and fall in birth rates. The difference in the time lag at different points in time may be due to multiple factors, but one important factor is the availability of contraceptive technologies. What took western European countries 30–40 years in the late 1800s and early 1900s, took eastern and southern European countries 10–20 years in the 1920s and 1930s, and has taken east Caribbean countries only 10 years in the 1960s and 1970s (Patel 1989). The historical nexus between child survival and decline in birth rates is the outcome of a process of family building that evolves through distinct phases as the mortality transition progresses (Lord & Ivanov 1988). A recent study in Turkey found that the previously observed time lag of 15 years between the fall in infant mortality rate and the fall in birth rate was reduced to 3 years in an area where child health and family planning services were integrated. The point to be made here is the *importance of exploiting the synergy between health services and family planning services.*

4. THE HEALTH OF MOTHERS AND CHILDREN

Breastfeeding exclusively for 4–6 months from birth is of well-known importance to infant nutrition, child survival and child spacing. Breastfeeding delays the return of fertility and increases the birth intervals; it is an important child survival and birth spacing strategy. The mucosal immunity of the new-born is enhanced by the secretory IgA produced by plasma cells migrating from Peyer's patches to the breast secretory tissue through the maternal entero–hepatic circulation (Short 1992).

Certain relationships between fertility patterns and maternal and child health are well established (Omran 1971; Royston & Armstrong 1989). There is increased risk of maternal and child mortality and morbidity associated with pregnancies too early, too many, too often, and too late. Factors such as timing and spacing of pregnancies, age at marriage and at first birth, the number of pregnancies, rapid childbearing and consequent displacement of the older sibling from the mother's breast, are well-known to exert a marked influence on the health of the mother and the child. I do not propose to repeat what is already a well-known set of phenomena. There are, however, a few points to be made in this connection:

1. A woman conceiving below the age of 15 is five times more likely to die than a woman who conceives in her 20s. Babies born to women under the age of 15 are twice as likely to die in infancy as those born to women in their 20s.
2. The chances of survival for the new-born are increased as the birth interval increases. Spacing pregnancies by two years reduces child mortality by 20%. Short birth intervals pose substantial risks to the offspring in their first five years.
3. For women over the age of 35, maternal mortality increases five-fold.

Even to this day, 500000 women lose their lives every year during pregnancy and labour, 99% of these deaths occurring in developing countries. It is here that the disparity between developed and developing countries is greater than for any other human development indicator. Women die and suffer ill health because of:

- neglect in childhood
- adolescent marriage
- poverty and illiteracy
- undernutrition and overwork
- harmful traditional practices
- denial of equal status; denial of social, economic and legal status
- denial of access to adequate family planning and maternal health services

The *root causes* of maternal mortality are ecological handicaps and socio—cultural traditions together with poverty, lack of educational opportunity and low societal status of women (Ramalingaswami 1992). They need to be addressed as part of an overall socio—economic development strategy. The *immediate* causes are medical in nature including haemorrhage, toxaemia, malnutrition, infections, obstructed labour and unsafe abortions. These are remediable by application of known medical technologies using community-based approaches with adequate referral services, equitable and accessible health care and the use of a high-risk approach. Certain practices occur which lead to alteration in infant mortality rates according to sex, for example, preference for male children and discriminatory practices against female children and women.

4.1 Abortion

Unsafe abortion constitutes a leading cause of maternal mortality. There are estimated to be 40–60 million abortions annually, of which fully one-half are believed to be illegal and unsafe (Sanström 1993). Legal restriction of abortions and inadequate family planning services lie at the bottom of the abortion tragedy. The experience of Romania is still fresh in our minds before and after lifting of the authoritarian imposition of highly restrictive anti-abortion legislation. India, Zambia and Uruguay are examples of countries where abortion for medical and social reasons is allowed. Provision of effective contraceptive services, with outreach and access to the community at large, is an essential step in avoiding unwanted pregnancies and the need for termination of pregnancies. However, that alone is not enough; nor is provision of legislation permitting abortion services. There must be, in addition, adequate abortion services which are accessible and affordable as a component of reproductive health care.

4.2 Adolescence

Sexual activity brings serious hazards to the health of those below the age of 18. These hazards are present throughout the world, developed or developing. Sexual relations in adolescence, particularly in developing countries, are likely to take place without the use of contraceptives or protection against sexually transmitted diseases (STDs) including HIV infection. At menarche, physical growth is not yet complete: increase in height to the extent of about 4% and in pelvic growth to the extent of 12% to 18% can be expected during this period. Profound psycho–social development and moulding are also taking place at this time. Pregnancies during the adolescent period are attended by high maternal mortality rates, especially in countries where reproductive health services are poorly developed and access to caring services is severely limited. Recourse to unsafe abortion practices leads to a variety of potentially fatal acute complications and a state of chronic morbidity. Adolescents seek help for their problems from friends, traditional healers, local chemists; the doors of the health care system are not freely open to this age group, despite their need for competent and confidential care (Friedman 1993).

4.3 AIDS

AIDS is increasingly becoming a problem of developing countries, and the gap between developing countries and developed countries is widening (Ramalingaswami 1992). Within developing countries, heterosexual transmission is the dominant mode, rising new infections and rapid spread are the rule, and men, women and children are affected. There are profound issues of human survival and human productivity in the long-term. The symbiotic relationship between AIDS and ulcerative genital disease caused by sexually transmitted infections provides a window of opportunity for controlling AIDS transmission through the control of STDs. Annually, 250 million new cases of STDs are believed to occur around the globe (Dixon-Mueller & Wasserheit 1991). Twenty different infections are sexually transmitted (Fathalla 1991). Nearly one-half of HIV infections occur in persons below 25 years of age; indeed the AIDS infection is actually being driven to a significant extent by young people. Vertical transmission of HIV from the mother to the offspring is of sinister significance, imparting an inter-generational quality to HIV infection. Migration of individuals and population groups tends to facilitate the spread of HIV. Poverty is a major factor leading to commercial sex and migration; a strategy for survival becomes a strategy for death. Women are the most vulnerable, subjected to sexual subordination, with double standards in marital fidelity; the subordination of women is a pervasive phenomenon educationally, economically, legally and sexually. Drug abuse is another factor serving a double conduit of HIV infection, through the use of contaminated injection equipment and heterosexual transmission. The future scenario of AIDS tends to overwhelm the health gains made in many parts of the developing world during the past three decades, especially in child survival. AIDS looms large over the horizon of population and health.

5. CONCLUSION

I would like to conclude by drawing attention to the policy and programmatic implications of the nexus between health and population:

1. Scientific evidence points to exclusive breastfeeding during the first 4–6 months of life, followed by complementary breastfeeding in the post-weaning phase up to two years of age, both as a health measure for the mother and child and as a population-limiting measure through its effect on increasing the inter-pregnancy interval.

2. Prenatal care including nutritional support is essential to decrease the cumulative reproductive stresses on the mother.

3. Discriminatory provision of health care, nutritional support and educational opportunity based on preference for sons is an issue at the societal level in some countries which needs to be addressed on an urgent basis because of its profound implications for the health, age and sex structure of the population.

4. Adolescent fertility and the social and health costs associated with it merits serious attention; whether the adolescent is married or not and whether the setting is a developed or developing country. Ending the system of early marriages is essential but not enough. There is need to help young adolescent girls from becoming mothers before they are physically and psychosocially mature and ready. The rate of abortion-related deaths among adolescents is tragically high. The widespread ignorance among young people in all countries of the risks of unprotected sexual activity and the ways of avoiding them must be addressed with a sense of urgency.

5. The availability and use of contraceptives will be facilitated if services are provided within a caring ambience of primary health care. Family planning and health services must be integrated truly and tightly. The separation of abortion from reproductive health issues has been unfortunate. Information and education on family planning by contraception is needed in the first place, with safe and accessible abortion as a back-up.

6. The persistence of high maternal mortality rates in the developing world, without much change in recent years, is a blot on society. Maternal health services, including family planning, coupled with broader inter-sectoral coordination to enhance women's education, economic potential and social status, are needed.

7. AIDS has numerous points of contact with population and development issues. A deeper understanding of sexual behaviour in different population groups is necessary for an educational strategy for prevention of the spread of HIV in an era when science offers promising approaches to its prevention and cure.

8. The relationships between health and population operate within and are

influenced by a broader framework in which educational level and status of women, childhood and gender disparities, overall living conditions and household food and nutritional security, are the key components.

9. Health is a major contribution to demographic transition. The interrelationships between health, nutrition and population have great relevance to policy and strategy formulation and programming for limiting population growth. Improved health conditions and the decline in birth rates have an extensive interface, with profound implications for policies and programmes.

REFERENCES

Dixon-Mueller, R. & Wasserheit, J. 1991 The culture and silence—reproductive tract infections among women in the third world. International Women's Health Coalition.

Fathalla, M.F. 1991 Reproductive health: a global overview. In *Frontiers in Human Reproduction.* Annals of the New York Academy of Sciences, June 28, 1–10.

Friedman, H.L. 1993 Marriage, pregnancy and sexually transmitted diseases, hazards to the health of young adolescents. Paper prepared for the Expert Committee on Maternal and Child Health and Family Planning in the 1990s and Beyond, Geneva: WHO, September.

Lloyd, C.B. & Ivanov, S. 1988 The effects of improved child survival on family planning and fertility. *Stud. in Fam. Planning* **19**, (3).

Omran, A.R. 1971 The health theme in family planning. Monograph No. 16, Chapel Hill: University of North Carolina Population Centre.

Patel, M.S. 1989 Eliminating social distance between North and South—cost-effective goals for 1990s UNICEF staff working paper No. 5, p. 224.

Ramalingaswami, V. 1991 Into inequity born: the state of health of the women of south Asia, *Science and Public Affairs* **6**, (1), 67–76.

Ramalingaswami, V. 1992 The implications of AIDS in developing countries, In *Science Challenging AIDS.* Proceedings based on the VII International Conference on AIDS, Florence, June 16-21, 1991, Karger pp. 24–32.

Royston, E. & Armstrong, S. 1989 *Preventing maternal deaths.* Geneva: WHO p. 233.

Sandstrom, K. 1993 Abortion—a reproductive health issue: executive summary. Stockholm, Washington, June.

Short, R. 1992 Breast-feeding, fertility and population growth. In *Nutrition and Population Links ACC/SCN Symposium Report.* Nutrition Policy Discussion Paper No. 11, May 33–46.

World Heath Organisation 1993 Health and Mortality. Contribution by HST to WHO policy paper on Population and Health for the International Conference on Population and Development. Geneva: WHO.

Population and Development:
Preparing for the 21st Century. A Statement
Nafis Sadik

Previous speakers have described very well how complex is the situation that faces the world. I would like to describe, very briefly, how we may change it.

1. CURRENT AND PROJECTED SITUATION

We should not underestimate how serious the problem is. The medium United Nations projections—which assume continued declines in fertility—indicate a world population of 8.5 billion by the year 2025 and 10 billion by 2050. Growth could readily be much higher: with slower fertility decline, the high projection reaches 12.5 billion in the year 2050. The difference between the medium and the high projection in 2050 is 2.5 billion—equal to the whole of the world population in 1950.

However, growth could also be lower. Assuming a sharper fertility decline, population could be slightly under 8 billion in 2050. That is, again, a difference of about 2.5 billion by 2050, but this time on the right side.

I believe we should aim for this more difficult goal. Although hard to reach, it is not unrealistic and the benefits offered are real and tangible. In its search for sustainable development, the world needs the breathing space that lower population growth rates will provide.

Men and women have a basic right to free choice in the size and spacing of the family. In this case, rights and necessity coincide. All the evidence points to the conclusion that if women and men are offered a fully informed and free choice, they will choose to have smaller families. That leaves us a clear course of action. Our efforts should concentrate first on establishing the scale of the unmet need for family planning and, second, on meeting it.

We should do this, starting now. One reason for urgency is that after the year 2000, the projections diverge more and more sharply. Fertility must fall in *this* decade to make sure of a declining trend in population growth during the first half of the next century.

Despite the seriousness and complexity of the problems connected to population, the experience of the last 25 years with population programmes demonstrates considerable success, and some reason for cautious optimism.

2. LESSONS LEARNED

In a wide variety of settings in the developing world, we have found:

First: population programmes can succeed, sometimes spectacularly, and to a large extent independent of the level of socio-economic development. This was not at all obvious at the start of the 1980s. Although balanced development reaching all sectors of society is the long-term aim, it can start in the social sector. Lower fertility need not wait for economic development — lower fertility and lower population growth can come first, and can even stimulate progress in reducing poverty and energising the economy.

Second: the majority of developing countries have made notable progress in adopting and implementing population policies and programmes. Indeed, several countries have been highly successful in drastically slowing population growth. Examples can be drawn from around the world: Colombia, Fiji, Indonesia, the Republic of Korea, Mauritius, Mexico, Sri Lanka, Thailand, and Tunisia. In addition, fertility declines are now evident in many more countries, including Botswana, Cape Verde, Egypt, Bangladesh, Kenya and Zimbabwe.

Third: contraceptive use is increasing. Since the early 1960s, contraceptive use has risen from around 10% of couples of reproductive age to around 53% today. Over the same period, the average number of births per woman dropped from over six to 3.7, a decline of almost half in just one generation.

Fourth: political commitment is the strongest influence on the strength of any population programme. Commitment is essential to ensure adequate resources for population programmes. It is also the precondition for change in favour of smaller family-size ideals.

Fifth: successful family planning programmes do not start with technology, they start with an idea. The idea is that each individual can make a choice about family size, and that it is a necessary part of everyday life. It must be based on full information about the services available, and counselling if necessary to assist in making it. It must be completely voluntary, not mere acquiescence to the wishes of a service provider. Once the choice is made, there must be adequate provision for follow-up and further counselling if necessary. At all points, the client must be treated with respect.

There is no substitute for this approach. I cannot say too strongly that if we do not meet the family planning needs of individual women — and men — in what remains of this century, then we have no hope of meeting the world's development needs in the next century.

Sixth: women must be at the centre of making and carrying out policy. In many societies, women are trapped in a web of tradition that determines their worth solely in terms of their reproductive role. Prevailing cultural patterns prevent women from developing a sense of self esteem, and customary practices make girls second-class citizens within their own households. For too many women, choice and opportunity are largely unknown experiences. Dr Ramalingaswami, in his presentation, vividly described the situation where women suffer ill-health and die from a number of causes and do not achieve their full potential.

There is no question that the conventional prescriptions for development have not worked, especially for women. A cornerstone of new development thinking is the full integration of women into the mainstream of development and concern for progress in all aspects of their lives — health, education, employment, nutrition, legal and political rights. In traditional development thinking, investment in social development was seen as a luxury, a fruit of economic success. However, we now know that the opposite is true: the basis of economic progress is a healthy and socially stable population growing in balance with socio-economic prospects and natural resources. Instead of being the fruit of development, social programmes, especially those addressing the status of women, are its very foundation.

If women are to realise their full potential in their productive and community roles, they must be guaranteed their reproductive rights and must be able to manage their reproductive role. The ability to decide freely and in an informed manner the number and spacing of one's children is the first step in enabling women to exercise choices in other areas. When a woman realises that she can make decisions regarding her reproductive function, this experience of autonomy spreads to other aspects of her life. It is a first, essential step on the road to empowerment and to making contributions to the real development of her society.

Seventh: in recent years, quality has emerged as a very important issue in family planning programmes. Empirical evidence shows that improvements in quality encourage acceptance and continuous contraceptive use.

Quality means that services take into account the needs and references of users, especially women. Women want clinics that are easily accessible. They want to be treated with respect and dignity in an environment of privacy and confidentiality. They want a wide range of safe, effective and affordable contraceptives. They want information and guidance that will allay their doubts and help them to make an informed choice. They also want a facility with a constellation of services, so that as many of their needs as possible can be met in one place.

Eighth: an important step is increasing investment in education. Education breeds confidence and encourages a woman's belief that she is in control of her life. It is a key factor in socio-economic development, in reducing maternal and infant mortality rates, as well as fertility. Educated women can explore and exercise their options instead of just following an assigned role of reproduction and service to their families.

3. WHAT CAN BE DONE IN THIS DECADE?

These, then, are some of the most important lessons about what is possible in the implementation of population policies. Much more can be achieved now, in the six remaining years of this millennium, in order to secure the demographic future.

The first step will be to meet existing demand for family planning. At least 350 million couples worldwide do not have access to the full range of modern methods of family planning. A large proportion of them would like to delay or space their pregnancies, or stop having children altogether. At least 120 million would use family planning now if services were available. Reaching only this group of motivated couples would go a long way towards meeting our goals for the year 2000.

Besides increasing family planning services, there are actions aimed at empowering women that should be made a priority: improving education, health and basic services for all, particularly for girls and women; providing economic opportunities for women to work; removing customary and legal barriers to women's full participation and equal treatment in the areas of marriage, property ownership and inheritance, politics, religion and the work place; and there are unstated but nevertheless real barriers in the form of different standards in respect of sexual behaviour as between men and women. All of these issues need full and open discussion in the widest possible context. In particular, open discussion is needed on how to change attitudes of men and women.

It is no longer sufficient for a government to draw up population policy only in broad and general terms. To be effective, policies must be sectoralised and adapted to local variations of circumstances and needs. This may imply a greater use of local government and non-governmental (NGO) structures, and more involvement in policy and implementation of programmes by all these institutions.

4. THE CHALLENGES AHEAD

Resources for population activities in developing countries lag far behind the actual needs. To reach global targets and to give all couples access to family planning would require a doubling of annual expenditures for population programmes from currently $4.5 billion to $9–11 billion annually by the year 2000. The governments of developing countries now finance at least three-quarters of the cost of those programmes. On the other hand, international population assistance has hardly increased at all in real terms over the past two decades, barely keeping up with the growth of numbers of couples of reproductive ages.

The latest data available show that less than 1.5% of ODA funding goes towards population programmes. We have long advocated that the share for population activities must be raised to 4%. With this small change in proportions, the extra billions of dollars needed would materialise and the goals I have alluded to could be realised.

It is equally vital to increase the priority of other social sectors, such as education and health. In our view, at least 20% of total international assistance should be earmarked for social sector programmes. We are also advocating that 20% of national budgets should be devoted to education and health in the social sector.

We have every incentive to spur our determination. Universal access to a wide range of safe, affordable and effective family planning choices would bring more benefits to more people at less cost than any other single technology currently available to the human race.

The demand is there. We know what to do. Now the main challenge for the population community is to raise resources to the level where demand can be met. The last decade of the 20th century offers a real possibility of achieving integrated goals in the areas of population, environment and socio-economic development.

Each of the scientific academies and the organisations represented here has a part to play. Many have already made important contributions. Your work will see its first fruit at the International Conference on Population and Development in Cairo next September, for which I have the privilege of serving as Secretary-General. The Cairo Conference will set the agenda for work in population for the next 20 years.

My colleagues and I in the Secretariat for the Cairo Conference are now preparing a first full draft of the proposed final outcome of the Conference. In doing so, we will study your deliberations and conclusions very carefully, and we also welcome your individual perspectives.

There is growing awareness that partnership between the scientific community, governments and the private sector is indispensable for a sustainable future. Your views are most important to political leadership and policy-makers in all areas and at all levels of national life. I urge you all to become involved both at the national and the international level in the remaining preparations for Cairo. On this most important issue of population and development, there is an increasingly receptive audience waiting to hear from you.

Introduction to Session 2:

LINKAGES BETWEEN POPULATION, NATURAL RESOURCES AND THE ENVIRONMENT

P.N. Tandon

The second session was devoted to discussing 'Linkages between Population, Natural Resources, and the Environment'. The carrying capacity of the Mother Earth is already under stress. Besides other factors, this process is integrally linked to the expansion of human numbers.

Dr Preston felt that the process is most readily recognized at the global level, but when analysis descends to smaller geographical units the relationship becomes more complex. He suggested that the advantages of slower population growth are felt across many environmental domains, whereas other approaches are often more limited in scope.

Dr Batliwala made a well-reasoned case to suggest that energy strategies could contribute to a reduction in population growth. Sufficient energy technologies exist that can contribute to an increase in living standards and thereby impact positively on the intensity of the population problem.

Professor Falkenmark discussed the role of the globally circulating water, the blood stream of biosphere, as the basic link-support of human population. Many low income countries have already crossed the optimal level of water-related population density. She warned that the escalating water scarcity will become critical by 2025 A.D., unless a proper ground-water management strategy and a 'global water ethics' are urgently evolved.

Dr Norman Myers, in his detailed analysis of ecological and economic values of biodiversity, examined the part played by the human population in the current crisis, differentiating between the role of the impoverished Southern nations and the rich Northern ones. He presented evidence that the fast growing numbers of shifting cultivators in the developing countries are the predominent cause of tropical deforestation. In contrast, the negligent and wasteful consumption in industrialised countries are the principal source of pollution-derived degradation of wild land habitats. He felt that the burners of fossil fuel are equally responsible as burners of the tropical forests in the loss of biodiversity, currently estimated to be 30,000 species per year.

Over the past 1000 years, the land area degraded by human activities has amounted to 2000 Mha observed Dr Zhao Qiguo. Consequent upon rapid population growth and mismanagement of the agroecosystem there is an annual loss of 5–6 Mha. He felt that the expertise developed by China for the prevention and control of land degradation could be of great significance to the rest of the world.

2/1

Population and the Environment:
The Scientific Evidence
Samuel H. Preston

ABSTRACT

Increasing food requirements are linked to contraction of forested land and to soil despoilation. The inadequacy of research design when describing the relationship of population growth and pollution is highlighted. Social models, e.g. of land tenure and their effects, are discussed, and obstacles to expansion of food production are noted.

1. INTRODUCTION

My assigned task was to review the scientific evidence linking population growth and environmental change. Clearly, I can only provide a brief introduction to this vast topic; the other papers in this session provide more detail on specific issues.

I will focus on the broad sweep of what we think we know and why we think we know it. The emphasis is on the quality of evidence available, evaluated according to what I take to be conventional scientific standards. This seems an appropriate emphasis in a meeting of the world's scientific academies. Unfortunately, the subject of population growth is one in which evidence is often intermingled with sentiment, strained metaphors, and apocalyptic visions.

As in any scientific evaluation, when we are examining evidence, we are dealing with the past. We look to the historical record in search of demographic footprints. We cannot look to the future for evidence. Computer simulations and projections of relations among populations, environments, and economies are useful for many purposes, but they are not evidence in the conventional sense; they are collections of hypotheses. Whether the hypotheses make any sense, individually or collectively, can only be evaluated by examining the historical record.

We have to begin by recognizing that the subject with which we are dealing is not one where investigators are permitted the luxury of controlled experimentation: thank goodness, I might add. Instead, they must attempt to interpret naturally-occurring events using research designs that come as close as possible to recapitulating the logic of experimental methods, so that they can try to establish cause and effect relationships. I have to say, however, that research designs in this area have not been notably ambitious. Most of what we know or think we know is a result of what can be called "informed observation"; that is, observation informed by what are usually very primitive, though often serviceable, models of human behavior. The data on which these observations are based are usually very slim in the environmental area.

Nevertheless, I believe that what we know at present supports the position that population growth has contributed and is contributing to a variety of environmental changes. Some, but not all, of these changes would be classified as ailments or degradations. These undoubtedly include the destruction of forests, especially tropical forests; soil erosion and degradation in certain major regions, especially within sub-Saharan Africa; and the loss of species of plants and animals.

2. BIOLOGICAL MODELS
2.1 Food production and agrarian resources
Let me be as explicit as possible about the model and evidence that supports the conclusion that the expansion of human numbers contributed to deforestation, soil degradation, and species loss. The basic element of the model recognizes man's prodigious need for food. To support more people, more food must be produced. To produce more food, more resources are required in food production. Some of these resources – in fact, the most important – are men's and women's labour, which is available in rough proportion to population size. But other resources include land and water. With more people, more of these resources will be devoted to food production, and fewer will be permitted to remain in their natural state or used for other purposes.

This model is so commonsensical that describing it may seem gratuitous, but I think that it is useful to acknowledge that what we think we know is based not only on empirical evidence but on evidence interpreted in light of this primitive model. The evidence on which the conclusion is based is, first of all, that patterns of land use have changed dramatically as human numbers have expanded. Forests that covered nearly all of Europe in 900 AD had virtually disappeared by 1900. They were converted primarily into agricultural fields and pastures to feed Europe's growing population (Wolman 1993). A similar process is occurring on a much-compressed time scale in most developing countries today. Sixteen million square kilometers of tropical forest have been reduced to eight over the last four decades, according to Norman Myers. The most significant agent of forest destruction is the encroachment of slash and burn cultivators (Myers 1991).

So there is clearly an association over time between population growth and loss of forest. There is also an association over space. During the 1970s, the correlation between a nation's rate of population growth and its proportionate change in forested area was –0.56 for 41 countries in the humid tropics (Grainger 1990; Mather 1986). These associations are what we would expect if population growth were driving the search for additional resources to be used in food production.

Associations do not establish causation, of course. We are convinced that we understand the direction of causation because we interpret it in light of the model I described. One alternative explanation of these associations is that both population growth and changes in land use were a product of a third factor, a change in productive technology. This interpretation is implausible, however, because the technology of forest clearance for food production is one of the oldest known to man. Furthermore, the acceleration in population growth rates is not for the most part attributable to changes in productive technology, but to the development and diffusion of methods to combat man's greatest natural enemy, disease-inducing microbes: bacteria, viruses, and parasites (Preston 1980). These were nature's first line of defence against the expansion of *Homo sapiens*. That line has been decisively breached. What we are essentially talking about at this meeting is man's assault on nature's second line of defence, the physical environment.

The changes in landscape that I have noted are not an unalloyed disaster for humans, although they certainly are for many other species. In traditional western thought, the wilderness was the useless and threatening home of wolves and bandits. Civilization came with the clearing of forests for permanent cultivation. It was only with the Romantic movement that the wilderness became potentially attractive and amusing (McNicoll 1991). Furthermore, the transformation of forest and swamp into cultivated land in Europe was not accompanied by soil degradation but, in general, by maintenance or improvement of soil quality (Wolman 1993; Ruttan 1993).

The situation is quite different in tropical areas. The population is growing at 2–3% a year, rather than less than 1% a year, a rate that was typical of Europe during its period of landscape transformation. This slower pace permitted the evolution of institutions and practices aimed at soil protection, for example, the enclosure movement (North & Thomas 1973). Furthermore, food production is less receptive to intensification in tropical areas because the soil is less responsive to additional applications of fertilizer (National Research Council 1986) and, in many cases, capital that would be necessary for agriculture intensification is lacking. The result is that, relative to Europe, the response to population growth in these areas more often takes the form of occupying new land rather than of intensifying production on old land (Grainger 1990). Not infrequently, these new lands are located in ecologically sensitive areas that are unusually vulnerable to permanent degradation, but the old lands are also more vulnerable to intensification in tropical areas because of soil and climatic conditions (Lele & Stone 1989). The combined effects of extensification and intensification, as estimated by the World Resources Institute (1993), are that agricultural activities have removed about 15% of organic carbon from the world's soil. Some 70 000 square kilometers of farmland are being abandoned each year because of soil exhaustion.

Data on species loss are notoriously poor (Simon & Wildavsky 1984) but the logic of accelerated loss is nevertheless compelling. Tropical forests have a much greater abundance of plant and animal species than do temperate forests, and it is tropical forests that are now disappearing most rapidly. In most cases, no agency is present to protect other species, in part because tropical forests are at the outer bounds of administrative structures. This is not evidence so much as it is theory, but the theory is sound. Nevertheless, the huge range of estimates of the rate of species loss is troublesome. For most purposes, even ethical accountancy, it matters whether the rate of loss is 100 per year or 100 000.

2.2 Industrial production

Man does not live by bread alone, and expanded human numbers are also accompanied by increased demand for other goods and services. The production and consumption of these goods and services very frequently has environmental implications as well. In particular, air and water resources often serve as a repository or sink for the byproducts of production. How much population growth contributes to the pollution of these resources has not, however, been established with any degree of precision.

Most analysts approach this question with the I = PAT equation, wherein the environmental impact is expressed as a product of population size, production per capita, and impact per unit of production. There are many problems with the way this equation has been used. It ignores interactions among the elements, for example the effect of population growth on per capita production (Demeny 1991) and the clear tendency of more affluent nations to choose technologies that are less polluting The World Bank's *World Development Report* for 1992 focused on the environment. Contrary to the implications of this formula, it concluded that higher levels of affluence were associated with lower levels of pollution and resource degradation. The formula is also very sensitive to the level of aggregation at which it is implemented. At present, population growth is concentrated in those regions where the impact multiplier of population growth is very low. Wolfgang Lutz (1992) has shown that failure to account for this regional pattern will lead to an overestimation of population's impact on carbon dioxide emissions by a factor of four.

But the most disappointing feature of this formula is that it defines away the issue. Whatever impact is on the left-hand side, the contribution of population growth to it will always be the same, equal to whatever the proportionate change in population is. The formula could have been written in terms of total production and the impact of each unit of production, in which case population would disappear from the accounting altogether. This kind of arbitrariness clearly violates normal standards of science.

Why this analytic problem is much less acute for analysis of food production and the resources devoted to it goes back to our recognition of biological requirements. People require at least 2200 calories a day for metabolism and basic activities, and resources *must* be reshuffled to ensure that these requirements are met. Otherwise, the population could not expand. This requirement simply does not come into play when we are dealing with automobile emissions or chlorofluorocarbons. We are left with the vague feeling that population growth is probably related to environmental pollution, but unable to say exactly how. Our research designs simply have not been up to the task.

3. SOCIAL MODELS

But we have gone about as far as a primitive biological model can take us. *Homo sapiens* is an intelligent, problem-solving, sociable and cooperative species. These features vastly complicate analysis of the relationship between population growth and environmental change. For example, food demands need not be satisfied within the ecological system whose population is growing but can be met by trade with other regions. People tend to move from areas with fewer economic opportunities to those with more. The smaller the area under study, the more confused these relations become, in part because local features influence population change. It is often no longer possible to treat population change as entirely exogenous, the feature that allows us to approximate the experimental method and to speak with more confidence at the global or highly aggregative level.

3.1 Institutions

In moving beyond the biological model, it is most important to recognize that humans create institutions that can mitigate the environmental impact of population growth. The most important of these institutions are those that govern ownership and access to natural resources, especially land. Over and over again in the literature, one finds that land tenure systems, which in many instances provide incentives for resource preservation, are a key variable conditioning the relationship between population growth and land use changes. These are stressed, for example, in a recent World Bank (1990) report on the population/agriculture/environment nexus in sub-Saharan Africa. In some places in Africa, ownership rights are acquired simply by clearing land. In other places, farmers who let their land lie fallow risk losing their ownership rights. In still other places, incentives for high fertility are provided by systems in which the allocation of land is a function of family size. In all of these instances, land tenure systems are not functioning effectively to preserve land resources for future generations. Examples are also provided where granting land ownership outright to farmers has led to the development and improvement of land resources by virtue of the incentives that owners acquire for land preservation.

Perhaps the most vivid such example is Michael Mortimore's (1993) careful analysis of environmental change in northern Nigeria. Mortimore has taken extensive samples of soil quality in a densely settled agrarian zone of rapid population growth in 1977 and 1990. He finds no evidence of soil deterioration during this period. Furthermore, the soil quality is equivalent to that in an uncultivated area with comparable ecological features. He concludes that "population growth and high population density are compatible with sustainable resource management by smallholders" (Mortimore 1993: 62). Where soil preservation is less successful, he suggests, incentives must be found for smallholders to invest in it, above all by providing secure ownership rights.

This is not the only example where population growth has proven compatible with sustainable resource management. The padi system for growing rice in Asia was developed in the 11th and 12th centuries and provided not only constant but increasing yields for nearly a thousand years (Wolman 1993). The potential for increased yields may now, however, be nearly fully exploited in the highest yield regions of Japan (Ruttan 1993).

The role of social institutions in environmental protection is also highlighted by a comparison of forest resources in China and Japan (Mather 1986). In China, the pressure of population on land resources, combined with weak administrative structures, led peasants to pursue short-term strategies of forest clearance. By the 19th century, the country had been almost entirely denuded of its forest cover. In Japan, on the other hand, the increasing demand for timber beginning in the 17th century was accompanied by an awareness of the adverse effects of deforestation. First the lords and later the imperial government prevented extensive depletion of forest cover. Since 1900, two-thirds of the forests have been in the hands of public institutions where they have been effectively preserved. Establishing clear lines of resource ownership is hardly a panacea, however. In many parts of Latin America, for example, the best land is heavily concentrated in the hands of large landowners whose output is sold mainly to the United States. Population growth must be accommodated disproportionately in marginal areas where resources are more vulnerable to degradation (Stonich 1989; Durham 1979).

In addition to land tenure systems that may provide incentives for land preservation, a second factor that affects the preservation of resources is the availability of credit. If farmers must borrow at real interest rates of 20%, or cannot borrow at all, they will not undertake the investments required to maintain soil fertility, especially if the return from such investments is only 15%.

Unfortunately, ownership rights are typically most ambiguous, administrative structures weakest, and credit markets most inefficient in the frontier areas of developing countries where forests are being destroyed. While it is useful to note that human institutions can intervene to prevent degradation, it is not realistic to suppose that such institutions will flourish in these areas. Mortimore (1993), in fact, suggests that resource degradation is actually more common in low density areas and is often reversed when higher densities are achieved. While this claim holds out hope for the longer term, there is little doubt that continued population growth in the shorter term increases the risk of continued deforestation and resource degradation in marginal areas.

3.2 Other factors and policy options

Population growth is not the only factor capable of affecting the extent of resource degradation. Depending on time, place, and criterion, it may not be the most important factor. The World Bank's (1990) review of population/environment/and agricultural linkages in sub-Saharan Africa lists a huge array of obstacles to expanded food production and better resource management. These include not only land tenure and credit systems, but also biased agricultural prices and exchange rates, adverse tax policies, weak agricultural extension services, excessive government control, and civil wars; but few if any of these problems will be resolved through rapid population growth. They are the context on which this growth will be imposed. According to the Bank, they have the effect of compelling growing populations to exploit ever more extensively the resources available.

Because they have multiple origins, it would be foolhardy to think that problems of food production and resource maintenance can or should be solved by population policy alone. There are times when certain biologists and ecologists appear to take this position. The reason is, I think, they are too wedded to the primitive, biological model of human beings, whereby humans are distinguished from ants or seagulls only by their greater capacity for ecological destruction. While this model helps us understand certain features of resource use, it is entirely inadequate as a guide to policy because it ignores the vast repertoire of social arrangements that humans have constructed to govern their behavior. Problems of poverty and resource degradation have multiple sources and admit to multiple forms of intervention.

The attractiveness of population policy in this array, and here I refer specifically to voluntaristic family planning programs, is that they are relatively cheap and, by assisting couples to have the number of children they desire, help to advance private goals as well as social goals. It is easy to forget in these large-scale discussions of population issues that private goals and social goals are often one and the same. For excellent reasons, most of the world's vital resources are privately owned and managed. The most important questions of population and resource balance in India should ultimately be answered not by the government's deciding whether it wants 1.4 or 1.6 billion people in 2040, but by millions of Indian couples deciding whether they want to divide their plot and patrimony among 2, 3, or 4 heirs. Family planning programs provide the means whereby population size and resources can be better balanced at the family level. They will not resolve all issues of population and environmental relations, but they surely deserve a prominent place in the array of policy initiatives.

ACKNOWLEDGEMENTS

I am grateful to Carole Jolly for bibliographic assistance and to Gordon Wolman for comments on an earlier draft.

REFERENCES

Demeny, P. 1991 Tradeoffs between human numbers and material standards of living. In *Resources, environment, and population: present knowledge, future options.* (eds. K. Davis & M. Bernstam). New York: Oxford University Press pp. 408–422.

Durham, W. 1979 *Scarcity and survival in Central America: the ecological origins of the soccer war.* Stanford, CA: Stanford University Press.

Grainger, A. 1990 Population as a concept and parameter in the modelling of tropical land use change. Presented at the Population–Environment Dynamics Symposium. Ann Arbor, MI: University of Michigan Oct. 1–3.

Lele, U. & Stone, S.W. 1989 *Population pressure, the environment and agricultural intensification: variations on the Boserup hypothesis.* MADIA Discussion Paper 4. Washington, DC: World Bank.

Lutz, W. 1992 Population and environment: what do we need more urgently, better data, better models, or better questions? Presented at the Annual Conference of the British Society for Population Studies, September 9–11. Exeter College, Oxford University.

Mather, A.S. 1986 Global trends in forest resources. In *Population and resources in a changing world.* pp. 289–304.

Mortimore, M. 1993 Northern Nigeria: land transformation under agricultural intensification. In *Population growth and land use change in developing countries: report of a workshop* (eds. C. Jolly & B.B. Torrey). National Research Council. Washington, DC: National Academy Press, pp. 44–70.

Myers, N. 1991 The world's forests and human populations: the environmental interconnections. In *Resources, environment, and population: present knowledge, future options.* (eds. K. Davis & M. Bernstam). New York: Oxford University Press, pp. 237–241.

McNicoll, G. 1993 Malthusian scenarios and demographic catastrophism. Population Council Research Division Working Papers **49**. New York.

National Research Council. 1986 *Population growth and economic development: policy questions.* Washington, DC: National Academy Press.

National Research Council. 1991 *Policy implications of greenhouse warming.* Washington, DC: National Academy Press.

North, D.D. & Thomas, R.P. 1973 *The rise of the western world: a new economic history.* Cambridge, UK: Cambridge University Press.

Preston, S.H. 1980 Causes and consequences of mortality change in less developed countries during the twentieth century. In *Population and economic change in developing countries.* (ed. R. Easterlin). Chicago: University of Chicago Press, pp. 289–360.

Ruttan, V. 1993 Population growth, environmental change, and innovation: implications for sustainable growth in agriculture. In *Population growth and land use change in developing countries: report of a workshop.* (eds. C. Jolly & B.B. Torrey). National Research Council. Washington, DC: National Academy Press, pp. 123–155.

Simon, J. & Wildavsky, A. 1984 On species loss, the absence of data, and risks to humanity. In *The resourceful earth: a response to global 2000.* (eds. J. Simon & H. Kahn). New York: Basil Blackwell, pp. 171–183.

Stonich, S.C. 1989 Processes and environmental destruction: a Central American case study. *Pop. Dev. Rev.* **15**: 269–296.

Wolman, M. 1993 Population, land use, and environment: a long history. In *Population growth and land use change in developing countries: report of a workshop.* (eds C. Jolly & B.B. Torrey). National Research Council. Washington, DC: National Academy Press, pp. 15–29.

World Bank. 1990 *The population, agriculture and environment nexus in sub-Saharan Africa.* Working Paper, World Bank Africa Region. Washington, DC: World Bank.

World Bank. 1992 *World Development Report: development and the environment.* Washington, DC: World Bank.

World Resources Institute. 1993 *Population and the environment.* Washington, DC: World Resources Institute. Forthcoming.

Energy Consumption and Population
Srilatha Batliwala and Amulya K.N. Reddy

ABSTRACT

The conventional approach to the energy–population nexus is that population exogenously determines energy consumption. This paper posits a dialectical relationship between the two, arguing that energy strategies contribute to a reduction of population growth rates. This linkage is further explored and elaborated.

The central hypothesis of the paper is that energy consumption patterns influence the rate of population growth through their effect on the relative benefits of fertility. The hypothesis is tested by exploring the influence of energy consumption on factors that affect population growth. This exploration is carried out at two levels—the micro, village level and the macro, global level. The gender dimension of energy consumption patterns and dependence on human labour of poor households is also brought out. Examples are given of energy strategies and alternative energy scenarios – based on efficient energy technologies – that can contribute to an increase in living standards and thereby impact positively on the intensity of the population problem. The paper concludes that changes in energy strategies are a necessary, though not sufficient, condition for reducing the desired number of births and perceptions of the relative benefits of fertility, a factor which has been totally ignored in population policy.

1. INTRODUCTION

The conventional approach to the energy–population nexus is that population levels determine energy demand—the larger the population, the more the total energy required, with the magnitude of this total energy depending on the per capita energy consumption. In other words, population exogenously determines energy consumption.

This exogenous impact of population on energy is the obvious aspect of the population–energy connection. If, however, energy consumption and population growth are a dialectical pair – each transforming the other, and each being the effect when the other is the cause – then the pattern of energy consumption should also have an effect on population growth, the other side of the coin. That energy strategies can contribute to a reduction of the intensity of the population problem has often been mentioned, but the linkage has not been elaborated sufficiently; hence, an attempt here to explore this other dimension of the energy–population nexus.

The exploration must begin with the general preconditions for a decline of fertility (Coale 1983):

- Fertility must be within the calculus of conscious choice. Potential parents must consider it an acceptable mode of thought and form of behaviour to balance advantages and disadvantages before deciding to have another child.
- Reduced fertility must be advantageous. Perceived social and economic

circumstances must make reduced fertility seem an advantage to individual couples.

- Effective techniques of fertility reduction must be available. Procedures that will, in fact, prevent births must be known, and there must be sufficient communication between spouses and sufficient sustained will, in both, to employ them successfully.

The central hypothesis of this paper is that energy consumption patterns influence the rate of population growth, through their effect on the desired number of births in a family and the relative benefits of fertility. Ultimately, these patterns tend to retard or accelerate the demographic transition (Goldemberg *et al.* 1988). This hypothesis will be examined by exploring the influence of energy consumption on population growth at two levels—the micro-level of villages and the macro-level of global levels.

2. THE ENERGY–POPULATION NEXUS AT THE VILLAGE LEVEL
2.1 Village energy consumption patterns

There have been several studies of the patterns of energy consumption in villages. Among the earliest of the studies was that of six villages in the Ungra region of Tumkur District, Karnataka State, South India (Ravinranath *et al.* 1979).

Pura (latitude: 12 49'00" N, longitude: 76 57'49" E, height above sea level: 670.6 m, average annual rainfall: 127 cm/year, population [in September 1977]: 357, households: 56) is one of the villages in Kunigal Taluk, Tumkur District, Karnataka State, South India.

The energy-utilizing activities in Pura consist of:

- agricultural operations (with ragi and rice as the main crops)
- domestic activities—grazing of livestock, cooking, gathering fuelwood and fetching water for domestic use, particularly drinking
- lighting
- industry (pottery, flour mill and coffee shop).

These activities are achieved with human beings, bullocks, fuelwood, kerosene and electricity as *direct* sources of energy.[1]

An aggregated matrix showing how the various energy sources are distributed over the various energy-utilizing activities is presented in Table 1 (Goldemberg *et al.* 1988).

The matrix yields the following ranking of sources (in order of percentage of annual requirement): (1) fuelwood 89%, (2) human energy 7%, (3) kerosene 2%, (4) bullock energy 1%, (5) electricity 1%. The ranking of these activities is as follows: (1) domestic activities 91%, (2) industry 4%, (3) agriculture 3%, and (4) lighting 2%.

Human energy is distributed thus: domestic activities 80% (grazing livestock 37%, cooking 19%, gathering fuelwood 14%, fetching water 10%), agriculture 12%, and industry 8%. Bullock energy is used wholly for agriculture, including transport. Fuelwood is used to the extent of 96% (cooking 82% and heating bath water 14%) in the domestic sector, and 4% in industry. Kerosene is used predominantly for lighting (93%) and, to a small extent, in industry (7%). Electricity flows to agriculture (65%), lighting (28%), and industry (7%).

There are several features of the patterns of energy consumption in Pura which must be highlighted:

Table 1. *Pura energy source* —activity matrix

	agriculture	domestic	lighting	industry	total
	(all x 10^6 kcals/year)				
human	7.97	50.78	—	4.97	63.72
(man)	(4.98)	(20.59)	—	(4.12)	(29.69)
(woman)	(2.99)	(22.79)	—	(0.85)	(26.63)
(child)	—	(7.40)	—	—	(7.40)
bullock	12.40	—	—	—	12.40
fuelwood	—	789.66	—	33.93	823.59
kerosene	—	—	17.40	1.40	18.80
electricity	6.25	—	2.65	0.71	9.61
totals	26.62	840.44	20.05	41.01	928.12

Total energy = 928 x 10^6 kcal/year; = 1.079 x 10^6 Wh/year; = 2955 kWh/day; = 8.28 kWh/day/capita

- What is conventionally referred to as *commercial* energy, i.e. kerosene and electricity in the case of Pura, accounts for a mere 3% of the inanimate energy used in the village, the remaining 97% coming from fuelwood. Further, fuelwood must be viewed as a *non-commercial* source since only about 4% of the total fuelwood requirement of Pura is purchased as a commodity, the remainder being gathered at zero private cost.[2]
- *Animate* sources, viz, human beings and bullocks, only account for about 8% of the total energy, but the real significance of this contribution is revealed by the fact that these animate sources represent 77% of the energy used in Pura's agriculture. In fact, this percentage would have been much higher were it not for the operation of *four* electrical pumpsets in Pura which account for 23% of the total agricultural energy.
- Virtually all of Pura's energy consumption comes from traditional renewable sources— thus, agriculture is largely based on human beings and bullocks, and domestic cooking (which utilizes about 80% of the total inanimate energy) is based entirely on fuelwood.[3]
- However, the environmental soundness of this pattern of dependence on renewable resources is achieved at an exorbitant price: levels of agricultural productivity are very low, and large amounts of human energy are spent on fuelwood gathering (on average, about 2–6 h and 4–8 km/day/family to collect about 10 kg of fuelwood).
- Fetching water for domestic consumption also utilizes a great deal of human energy (an average of 1–5 h and 1–6 km/day/household) to achieve an extremely low *per capita* water consumption of 17 litres/day.
- 46% of the human energy is spent on grazing livestock (5–8 h/day/household), a crucial source of supplementary household income.

- Children contribute a crucial 30%, 20%, and 34% of the labour for gathering fuelwood, fetching water and grazing livestock, respectively. Their labour contributions are vital to the survival of families, a point often ignored by population and education planners.
- Only 25% of the houses in the 'electrified' village of Pura have acquired domestic connections for electric lighting; the remaining 75% of the houses depend on kerosene lamps and, of these lamps, 78% are of the open-wick type.
- A very small amount of electricity, viz, 30 kWh/day, flows into Pura, and even this is distributed in a highly inegalitarian way—65% of this electricity goes to the four irrigation pumpsets of three landowners, 28% to illuminate 14 out of 56 houses, and the remaining 7% for one flour-mill owner.

Table 2 and Figure 1 shows the end-uses of human energy in Pura. It is obvious that the inhabitants of Pura, particularly its women and children, suffer burdens that have been largely eliminated in urban settings by the deployment of inanimate energy. For example, gathering fuelwood and fetching water can be eliminated by the supply of cooking fuel and water, respectively. There are also serious gender and health implications of rural energy consumption patterns (Batliwala 1982).

Since then, there have been innumerable studies of rural energy consumption patterns (Barnett *et al.* 1982). The precise details show differences depending upon the region of the country, the agro-climatic zone, the proximity to forests, the availability of crop residues, and prevalent cropping patterns, but the broad features of the patterns of energy consumption in Pura that have been highlighted above are generally valid.

2.2 Population implications of village energy consumption patterns

To understand the population implications of these features of the patterns of energy consumption in villages, it is necessary to consider how these features influence the

Table 2. *End-uses of human energy in Pura*

human activity	human energy expenditure		
	h/year	h/day/household	kcal/year (x10⁶)
domestic	255506	12.5	50.8
livestock grazing	(117534)	(5.7)	(23.4)
cooking	(58766)	(2.9)	(11.7)
fuelwood gathering	(45991)	(2.3)	(9.1)
fetching water	(33215)	(1.6)	(6.6)
agriculture	34848	1.7	8.0
industry	20730	1.0	5.0
total	311084	15.2	63.8

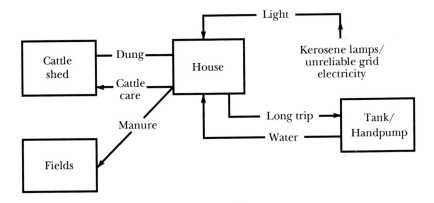

Figure 1. Traditional system of obtaining water, light and fertilizer.

desired number of births in a family and the relative benefits and costs of fertility.

Whereas the exercise of choice in matters of fertility is a culture-dependent issue, and the awareness and availability of fertility-reduction techniques depends upon specific technologies and the success with which they are spread, the desired number of births and therefore the relative benefits and costs of fertility depend upon socioeconomic factors such as:

- infant mortality and the probability of offspring surviving—the lower this probability, the larger the number of children aspired for and the greater the exposure of the mother to the possibility of additional pregnancies
- the role of women in arduous time-consuming household chores—the greater this role, the less the emphasis on women's education and the lower the age of marriage
- the use of children for the performance of essential household tasks—the greater the use of children for these tasks, the more they become essential for the survival of the household
- the opportunities for children to earn wages—such wage-earning children become desirable and wanted as economic assets.

These are only a few of the factors that enter the perceptions of advantages and disadvantages of larger family size and greater fertility. However, it is clear that the reduction of desired family size and fertility and, therefore, the acceleration of the demographic transition, depends upon crucial developmental tasks such as increase of life expectancy, improvement of the environment (drinking water, sanitation, housing, etc), education of women, and the diversion of children away from life-support tasks and employment to schooling.

Almost every one of these socioeconomic preconditions for smaller family size and fertility decline depends upon energy-utilizing technologies:

- infant mortality has much to do with adequate and safe supplies of domestic water and with a clean environment

- the conditions for women's education become favourable if the drudgery of their household chores is reduced, if not eliminated, with efficient energy sources and/or devices for cooking and with energy-utilizing technologies for the supply of water for domestic uses
- the deployment of energy for industries which generate employment and income for women can also help in delaying the marriage age, which is an important determinant of fertility
- if the use of energy results in child labour becoming unnecessary for crucial household tasks (such as cooking, gathering fuelwood, fetching drinking water, and grazing livestock), an important rationale for large families is eliminated.

From this standpoint, it is obvious that the prevailing patterns of energy consumption in villages such as Pura do not emphasize energy inputs for

- provision of safe and sufficient supplies of drinking water
- the maintenance of a clean and healthy environment
- the reduction, if not elimination, of the drudgery of household chores traditionally performed by women
- the relief of menial tasks carried out by children
- the establishment of income-generating industries in rural areas.

Thus, current energy consumption patterns exclude the type of energy-utilizing technologies necessary to satisfy the socioeconomic preconditions for fertility decline. In fact, they encourage an increase in the desired number of births in a family and an increase in the relative benefits of fertility.

Alternative energy strategies can contribute to a reduction in the rate of population growth if they are directed preferentially towards the needs of women, households and a healthy environment (Reddy *et al.* 1979). Energy strategies must provide the mundane, but momentous, energy inputs that would encourage a smaller family size and lower fertility, and thereby facilitate the demographic transition. Otherwise, the strategies would be missing an opportunity to contribute to a reduction of the intensity of the population problem.

2.3 A population-related village-level energy intervention

An example of an energy intervention which would be a small step towards establishing village-level conditions that would play a role in discouraging large families will now be described. Fortunately, the intervention is in the same village of Pura, the energy consumption pattern of which has just been described.

The traditional system of obtaining water, illumination and fertilizer (for the fields) in Pura village is as described in 2.1. This traditional system was replaced in September 1987 with a community biogas plant system (Reddy & Balachandra 1991) (Figure 2).

A comparison of the community biogas plants system with the traditional system of obtaining water, illumination and fertilizer, shows that the households are winners on all counts. Not only have they lost nothing, but they have gained the following:

- deep-bore well water which is better and safer than the water from the open tank
- less effort to get this improved water

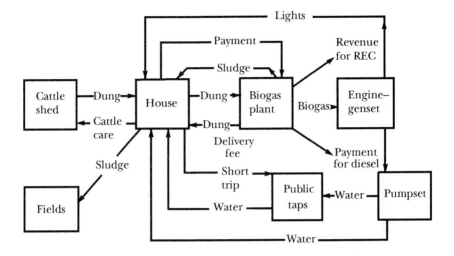

Figure 2. The present community biogas plant system at Pura.

- reduction in the incidence of water-borne intestinal diseases and therefore noticeable improvement in the health of children
- better illumination than the traditional kerosene lamps or even the unreliable, low-voltage grid electricity
- cheaper illumination for the households using kerosene lamps
- less pressure on the women to finish their chores during daylight
- improved fertilizer which has greater nitrogen content and is less favourable to the growth of weeds and proliferation of flies compared to farmyard manure.
- a dung delivery fee to those (mainly women and children) who deliver the dung to the plants and take back the sludge.

The system is still under development and has much further to go. The next stages include the provision of efficient cooking fuels/devices to households to reduce the burden of fuelwood gathering and the health hazards associated with current cooking patterns. However, even the first phase suggests the type of energy interventions that can influence the rate of population growth.

3. THE ENERGY POPULATION NEXUS AT THE GLOBAL LEVEL

Over the past decade and a half, there have been a number of conventional global energy scenarios. Almost every one of them show

- a growing disparity in the energy consumption of industrialized and developing countries
- virtually no improvement, even over several decades into the future, in the level of energy services for the populations of developing countries.

Goldemberg *et al.* (1985, 1988) constructed what has come to be known as a *1 kW per capita scenario* based on a "thought experiment" in which the following question was explored:

if all developing countries achieved a level of energy services equivalent to that obtained in Western Europe in the 1970s, and if they deployed the most efficient energy technologies available today, what would be the *per capita* energy consumption corresponding to this vastly improved standard of living?

The surprising result was that *a mere 10% increase in the magnitude of energy would be required for the populations of developing countries to enjoy a standard of living as high as that which obtained in Western Europe in the 1970s, provided that the best energy-efficient technologies available today are implemented.* In other words, under the conditions of this scenario, energy supplies need not become a constraint and dramatic increases in standards of living can be attained in the developing countries.

It follows that, if energy-efficient technologies are implemented to enable the populations of developing countries to realize a better standard of living, then it is likely that this standard of living is very likely to result in the low growth rates of the populations of developing countries characteristic of West European countries.

In addition to dramatic increases in standards of living for the populations of developing countries, the *1 kW per capita scenario* also led to a global energy scenario in which

- the total global energy requirement was only about 60% and 40% of that indicated by the IIASA Low and High projections
- there was, in stark contrast to all the other scenarios, a *convergence* of the per capita consumptions of the industrialized and developing countries.[4]

4. CONCLUSIONS

By considering the energy–population nexus at the village micro-level and the global macro-level, it has been shown that the pattern of energy consumption can influence population growth by retarding or accelerating the demographic transition. Illustrative examples of energy strategies that can contribute to a reduction of the intensity of the population problem have been briefly described—a biogas-based electricity-generation system at the village level and the *1 kW per capita scenario* at the global level. The essence of these energy interventions and alternative energy scenarios is the overriding emphasis on efficient energy technologies.

It is not the claim here that energy strategies alone will achieve a reduction in the desired number of births in a family and a decrease in the relative benefits of fertility. However, they are a necessary condition, if not sufficient. Unfortunately, they have been largely ignored as crucial interventions in the population problem. This lacuna must be corrected.

End note: Attention must be drawn to the growing view that population increases in the developing countries represents the most serious threat to the global atmosphere through the phenomenon of global warming. A counter view is that the patterns of energy consumption in the rich industrialized and poor developing countries, and the rich and the poor within developing countries, are such that the industrialized countries, and the rich within developing countries, have via their energy-intensive consumption patterns, far greater per capita impact on the global atmosphere, and therefore the greater rates of population growth of the poor developing countries, and the poor within developing countries, are far less relevant to global warming than the lower rates of population growth of the industrialized countries, and of the rich within developing countries.

REFERENCES

ASTRA 1982 Rural energy consumption patterns—a field study. *Biomass* **2**, No.4, September, 255–280.

Barnett, A., Bell, M. & Hoffman, K. 1982 Rural energy and the third world, Oxford UK: Pergamon Press.

Batliwala, S. 1982 Rural energy scarcity and nutrition—a new perspective. *Economic and Political Weekly* **XVII**, No.9, February 27.

Batliwala, S. 1984 Rural energy situation: consequences for women's health. *Socialist Health Review* **1**, No.2, 75, September.

Batliwala, S. 1987 Women's access to food. *Indian Journal of Social Work* XLVIII, No.3, 255–271, October.

Coale, A.J. 1983 Recent trends in fertility in less developed countries. *Science* **221**, 828–832, August.

Coale, A.J., India Coordinators, DAWN (Development Alternatives with Women for a New Era), c/o 751 8th Main, III Block, Koramangala, Bangalore, 560 034, India.

Goldemberg, J., Johnansson, T.B., Reddy, A.K.N. & Williams, R.H. 1985 Basic needs and much more with one kilowatt per capita. *Ambio* **14**, No. 4–5, 190–200.

Goldemberg, J., Johansson, T.B., Reddy, A.K.N. & Williams, R.H. 1988 Energy for a sustainable world, New Delhi: Wiley-Eastern.

Rajabapaiah, P., Jayakumar, S. & Reddy, A.K.N. 1993 In Biogas electricity—the Pura village case study. Ch 19, *Fuels and electricity from renewable sources of energy*, (eds. T.B. Johansson & H. Kelly, A.K.N. Reddy & R.H. Williams). Island Press.

Ravinranath, N.H., Somasekhar, H.I., Ramesh, R., Reddy, A, Venkatram, K. & Reddy, A.K.N. 1979 The design of a rural energy centre for Pura village, Part I: its present pattern of energy consumption. *Employment Expansion in Indian Agriculture*, International Labour Office, Bangkok: pp. 171–187.

Reddy, A.K.N. & Balachandra, P. 1991 In *Power generation through renewable sources of energy* (eds. B.R. Pai & M.S. Rama Prasad). New Delhi: Tata McGraw-Hill Publishing Company Limited, Ch 7, pp. 66–75.

Reddy, A.K.N. & Batliwala, S. 1979 Energy to liberate children, *Ceres*, **71**, 42–46, September – October.

NOTES

[1]   Transport has been included in agriculture because the only vehicles in Pura are bullock carts and these are used almost solely for agriculture-related activities such as carrying manure from backyard compost pits to the farms, and produce from farms to households.

[2]   Pura uses about 217 tonnes of firewood per year, i.e. about 0.6 tonnes/day for the village, or 0.6 tonnes/year/capita.

[3]   Unlike some rural areas of India, dung cakes are not used as cooking fuel in the Pura region. In situations where agro-wastes (e.g. coconut husk) are not abundant, it

appears that, if firewood is available within some convenient range (determined by the capacity of head-load transportation), dung-cakes are never burnt as fuel; instead, dung is used as manure.

⁴   The thought experiment was not intended to recommend Western European living standards as the goal for developing countries or to establish activity level targets for these countries to be achieved by some particular future date. The appropriate mix and levels of activities for the future in developing countries will have to be different to be consistent with the climate, culture and overall development goals. Rather, the purpose was to show that it is possible not only to meet basic human needs, but also to provide improvements in living standards that go far beyond the satisfaction of basic needs, without significant increases in per capita energy use. Thus, energy supply availability *per se* need not be a fundamental constraint on development.

Landscape as Life Support Provider
Water-related Limitations

Malin Falkenmark

ABSTRACT

Development takes place by the interaction of two different worlds: a) the landscape reality, controlled by a set of natural laws, and managed by man by help of varying technologies; b) the human mind and its perceptions, controlling the attitudes and general governance patterns. Basic to life is the continuously circulating water, a non-substitutable life-supporting substance, provided from the atmosphere in a climatically defined manner, and consumed in biomass production in dry climates at the rate of 1000 cubic metres of water per tonne biomass produced. The remainder goes to recharge aquifers and rivers, where it can be put to societal use while passing through any particular landscape. This amount limits the possible water-dependent activities.

At the same time, human production activities in the landscape produce threats to sustainability in two ways: by land manipulation in areas with particular environmental vulnerability; and by waste production and poor waste handling, allowing pollutants to escape into the landscape, where they are caught by the circulating water and carried to the ecosystems. Population growth produces multiple sustainability threats: in terms of famine-proneness due to both water scarcity and food scarcity, and in terms of water quality deterioration producing health and protein deficiency threats. A fundamental dilemma today is that the main part of the unavoidable population growth takes place in the environmentally most vulnerable regions.

The world academies, in a huge scholarly effort, are confronting two main problems and how best to cope with them:

1. *rapidly escalating water scarcity*, expected to increase tenfold in the next few decades in response to an unavoidable population growth, related to females already born.
2. *landscape vulnerability*, which threatens water quality and land fertility.

1. INTRODUCTION

The diagnosis of the population–environment–development dilemma suffers from some fundamental problems. The UNCED process—although maybe the most comprehensive effort performed in this field—addressed the problems according to an issue-oriented model, neglecting focus on the linkages, for instance between land use and water-related constraints. The literature from recent years includes many awareness-raising papers drawing attention to linkages (Myers 1992), although remaining on a rather simplistic level. Even studies on global food supply tend to be rather crude and simplistic.

What is still lacking seems to be a clearer idea of the system that provides the human population with its life support and its natural resources. This author has engaged in a series of studies with the purpose of developing a mental image that pays adequate attention to the crucial role of water and water-related functions and constraints in the life support system. Without such an image, it is in fact difficult to formulate the development problems, and how they might be coped with in the dry climate tropics and subtropics. Accepting the argument of Hägerstrand (1989) that all disciplines meet in the same landscape, the author has proposed a landscape-oriented mental image (Falkenmark & Suprapto 1991).

In this image, the development process is seen as the result of long-term interactions between the natural landscape with all its physical, chemical and biological interactions, and the noosphere, containing man's actions, needs and aspirations. The landscape provides the natural resources on which human progress depends (biomass production, water, energy, minerals). Access to the resources generally depends on manipulations of the landscape, driven by human needs and therefore population growth on the one hand, and human aspirations and access to technology on the other. The undesirable side effects, developing in response to such manipulations, were in earlier days met by human adaptation. Today, the constellation of manipulation is so complex that it is difficult to judge the possible causes of experienced changes. This has raised the issue of how far the sustainability limits may in fact be met.

In order to come to grips with the whole environment–development dilemma, unprecedented multidisciplinary efforts will be needed, joining on the one hand social and behavioural scientists, with their focus on the driving forces and the societal response to environmental change, and on the other natural scientists, with their focus on the livelihood-providing natural system, and its response to human manipulations.

In the simplistic approaches taken in the past to this whole realm of human survival issues, there has been both overshoot and undershoot (Svedin 1990). A huge amount of work has for instance been dedicated to the ecology of natural systems but without adequate attention to the humans depending on those systems. Energy flow analysis has been an important mode of approach, whereas water flow analysis seems to be quite exceptional.

Rather, water has been addressed in an oversimplistic way with focus on water supply technicalities, and water habitats in needs of protection. By the conventional neglect of the basic fact that all life is at the mercy of the water cycle, the whole environmental debate—including UNCED—continues to be severely distorted. Environmental texts largely reflect the pollution-related perspective of the north. Much less interest has gone into the landscape manipulation perspective of relevance to the south, except for focus on deforestation and desertification as isolated impact-oriented issues. There has been almost a conspiracy of silence around the particular environmental vulnerability of tropical and subtropical regions.

This paper will try to remedy the water blindness that goes through so much of what has been written in past studies on environment—population—development. It will address the issue from the perspective of the water cycle. The water that occupies 2/3 of the human body, and is the very life-blood of the terrestrial ecosystems, from which the human population gets its food, fodder, fuelwood and timber. The water that has played the role of a fundamental lubricant of industrial development in the temperate zone. Particular interest will be paid to the issues of livelihood security to an exploding human population, mainly in the tropics and subtropics, expanding with some 90 million additional inhabitants every year. This is equivalent to another China being added every decade in the next 20 to 30 years.

The aim of the paper is twofold:

- system analysts are invited to enter water's key functions into the next generation of models applicable to third world development problems
- demographers are urged to pay increased attention to defining natural resource constraints in their predictions, for example, possible morbidity/mortality change scenarios as population approaches the life support capacity of a region.

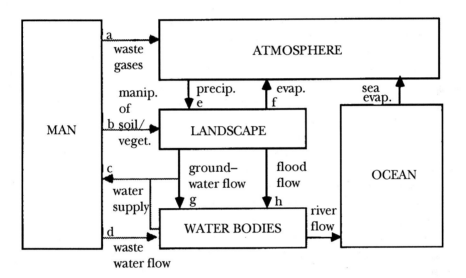

Figure 1. Water perspective of the Total Earth system with the water cycle as the central clockwork of the biosphere, and four main modes of human interventions. Black arrows (e, f, g, h) indicate water flows. The four main categories of human influences are indicated by grey arrows (a, b, c, d) showing what part of the water cycle they primarily disturb. Any disturbances are caught, carried and propagated onwards by the water cycle, finally reaching the ecosystems (terrestrial, aquatic, marine).

2. CONCEPTUAL FRAMEWORK

2.1 Life on this planet is based on circulating water

Although incessantly stressed already at the time of the Bible and the Koran, the importance of water for life has never been really clarified in terms of its implications. The fact that this is the only planet in the solar system whose temperatures allow liquid water to exist had escaped general attention, until the time when NASA returned from its excursion to planet Mars (Dooge 1992).

Life processes depend on water's highly specific and peculiar properties. On a global scale, solar energy and the circulation of water between the ocean, the atmosphere, and the continents constitutes the very clockwork of the biosphere and its climate patterns (Figure 1). Land and climate together define the natural vegetation in any region: desert, semi-desert, steppe, prairie, savannah, coniferous or deciduous forest (Budyko 1986).

As a consequence of the fundamental functions of water, the endogenous *carrying capacity of a region is water-dependent*, the term endogenous here indicating self-reliance without food import. The biomass productivity in terms of tonnes of plant material per unit of land area is much larger in the humid tropics than in the dry tropics, since there is not only plenty of energy but also plenty of water. In the former, plant production is also much more efficient in terms of water consumption, so that only some 200 cubic metres of water is needed to produce each tonne of biomass. As a contrast, the dry climate areas need five times as much water: some 1000 cubic metres of water per ton biomass produced, partly due to the sparse vegetation, allowing large evaporation losses from naked soil between the plants (Falkenmark 1986).

Water availability in other words determines the number of individuals that can be sustained from locally produced biomass. Consequently, the dry tropics have greater difficulty in feeding its population than the humid tropics, where the vegetation is rich and luxuriant. This simple fact is illustrated by the fact that Africa—except for the Congo basin an extremely dry continent—now stands out as the most problematic continent in terms of development.

2.2 The dilemma of the lowest-income countries

On the one hand, the lowest income countries tend to remain highly dependent on agriculture in terms of its share of the GNP (van den Oever 1992). If the agricultural potential is for some reason limited, population growth exacerbates the shortages.

On the other hand, most of these countries are located in the tropical/subtropical region where there is lack of water at least part of the year; where recurrent droughts are part of the climate; and where the evaporative demand of the atmosphere is particularly high (at least three times as high as in Scandinavia) (Falkenmark 1991).

2.3 Avoidable and unavoidable landscape manipulations

It is essential to develop a perception of Man and landscape that makes sense both in the north and in the south, and such that both similarities and differences can be properly distinguished (Falkenmark & Suprapto 1992). Humans have always *manipulated the landscape* in order to secure the resources needed for livelihood security—water, food, fodder, fibre, fuelwood, timber and energy. They drain the land, dig wells, pipe water, clear the vegetation, till and fertilise it, and control its pests. This manipulation is unavoidable in securing the biomass needed to feed and support the population. Population growth will call for even more intensive land manipulations. The sustainable manipulation level will depend on the environmental vulnerability of a particular area. All such manipulations—besides the intended benefits—produce environmental side-effects, due to the intricate interaction of water–soil/vegetation–man–other species (Figure 2).

At the same time, human activities *produce waste* from households, industry, agriculture and other activities. As a result of the waste production, water systems get polluted: leachants move into groundwater aquifers below the land surface, and surface waters into the rivers and water bodies draining the landscape. Since the water is an excellent solvent, the pollutants arrive in the coastal waters. This waste production can principally be managed by various methods for minimising the output of polluting substances, thereby controlling the pollution of the water that passes through a particular area. It is, in this sense, if not totally *avoidable*, at least possible to minimise.

Sustainable livelihood conditions demand that the land productivity and water quality are protected so that food can continue to be grown to feed the local population and possibly for export, and so that water can be safely used also for other purposes. Trespassing these very basic ethical rules would involve threats to future food supply, water supply and human health. The result would be migration and increasing morbidity/

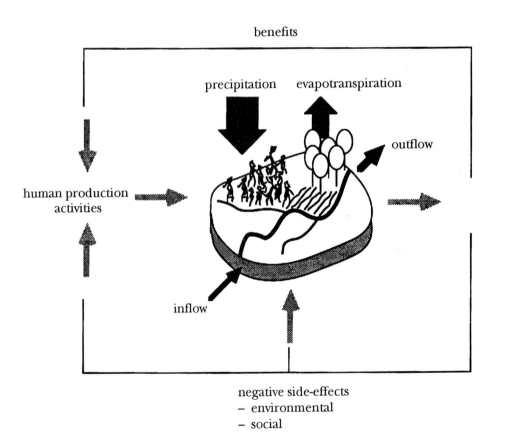

Figure 2. Man-induced environmental problems are often side-effects of human production activities in the landscape, aimed at achieving benefits for life quality and economic development. See text.

mortality. *Sustainability criteria can in this sense be seen as equivalent to carrying capacity limitations, since they define the population that can be locally supported.*

2.4 Environmental vulnerability

The acceptable level of landscape manipulation is controlled by environmental vulnerability, and consequently the population that may be supported is limited by the same conditions. Today's world has arrived in a highly frustrating dilemma: *the population growth is largest in the most vulnerable regions.* This makes it essential to find out where the limits are in terms of *inter alia* the amount of food that can be produced, and the amount of water that can be made accessible.

Environmental vulnerability is climate- and soil-dependent and therefore differs between regions. There are principally three dimensions of environmental vulnerability in the tropical/subtropical regions:

- *recurrent droughts* as part of the climate
- *water stress* in terms of population pressure on the water passing through
- *land impermeabilisation* as a consequence of human manipulations of the land.

The two first are limited to the arid tropics and subtropics, whereas the third is typical for both the arid and the humid tropical regions.

Recurrent droughts imply that there is deficient rainfall during intermittent dry years. Since the rainfall is typically sporadic in the arid regions, with very high variability both in space and time, droughts may occur also as dry spells during the rainy season. Returning dry spells are equivalent to vulnerability to crop failure. To secure the high yields needed to support a growing population, root-zone water security is crucial—it is important to stress (Falkenmark 1990) that safe crop yields cannot be achieved in drought-prone regions just by means of adding 'dry' technology components like tractors, fertilisers, pesticides—the way in which yield increase is too often discussed.

3. WATER DEPENDENCE

3.1 Water need for livelihood security

FAO-based experience tells us that in dry regions irrigation-based crop production on a subsistence level represents a per capita need of 500–2500 cubic meters per year (Higgins *et al.* 1988). Let us therefore assume that—when compared to an amount H needed for household purposes under good life quality conditions (H assumed to be 100 litre per person and day)—food security based on irrigation would correspond to some twenty times this amount, or to a need of 20H (corresponding to about 750 cubic metres per person per year).

The daily water needed in a region would therefore be 20H for food production, plus H for household needs and whatever amount will be needed for local industry which is generally also water-dependent. If we are extremely conservative, maybe H will do also for that purpose, so that the overall need for basic life support at an acceptable level would sum up to 22H as a minimum.

3.2 Water availability constraints

If we assume that 22H is the *per capita* amount of water needed in a dry-climate society to support local livelihood security in, say, a region of villages or small towns fed by the surrounding agriculture, then the question is: how much water is in fact passing through that particular landscape, accessible for withdrawal and use for these three purposes?

The water cycle carries a certain amount of water to any inhabited area. Plant growth and evaporation sends part of the rainwater back to the atmosphere—more in a hot, dry atmosphere. The remainder passes through the landscape above and below the ground—this is the amount available to satisfy the societal needs just discussed, adding up to 22H (Figure 3a).

As long as the climate does not change, the long-term average of the amount of available water is *finite, although fluctuating between wet and dry years:* the long-term average corresponds to a certain number of flow units of water (Figure 3a-b). Most of that water passes through the area as rapid flood flows during the wet season, whereas the time-stable part available on a year round basis is limited. Under dry climate only some 10% of the overall availability is time-stable.

This amount can however be *increased by storing the flood water in reservoirs.* When only moderate extra storage is available, maybe some 20% of the overall availability can be made accessible. Translated into population pressure on the total amount of water passing through the area, this means that wherever there are fewer than 250 people per flow unit of water (one unit being one million cubic metres per year), 22H can be provided. Under more favourable storage possibilities, maybe even 50% can be mobilised on a year-round basis, implying that self-reliance would be possible up to a population density of around 600 persons/flow unit of water (Figure 3b).

3.3 What are the options of mobilising more of the renewable water?

Storing wet-season surplus evidently calls for reservoirs. Dam-building is, however, a highly controversial issue, due to the side-effects produced when introducing a dam: local population has to be resettled, interfering with human rights principles; the local ecology in the river will change; coastal fishery will be reduced while local fishery in the reservoir will increase. In regions with land mismanagement and erosion, sediments will be trapped in the reservoir and therefore impeded from reaching the delta. And so on (Biswas 1992).

If we, nevertheless, for a moment go for finding the *ultimate* limits, let us assume that reservoirs will become accepted as a major tool in eradication of poverty in drought-prone regions; that most of the flood flow can be stored; and that the costs for the structures and side-effect compensations can be financed. Taking into account the large evaporation losses from the reservoirs, the water ceiling would then probably be some 50% of the total water availability, i.e. as already indicated allowing food self-reliance up to 600 people per flow unit of water.

The conclusion is that food security would, from the particular perspective of water availability, be possible under the population pressure on water typical for most developing countries *at present*—provided that massive water storage could be provided; and that regional agreements were possible to reach between upstream and downstream countries on international rivers.

Figure 3c shows the prospects of having access to this amount of water on the different

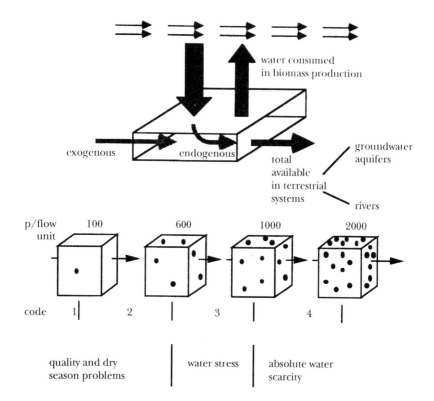

Figure 3. Water availability as seen on a regional (country) scale. Upper figure (a) illustrates water availability as composed of an endogenous component, emerging from rainfall over the territory, and an exogenous component, emerging from rainfall over upstream countries. Lower figure (b) visualises growing population pressure on a finite availability. Each cube represents one flow unit of water of one million cubic metres per year, each dot 100 individuals jointly depending on that water. The code numbers indicate intervals of increasing water stress. Figure (c) (opposite) indicates number of people by 1990 and 2025 AD, living in water-stressed countries (code intervals 3, 4 and 5 in fig b), defined as more than 600 people per flow unit of available water (one million cubic metres per year). Columns show the different continents and the gross total (Arnestrand, 1992).

continents in a time perspective of some three decades (Arnestrand 1992). Calculations suggest that by 1990 300 million people were living in countries with more than 600 p/flow unit. By 2025 AD this number will have *ten-folded* up to 3040 millions. The conclusion is evident: *water scarcity constraints are becoming a major development problem.* Moreover, these constraints will produce problems *before* the global warming will be apparent—generally assumed to be around 2030.

3.4 What are the threats if unsuccessful?

What are, on the other hand, the general threats if water-security cannot be achieved

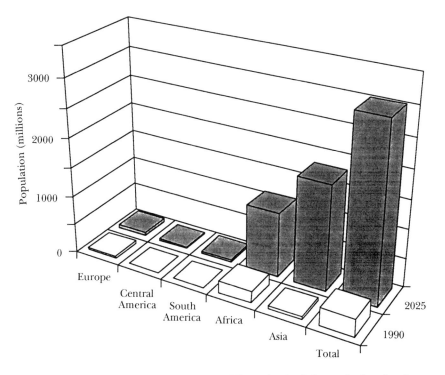

in a poverty-stricken drought-prone region? The principal threat is that famines would tend to develop during recurrent drought years in the same way as we have been witnessing in Africa: in the Sahel region in the 1970s; in all the 20 countries along the hunger crescent during the 1984/85 drought; and in southern Africa during the most recent drought.

Since the population would have grown since the preceding drought, every new drought would threaten an even larger population than last time. We may speak of a *risk spiral* (Falkenmark 1989). There is a basic vulnerability related to the dry climate, reflected in a limited growing period (water scarcity for food production, denoted as type A), implying a general vulnerability to crop failures during disturbances of any sort (Falkenmark *et al.* 1989). Land impermeabilisation due to poor land management or overuse would add to this vulnerability (water scarcity C, see below). The intermittent drought years (water scarcity B) would trigger famines that might hit larger and larger populations. In the meantime, also the population pressure on the passing water will have increased (water scarcity D) so that food security is more and more elusive. Figure 4 tries to summarise the predicament caused by environmental vulnerability in combination with rapid population growth.

4. WHAT DEFINES SUSTAINABILITY LIMITS?

Environmental sustainability demands that both land productivity and water quality be protected. These are necessary conditions for quality of human life and for biodiversity. Human–ecological criteria demand that groundwater remains drinkable; crop, fish and meat remain edible, and that soils remain productive. Biological criteria prescribe that biodiversity be protected, a protection which will depend on strict control of water quality in aquatic and marine habitats, and in root-zone water on which terrestrial ecosystems depend. Meeting these criteria has implications in terms of acceptable manipulations of soil and vegetation for biomass production and harvesting, on the one hand, and for waste production and handling on the other.

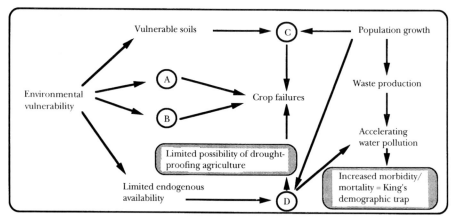

Figure 4. Threats developing from the environmental vulnerability characterising the dry climate tropics and subtropics, as affected by rapid population growth. First and second order components are four main modes of water scarcity (A, B, C, D, see text) and particularly vulnerable soils. The grey fields indicate the main threats.

4.1 Land vulnerability-related constraints

Adequate water is not enough in itself to produce good yields. The soil has also to *allow the water to infiltrate* into the root-zone; there has to be a good balance in the soil between water and air; and the chemical composition of the soil water has to be adequate for the plants. These requirements are, however, subject to severe disturbances, causing water-related land degradation from

- salinisation/waterlogging from poor irrigation management
- effects of acid rain originating from air emissions
- reduced water-holding capacity due to reduced use of organic fertilisers, and removal of organic matter from the soil
- land permeability degradation due to mismanagement

Land permeability degradation poses threats of desiccation. Vulnerability to *soil impermeabilisation* (water scarcity C, 'desertification') is constraining land use in both the arid and the humid tropics. The problem is related to the tendency of crustal formation, typical for tropical soils. The immediate causes may be physical (trampling, raindrop hammering, water erosion clogging the surface), or chemical (laterisation). The physical processes are generated by human action: clearing/deforestation; exposing the soil surface to heavy rains; overuse of land such as overgrazing; or poor agricultural practices, exposing the naked soil.

Agricultural production is threatened when water cannot infiltrate into the root zone. The driving forces are social and economic, forcing poor farmers up into the hills or out onto marginal lands. These phenomena are in their turn side-effects of population growth, as exemplified by the current development in the Philippines (Myers 1992).

The result is a *land-vulnerability-related limitation of the carrying capacity*. As long as restoration is possible, the degradation is not absolute, but can be reversed by active soil conservation activities.

4.2 Water quality-related constraints

There is also a vulnerability to water quality degradation. A growing population causes increasing waste production under conditions of diminishing *per capita* dilution capacity, since water amounts are finite.

We may distinguish two types of waste: *organic wastes* from humans, from cattle and from food industry. The first two in particular involve disease vectors by their content of infectious matter. *Development-related waste* emanates from process industry, mining, and commercial agriculture, producing heavy metal pollutants, excess nutrients, pesticides and other toxics.

The resulting water quality deterioration threatens coastal fisheries and aquaculture, directly involving important food sources, and ultimately the health of humans as well as the ecosystems on which they depend. A let-go attitude accepting increasing morbidity and mortality has been indicated as the closing stage of the demographic trap (King 1990). Large-scale pollution abatement is the only alternative.

4.3 The overall threat—multicause global change

The global scale of what has been discussed in the earlier sections of this paper makes us entitled to speak of the different phenomena as a set of determinants of *global change:*

- population-growth-driven rapidly expanding water scarcity
- population-growth-driven land use intensification, increasing the threat of land degradation with its consequences in terms of reduced carrying capacity
- population-growth and development-driven water quality degradation, involving threats to health and protein supply

In addition to these different modes of global change there are the consequences from the greenhouse-gas-driven climate change. Any changes in the climate will evidently produce changes also in the ecological limits by:

- altering the wetting of the landscapes, changing the cropping patterns and water supply
- producing new vulnerabilities to extremes in terms of floods and droughts

It is essential to realise that the population-growth driven global change will manifest itself in the next few decades, before the greenhouse-gas driven change predicted for the 2020s and beyond.

5. CONCLUSIONS
5.1 Summing up

Some *implications of the fact that life is based on the continuous circulation of water* have been set out. The simple fact of water as a necessary condition for life—evident to our ancestors in the arid subtropics—seems to have slipped from the minds of the present generations in the north, where water is easily accessible even in private homes. It has been shown that a hydroclimatically defined amount of water is locally available for use while passing through aquifers and rivers in any particular landscape. This amount consequently limits water-dependent activities: household supply, industry, extra water to dryland agriculture to secure good yields in spite of dry spells and dry years.

Human production activities in the landscape produce threats to sustainability in two ways: by land manipulation due to the particular environmental vulnerability in certain zones; and by waste production and poor waste handling, allowing pollutants to escape into the landscape. Population growth produces multiple sustainability threats: to famine-proneness in terms of both water scarcity and food scarcity, and to water quality deterioration in terms of health threats and protein deficiency threats. Climate change will add new vulnerabilities: extreme events during the next few decades may trigger famines and morbidity events; later changes of rainfall patterns will involve perturbations of the present climate, producing more agricultural problems.

5.2 The basic problem

A fundamental dilemma today is that the main part of the population growth takes place in the environmentally most vulnerable regions. The world academies must develop an understanding of the problems to be addressed, and how they may best be coped with. Scientists from many different fields must be involved but depend for their successful communication on sharing a basic mental image of man–environment–development interactions. It has to be simple enough so that the dialogue is not unnecessarily complicated, but still containing the most fundamental factors in order to avoid biasing distortions.

Human prospects are deeply influenced by the hydroclimatically limited water availability. Water is a non-substitutable life-supporting substance, provided from the atmosphere in a climatically defined manner, and consumed in biomass production, in dry climates at the rate of 1000 cubic metres of water per ton biomass produced. The remainder goes to recharge aquifers and rivers, where it can be put to societal use while passing through any particular landscape. The paper has clarified some roles of the circulating multifunctional freshwater as a crucial ingredient in the tropical and subtropical landscapes where the rapid population growth introduces severe sustainability problems. Two main challenges have emerged from the discussion:

- *rapidly escalating water scarcity*, expected to increase tenfold in the next few decades in response to an unavoidable population growth related to the mothers already born
- *landscape vulnerability* typical for these zones. What has in particular to be protected is water quality in order to avoid the threat of water-related diseases such as cholera, and land fertility to protect from the threats of famines due to crop failures and degradation of arable land

The complementary character of the vertical and horizontal water flows, as well as water's non-substitutable role in both biomass production and much of the economic production makes it *crucial to merge food and water issues in future life support discussions*. Biomass production cannot be discussed without proper attention to a) moisture preconditions; b) consequences for rainwater partitioning and recharge of aquifers and rivers.

The eradication of poverty in the lowest income countries is a huge life support problem. Escalating water scarcity in response to an unavoidable population growth and the gigantic food and water needs that go with it forms the greatest challenge for mankind to address. This water scarcity forms a fundamental component of an ongoing global change. *It is expected to increase tenfold before the climate change will manifest itself on a larger scale.*

5.2 Closing remarks

The paper has also suggested that development takes place by the interaction of two different worlds: the *landscape reality*, controlled by natural laws and managed by man; and the *world of the human mind and its perceptions*, focusing on attitudes and mechanisms of economy and administration.

'A fundamental problem is the dominance of the temperate zone perceptions' (Biswas 1992). In the past, this has materialised in a certain 'temperate zone imperialism' in discussing third world problems. For example, the Brundtland Commission totally ignored the accelerating water scarcity and its implications for development.

Another problem is the absent discussion of the implications of the *unavoidable* part of the population growth, even at the UNCED Conference in Rio. *In other words, the most essential of all problems determining the relation between environment and development in the next few decades was not addressed in Rio:* the issue of how to balance growing human needs versus the limited carrying capacity.

Demographers are essential participants in addressing the extremely fundamental development problems. It is high time for them to *start studying the influence on population dynamics of natural resource constraints*. For example: where and when will water availability limitation generate a morbidity increase, influencing demographic projections? Three possibilities can be seen: water quality deterioration, food scarcity in general, and crop failure during recurrent drought, producing increasingly severe famines of the types manifested in sub-Saharan Africa in recent decades. Demographers might also be involved in interdisciplinary research in order to produce awareness of the threatening future, so that realistic options to reduce the threats can be defined and urgently developed.

It is finally essential to acknowledge the difference between population development in a resource-rich world, where technology and trade can release the constraints as they develop, and population responses when maximum carrying capacity is being approached in terms of limitations of the basic life-support systems.

REFERENCES

Arnestrand, M. 1992 Recent calculations. Research Group on International Hydrology, Swedish Natural Science Research Council, Stockholm.
Biswas, A. 1992 The Aswan Dam revisited. *Ecodecision*, Sept 1992, 67–69.
Budyko, M.I. 1986 *The evolution of the biosphere.* D. Reidel Publishing Company.

Dooge, J.C.I. 1992 Keynote lecture. *Proceedings from the Stockholm Water Symposium 1992.* Stockholm Water Ltd.

FAO/UNEP/IIASA 1983 *Potential population supporting capacities of lands in the developing world.* Land resources for population of the future. FAO Technical Report of Project, FPA/INT/ 513, Rome.

Falkenmark, M. 1986 Fresh water—time for a modified approach. *Ambio* **4**, 192–200.

Falkenmark, M. 1989 The massive water scarcity now threatening Africa – why isn't it being addressed? *Ambio* **2**, 112–118.

Falkenmark, M. 1990 Water scarcity management and small-scale irrigation in traditional agriculture. Inter-Agency Preparatory Meeting on Water and Sustainable Agricultural Development, 21–23 February 1990. UNFAO, Rome.

Falkenmark, M. 1991 Environment and development. Urgent need for a water perspective. Chow Memorial Lecture, IWRA Congress, Rabat, May 1991. *Water International* **16**, 229–240.

Falkenmark, M. & Suprapto, R.A. 1992 Population-landscape interactions in development. A water perspective to environmental sustainability. *Ambio* **1** , 31–36.

Hägerstrand, T. 1989 The landscape as a garden (In Swedish). Report from a Future Seminar on Natural Resources and Landscape Transformation. Ministry of Housing, Stockholm.

Higgins, G.M., Dielemann, P.J. & Albernethy, C.L. 1988 Trends in irrigation development, and their implications for hydrologists and water resources engineers. *J. Hyd. Sci.* **1/2**, 43–59.

King, M. 1990 Health is a sustainable state. Lancet 336, l990.

Myers, N. 1992 Population/environment linkages: discontinuities ahead? UN Expert Group Meeting on Population, Environment and Development, New York 20–24 Jan l992. UN Doc. IESA/P/AC.34/3.

van den Oever, P. 1992 Population, natural resources and development interactions: issues for the 1990s. UN Expert Group Meeting on Population, Environment and Development, New York 20–24 Jan 1992. UN Doc. IESA/P/AC.34/1.

Svedin, U. The societal context. In *Water awareness in planning and decision-making.* (eds. R. Castensson, M. Falkenmark & J-E. Gustafsson). Swedish Council for Planning and Coordination of Research, Stockholm. FRN Report **90:9**, 13–16.

Population and Biodiversity
Norman Myers

ABSTRACT

The paper opens with a brief account of the nature and extent of biodiversity, and some of its values to humankind, notably bio-ecological and economic values. It goes on to review the scope and scale of the biotic crisis unfolding, with its potential to precipitate a mass extinction of species to match most such episodes in the prehistoric past. The assessment focuses on tropical moist forests as the biome by far the richest in species and undergoing the most rapid depletion. The paper engages in a detailed examination of the part played by human population in the crisis, differentiating between the role of developing and developed nations. It emphasises the fast-growing numbers of displaced peasants as the predominant cause of tropical deforestation, and of negligent and wasteful consumption in industrialised countries as the principal cause of pollution-derived degradation of wildland habitats. The paper concludes with a selective appraisal of policy responses to safeguard biodiversity.

1. INTRODUCTION

Biodiversity can be roughly defined as the sum total of life forms at all levels of organisation in biological systems. The most readily defined and recognised manifestation lies with species, so they are the chief focus of this paper.

However, biodiversity occurs at subspecies level too. If, as is likely, an average species comprises hundreds of genetically distinct populations, there could be billions of such populations worldwide (Ehrlich & Daily 1993). Because of their ecological differentiation, some populations will be better equipped than others to adapt to the swiftly changing environmental conditions of the foreseeable future. We may well find that if the depletion of biodiversity continues unabated, the loss of sub-species and populations will eventually induce adverse biospheric repercussions on a scale to rival those arising from the loss of species themselves.

Biodiversity is the key characteristic of our planet, possibly unique in the universe. Yet this distinctive phenomenon is being depleted at ever-more rapid rates. Moreover, the biodepletion problem differs from other environmental problems. Soil loss, desertification, deforestation, ozone-layer thinning and the rest could eventually be made good over a period of a few centuries at most. Biodepletion, by contrast, is irreversible within conventional time horizons: it will impoverish the biosphere for millions of years. Hence the issue deserves special attention.

Biodepletion stems almost entirely from loss of habitat. It turn, this derives from the expansion of human activities—partly due to growing human numbers, partly to growing human aspirations, and partly to growing human techno-capacity to exploit environments and their natural resources. Note in particular that the human species is already appropriating 40 percent of net primary production (NPP), leaving the rest for millions of other species (Vitousek *et al.* 1986). What when humans number twice as many as today, as is projected within a few decades' time—and, given recent trends of humans' intensifying exploitation of NPP, the ratio may become still more disproportionately skewed? Note too that one third of Earth's vegetated surface has undergone human-induced land degradation through reduction of its potential biotic productivity; and that the degradation rate is accelerating almost everywhere, certainly in the most populous nations (Daily 1993; Woodwell 1990, 1992).

The role of population, viz. human numbers and their growth rate, is central to biodepletion. But is it prominent, predominant, or overwhelming? The issue is subject to much debate, as this paper reveals.

2. BIODIVERSITY—VALUES TO HUMANKIND

Biodiversity supplies abundant values to humankind, and its decline is to be deplored on many counts. The richness of species and their sub-units contributes to ecological complexity, which in turn can be associated with ecosystem stability, resilience and other salient attributes (Meffe & Carroll 1994; Odum 1993; Solbrig 1991). In a world that seems set to experience increasing environmental turmoil of many sorts, we can ill afford to forego the ecological benefits of a full planetary complement of species. Biodiversity supplies a host of further environmental services such as controlling the gaseous mix of the atmosphere, generating and maintaining soils, controlling pests and running biogeochemical cycles, among other biospheric functions for the transfer of matter, nutrients and energy—all of which are vital to human societies everywhere (Ehrlich & Ehrlich 1992).

Consider, for instance, some services supplied by insects. One third of the human diet derives from fruits, vegetables and other food plants pollinated by insects. In the United States, bees (both wild and honey bees) pollinate more than 40 crops worth $30 billion a year. Because of decline in wild populations, many American farmers now have to rent bees (Pimentel *et al.* 1992). As we shall see, tens of thousands of insect species become extinct each year.

The values of biodiversity for humankind are further apparent through the myriad contributions of species and their genetic resources to plant-based medicines, drugs and pharmaceuticals (Myers 1983; Oldfield 1989). The cumulative commercial value of these products, mostly derived from tropical plants in the territories of developing nations, is estimated to amount during the 1990s to $500 billion (1984 dollars) for the developed nations alone (Principe 1991, 1993; see also Farnsworth & Soejarto 1985). To put the figure of $500 billion in perspective, it is equivalent to more than half the GDP of Britain or India. Moreover, the calculation applies only to the commercial value of the products as reflected through sales. Their economic value, including the benefits of reduced morbidity and mortality, worker productivity maintained and the like, is several times larger. It is anticipated that in the absence of greatly expanded conservation efforts, we shall witness an average extinction rate of one species every two years until 2050 of plants with potential to produce a drug. The cumulative retail-market loss from each such plant extinction will amount to $12 billion in the United States alone (Principe 1991, 1993).

A number of plants generate anticancer drugs, along the lines of vincristine and vinblastine used against childhood leukemia and derived from the rosy periwinkle of Madagascar. Each year, around 30,000 lives are saved in the United States thanks to plant-derived anti-cancer drugs. Using OCED price indices, and an estimate of $12 million for the value of a human life, the annual economic benefits of anti-cancer plant materials in the United States already amount to $370 billion in terms of lives saved, let alone reduced morbidity and the like. We can realistically triple these figures to derive values for all developed nations (Principe 1991, 1993). Most anticancer plants are to be found in the tropics, meaning for the most part the developing nations. This, too, is where the great majority of extinctions are occurring.

Similar considerations apply in agriculture. In the late 1970s a wild species of maize was discovered in a montane forest of south-central Mexico, being the most primitive known relative of modern maize (Iltis *et al.* 1979). At the time of its discovery, it was surviving in three forest patches covering a mere four hectares, a habitat threatened with imminent destruction by agricultural settlement. The wild species is a perennial, unlike all other forms of maize. Cross-breeding with established commercial varieties of maize has opened up the prospect that maize growers (and maize consumers) can be spared the seasonal expense of ploughing and sowing, since the plant springs up again of its own accord like grass. Even more important, the wild maize offers resistance to four of eight major viruses and mycoplasmas that have hitherto baffled maize breeders (Nault & Findley 1981). These four diseases cause at least a 1% loss to the world's maize harvest each year, worth more than $500 million in 1980 dollars. Equally to the point, the wild maize grows at elevations above 2500 metres, and is thus adapted to habitats cooler and damper than established maize-growing lands. This offers scope for expanding the cultivation range of maize by as much as one-fifth. The overall commercial benefits supplied by this wild plant, surviving when first found in the form of no more than a few thousand stalks, could be worth at least $4 billion per year (1980 dollars) (Fisher 1982).

In summary, species and their genetic constituents supply many marketplace benefits to humans, even though pharmacognosy scientists and agronomic experts have undertaken detailed examination of only one plant species in one hundred, and fewer than one animal species in five thousand, to assess their potential for medicine and agriculture. Indeed, the scope for further plant-derived contributions to industry remains largely unexplored even though we already enjoy multiple applications in the form of fibres, exudates, oils, waxes, acids, sterols, esters, phenols, elastomers and polystyrenes. All in all, we can reasonably assert that the planetary spectrum of species represents the most abundant and diversified, the least exploited, and the most rapidly declining stock of natural resources with which humankind can tackle many of its most fundamental challenges. Yet—and to reiterate a prime point—the principal values of species for humankind rest with their ecological services and environmental benefits of numerous sorts. These remain even less explored and understood than the direct utilitarian contributions cited. It may well be that we shall not appreciate these larger values except by experiencing the rigours of a biosphere impoverished through gross biodepletion.

3. DEPLETION OF BIODIVERSITY

3.1 Mass extinction of species

There is much evidence that we are into the opening phase of a mass extinction of species (Ehrlich & Ehrlich 1981; Myers 1976, 1990a; Raven 1990; Soule 1991; Western & Pearl 1989; Wilson 1992). A mass extinction can be defined as an exceptional decline in biodiversity that is substantial in size and generally global in extent, and affecting a broad range of taxonomic groups over a short period of time (Jablonski 1986). In this sense, the present mass extinction—if it remains unchecked by conservation action of appropriate scope and scale—will rival and conceivably surpass the numbers of species lost during the mass-extinction episodes of the prehistoric past (Myers 1990a).

Earth's stock of species is widely estimated (Gaston 1991; May 1988; Soule 1991) to total a minimum of 10 million. Some scientists (Erwin 1991; Ehrlich & Wilson 1991; Wilson 1992) believe the true total could well be 30 million, possibly 50 million and conceivably 100 million. Of the conservative estimate of 10 million species, around 90% are usually considered to be terrestrial (Raven *et al.* 1993); and of the terrestrial species, roughly 80% or more than seven million are believed to occur in the tropics (Stevens 1989), with roughly five million in tropical moist forests (Ricklefs & Schluter 1992). As we shall see, these tropical forests are not only the richest biome biotically but that where habitat depletion is occurring most rapidly—'depletion' including not only outright destruction but gross disruption (fragmentation, etc.) with loss of many ecosystem attributes including food webs. So this is the prime locus of the mass extinction underway, and it is the main focus of the present analysis.

Consider again the higher estimates for the planetary spectrum of species, between 30 million and 100 million (Erwin 1991; Wilson 1992; for critiques, see Adis 1990; Gaston 1991; Hodkinson & Casson 1991; May 1992). Since many if not most of the additional species are believed to occur in tropical forests, the true planetary total is not only a matter for speculation. If the real total is 30 million species, the extinction rate will be much higher than the rate postulated on the basis of only 10 million species. But for the sake of being cautious and conservative, let us accept a total of 10 million species. As noted, at least half of these species live in tropical forests, even though remaining forests cover only 6% of Earth's land surface.

Tropical moist forests are being destroyed at a rate around 150000 square kilometres per year (Myers 1989, 1992a and b; for a slightly lower estimate, see Food and Agriculture Organization 1993). In addition to this outright destruction, an expanse at least as large is being grossly disrupted through over-heavy logging and slash-and-burn cultivation, with much degradation and impoverishment of ecosystems. But in the interests of being cautious and conservative again, let us consider only forest destruction. The current annual loss represents 2% of remaining forests; and the amount increased by 89% during the 1980s. If present patterns and trends of forest destruction persist, leading to still more acceleration in the annual rate, the current annual destruction of 2% of remaining forests may well double again by around the year 2000.

How shall we translate a 2% annual rate of forest destruction into an annual species extinction rate? An analytic approach is supplied by the theory of island biogeography (MacArthur & Wilson 1967), a well established theory with much empirical evidence from on-ground analyses around the world (Case & Cody 1987; Heaney & Paterson 1986; Ricklefs 1990; Shafer 1991; Wilcove 1987; for some dissident views, see Burgman *et al.* 1988; Soule & Simberloff 1986; Zimmerman & Bierregaard 1986). The theory states that the number of species in an area falls as approximately the fourth root of the area remaining, with actual values varying between the third and fifth roots. So when a habitat loses 90% of its original extent, it can generally support no more than about 50% of its original number of species.

The calculation is cautious and conservative. It depends critically upon the status of the remaining 10% of habitat. If this relict expanse is split into many small pieces (as is often the case with remnant tracts of tropical forests), a further 'islandising effect' comes into play, reducing the stock of surviving species still more. It is not clear how severe this additional depletion can be. Informed estimates (Wilson 1992) suggest the 50% can readily be reduced to 40%, more generally to 30%, sometimes to 20%, and occasionally even to 10%. Similarly, if most species concerned occur in small, local endemic communities, the percentage loss of species can readily approach the percentage loss of area. Moreover, isolated remnants of forest become prone to additional impoverishing processes such as 'edge effects', also to desiccating effects due to local climate change (Myers 1992c). So the 90/50 calculation for island biogeography extinctions should be viewed as a minimum estimate.

The most broad-scale application of island biogeography to tropical deforestation and species extinctions has been presented by one of the authors of the original theory, Prof Edward O. Wilson of Harvard University (1992). He estimates a current annual loss of 27,000 species in the forests. As he emphasises repeatedly, this estimate is extremely optimistic. If we employ a more 'realistic' reckoning by qualitatively incorporating a number of other bioecological factors such as alien introductions, over-hunting and diseases, the annual total will become larger. [Indeed an alternative analysis (Ehrlich & Ehrlich 1992) proposes that 60,000 to 90,000 species are lost in tropical forests each year.] In addition, a large number of species, albeit undetermined in even preliminary terms, are presumably disappearing in other parts of the world. Suppose we accept a bare minimum estimate of 30,000 species eliminated worldwide per year. This means we are witnessing a rate at least 120,000 times higher than the 'natural' rate of extinctions before the advent of the human era, considered to be perhaps one species every four years (Raup 1991).

True, the tropical-forest calculation is a broad-brush affair, viewing the forests as a single homogeneous expanse, even though they are highly heterogeneous. So the island biogeography approach needs to be complemented by a local-scale assessment, available in the form of a 'hot spots' analysis. Hot spots are areas that (a) feature exceptional concentrations of species with exceptional levels of endemism, and (b) face exceptional threats of imminent habitat destruction. There are 14 such hot spots in tropical forests and another four in Mediterranean-type zones (plus others, unappraised as yet, in coral reefs, wetlands, montane environments and many islands among other species-rich localities). Collectively, these 18 hot spots contain 50000 endemic plant species, or 20% of all Earth's plant species confined to 0.5% of Earth's land surface. So far as we can determine, they contain an even larger proportion of Earth's animal species with highly localised distributions. Most of these hot spots have already lost the great bulk of their biodiversity habitats, and it is reasonable to suppose that many thousands of species are disappearing annually in hot-spot areas alone (Myers 1988, 1990b).

So much for the current extinction rate. What of the future? Through detailed analysis backed by abundant documentation, Wilson (1992) considers we face the prospect of losing 20% of all species within 30 years and 50% or more thereafter. Another long-experienced expert, Raven (1990), calculates that half of all species exist in those tropical forests that, in the absence of adequate conservation measures, will be reduced to less than one tenth of their present expanse within the next three decades. In accord with island biogeography, Raven concludes—and he stresses this is a conservative prognosis—that one quarter of all species are likely to be eliminated during the next 30 years. Worse, 'fully half of total species may disappear before the close of the 21st century.' Another two biodiversity analysts, Paul and Anne Ehrlich (1992), assert that 'If the current accelerating trends [of habitat destruction] continue, half of Earth's species might easily disappear by 2050.' These estimates are in line with those of several other biodiversity specialists (Diamond 1989; May 1992; Myers 1990a and b). If we accept, then, that half of all species are likely to be eliminated within the foreseeable future, this all means, moreover, that two-fifths of the problem is confined to the 18 hot-spot localities.

3.2 Consequences for evolution

The loss of large numbers of species will not be the only outcome of the present biotic debacle, assuming it proceeds unchecked. There is likely to be a significant disruption of certain basic processes of evolution (Myers 1986a, 1993a). The forces of natural selection and speciation can work only with the 'resource base' of species and sub-units available (Eldredge 1991; Raup 1991)—and as we have seen, this crucial base is being grossly reduced. To cite the graphic phrasing of Soule and Wilcox (1980) 'Death is one thing; an end to birth is something else.' Given what we can discern from the geologic record, the recovery period, that is, the interval until speciation capacities generate a stock of species to match today's in abundance and variety, will be protracted. After the late Cretaceous crash, between five and ten million years elapsed before there were bats in the skies and whales in the seas. Following the mass extinction of the late Permian when marine invertebrates lost roughly half their families, as many as 20 million years were needed before the survivors could establish even half as many families as they had lost (Jablonski 1991).

The evolutionary outcome this time around could prove yet more catastrophic. The critical factor lies with the likely loss of key environments. Not only do we appear set to lose most if not virtually all tropical forests. There is progressive depletion of tropical coral reefs, wetlands, estuaries and other biotypes with exceptional abundance and diversity of species and with unusual complexity of ecological workings. These environments have served in the past as pre-eminent 'powerhouses' of evolution, meaning that they have thrown up more species than other environments. Virtually every major group of vertebrates and many other large categories of animals have originated in spacious zones with warm, equable climates, notably the Old World tropics and especially their forests (Darlington 1957; Mayr 1982). The rate of evolutionary diversification—

whether through proliferation of species or through emergence of major new adaptations—has been greatest in the tropics, especially in tropical forests. Tropical forest species appear to persist for only brief periods of geologic time, which implies a high rate of evolution (Jablonski 1993; Stanley 1991; Stenseth 1984).

As extensive environments are eliminated wholesale, moreover, the current mass extinction applies across most if not all major categories of species. The outcome will contrast sharply with that of the end of the Cretaceous, when not only placental mammals survived (leading to the adaptive radiation of mammals, eventually including man), but also birds, amphibians, and crocodiles among many other non-dinosaurian reptiles. In addition, the present extinction spasm is eliminating a large portion of terrestrial plant species, by contrast with mass-extinction episodes of the prehistoric past when terrestrial plants have survived with relatively few losses (Knoll 1984)—and have thus supplied a resource base on which evolutionary processes could start to generate replacement animal species forthwith. If this biotic substrate is markedly depleted within the foreseeable future, the restorative capacities of evolution will be the more diminished.

All this will carry severe implications for human societies, extending throughout the recovery period estimated to last at least five million years, possibly several times longer. Just five million years would be twenty times longer than humankind itself has been a species. The present generation is effectively imposing a decision on the unconsulted behalf of at least 200,000 follow-on generations. It must rank as the most far-reaching decision ever taken on the behalf of such a large number of people in the course of human history. Suppose that Earth's population maintains an average of 2.5 billion people during the next five million years, and that the generation time remains 25 years: the total affected will amount to 100 trillion people (Myers 1993b).

4. BIODIVERSITY AND POPULATION
4.1 The role of developing countries
The broadscale decline of biodiversity has been underway since roughly 1950, when there began a major increase in human encroachment onto wildland environments. Since that time too, the population of developing countries has expanded from 1.7 billion to 4.3 billion people, more than a 150% increase. But this is not to say that more people must *necessarily* mean fewer species habitats. Many other variables are at work, notably poverty, inefficient agriculture, poor land-use planning, inadequate technology and deficient policy strategies among other prominent factors of countries concerned; plus adverse exogenous factors of aid, trade, debt, investment and South/North relationships generally. There are abundant linkages that make the picture far more complex than a simple population/biodiversity equation (Davis & Bernstam 1991; Leonard 1987; Myers 1991, 1994a; Repetto 1987).

Let us establish a rough analytic framework within which to evaluate the impact of population growth on wildland environments. The sudden upsurge in human numbers has often exacted a toll in terms of the environmental underpinnings of human societies, as witness tropical deforestation, desertification, soil erosion and the like. But population growth has not been the only factor at issue. Soil erosion is as severe in Indiana as in India, even though Indiana's population pressures *per se* are only a fraction of those of

India. One of the fastest desertifying countries is Botswana, with only 1.4 million people in a territory the size of Spain or Texas—and a country where most desertifying processes are due to the activities of a few hundred largescale cattle ranchers who make up only 5% of the livestock-owning sector.

So population growth is no more than one among many variables, even though it can often rank as *primus inter pares*. Important too are technology types, energy supplies, economic systems, trade relations, political persuasions, policy strategies and a host of other factors that either reduce or aggravate the impact of population growth. All the same, population growth can be a prominent if not pre-eminent factor when it exceeds the capacity of a country's natural-resource base to sustain it, and likewise exceeds the capacity of development planners to accommodate it (Ehrlich & Ehrlich 1990; Myers 1992d; Ness *et al.* 1993). In these circumstances it causes—or at the very least it makes a major contribution to—a spillover of human communities onto biodiversity habitats.

Consider the case of Kenya, a country with exceptional biodiversity. The 1993 population of 27 million people is projected to expand to well over 100 million by the time zero growth is attained in the 22nd century. Yet even if the nation were to employ Western Europe's high-technology agriculture, it could support no more than 52 million people off its own lands (Food and Agriculture Organization 1984); and even if Kenya were to achieve the two-child family forthwith, its population would still double because of demographic momentum (49% of Kenyans are under the age of 15, meaning that large numbers of future parents are already in place). So Kenya will have to depend on steadily increasing amounts of food from outside to support itself. Regrettably, and in large part because of its high population growth rate (around 4% during the 1980s), its *per-capita* economic growth has been well under 2% (World Bank 1993). Worse, Kenya's terms of trade have long been declining until they are barely positive today, meaning the country faces the prospect of diminishing financial reserves to purchase food abroad. Its export economy will have to permanently flourish in a manner far better than it has ever achieved to date if the country is to buy enough food to meet its fast-growing needs. Worst of all, the country will have to undertake this challenge with a natural-resource base from which forests have almost disappeared, watershed flows for irrigation agriculture are widely depleted, and much topsoil has been eroded away (World Resources Institute 1992).

We must anticipate, then, that Kenya will continue to feature growing throngs of impoverished peasants who will encroach onto whatever environments are available for them to gain their subsistence livelihoods. Since that will usually mean more cutting down of forests, digging up of grasslands and cultivation of steep slopes (the phenomenon of 'marginal people in marginal environments'), these peasant farmers have the capacity to induce exceptionally pervasive injury of Kenya's wildlands throughout the foreseeable future. The country's forests, being the most species-rich habitats, covered 12% of national territory in 1960, when the population was only six million. Since the forests often occupy fertile lands where property rights are vague at best, they have been a prime focus for agricultural settlement on the part of landless peasants, until today they occupy only 2% of Kenya's land area.

4.2 Tropical forests and the shifted cultivator

Let us now move on to a larger-scope perspective and examine the generic case of tropical forests. As we have seen, these forests contain at least 50% of all species in only 6% of Earth's land surface; and they are being depleted faster than any other largescale biome. This is where the mass extinction envisaged will largely occur—or be contained. If we allow the forests to be virtually eliminated within the next few decades, there will be a massive loss of species regardless of our conservation efforts in the rest of the world; but if we manage to save most of the forests while allowing other major environments to be widely depleted, we shall surely avoid a mass extinction when viewed in proportion to the planetary complement of species. Tropical forests are uniquely critical to the biodiversity prospect writ large, hence they receive special emphasis here.

Of current deforestation, only one fifth is due to excessive logging, which has hardly increased since the early 1980s. Roughly one tenth is due to cattle ranching, which has actually declined somewhat. One seventh is due to road building, dam construction, commercial agriculture, fuelwood gathering and other peripheral activities, which have likewise shown scant increase. Almost three-fifths is attributable to the slash-and-burn farmer, with fast-expanding impact (Myers 1992c, 1994b). This principal agent of deforestation operates not so much as the 'shifting cultivator' of tradition: rather, he is a displaced peasant who finds himself landless in established farming areas of countries concerned and feels obliged to migrate to the last unoccupied public lands available, tropical forests (Manshard & Morgan 1988; Palo & Salmi 1988; Peters & Neuenschwander 1988; Schuman & Partridge 1989; Theisenhusen 1989). Driven significantly by population growth and resultant pressure on traditional farmlands (albeit often cultivated with only low or medium levels of agrotechnology, hence cultivated in extensive rather than intensive fashion), slash-and-burn agriculture is the main source of deforestation in such leading tropical-forest countries as Colombia, Ecuador, Peru, Bolivia, Ivory Coast, Zaire, Madagascar, India, Nepal, Sri Lanka, Thailand, Indonesia and Philippines, often too in Mexico, Brazil, Myanmar and Vietnam (Myers 1989). These countries with acute population pressures include nine of the fourteen tropical-forest hot spots, with endemic plant species comprising 9% of the planetary total.

Being powerless to resist the factors that drive him into the forest, the shifted cultivator is no more to be 'blamed' for deforestation than a soldier is to be held responsible for starting a war. His lifestyle is determined by a host of factors—economic, social, legal, institutional, political—of which he has scant understanding and over which he has virtually no control (Colchester & Lohmann 1993; Westoby 1989). But he advances on forest fringes in ever-growing numbers, pushing deeper into forests year by year. Behind come more multitudes of displaced peasants. By contrast with the shifting cultivator and his sustainable use of forest ecosystems, the shifted cultivator is unable to allow the forest any chance of regeneration.

To reiterate, many other factors are at work in the shifted cultivator phenomenon. While tropical-forest countries' populations expanded by amounts ranging from 15 to 36% during the 1980s, deforestation expanded by almost 90% (Myers 1989). Malaysia has only one tenth as many people as Indonesia, yet it has lost 40% as much forest as Indonesia. While the amount of forest destroyed per person in India is less than 0.2

hectare, the corresponding figure is six times higher in both Ivory Coast and Colombia (World Bank 1992). Vietnam, Peru and Papua New Guinea are each clearing forest at a rate of 3500 square kilometres per year, though annual population increase is 1.6 million in Vietnam, 458,000 in Peru and 90,000 in Papua New Guinea (World Resources Institute 1992).

So the further factors displacing peasants into the forests are critically important too. They include peasant poverty, maldistribution of established farmlands, inequitable land-use systems, lack of property rights and tenure regimes, low-level agrotechnologies, insufficient policy support for subsistence farming, deficient rural infrastructure and inadequate development overall (Repetto & Gillis 1988; Westoby 1987). But population growth is likely to be a prominent if not the predominant factor in the progressive expansion of shifted cultivator numbers foreseeable, and hence in the accelerating rates of deforestation and of species extinctions (Grainger 1993; Lynch 1991; Myers 1991).

Given the demographic momentum built into population-growth processes in countries concerned, and even allowing for expanded family-planning programmes, population projections (Table 1) suggest that in those countries where economies appear likely to remain primarily agrarian, there will surely be progressive pressures on remaining forests, extending for decades into the future. For instance, Peru's population is projected to grow from 23 million in mid-1993 to 48 million (an increase of 110%) before it attains zero growth in about one century's time; Cameroon's from 13 million to 56 million (338%); Madagascar's from 13 million to 49 million (268%); Myanmar's from 44 million to 96 million (121%); and Vietnam's from 72 million to 159 million (121%).

Again, we must be careful not to over-state the case. In the island of New Guinea, population pressures are slight to date (eight million people in 827 000 square kilometres), and appear unlikely to become unduly significant within the foreseeable future. Much the same applies to the countries of the Zaire Basin in central Africa; to the countries of the Guyana shield, viz. Guyana, Suriname and French Guiana; and to the western sector of Brazilian Amazonia. All in all, these areas comprise roughly three million square kilometres of tropical forest, or two-fifths of the remaining biome.

As a measure of the scope for increasing streams of shifted cultivators to migrate into the forests, consider three salient factors. First, tropical forest countries will not only account for the bulk of population growth, an extra three billion people, within the next forty years (for details, see Table 1). More significantly, the numbers of shifted cultivators have recently been growing far faster than national populations, usually at rates between 4% and 16% annually (Myers 1992c), meaning their projected doubling time is between 17.25 and 4.3 years.

Secondly, alternative forms of livelihood for landless peasants are becoming still more limited by unemployment problems. Developing countries need to generate 600 million jobs (as many as all jobs in developed countries today) during the next 20 years simply to accommodate new entrants into the labour market, let alone to relieve present unemployment and underemployment which often amount to 30% to 40% of the work force. In Brazil 1.7 million new people seek jobs each year, over half of them failing to find enough employment to support themselves, and many of them join the migratory surge toward Amazonia.

Table 1. *Population growth and socioeconomic factors in leading tropical forest countries*

	population (millions)		population growth rate (%)	population in rural areas (%)	population projected (millions)		projected size of stationary population (millions)	per-capita GNP (US$)	foreign debt (billions US$)
	1950	1993	1993	1993	2000	2025		1991	1991
Latin America									
Bolivia	3	8	2.7	49	9	14	22	650	4
Brazil	53	152	1.5	24	172	205	285	2920	117
Colombia	12	35	2.1	32	38	51	63	1280	17
Ecuador	3	10	2.5	45	13	17	25	1020	13
Mexico	27	90	2.3	29	99	138	182	2870	102
Peru	8	23	2.0	28	26	36	48	1020	21
Venezuela	5	21	2.6	16	23	33	41	2610	34
Asia									
India	362	897	2.1	74	1017	1380	1886	330	72
Indonesia	77	188	1.7	69	206	278	354	610	74
Malaysia	6	18	2.3	49	22	33	43	2490	21
Myanmar	18	44	1.9	78	51	70	96	n/a	5
Papua New Guinea	2	4	2.3	87	5	7	12	820	3
Philippines	20	65	2.5	57	74	101	140	740	32
Thailand	20	57	1.4	81	65	76	105	1580	36
Vietnam	24	72	2.2	80	82	107	159	n/a	n/a
Africa									
Cameroon	5	13	2.9	60	16	33	58	940	6
Congo	1	2	2.8	59	3	5	15	1120	5
Gabon	n/a	1	2.4	54	2	2	7	3780	4
Ivory Coast	3	13	3.5	60	17	38	67	690	19
Madagascar	5	13	3.3	76	15	34	49	210	4
Zaire	14	41	3.3	60	50	105	172	220	10

n/a = not available.

Sources: United Nations 1992; World Bank 1992, 1993

Thirdly, there is a pervasive problem of farmland shortage in many if not most developing countries, where land provides the livelihood for around three-fifths of populations and where the great bulk of the most fertile and accessible land has already been taken (Harrison 1992; Myers 1994a). A full 200 million farmers have too little land for subsistence needs of food and fuel (El-Ghonemy 1990). For some sample figures for leading tropical forest countries, note that of Indonesia's and Thailand's rural populations in the late 1980s, 15% were landless; of Peru's, 19%; of Myanmar's, 22%; and of the Philippines', 34%. This translated into a total in Thailand of 6.4 million people landless, in Myanmar, 6.7 million, in the Philippines, 11.9 million, and in Indonesia, 19.2 million (Jazairy *et al.*, 1992).)

Many rural poor are increasingly encroaching onto tropical forests among other low-potential lands, where they have no option but to over-exploit environmental resource stocks in order to survive (Oodit & Simonis 1992; World Bank 1990). Worse, farmland shortages continue to spread among the rural poor at rates between 3% and 5% a year, i.e. faster than population growth rates—though much of the problem has been set up by population growth in the past (Jazairy *et al.* 1992).

These two last considerations also apply to wildland environments and hence to species habitats in zones other than tropical forests—zones where population pressures already cause much decline in biodiversity. According to the most comprehensive and systematised analysis to date (Harrison 1992), population growth in developing countries accounted for (a) 72% of expansion of arable lands during 1961—85, leading to the decline of many natural environments, not only through deforestation but desertification and other forms of land degradation; and (b) 69% of the increase in livestock numbers during 1961—85, leading to soil erosion and desertification. Several other analyses (e.g. Ehrlich & Ehrlich 1990; Davis & Bernstam 1991; Food and Agriculture Organization 1993; Ness *et al.* 1993; Myers 1993c, 1994a) supply similar findings, albeit with marginally different statistical conclusions.

Of course, these calculations can appear over-simplified, even simplistic. A situation with multiple complexities is the opposite of simple. The multiple linkages are not all direct in their operation, still less are they exclusively causative. But they are there. Just because they cannot be demonstrated and documented in detail does not mean they are any less real than more readily defined linkages. They exert their effect, and they are growing stronger and more numerous. The fact that it is difficult to perceive all the linkages in question may tell us less about the linkages than about our limited capacity to think concisely and systematically about them in their full scope. To the extent that environmental scientists are sometimes reluctant to assert a population–deforestation linkage because they lack information of conventional quantity and quality, they might reflect that, all too unwittingly, an unduly cautious approach to linkage analysis could prove erroneous.

This relates particularly to the response of the policy maker, who may feel that absence of evidence about a problem implies evidence of absence of a problem—whereupon he or she may decide to do nothing, even though that is to decide to do a great deal in a world that is not standing still. The asymmetry of evaluation means that we should be wary of being preoccupied with what can be counted if that is to the detriment of what ultimately counts. As in other situations of uncertainty where a negative outcome carries exceptionally adverse consequences, it will be better for us to find we have been roughly right than precisely wrong.

4.2 The role of developed countries

Population growth in developed countries, in conjunction with related factors of excessively consumerist and wasteful lifestyles, also contributes to the decline of biodiversity. (For a singularly illuminating analysis of energy consumption, see Ehrlich 1994.)

Consider first the role of developed countries in tropical deforestation. There are the well-known linkages of the hamburger and cassava connections, also the tropical timber trade, whereby developed countries' consumerist lifestyles, working in conjunction with inequitable trading patterns, generate marketplace pressures that induce deforestation (Myers 1986b, 1993d). Not so well known is the debt connection. Tropical forest countries owe roughly two-thirds of international debt totalling $1.3 trillion (for details, see Table 1). Debt-burdened countries often feel inclined to over-exploit their forest resources in order to raise foreign exchange. More importantly, debt leaves them with fewer financial resources to tackle problems of peasant poverty, landlessness and unemployment. So strong is this linkage in certain instances that a $5 billion reduction in a country's debt can lead to a reduction of anywhere between 250 and 1000 (occasionally more) square kilometres of annual deforestion (Kahn & McDonald 1992; see also Gullison & Losos 1993). Debt relief could be a potent factor in the case of, for example, Peru with its $21 billion debt and annual deforestation of 3500 square kilometres, and Philippines with debt of $32 billion and annual deforestation of 2700 square kilometres.

At the same time, much biodiversity is threatened within developed countries. In the United States, for instance, more than 2250 plant species, 12% of the total, face extinction within less than ten years (many species are restricted to a single population) (Robert 1988). At least half the country's freshwater animal species are severely endangered through disruption of rivers, lakes and other wetlands (Williams *et al.* 1989). Two Mediterranean-type hot spots are located in California and south-western Australia, where almost 5000 endemic plant species and a still larger number of endemic animal species are confined to habitats undergoing progressive depletion (Myers 1990b). (To put this plant figure in perspective, note that the British Isles' flora amounts to only some 1600 species, fewer than 20 of which are endemic.) There are many such instances of species concentrations threatened in developed countries, albeit with not nearly such large totals as in tropical forests (McNeely *et al.* 1990).

Present threats to biodiversity worldwide are not to be compared, however, with those that could lie ahead through climate change. Global warming, mainly induced to date through profligate consumption of fossil fuels in developed countries, would likely cause widespread depletion of habitats in many parts of the Earth (Gates 1993; Peters & Lovejoy 1992; Woodwell 1990). Indeed, burners of fossil fuel could eventually rank second to burners of tropical forests as a source of mass extinction.

The study of population growth effects yields surprising results. While developed-country population growth rates are generally low, they count. Britain, for example, with a 0.2% annual population growth rate, features a net increase through natural growth of 116000 persons per year. By contrast, Bangladesh, with a 2.4% annual growth rate, features a net increase of 2.7 million persons, 23 times larger. But because the fossil-fuel consumption of each new British person is more than thirty times that of a Bangladeshi, Britain's population growth contributes 3.9 times as much carbon dioxide to the global atmosphere, and hence to global warming, than does Bangladesh's. (The average British family comprises less than two children, but when we factor in resource consumption and pollution impacts, and then compare the British lifestyle with the global average, the 'real world' size of a British family is more like ten children.) Ironically, Britain—a country where family planning benefits exceed costs by a ratio of 5:1 (Estaugh & Wheatly 1991)—could achieve zero population growth by the simple expedient of eliminating unwanted births.

Population growth in all developed countries will contribute more to buildup of carbon dioxide in the global atmosphere during the 1990s than will population growth in developing countries (Harrison 1992). Much the same applies to emissions of ozone-depleting chemicals and toxic substances that likewise degrade extensive sectors of the biosphere. Yet not a single developed country has formulated a population policy within a context of environmental linkages overall.

5. POLICY RESPONSES

Fortunately, there are many policy responses available in both the biodiversity and population fields. The population options are dealt with in other Delhi Conference papers, so they are not touched on here—except to emphasise the need for population policies, grounded in an assessment of key factors such as carrying capacity and optimum population size in all countries, including developed countries.

Consider the particular scope to tackle the leading biodiversity problem through measures to reduce tropical deforestation on the part of the shifted cultivator. Unless there is a reduction of population growth together with a resolution of landlessness (the latter prospect appears distinctly unpromising (Jazairy *et al.* 1992; Salmi 1988; World Bank 1990)), it is difficult to forecast that much forest will remain in a few decades, in most countries in question. The shifted cultivator problem is complex and taxing: whereas it would be fairly straightforward to relieve deforestation pressures from the commercial logger (by growing timber in plantations on deforested lands) and from the cattle rancher (by expanding sustainable beef production on established pasturelands), no such 'easy fix' is available for the shifted cultivator. His needs can be addressed only through a broad-scale effort to bring him into the development process through socioeconomic advancement, redistribution of existing farmlands, reform of land-tenure systems, build-up of agricultural extension services, improvement of rural infrastructure, and provision of agrotechnologies that enable the impoverished peasant to practise more intensive and sustainable farming in traditional agricultural areas, viz. the areas from which he feels obliged to migrate.

To date, there seems limited prospect of the shifted cultivator problem being resolved within a time horizon that will assist tropical forests, unless much more attention is directed by governments concerned, also international development agencies, to the particular development challenges he poses. It is a measure of how far his cause is systematically neglected that we have no sound idea of how numerous his communities are, beyond estimates that range from 300 million to 600 million (Lynch 1991; Myers 1992b). If the latter total is correct (it may well be an under-estimate), the shifted cultivator accounts for over one in ten of humankind. Yet he remains a forgotten figure. Although the issue was identified as long ago as the late 1970s (Myers 1979; UNESCO 1978), the amount done to tackle the problem through policy reform of appropriate scope and scale is scant at best.

Most measures to tackle deforestation seek to relieve problems within the forests, even though these measures respond to less than half the problem overall, located as it is in the shifted cultivator issue originating in lands well outside the forests. Many anti-deforestation measures, for example, more protected areas, reflect efforts to tackle symptoms rather than sources of problems, given that—to reiterate the principal point— the ultimate source of the biggest problem lies in lands far outside the forests. This dimension to the deforestation issue remains beyond the policy purview of most tropical forest planners.

The shifted cultivator issue demonstrates that there is limited scope for biodiversity protection in the traditional strategy of parks and reserves. This is not to say there is not great need for many more such areas. Ecologists and biogeographers consider that in tropical forests alone, we should at least triple the expanse protected (World Conservation Monitoring Centre 1992), while recognising that one third of existing parks and reserves are already subject to agricultural encroachment and other forms of human disruption. Additional forms of degradation are likely to stem in the future from pollution: as much as one million square kilometres or almost 15% of remaining forests could soon become subject to acid precipitation (Rodhe & Herrera 1988). There could eventually be further and more widespread depletion from global warming (Hartshoorn 1992; Shugart *et al.* 1986).

This means that protected areas are becoming far less of the sufficient conservation response that they were once considered to be. The time has arrived when, as a bottom-line conclusion, we must recognise we can ultimately safeguard biodiversity only by safeguarding the biosphere—with all that entails for agriculture, industry, energy and a host of other sectors, especially the growth of both population and consumption. Increasingly too it is apparent that we may ultimately find we inhabit a world where there are no more protected areas: either because they have been over-run by landless peasants and grand-scale pollution, or because we have learned to manage all our landscapes in such a manner that there is automatic provision for biodiversity (McNeely 1990).

The Global Environment Facility is providing $350 million dollars over three years to assist biodiversity. This is quite the largest such dispensation ever made. But compare it with what is at stake. Every year, just the commercial value to just the rich nations of just the present array of plant-derived pharmaceuticals is over 140 times greater. More significant still, the worldwide amount spent annually on 'perverse' subsidies, that is, subsidies that inadvertently foster over-loading of croplands, over-grazing of rangelands, profligate burning of fossil fuels, wasteful use of water, over-cutting of forests and over-harvesting of fisheries (to cite but a few examples of activities that also reduce biodiversity) is twenty times greater again. Note too that the shortfall in spending to support those 300 million developing-world women who possess the motivation to reduce their fertility but lack the family planning facilities, is $6 billion per year. If we were to take care of these unmet needs—which should be catered for on humanitarian grounds even if there were no population problem at all—we would reduce the ultimate world population size by 2.0 to 2.5 billion people.

ACKNOWLEDGEMENTS

It is a pleasure to recognise substantive critiques from Dr. Gretchen Daily of the University of California at Berkeley and from Professor David Pimentel of Cornell University. In addition and as usual, I have received back-up support in the form of many illuminating ideas from my Research Associate, Jennifer Kent.

REFERENCES

Adis, J. 1990 Thirty million arthropod species—too many or too few? *J. Trop. Ecol.* **6**, 115–118.
Burgman, M.A., Akcakaya, H.R. & Loew, S.S. 1988 The use of extinction models for species conservation. *Biol. Cons.* **43**, 9–25.
Case, T.J. & Cody, M.L. 1987 Testing theories of island biogeography. *Am. Scient.* **75**, 402–411.
Colchester, M. & Lohmann, L. eds. 1992 *The struggle for land and the fate of the forests.* London: Zed Books.
Daily, G.C. 1993 Personal communication, letter of October 10th, 1993. Berkeley, California: Energy and Resources Group, University of California.
Darlington, P.J. 1957 *Zoogeography: the geographical distribution of animals.* New York: Wiley.
Davis, K. & Bernstam, M.S., eds. 1991 *Resources, environment and population: present knowledge, future options.* New York: Oxford University Press.
Diamond, J.M. 1989 The present, past and future of human-caused extinction. *Phil. Trans. Soc. Lond.* B 325, 469–478.
Ehrlich, P.R. 1994 The scale of the human enterprise and the biodiversity loss. *Phil. Trans. Soc. Lond.* (in press).
Ehrlich, P.R. & Daily, G.C. 1993 Population extinction and saving biodiversity. *Ambio* **22**, 64–68.
Ehrlich, P.R. & Ehrlich, A.H. 1981 *Extinction: the causes and consequences of the disappearance of species.* New York: Random House.
Ehrlich, P.R. & Ehrlich, A.H. 1990 *The population explosion.* New York: Simon and Schuster.
Ehrlich, P.R. & Ehrlich, A.H. 1992 The value of biodiversity. *Ambio* **21**, 219–226.
Ehrlich, P.R. & Wilson, E.O. 1991 Biodiversity studies: science and policy. *Science, Wash.* **253**, 758–762.
Eldredge, N. 1991 *The miner's canary.* New York: Prentice-Hall.
El-Ghonemy, R.M. 1990 *The political economy of rural poverty: the case for land reform.* London: Routledge.
Erwin, T.L. 1991 How many species are there?: revisited. *Cons. Biol.* **5**, 330–333.
Estaugh, V. & Wheatly, J. 1991 *Family planning and family well-being.* London: Family Policy Studies Centre.
Farnsworth, N.R. & Soejarto, D.D. 1985 Potential consequences of plant extinctions in the United States on the current and future availability of prescription drugs. *Econ. Bot.* **39**, 231.
Fisher, A.C. 1982 *Economic analysis and the extinction of species.* University of California: Department of Agriculture and Resource Economics.
Food and Agriculture Organization. 1984 *Potential population supporting capacities of lands in the*

developing world. Rome: FAO.

Food and Agriculture Organization. 1988 *World agriculture: towards 2000*. London: Belhaven Press.

Food and Agriculture Organization. 1993 *Tropical forest resources assessment*. Rome: FAO.

Gaston, K.J. 1991 The magnitude of global insect species richness. *Cons. Biol.* 5, 283–296.

Gates, D.M. 1993 *Climate change and its biological consequences*. Sunderland, MA: Sinauer Associates.

Grainger, A. 1993 *Controlling tropical deforestation*. London: Earthscan Publications.

Gullison, R.E. & Losos, E.C. 1993 The role of foreign debt in deforestation in Latin America. *Cons. Biol.* **7**, 140–147.

Harrison, P. 1992. *The third revolution: environment, population and a sustainable world*. London: Tauris.

Hartshorn, G.S. 1992 Ten possible effects of global warming on the biological diversity in tropical forests. In *Global warming and biological diversity*, (eds. R.L. Peters & T.E. Lovejoy). New Haven: Yale University Press pp. 137–146.

Heaney, R. & Paterson, B.D. 1986 *Island biogeography of mammals*. New York: Academic Press.

Hodkinson, I.D. & Casson, D. 1991 A lesser predilection for bugs: *Hemiptera* (Insecta) diversity in tropical rain forests. *Biol. J. Linn. Soc.* **43**, 101–109.

Iltis, H.H., Doebley, J.F., Guzman, R.M. & Pazy, B. 1979 *Zea diploperennis* (Gramineae), a new teosinte from Mexico. *Science* **203**, 198–188.

Jablonski, D. 1986 Causes and consequences of mass extinctions: a comparative approach. In *Dynamics of extinction* (ed. D.K. Elliott). New York: Wiley, pp. 183–229.

Jablonski, D. 1991 Extinctions: a palaeontological perspective. *Science* **253**, 754–757.

Jablonski, D. 1993 The tropics as a source of evolutionary novelty through geological time. *Nature, Lond.* **364**, 142–144.

Jazairy, I., Alamgir, M. & Panuccio, T. 1992 *The state of world rural poverty: an inquiry into its causes and consequences*. London: Intermediate Technology Publications.

Kahn, J.R. & McDonald, J.A. 1992 *Third world debt and tropical deforestation*. Binghamton, NY: State University of New York.

Knoll, A.H. 1984 Patterns of extinction in the fossil record of vascular plants. In *Extinctions* (ed. M.H. Nitecki). University of Chicago Press, pp. 21–68.

Leonard, H.J. 1987 *Natural resources and economic development in central america*. New Brunswick, NJ: TransAction Books.

Leonard, J. 1989 *Environment and the poor: development strategies for a common agenda*. New Brunswick, NJ: TransAction Books.

Lynch, O.J. 1991 *Community-based tenurial strategies for promoting forest conservation and development in South and South-East Asia*. Washington DC: World Resources Institute.

MacArthur, R.H. & Wilson, E.O. 1967 *The theory of island biogeography*. Princeton, NJ: Princeton University Press.

Manshard, W. & Morgan, W.B., eds. 1988 *Agricultural expansion and pioneer settlements in the humid tropics*. Tokyo: United Nations University.

May, R.M. 1988 How many species are there on Earth? *Science, Wash.* **241**, 1441–1449.

May, R.M. 1992 How many species inhabit the Earth? *Scient. Am.* **267**, 42–48.

Mayr, E. 1982 *The growth of biological thought: diversity, evolution and inheritance*. Cambridge, MA: Harvard University Press.

McNeely, J.A. 1990 The future of national parks. *Environment* **32**(1),16–20, 36–41.

McNeely, J.A., *et al.* 1990 *Conserving the world's biological diversity*. Gland, Switzerland: International Union for Conservation of Nature and Natural Resources.

Meffe, G.K. & Carroll, C.R., eds. 1994 *An introduction to conservation biology*. Sunderland, MA: Sinauer Associates (in press).

Myers, N. 1976 An expanded approach to the problem of disappearing species. *Science, Wash.* **193**, 198–202.

Myers, N. 1979 *The sinking ark.* Oxford: Pergamon Press.

Myers, N. 1980 *Conversion of tropical moist forests.* Washington DC: National Research Council.

Myers, N. 1983 *A wealth of wild species: storehouse for human welfare.* Boulder, CO: Westview Press.

Myers, N. 1986a *Tackling mass extinction of species: a great creative challenge.* Berkeley, CA: Horace M. Albright Lecture in Conservation, University of California.

Myers, N. 1986b Economics and ecology in the international arena: the phenomenon of "linked linkages". *Ambio* **15**(5): 296–300.

Myers, N. 1988 Threatened biotas: "hot spots" in tropical forests. *The Environmentalist* **8**, 187–208.

Myers, N. 1989 *Deforestation rates in tropical forests and their climatic implications.* London: Friends of the Earth.

Myers, N. 1990a Mass extinctions: what can the past tell us about the present and the future? *Global and Planetary Change* **82**, 175–185.

Myers, N. 1990b The biodiversity challenge: expanded hot-spots analysis. *TheEnvironmentalist* **10**, 243–256.

Myers, N. 1991 *Population, resources and the environment: the critical challenges.* New York: United Nations Population Fund.

Myers, N. 1992a *Future operational monitoring of tropical forests: an alert strategy.* Ispra, Italy: Joint Research Centre, Commission of the European Communities.

Myers, N. 1992b *The primary source: tropical forests and our future.* New York: W.W.Norton.

Myers, N., ed. 1992c *Tropical forests and climate.* Dordrecht: Kluwer.

Myers, N. 1992d *The environmental consequences for the European Community of population factors worldwide and within the community.* Brussels: European Commission.

Myers, N. 1993a Questions of mass extinction. *Biodiversity and Conservation* **2**, 2–17.

Myers, N. 1993b Biodiversity and the precautionary principle. *Ambio* **22**, 74–79.

Myers, N. 1993c Population, environment and development. *Env. Cons.* **20**.

Myers, N. 1993d The question of linkages in environment and development. *BioScience* **43**, 302–310.

Myers, N. 1994a *Scarcity or abundance: a debate on the environment.* New York: W.W.Norton (in press).

Myers, N. 1994b. Tropical deforestation: population, poverty and biodiversity. In *Cambridge symposium on biodiversity decline: the driving forces* (ed. T.M. Swanson) (in press).

Nault, L.R. & Findley, W.R. 1981 Primitive relative offers new traits for corn improvement. *Ohio Report* **66**(6), 90–92.

Ness, G.D., Drake, W.D. & Brechin, S.R., eds. 1993 *Population–environment dynamics: ideas and observations.* Ann Arbor, MI: University of Michigan Press.

Odum, E.P. 1993 *Ecology and our endangered life-support systems.* Sunderland, MA: Sinauer Associates.

Oldfield, M.L. 1989 *The value of conserving genetic resources.* Sunderland, MA: Sinauer Associates.

Oodit, D. & Simonis, U.E. 1992 *Poverty: environment and development.* Berlin: Wissenschaftzentrum.

Palo, M. & Salmi, J., eds. 1988 *Deforestation or development in the third world?* Helsinki: Finnish Forest Research Institute.

Peters, W.J. & Neuenschwander, L.F. 1988 *Slash and burn farming in third world forests.* Moscow, ID: University of Idaho Press.

Peters, R.L. & Lovejoy, T.E., eds. 1992 *Consequences of the greenhouse warming to biodiversity.* New Haven, Conn.: Yale University Press.

Pimentel, D. & eight others 1992 Conserving biological diversity in agricultural/forestry systems. *BioScience* **42**, 354–362.

Principe, P. 1991 Valuing diversity of medicinal plants. In *Conservation of medicinal plants* (eds. O. Akerele, V. Heywood & H. Synge). Cambridge, UK: Cambridge University Press, pp. 70–124.

Principe, P. 1993 Monetizing the pharmocological benefits of plants. In *Tropical forest medical resources and the conservation of biodiversity* (eds. M.J. Balick, et al.) New York: Columbia University Press (in press).

Raup, D.M. 1991 *Extinction: bad genes or bad luck?* New York: W. W. Norton.

Raven, P.R. 1990 The politics of preserving biodiversity. *BioScience* **40**(10), 769–774.

Raven, P.H., Berg, L.R. & Johnson, G.B. 1993 *Environment.* New York: Saunders College Publishing.

Repetto, R. 1987 *Population, resources, environment: an uncertain future.* Washington DC: Population Reference Bureau.

Repetto, R. & Gillis, M. 1988 *Public policy and the misuse of forest resources.* Cambridge: Cambridge University Press.

Ricklefs, R. 1990 *Ecology* (3e). San Francisco, CA: W.H. Freeman.

Ricklefs, R. & Schluter, D., eds. 1992 *Species diversity: geographical and historical aspects.* Chicago, IL: University of Chicago Press.

Robert, L. 1988 Extinction imminent for native plants. *Science, Wash.* **242**, 1508.

Rodhe, H. & Herrera, R., eds. 1988 *Acidification in tropical countries.* Chichester: Wiley.

Salmi, J. 1988 Land reform—a weapon against tropical deforestation? In *Deforestation or development in the third world,* Vol. II (eds. M. Palo & J. Salmi). Helsinki: Division of Social Economics of Forestry, Finnish Forest Research Institute, pp. 159–180.

Schugart, H.H., Antonovsky, M. Y., Jarvis, P.G. & Sandford, A.P. 1986 Assessing the response of global forests to the direct effects of increasing CO_2 and climate change. In *The greenhouse effect, climatic change and ecosystems* (eds. B. Bolin, B.R. Doos, J. Jager & R.A. Warrick). Chichester: John Wiley and Sons, pp. 475–521.

Schuman, D. & Partridge, W.L. 1989 *Human ecology of tropical land settlement in Latin America.* Boulder, CO: Westview Press.

Shafer, C.L. 1991 *Nature reserves: island theory and conservation practice.* Washington DC: Smithsonian Institution Press.

Solbrig, O.T. 1991 *From genes to ecosystems: a research agenda for biodiversity.* Paris: International Union of Biological Sciences.

Soule, M.E. 1991 Conservation: tactics for a constant crisis. *Science, Wash.* **253**, 744–750.

Soule, M.E. & Wilcox, B.A. 1980 Conservation biology: its scope and its challenge. In *Conservation biology: an evolutionary–ecological perspective* (eds. M.E. Soule & B.A. Wilcox). Sunderland, MA: Sinauer Associates. pp. 1–8.

Soule, M.E. & Simberloff, D. 1986 What do genetics and ecology tell us about the design of nature reserves? *Biol. Con.* **35**, 19–40.

Stanley, S.M. 1991 *The new evolutionary timetable.* New York: Basic Books.

Stenseth, N.C. 1984 The tropics: cradle or museum? *Oikos* **43**, 417–420.

Stevens, G.C. 1989 The latitudinal gradient in geographical range: how so many species coexist in the tropics. *Am. Nat.* **133**, 240–256.

Thiesenhusen, W.C., ed. 1989 *Searching for agrarian reform in Latin America.* Boston, MA: Unwin Hyman.

UNESCO. 1978. *Tropical forest ecosystems: a state-of-knowledge report.* Paris: Natural Resources Research XIV, UNESCO.

United Nations. 1992 *Long-range world population projections.* New York: United Nations.

Vitousek, P.M., Ehrlich, P.H., Ehrlich, A.H. & Matson, P.A. 1986 Human appropriation of the products of photosynthesis. *BioScience* **36**, 368–373.

Western, D. & Pearl, M., eds. 1989 *Conservation for the twenty-first century.* Oxford: Oxford

University Press.

Westoby, J. 1987 *The purpose of forests: follies of development.* Oxford: Basil Blackwell.

Westoby, J. 1989 *Introduction to world forestry.* Oxford: Basil Blackwell.

Wilcove, D.S. 1987 From fragmentation to extinction. *Nat. Areas Journal* 7, 23–29.

Williams, J.E., Johnson, J.E., Hendrickson, D.A., Contraras-Balderas, S., Williams, J.D., Navarro-Mendoza, M., McAllister, D.E. & and Deacon, J.E. 1989 Fishes of North America endangered, threatened or of special concern, 1989. *Fisheries* **14**(6), 2–38.

Wilson, E. O. 1992 *The diversity of life.* Cambridge, MA: Harvard University Press.

Woodwell, G.M., ed. 1990 *The earth in transition: patterns and processes of biotic impoverishment.* New York: Cambridge University Press.

Woodwell, G.M. 1992 When succession fails... In *Ecosystem rehabilitation, Vol. 1: Policy issues* (ed. M.K. Wali). SPE The Hague: Academic Publishing, pp. 27–35.

World Bank. 1990 *World Development Report: Poverty.* New York: Oxford University Press.

World Bank. 1992 *World Development Report: Environment and Development.* New York: Oxford University Press.

World Bank. 1993 *World Development Report: Investing in Health.* New York: Oxford University Press.

World Conservation Monitoring Centre. 1992 *Global biodiversity: status of the earth's living resources.* London: Chapman and Hall.

World Resources Institute. 1992 *World Resources 1992-93.* New York: Oxford University Press.

Zimmerman, B.L. & Bierregaard, R.O. 1986 The relevance of the equilibrium theory of island biogeography and species-area relations to conservation with a case from Amazonia. *J. Biogeog.* **13**, 133–143.

2/5

Land Degradation and Improvement
Zhao Qiguo

ABSTRACT

Degradation of the land resource is the fundamental constraint to sustainable development. Over the past 1000 years, the land area degraded by man's activities has amounted to 2000 million ha (Mha). Rapid population growth and consequent expansion of agriculture on marginal lands plus mismanagement of good land has accelerated the annual loss to 5–6 Mha. An estimate in 1974 indicates that degradation induced by anthropogenic exertions has resulted in a loss of about 10% of arable land over the world. Recent research shows that about 1230 Mha of terrain is degraded as a consequence of mismanagement of cropland and overgrazing, suggesting that some 25% of the agricultural land is affected by human-induced soil degradation.

In many countries, soil loss through erosion by wind and water represents one of the major consequences of agroecosystem mismanagement. Brown's figure for erosion in excess of formation of new soil was 23×10^9 tonnes/year, which means a jump of more than 50% over an 18 year period (Brown 1984). The increased rate is alarming enough, but if we consider that the global population in 1968 was about 3.7×10^9, and by 1984 it had risen to 4.8×10^9, the per capita loss of soils had increased from 4.0 to 4.8 tonnes/year.

There is also increasing evidence for declining base yield of crops of the order of 2–10% per year (Twyford 1988). Much of this decline is related to physical and chemical damage through the loss of plant nutrients by erosion; from soil acidification because of mismanagement of fertilizer practices; and as a result of nutrient mining. For example, in some East African countries, where only small amounts of fertilizers are used and soil erosion is also serious, net country-wide average rates of nutrient loss as high as NPK 80kg/hectare/annum have been estimated in a recent study commissioned by FAO (Stoorvogel 1990).

China has accumulated an abundance of experience in the utilization of land resources and prevention of land degradation. The land degradation can be overcome if comprehensive principles of management are adopted suiting the measures to differing conditions, with full use of scientific and technological advances. The experience of prevention and control of land degradation in China has been shown to be of great significance to the world.

1. INTRODUCTION

Land degradation is one of the most pressing problems facing the world, and affects both the fabric of mankind and the general environment. Globally, the extent and impact of land degradation on the utilization of natural resources, causing environmental deterioration and decreased production from agriculture, forest, and animal husbandry is greater than ever. Consideration of studies on land degradation, and its prevention

137

and control in China, should therefore be of significance.

2. GENERAL ASPECTS OF LAND DEGRADATION

Land degradation is an outcome of depletive human activities and their interaction with natural land resources. Generally speaking, land degradation is defined as the process of decline in land quality through its misuse by humans. There are three main consequences:

- land degradation undermines the productive capacity of an ecosystem
- global climate is affected through alterations in water and energy balance and disruptions in cycles of carbon, nitrogen, sulfur, and phosphorus
- land degradation leads to political and social instability via, for instance, enhanced rate of deforestation, soil erosion, pollution of natural waters, and emission of greenhouse gases into the atmosphere.

Historical records show that most ancient civilizations (for instance, Egypt, India) flourished on fertile soils, yet land degradation is responsible for extinctions in western India, western Asia and Central America. The statistics gathered by FAO/UNEP in 1986 point out that over the millennia as much as two billion hectares of land have been rendered unproductive through soil degradation. Furthermore, the current rate of land degradation is estimated at 5–6 Mha/year and, if these statistics are only nearly correct, almost one-third of total arable land will have been destroyed by the turn of the century. If no conservation-effective measures are taken, the grain output of 117 developing countries in the world will decrease by as much as 19% of average rate. By the end of this century, the South-East Asian region will feed only 85% of its estimated population.

Degradation of the land resource is the fundamental constraint to sustainable development. Over the past 1000 years, the land area degraded by man's activities has amounted to 2000 Mha. Rapid population growth and consequent expansion of agriculture on marginal lands plus mismanagement of good land has accelerated the annual loss to 5–6Mha. An estimate in 1974 indicates that anthropogenic degradation has resulted in a loss of about 10% arable land over the world. Recent research shows that about 1230 Mha of terrain has been degraded as a consequence of mismanagement of cropland and overgrazing, suggesting that some 25% of the agricultural land is affected by human-induced soil degradation (Table 1).

Table 1. *Areas of developing countries moderately, severely or extremely affected by human-induced land degradation* (Oldeman *et al.*, 1990)

type	land area (Mha)		
	Africa	Asia	South and Central America
water erosion	170	315	77
wind erosion	98	90	16
nutrient loss	25	104	3
salinization	10	26	–

In many countries, soil loss through erosion by wind and water represents one of the major consequences of agroecosystem mismanagement. Brown's figure for erosion in excess of new soils produced was 23 x 10^9 tonnes/year, which means a jump of more than 50% over 18 years (Brown 1984). The increased rate is alarming enough, but if we consider that the global population in 1968 was about 3.7 x 10^9 and by 1984 it had risen to 4.8 x 10^9, the per capita loss of soils had increased from 4.0 to 4.8 tonnes/year.

There is also increasing evidence for declining base yield of the order of 2–10% per year (Twyford 1988). Much of this decline is related to physical and chemical damage through the loss of plant nutrients by erosion; from soil acidification because of mismanagement of fertilizer practice; and as a result of nutrient mining. For example, in some East African countries, where only small amounts of fertilizer are used and soil erosion is also serious, net country-wide average rates of nutrient loss as high as NPK 80 kg/hectare/annum have been estimated in a recent study commissioned by FAO (Stoorvoge 1990).

3. LAND DEGRADATION AND IMPROVEMENT IN CHINA

China is an old agricultural country with a long history. By means of radiocarbon dating, the carbonized grains excavated from the Xian Banbo Relic were identified as remains of 6000 years ago, and the traces of carbonized rice grains unearthed in the Hemudu Relic in Zhejiang Province are believed to be 7000 years old, while the applications of limes in the flooded calcareous paddy soils in Southern China are over 1600 years old. This is convincing evidence of several thousand years of human activities in China. Increasing population pressure and the inappropriate utilization of land have increased land degradation considerably. There are about 33 Mha in China with restricted use because of their low-lying or acid situation. Each year, occupation of arable land accounts for 6.6 Mha while 20 Mh of cultivated land suffer fertility depletion from various causes. There is a severe threat to utilization of land in China – an urgent problem to be solved immediately.

3.1 Types of land degradation

There are three principal types of degradation: physical, chemical and biological (Table 2).

3.1.1 Physical degradation of soil

This includes erosion and desertification, compaction and hard setting as well as laterization. Soil erosion is preceded by nutrient depletion and excessive leaching. Of the total land area, 27% is subject to erosion, and the yearly loss of land amounts to 6–7 Mha. In general, soil erosion can be divided into water and wind erosion.

In China, water erosion redistributes land in the Loess Plateau, Northwest China and hilly–mountainous regions, and in Southern China. With an area of 1.5 Mha, the affected land occupies one-sixth of the total cultivated land area of the country. That amounts to 5 billion tonnes of soils being destroyed every year.

Wind erosion is considered in association with the process of desertification. The arid and semi-arid region in China involves 11 provinces, with an area of 1.49 Mha, of which

Table 2. *Types and processes of soil degradation*

type of degradation	process	effects
physical	compaction and hardsetting	loss of porous structure leading to diminished aeration and water drainage
	laterization	formation of iron and aluminium hydroxides
	wind erosion	loss of topsoil leading to desertification
	water erosion	loss of topsoil leading to desertification
chemical	pollution by landfill, pesticides	accumulation of toxic substances
	nutrient depletion by leaching	acidification alkalization salination
biological	decline in organic matter	reduction in microfauna including loss of soil nitrifying bacteria leading to nitrate depletion
		loss of pore structure leading to waterlogging or rapid drainage

the area of the cross bedding region of agriculture and animal husbandry directly affected by wind and desertification amounts up to 0.33 Mha.

Compaction and hardsetting are the processes that cause soil to set to a hard, poreless, structureless mass because of unreasonable agricultural traffic or trampling and erosion conditions. In the Taihu Lake region of China, almost 80% of paddy soils were found to be compact and puddling after the triple cropping system was adopted. In Northeast China, hardsetting was identified in black earths under mechanical cultivation. Red soils in tropical and subtropical China were also affected in a similar manner.

3.1.2 Chemical degradation of soil

This involves soil element imbalances leading to acidification or alkalization as well as chemical pollution. Soil element imbalance is caused by depletion of soil nutrients by long-term cropping without appropriate management, resulting in serious decline of soil fertility. Under cultivation for ten years and without fertilization, the total N content of black soils in Northeast China has declined from 0.33 to 0.26%, which will further decrease from 0.26 to 0.15% in the coming 50 years (Table 3). Correspondingly, the output of wheat will also decrease by 30–50%. In summary, the decrease of crop yield and deterioration of the soil fertility are mainly caused by soil acidification and secondary salinization as well as pollution.

3.1.3 Biological degradation of soil

Reduction in soil organic matter content and decrease in activity and diversity of soil macro and microfauna are effects of biological degradation. Owing to neglect of effective management, the ten years reclamation of bog soils in China for crop cultivation has brought about an organic matter decrease of 30.6%, which will become more severe in the coming 50 years. The depletion of soil fauna is more severe in the tropics than in the temperate zone. Although China has abundant natural forest resources, the average coverage of forest per capita constitutes only 15% of the world average, with forest cover to its territory of only 12%. China has 40 Mha of grasslands, of which about 30% have been seriously degraded. The output of animal products in China is only one-twentieth that of the United States.

Table 3. *Variation of nitrogen content of soils under natural vegetation and cultivation (%)*

soils	under natural vegetation	cultivated land (for 200–500 yrs)
black soil	0.256 – 0.695	0.150 – 0.348
cinnamon soil, burozem	0.064 – 0.145	0.030 – 0.099
red earth	0.101 – 0.340	0.050 – 0.115
latosol	0.090 – 0.305	0.070 – 0.183

3.2 Land degradation and human activities
3.2.1 Water erosion in the Loess Plateau

The population in the Loess Plateau has doubled from the 1950s to the 1980s following deforestation. The forest line of the Ziwu mountain has drawn back by 20 km. According to the statistics, whenever one person comes into the world, about 0.3 ha of the land in the region must be reclaimed. A huge area of the slopes has been opened for cropping in the last three decades, leading to severe water erosion. This has increased from 1.3×10^9 tonnes to 2.2×10^9 tonnes in the last 100 years. Soil erosion is not only hindering production, but also threatening the safety of the people.

3.2.2 Wind erosion and desertification of agriculture and pasture

Since its foundation in 1949, modern China has seen up to 100 Mha of grasslands desertified in the semi-arid interlocking regions of agriculture and pasture, constituting one-third of the total national grasslands. For example, Shangdu County of the Southern Wulanbu grassland was a virgin grassland 100 years ago, in 1885. In the 1920s, transmigrants settled there. By the 1980s, both population and cultivated land increased

Table 4. *Land area subjected to desertification in North China* (Zhu *et al.* 1988)

causes of desertification	total area (%)
over-cultivation	25.4
over-grazing	28.3
deforestation	31.8
construction industries, mines, communications	0.7
water conservation	8.3
sand dune advance	5.5

by four times while the area of grassland decreased by 50% — about one-third of the arable land suffering from desertification, resulting in an area of 0.21 Mha of land desertified annually. The prevention of desertification is a major problem worthy of our immediate attention (Table 4).

3.2.3 Soil salinization in arid and semi-arid region

The North China Plain had about 250,000 ha of salinized soils in the 1950s. Due to irrational irrigation and cultivation, severe secondary salinization occurred and the area of salinized soils increased to 4 Mha. The saline area of Hetao region in Inner Mongolia increased by 43–47% in the period 1954 to 1974, an expansion rate of 1–3% annually. Statistics indicate that China has an area of nearly 10 Mha of salified soils, of which there are about 1.7 Mha of soil in potential salinization, amounting to 17.5%. The salified soils covering nearly 1 Mha of the arable land in China are great obstacles to the development of agriculture.

3.2.4 Degradation of soil fertilities in farming areas

The available nutrients in a soil are renewable in a distinct cycling period. While this is 20 to 40 years for nitrogen and 10 to 20 years for phosphorus, 80 to 130 years are required for potassium. In Northeast China, the organic matter of black soils has decreased by 1–2% under cultivation of around 10 years; it would take 100 years to rebuild organic levels in balance. The soil humic contents will be reduced by 30–60% in 10 years.

When the multiple cropping index was increased considerably, the cultivated layer was shallower and the plowpan heavier in some paddy soils of the Taihu Lake Region, South China. This brought about a rice yield decrease of 50% (Tables 5 and 6).

3.2.5 Soil pollution

Statistically, about 50 000 ha of land have become the final solution for 80% of industrial waste disposal in China, constituting 8 000 ha cultivated land. In addition, 1.3 Mha of land suffer from accumulation of toxic pesticides. These human-induced products are increasingly diverse and many are potentially toxic to humans and to micro and macrofauna.

Table 5. *Composition of organic matter and nutrients in soils after cultivation*

soils	period of cultivation	O.M	total N (%)	total P (%)	total K (%)
meadow soil	waste land	8.83	0.508	0.284	2.00
(sand loam)	abandoned, and land	7.76	0.439	0.261	2.06
	cultivated for 29 years	6.83	0.228	0.238	2.12
black soil	waste land	6.31	0.268	0.175	–
(sand loam)	land cultivated for 20 years	2.34	0.115	0.086	–
black soil	waste land	7.09	0.335	0.133	2.30
	land cultivated for 10 years	4.58	0.268	0.118	2.48
	land cultivated for 50 years	2.93	0.157	0.092	2.30
marshes	waste land	6.84	0.352	0.183	2.26
black soil	land cultivated for 9 years	5.81	0.298	0.178	2.32
	land cultivated for 50 years	5.19	0.278	0.164	–
	land cultivated for 100 years	4.11	0.210	0.137	2.28

3.2.6 Destruction of forest and grass

Deforestation is greater than afforestation by 10.6%. Actual cut of forest is greater than that grown by 10%, and so is the degraded area of grassland, with an annual rate of 61 000 ha.

3.2.7 Occupation of land

Occupation of land is another severe problem of land degradation. In the 1950s, the total cultivated land in China was 97 Mha and, in 1982, the cultivated land amounted to 99.3 Mha and, although 21.3 Mha had been reclaimed, the area occupied had even reached 460 000 ha yearly. So, instead of an increase, the cultivated land will be reduced by 12 Mha, only 0.06 ha per capita by the end of this century. Although soil productivity can be improved, the productive potential of land resources must be finite. The occupation of land inevitably results in destruction of productive capacity. The prospect is gloomy if the conflict of increasing population and decreasing land continues.

3.3 Prevention of land degradation
3.3.1 Comprehensive management in line with local conditions

Comprehensive measures should be taken, with biological as well as environmental factors being considered.

In the loessal region of Northwest Plateau, water and soil conservation should be emphasized in combination with the extensive seeding of grasslands and afforestation, and moderate cultivation of the agricultural soils with the aim of increasing the crop yield per unit area. Cultivation of the steep slopes should be strictly forbidden. The Huang-Huai-Hai plain of North China should be improved in fertility so that the multiple cropping index increases. In the hilly-mountainous regions of South China,

Table 6. *Variation of composition of humus under black soils after cultivation (all %)*

years of cultivation	humus	humic acid (HA)	fulvic acid (FA)	HA/FA ratio	active humic acid
waste land	5.97	1.20	0.75	1.60	0.55
land cultivated for 10 years	4.14	0.74	0.39	1.90	0.30
land cultivated for 50 years	2.69	0.60	0.40	1.50	0.41

comprehensive management of agriculture, forestry, pasture and cultivation of economic crops should be emphasized on the basis of prevention and control of soil erosion. In the crossing regions of agriculture and pasture in North China, prevention and control of wind erosion and desertification should be emphasized by means of comprehensive measures of afforestation (including arbor and shrub forests) or the seeding of grasslands, while ploughing for cropping should be forbidden. In the tropical region, more attention should be paid to conserving natural reserves and to vertical layouts of crops.

3.3.3 Control of desertification

Experience has shown that desertification can be prevented through control. The area of running sand in Keerxin Region of Inner Mongolia in 1984 was 1000 ha, the forest coverage less than 10%, and total grain yield 15 000 kg. After four years control, the area of running sand in 1988 occupied less than one-third, and grain yield increased by 250 000 kg. In Maowushu Region, the area of desertification declined by 12% in five years of control, with the grass output increased by 240 kg/ha to 1320 kg/ha. Starting in the Eighth Five-year Plan (1991–95), eight demonstration zones, with studies on the process of land desertification and the ecological systems of sandy land and grassland, are in progress. It is expected that the coverage of forest and grass will increase by 100% in the major forest areas, with an increase by 50% of output value of agriculture and pasture, and a decrease by 30–40% of "running sand". The aim is for the income per capita to be as high as the national average.

3.3.3 Control of erosion

By means of control of desertification conducted at 11 experimental demonstration zones in the loess areas, the grain output of these zones has now become basically self-sufficient, with 400–500 kg per capita, and an increase by 13% of income per capita, while the runoff volume of running sands decreased by 50%, and the erosion index of steep slopes declined by 45–90%. During the Eighth Five-year Plan (1991–1995), 12 other experimental demonstration zones in the region, with regional characteristics of soils and water, are in progress. By taking comprehensive measures, these experimental demonstration zones will increase grain output 30%, income per capita 50%, and decrease running sand by 30%. During the Seventh Five-year Plan (1985-1990), the income per capita in the Anshi Region, Northern Shannxi Province, rose by four times while its grain yield per unit was 30–70 kg. This region is expected to be built up as a soil and water conserving and ecological agricultural base in 10 years time.

3.3.4 Control of alkalization

By means of comprehensive control conducted in the alkali and saline soil districts of Fengqiu County, Henan Province, from 1983 to 1989, the grain output increased by 185 kg to 583 kg, and the income per capita from 154 Yuan to 628 Yuan. The yield of grain recorded was a historic high. At the same time, the yield of grain per unit in Yucheng County of Shangdong Province increased by 200 kg to 700 kg with management of alkali and saline soils. The programme on comprehensive control and conservative use of water resources in this region will, by the end of this century, make it possible to boost agricultural production by an output increment of 15 billion kg of grain, 1 million dan (50 kg) of cotton, 1.5 million tonnes of oil crops, and 2 million tonnes of meat.

3.3.5 Correction of infertility

There are about 13 Mha of arable land in the red soil hilly regions, in which land with acidification, concretion and poor nutrients accounts for 60%. However, productive potential is significant. The experience obtained from the Qianyan Zhou Experimental Zone indicates that through integrated development based on the reclamation of 236 hectares of bare land, the total output value in the zone has increased by 580 Yuan to 390 000 Yuan (77 times), while the net income per capita has increased during the six years (1983–1988) by 130 Yuan to 1078 Yuan (8 times). In Yingtan Experimental Station, with emphasis on soil and water conservation, and soil fertilization as well as the establishment of parallel layout of agriculture, pasture and animal husbandry, the grain output in 3 years increased by 500 kg to 1800 kg, while the tea output doubled. In the Eighth Five-year Plan (1991–1995), the red soil hilly regions set up other 12 demonstration zones, aiming to speed the experience obtained from the demonstration zones and comprehensively control soil degradation. The grain output is expected to rise by as much as 20 billion kg, with great development of economic crops in tropical and subtropical zones as well as obvious improvement of soil and water conservation and ecological environments.

3.3.6 Management of boglands

In the Three-River Plain (the Heilongjiang River, Wusulijang River and Songhuajiang River), Northeast China, there used to exist about 2.3 Mha of bog soils. Because of insufficient drainage, flood threat, soil infertility, degradation, and low resistance to natural diseases, the grain output in some cultivated land was only a little more than 1.5 tonne/ha.

By demonstration and adoption of comprehensive ways of utilization of rice growth, reed planting and fish cultivation in bog fields, the output of grain and reed has presented as 10 tonne and 2 tonne/ha, respectively, with the output value of fish doubling as well. During the Eighth Five-year Plan (1991–1995), several demonstration zones will be set up, including a wet soil ecological engineering project on the adjustment of water levels, in a bid to improve soil fertility which should raise the output value of grain from bog soils by 200 Yuan, while the output of grain in the region will increase by 2.5 billion to 5.0 billion kg.

3.3.7 Management of ecological systems

Comprehensive management of forest and grasslands should be put into operation so as to strengthen the protection of biological resources.

The fauna in China constitutes 10% of that in the world, microbiological species 40%, and China's biological diversification occupies the eighth place.

3.3.8 Protection of arable land and enforcing legislation and legal systems

Statistics have shown that China has only 31 Mha of land reserves, of which 16 Mha will be pasture, 3 Mha for economic timber cultivation, 13 Mha for agriculture, and 130,000 ha for coastal beach land. Under the situation of increasing population and decreasing land, arable land must be strictly preserved; one metre of land saved is as valuable as one ounce of gold in mind!

Restrictive policies and legislative measures (such as the adoption of laws on soil and water conservation) are needed for both corrective and preventive land planning, together with strict control of population.

4. RESEARCH AND DATA NEEDS FOR LAND DEGRADATION

Action is needed at three levels: first, the creation of baseline data sets on key indicators of degradation to clarify long-term trends; second, physical and economic research on degradation processes, impacts, and control; and third, minimum standards for ecologically sound and sustainable production and land use.

4.1 Data collection

The principal step is estimation and monitoring of actual land use. This will require improved Geographical Information Systems (GIS) that can bring together land use data with socio-economic information. The second is the establishment of a global monitoring network.

4.2 Degradation processes and impacts

Priorities include research on:

(a) The general processes and mechanisms, especially the rehabilitation and restoration of different types of global soil degradation, and the theory and practice of controlling them.

(b) Technology for monitoring the global changes of land use and the dynamics of soil degradation as well as the methodology of soil degradation evaluation.

(c) The function of agroecosystem and its relationship with land use changes and soil degradation. Various simulation methods and modelling may be employed to predict the existing and new management measures, and the long-term effect of varying climates on soil quality and agricultural productivity, so as to build optimized artificial agroecosystems.

(d) The rate and consequences of deforestation. This should involve the monitoring of the dynamics of deforestation rate and its effect on rivers, soil erosion, agricultural productivity, fuel wood supply and the loss of biodiversity, as well as the local and global weather.

(e) The monitoring and evaluation of the global dynamics of soil erosion (quantity and rate) to identify environmentally critical areas.

(f) Minimum standards for ecologically sound production so that the land degradation costs of traded commodities can be reflected in export prices.

4.3 Standards for land restoration and sustainable production

Prime candidates here are:

(a) Development of sustainable production systems, and their component technologies, notably to maintain or increase soil fertility through integrated plant nutrition principles that avoid soil acidification.

(b) Development of improved forest and agro-forestry practices for land stabilization and sustainable multipurpose land use.

(c) Adoption of biotechnology-derived crops that confer resistance to pests, that will provide alternatives to traditional toxic pesticides that currently degrade land, environment and ground water through accumulation of pesticide residues.

(d) Use of biotechnology to develop higher yielding crops and to process agricultural wastes, such as bagasse, oil cake and straw, to upgrade their nutrient content for livestock feed or to promote their use as fuel substitutes.

5. CONCLUSIONS

Degradation of the land resource is the fundamental constraint to sustainable development. Over the past 1000 years, the land area degraded by man's activities has amounted to 2000 Mha. Rapid population growth and consequent expansion of agriculture on marginal lands plus mismanagement of good land, has accelerated the annual loss to 5–6 Mha. An estimate in 1974 indicates that anthropogenic degradation has resulted in a loss of about 10% arable land over the world. Recent research shows that about 1230 Mha of terrain is degraded as a consequence of mismanagement of cropland and overgrazing, suggesting that some 25% of the agricultural land is affected by human-induced soil degradation.

China has accumulated an abundance of experience for the utilization of land resources and prevention and control of land degradation. The land degradation can be overcome if the comprehensive management conditions, following the principle of suiting the measures to different conditions and utilization in an all-round way, implementation of policies, strengthening the input as well as adoption of science and technology. The experience of prevention and control of land degradation in China has been shown to be of great significance to the world.

REFERENCES

Cheng Yongzhong, 1988 Jingke: present erosion and control in the Loess Plateau. Science Press.
FAO 1984 *Land, food and population*, Rome.

Lal, R. & Stewart, B.A. 1984 *Soil degradation— a global threat*. Advanced agronomy.

Norse, D., James, C., Skinner, B.J. & Zhao Q. 1991 *Agriculture, land use and degradation: an agenda of science for 21st century,* Cambridge: CUP.

Zhu Zhengda, Liu Su *et al*. 1989 China's desertification and its control. Science Press.

Introduction to Session 3:

DEMOGRAPHIC TRANSITION IN A GENDER PERSPECTIVE

P.N. Tandon

A recurring theme of the conference was the pivotal role of women in bringing about demographic transition. Although this was referred to by most speakers in the other sessions (Keyfitz and Lindahl-Kiessling, Sadik, Ramalingaswami and Gita Sen), the third session primarily focused on gender perspectives.

Professor Partha Dasgupta presented evidence that there was a serious population problem in many countries which in varying degrees is synergistically related to poverty, to communal sharing of child rearing and possibly also to an erosion of the local environmental-resource base. He discussed the private versus social returns of having children, which influences the choice of family size. He felt that measures directed at the alleviation of poverty, such as improved credit and savings markets, ready availability of basic household needs like water and fuel, by reducing the private benefits of procreation, would help in breaking the vicious cycle of increased fertility rate, erosions of common property resources, need for more hands for household requirements and therefore rejection of population control measures.

Dr. K. Srinivasan analysed the factors underlying the rapid decline in fertility rate, observed recently in some of the developing countries. Although political will, reduction in infant mortality, and availability of well-managed family planning programmes were important, the most important single factor identified was female literacy, irrespective of all other parameters.

Professor Lydia Makhubu pointed out the positive aspects of women's roles for the preservation of culture and the promotion of social transformation. These roles constitute strong potential for women to contribute to all aspects of environmental protection and management, and the implementation of strategies for sustainable development.

Dr Mayra Buvinić advocated the need for the family planning programmes to be based on the reproductive health needs of women, including, but not limited to, their need for contraception, designed to respond to both women's needs and rights, and taking into consideration the consequences of these programmes for women's lives and their economic roles.

Professor John Cleland, in a study of different pathways to demographic transition observed the diversity of conditions under which fertility has declined in several countries in South and South-East Asia (parts of India, Bangladesh, Pakistan, Indonesia, Philippines and Nepal). His analysis warns against a simple mono-causal explanation for this complex problem.

3/1

The Population Problem
Partha Dasgupta

ABSTRACT

This article applies economic analysis to rural households in poor countries to see what one may mean by a "population problem". It is argued by an appeal to evidence that there is a serious population problem in these parts, and that it is in varying degrees related synergistically to poverty, to communal sharing of child rearing, and possibly also to an erosion of the local environmental resource base. One manifestation of the problem is that very high fertility rates are experienced by women, bearing risks of death that should now be unacceptable. An argument is sketched to show how the cycle of poverty, low birth weight and stature, and high fertility rates can perpetuate within a dynasty. The one general policy conclusion that may be novel is that a population policy in these parts would not only contain such measures as family planning programmes and increased female education and employment opportunities, but also those measures that are directed at the alleviation of poverty, such as improved credit and savings markets, and a ready availability of basic household needs, such as water and fuel. It is argued that these latter measures lower the private benefits of procreation.

1. POPULATION AND DEVELOPMENT

With the exception of sub-Saharan Africa, over the past 25 years or so gross income per head has grown in nearly all poor regions since the end of the second world war. Moreover, growth in world food production since 1960 has exceeded the world's population growth rate: by an annual 0.8% during 1960–70, by an annual 0.5% during 1970–80, and by an annual 0.4% during 1980–87 (World Bank 1984, Table 5.6; FAO 1989, Annex, Table 2). This has been accompanied by improvements in a number of indicators of human well-being, such as the infant survival rate, life expectancy at birth, and literacy. In poor regions, all this has occurred in a regime of population growth rates substantially higher than in the past. Except for parts of East and South-East Asia, modern-day declines in mortality rates have not been matched by reductions in fertility (World Bank 1993). Moreover, a number of places that did experience a decline in fertility rates for a while (for example, Costa Rica and India), have stabilized at levels well above the population replacement rate (the fertility rate at which population size would be expected to stabilize in the long run; a figure just over 2.1). The accompanying table presents *total fertility rates* in several areas (Table 1). Towards the end of the 1980s, the total fertility rate in the World Bank's list of low-income countries (excluding China and India) was 5.6. The figure for China and India were 2.3 and 4.2, respectively.[1†] The oft-expressed fear that rapid population growth will accompany deteriorations in living standards has not been borne out by experience so far; at least, not when judged from the vantage of the world as a whole.

† Numbers in this form refer to notes at the end of the text.

Table 1. *Total fertility rates in the late 1980s* (World Bank 1990)

	total fertility rate
India	4.2
China	2.3
sub-Saharan Africa	6 – 8
Japan, and western industrial democracies	1.5 – 1.9

The effects of population growth on economic development have been a recurring theme in the development literature (National Research Council 1986). These inquiries are of very limited value, for neither the population growth rate in a country nor its pace of economic development (as measured by, say, increases in national income per head) is given from outside. They are both determined jointly by a complex combination of private and public opportunities, human motivation and needs, ecological possibilities, public policy, and chance factors. In short, neither is an exogenous factor shaping a country's state of affairs. Furthermore, each would be expected to affect the other. It therefore makes at least as much sense to inquire into the effects of economic development on population growth. As would be expected, this, too, has been much studied, mainly in the demographic literature (e.g. the quarterly, *Population and Development Review*).

What do we know of their mutual influence? The accompanying diagram (Figure 1) provides information at the national level concerning 98 so-called developing countries, in the period from the late 1970s to the early 1980s. It reveals a negative relationship between the (total) fertility rate and national income per head. China, Sri Lanka, Thailand, and South Korea are outliers, with fertility rates much lower at their levels of income than would be predicted by the statistical relationship. So are most nations of the sub-Saharan Africa outliers, but they all lie on the other side of the curve. The diagram suggests that there is a link between income and fertility. A regional breakdown of even the Chinese experience displays the general pattern: fertility is lower in higher-income regions (Birdsall & Jamison 1983). With the notable exception of China and Sri Lanka, poor countries are a long way from the so-called *demographic transition*, that is, the transition to a regime of low fertility and low mortality rates from one of high fertility and mortality rates.[2]

Both historical trends in advanced regions and, as we have just observed, current data for low-income countries are suggestive of a negative relationship between fertility rates and national income per head. The evidence also suggests a negative relationship between national income per head and mortality rates (Coale & Hoover 1958). That mortality rates would decrease with increasing income is something to be expected. Rising income usually carries with it more education, improved diet, and better health-care and sanitation.[3] However, a decline in the fertility rate is not self-evident. Understanding why fertility rates have fallen in many societies, and why at the same time the decline has been so sluggish in so many others (even while the mortality rate has been falling, as in sub-Saharan Africa), has been a central point of inquiry in modern demographic research.

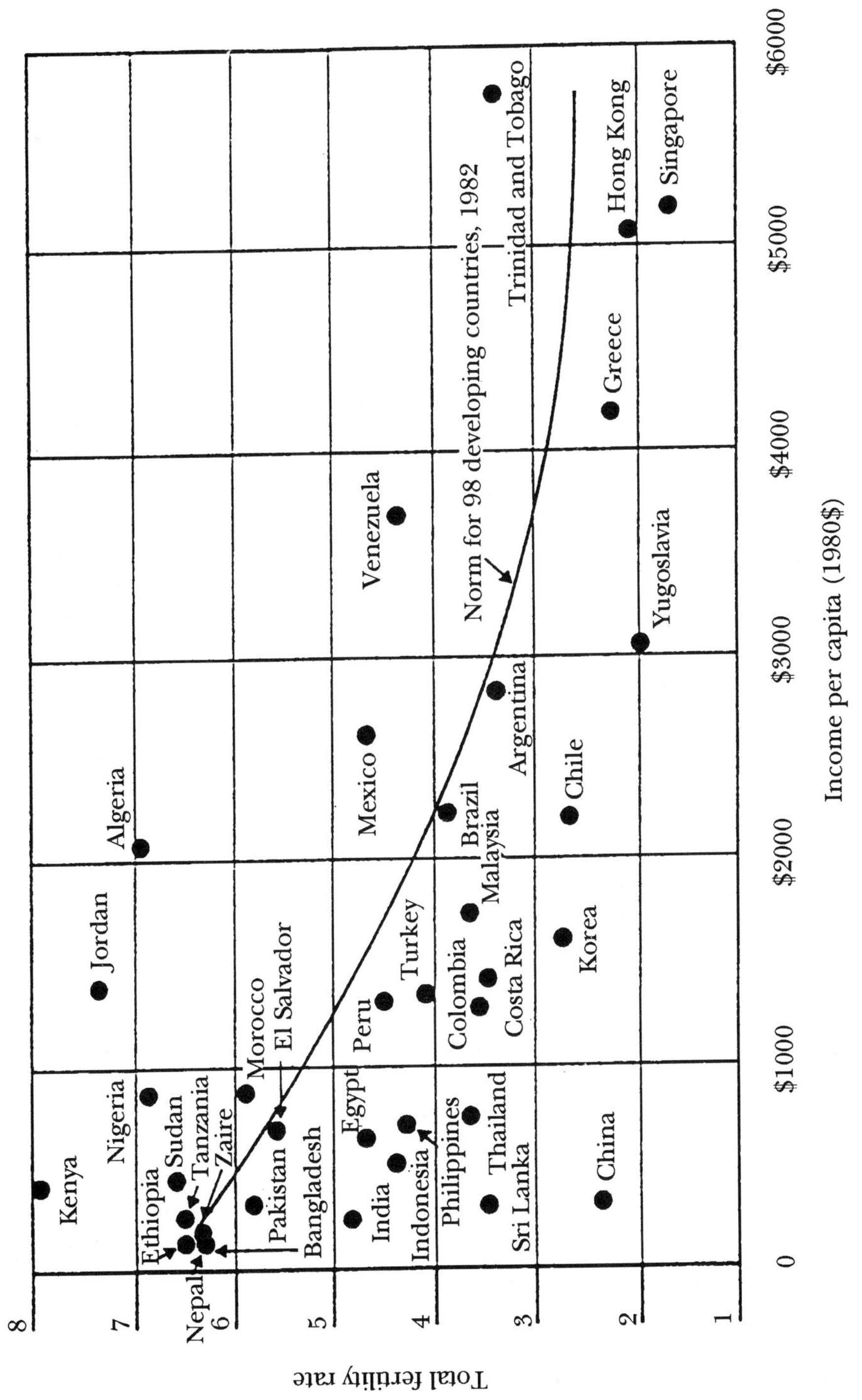

Figure 1. Fertility in relation to income in developing countries, 1982 (Birdsall 1988).

To effect an answer, however, requires an account that peers into the locus of decision-making about fertility matters. As human society is currently organized, this locus is in large measure the *household*.[4] So, in building any reasonable account of the matter we need to study the household. One of my purposes in this essay is to collate the kinds of argument that go towards constructing such an account.

2. POPULATION AND ENVIRONMENT

Talk of income smacks of commodity production, not the commodity basis of production. Moreover, statistics on past movements of income and agricultural production per head can lull us into neglecting the environmental-resource basis of human well-being (e.g. soil and its cover, fresh water, fisheries, and forests). They can encourage the thought that human ingenuity can be relied upon to overcome the stresses that growing populations would otherwise impose on the natural environment (Simon 1981; Simon & Kahn 1984). They may even explain why environmental resources have until recently been so confidently neglected in the economics of poor countries. However, current income does not capture declines in future consumption possibilities caused by a deterioration of the natural environment. By concentrating on (gross) income, we allow ourselves to bypass the very concerns that environmentalists have repeatedly expressed, namely, about the strong links that exist between continual population growth and the state of the environment.[5] The account we should be constructing ought to recognize these links as well.

The literature on population and the environment has a different style from the one on population and development. Thus, it is a commonplace in the former to read estimates of declining land—man ratios and the dwindling natural resource base associated with increases in the size of populations. That rising numbers in the face of finite resources may well have catastrophic effects has been argued by Ehrlich and Ehrlich (1990) and Keyfitz (1991), among others. The assertion here is that, beyond a point, there are no substitution possibilities between environmental resources (e.g. genetic diversity, fresh water, breathable air, and so forth) and manufactured goods. It is argued that policy-makers are often less than sensitive about the limits to the resilience of ecological processes. Qualitative knowledge about such matters is often held by people who have historically relied on them directly for their livelihood, to wit, the rural poor, and their voice is often not heard during the process of economic development. In addition, as long as uncertainty about the value of natural resources is great and environmental destruction is not wholly reversible, there is a case for awarding special weight to keeping our future options open. In the present context, the implication of this is that we ought to pursue what one could call a "conservationist" approach to environmental policy: we should preserve more than what standard cost-benefit analysis of the use of environmental resources will warrant (Arrow & Fisher 1974; Henry 1974). This is at the intellectual heart of the ecological movement.

3. THE PROBLEM

Except under conditions of extreme nutritional stress, nutritional status does not appear to affect fecundity (Bongaarts 1980; Menken, Trussell & Watkins 1981). During the 1974 famine in Bangladesh, the rural population lost over 1.5 million additional children; the stock was replenished within a year (Bongaarts & Cain 1981). Of course, undernourishment can still have an effect on sexual reproduction through its implications on the frequency of still-births, maternal and infant mortality, and a possible reduction in the frequency of sexual intercourse. The central questions in economic demography are then these: what determines fertility, and are there grounds for thinking that fertility rates in the poorest countries are too high? This essay addresses both questions.

My aim here is to put economic analysis to work on findings in applied demography so as to identify what we could today call *the population problem* in the poorest regions of the world: the Indian sub-continent and sub-Saharan Africa. I will argue that current rates of population growth in these regions are overly high, and I will try to identify the directions in which public policy needs to be put into effect. In addition to the ecologist's concerns, the population problem in these parts displays itself starkly in the form of unacceptable risks of maternal death for poor, illiterate women, and of new lives doomed to extreme poverty (see below). This identification has the air of banality about it, but it needs to be made. I have not found in the literature (e.g. National Research Council 1986; and the technical essays in Johnson & Lee 1987, upon which the former was based) an exploration of household behaviour that yields anything like the population problem we will uncover here.

Demographers typically study the determinants of fertility behaviour. As a general rule, they have shied away from identifying social mechanisms in which a myriad of individual household decisions can lead to outcomes that are a collective failure.[6] For example, even in the influential and informative report on population and development by the World Bank (World Bank 1984), there are only three pages (pp. 54–6) devoted to the question why households may be producing too many children. Moreover, the answer it offers is rough and limiting. The report says that in making fertility decisions, households can get locked into the Prisoners' Dilemma game, a well-known class of social environments in which individually rational acts yield outcomes that are collectively not rational.[7] The report also said that poor folk are typically ignorant of family planning measures.

I shall argue (Section 10) that there are several other reasons why we should not expect individual and collective rationality to be consonant over fertility matters. We will find that there is a lot more to the population problem than the Prisoners' Dilemma and ignorance (or fear) of modern birth-control techniques. It will be seen that the population–poverty–environment nexus in the Indian sub-continent and sub-Saharan Africa is harsh not only because credit and savings markets work badly there, but also because poor households cannot readily obtain potable water and fuel supplies. I shall argue that in order to circumvent some of the limitations in transaction possibilities, rural households forge a link between their decisions in different spheres of life. To cite an example, children in poor households are not only valued for their own sake (Section 7), they also play a role in providing their parents' labour and old-age security (Sections 7–9).

The implications of such linkages for public policy are a central concern of this essay (Section 11). Among other things, we will find that, for poor rural households, environmental degradation (for example, vanishing sources of water, receding sources of fodder and household fuel) can be both a cause and an effect of an increase in the net reproductive rate. To the best of my knowledge, this last has not been given any attention in the applied demographic literature. Except for a weak empirical substantiation in World Bank (1991), I have not been able to locate any empirical work that tests the thesis. It is not known how powerful the mutual feedback is in the rural communities we know. Should it prove important, the policies that governments will be urged to pursue for bringing down fertility rates will be of a different nature from the ones usually espoused (Section 11). It would also go some way towards explaining the fact that fertility rates in sub-Saharan Africa have not responded to a decline in infant mortality rates. The theory deserves investigation, and it explains why I shall lay stress on it.

Having said this, it is as well to note that to anyone who is not a demographer, economic demography is a most frustrating subject. It would seem that for any theoretical prediction, say, on fertility matters, no matter how innocuous, there is some set of data from some part of the world over some period that is not consonant with it. The springs of human behaviour in an activity at once so personal and social as procreation are so complex and interconnected that empirical confirmations of ideas are always shot through with difficulty.

Faced with this, there are two avenues that are open to me here. One would be to try to collate what we know about fertility matters from international and interregional data. The other is to appeal to simple theoretical constructs and highlight a few of the forces that we may expect to have an important effect on the demographic structure of a community. World Bank (1984) and Cochrane and Farid (1989) provide excellent illustrations of the former route. I shall follow the latter route here. In Sections 4–9, we will study how fertility behaviour responds (and how it would be expected to respond) to changes in the parameters households face, such as prices of goods and services, community rules and regulations, employment opportunities for men and women, and distances to sources of water and fuelwood. I will be concerned with the directions of these responses (viz. greater or less), not their strengths, because the latter can most certainly be expected to differ widely across communities and cultures.[8] However, even the directions are sometimes ambiguous, and they have been observed to differ across regions as well (Easterlin, Pollak & Wachter 1980).

Now many of the parameters that households face (prices of goods and services, costs of rearing children, and so forth) are, in fact, variables that assume the values they do through interactions among households and firms, and through public policies. In Section 10 we will study examples of how they get determined and identify types of interactions in which individual and collective rationality can be expected to be dissonant. Finally, in Section 11, I will summarize our findings by identifying desirable public policies for reducing the population problem in poor countries.

4. THE GENDERS: DIFFERENTIAL FERTILITY COSTS AND BENEFITS

Economists typically interpret household behaviour by imagining that it pursues well-defined goals, subject to it being guided by norms and values. The theory assumes that household choices reflect this. This interpretation makes for a perfectly consistent analysis, but it puts strain on the normative significance of household choice. Choice may reflect decisions that systematically favour some members (for example, males), and it may discriminate against others (for example, higher birth-order girls and elderly relatives). Household choice assumes strong normative significance only when the underlying basis upon which it is made takes each member's interests into reasonable account. This may not be common, however; at least, not when the family is impoverished and the stresses and strains of hunger, illness, and physical weakness makes themselves felt.

The matter is a delicate one. Interference by the state with household choice can have catastrophic consequences, if recent evidence in a number of poor countries is any guide. Nevertheless, there are indirect levers the state can pull which do not amount to direct interference with what happens inside the household, but which protect vulnerable members and enable them to reach a stronger strategic position. In this essay I shall be much concerned with identifying such levers. Modelling household fertility decision is not for the faint- hearted, however; the motivations of the two central parties to a decision may well be quite different. Fortunately, I will lose nothing qualitatively in what follows by not specifying the household model in any sharp detail. I want to avoid doing the latter in any case. These are early days yet in our understanding of the exact springs of household behaviour, even in poor countries. It is therefore better to squeeze as much out of a partially unspecified model than to start with a precise model and work through its implications. In any event, this is how I will proceed.

Our interest lies in those situations where the two central parties perceive that they add something by acting together (there are gains in forming a household and cooperating), where the pair can break up should either party be placed under undue stress (there is an outside option for each party), and where the parties' motivations are not the same. This is not to say that mutual care and concern are absent, but it is to say that we should not expect a complete identification of personal interest.

As an example, consider the costs of bearing and rearing children. They are different for the genders. Pregnancy involves lost opportunities for work among women. Each successful birth involves a year-and-a-half of pregnancy and breast-feeding—it can be longer if really extended breast-feeding is practised, as in sub-Saharan Africa. On making the obvious corrections, we can then conclude that in a society where female life expectancy at birth is 50 years, and where the total fertility rate is 7 (this is approximately the average figure in sub-Saharan Africa today), nearly half of a woman's expected adult life will be spent either carrying a child in her womb or breast-feeding it; and we have not allowed for unsuccessful pregnancies.[9]

Reproduction also involves additional risk of death among poor women. In most poor countries, maternal mortality is the largest single cause of death among women in their reproductive years, nutritional anaemia playing a central role in this. In sub-Saharan Africa (e.g. Ethiopia), maternal mortality rates as high as 1 in 50 have been recorded.[10] We may conclude that, at a total fertility rate of 7 and over, the chance such a woman entering her reproductive years will not survive them is about 1 in 6. The reproductive cycle in this woman's life involves her playing Russian roulette. This is one manifestation of the population problem. It is unacceptable.

The benefits from reproduction are also different for the genders. This may be inferred in part from differences in the care they give to their young. A number of studies on family health and nutrition have found that unearned income in the hands of the mother has a bigger effect on her family's health (e.g. child survival rate) than income under the control of the father. In some studies, there is evidence also of differences in attitudes towards sons and daughters: mothers prefer to devote resources to improve the nutritional status of their daughters, fathers for their sons.[11] In some regions, e.g. sub-Saharan Africa, the cost of rearing children is shared among the kinship (Bledsoe 1990). In societies characterized by weak conjugal bond (as in much of sub-Saharan Africa and the Caribbean), male parents often bear little of the cost of rearing children. Here, then, we would expect to see another source of differences in parental motivations concerning reproduction. Men's desire for children would, on balance, be expected to exceed that of women by far, and this would bring in its wake the attendant implications we observe in the data.

Unlike the Indian sub-continent, the "household" is not a very meaningful unit for organising production, consumption, and fertility decisions in sub-Saharan Africa (Caldwell 1975; Cain 1984; Bleek 1987; Caldwell & Caldwell 1987, 1990; Kamarck 1988; Goody 1990). Often, there is no common budget for a man and wife. Polygyny is widely practised. In the late 1950s, some 35% of all married men in sub-Saharan Africa were polygynists (Goody 1976). In rural areas, matters would not appear to have changed much (Farooq, Ekanem & Ojelade 1987). Recall also that the dowry system is virtually non-existent in sub-Saharan Africa. For the most part, it is the men's family that has to accumulate wealth to obtain a bride. This affords a reason why the median age difference between spouses in Africa is large; a fact of considerable importance, since it enables women to have spouses despite the prevalence of polygyny. Women on average become widows at an early age, and widow remarriages are not only permissible, they are a commonplace.

The sexual division of labour in sub-Saharan Africa is powerful, but it assumes a different form from that in the Indian sub-continent. Even though women do not inherit land, the primary responsibility for raising subsistence crops for the household usually rests with women who, as a consequence, have greater power and control over food distribution than their counterparts in the Indian sub-continent. Over 30% of rural households are headed by women; the men are absent (Jazairy, Alamgir & Pannucio 1992).[12] Nevertheless, women's sexuality and labour power are firmly under control by the husband's lineage. Among other things, it is the extent of kinship control of women that differentiates societies in sub-Saharan Africa from those in the Indian sub-continent. Until relatively recently, the fallow land was communally owned within kinship groups. All this makes for a considerable difference in the resource implications of having offspring.

Cochrane and Farid (1989) remark that the high levels of fertility in sub-Saharan Africa are a consequence of early and universal marriage, allied to little reliance on contraception. Thus, average age at marriage for sub-Saharan women is 18.9, and the proportion of those 15–19 years of age who are married is 40%. The comparable figures for Asia are 21.3 years and 26%, respectively, and, for Latin America, 21.5 years and 19.8%, respectively. The overall usage of contraceptives is very low in sub-Saharan Africa:

even among the most educated of people, the prevalence is only 20% or so. However, the proximate causes identified by Cochrane and Farid are themselves in need of explanation, and we will look into it. The importance of women in farming has often been adduced to explain in part sub-Saharan Africa's marriage patterns. However, differences between the genders in the net benefits of having children are a key ingredient in the population problem, both in the Indian subcontinent and in sub-Saharan Africa.

5. BIRTH CONTROL

People in all societies practice some form of birth control. Fertility is below the maximum possible in all societies. Even in poor countries, fertility is not unresponsive to the relative prices of goods and services.[13] Extended breast-feeding and post-partum female sexual abstinence have been common practice in Africa. In a noted study on !Kung San foragers in the Kalahari region, Lee (1972) observed that among them the nomadic, bush-dwelling women had an inter-birth interval of nearly four years, while those settled at cattle-posts gave birth to children at much shorter intervals. From the perspective of the individual nomadic !Kung San woman, it is significant that the social custom is for mothers to nurse their children on demand, and to carry them during their day-long trips in search of wild food through the children's fourth year of life. Anything less than a four-year birth interval would therefore increase mothers' carrying loads enormously, impose a threat on their own capacity to survive, and reduce their children's prospects of survival. In contrast, cattle-post women are sedentary, and are able to wean their children earlier.[14]

The first and most obvious determinant of fertility is the nature of the available technology of fertility control. (Bongaarts 1978; World Bank 1984, contain good discussions.) Traditional methods have consisted of abortion, abstinence or rhythm, prolonged breast- feeding, and coitus interruptus. These options are often inhumane and unreliable. Modern contraceptives are superior. Nevertheless, their use has been uneven within poor countries. In East Asia, over 65% of married women in the age range 15–49 years use contraceptives as against somewhat under 10% in sub-Saharan Africa. In South Asia as a whole, the figure in the early 1980s was about 25%, but in Sri Lanka it was a high 55% (World Bank 1984; Table 7.1). These large variations across regions not only reflect a divergence in the public provision of family planning and health-care services, they reflect variations in demand as well. Surveys indicate that women themselves perceive an unmet need for access to methods for reducing their fertility (Bongaarts 1991). However, the extent of this felt need varies across regions substantially (World Bank 1984; Cochrane & Farid 1989; Chomitz & Birdsall 1991; Hill 1992). Successful family planning programmes have proved more difficult to institute than could have been thought possible at first. At one extreme (East and South-East Asia, Sri Lanka, and the state of Kerala in India), household demand and state commitment to family planning programmes and public-health services have merged in a successful way. China, in particular, has pursued an active policy of limiting family size. Total fertility rate was brought down to a remarkable 2.3 by 1978 from a high 5.9 in 1960.[15] At another extreme (most of sub-Saharan Africa), little has been done at the State level to supply such services. As we have noted earlier, however, the parental demand for children there is high as well. The population growth rate has increased during the two decades 1960–80 from about 2.5% per year to something like 2.9% per year. We will see below that the absence of conjugal bond (in particular, the practice of polygyny) as a norm in sub-Saharan African has something to do with such high rates, but it has little to do with the fact that fertility rates have not declined there. We will have to seek some other explanation for the latter (see Section 8).

We should not be surprised that, in those regions where family planning programmes have had an impact, it has occurred mostly in the initial stages. Couples would be expected to adopt new methods of birth control to satisfy unmet needs. However, over time it is the net demand for children that would be expected to dominate household decisions. Here is a substantiation. Starting in 1977, 70 "treatment" villages were serviced by a programme of birth control in the famous experiment in Matlab Thana in Bangladesh, while 79 "control" villages were offered no such special service. The contraceptive prevalence in the treatment villages increased from 7 to 33% within 18 months, and then more gradually to a level of 45% by 1985. The prevalence also increased in the control villages, but only to 16% in 1985. The difference in total fertility rates between the two groups reached a figure of 1.5 (Phillips *et al.* 1988; Hill 1992).[16]

6. FEMALE EDUCATION AS A DETERMINANT OF FERTILITY BEHAVIOUR

In the initial stages, family-planning programmes would appear to have greater effect if women have a measure of education and autonomy. This has been a conclusion of a number of empirical studies. Indeed, the beneficial effects of parents' education, particularly mothers' education promote the well-being of children. For the most part, the studies have explored the effect of some 6 to 7 years of schooling, no more.[17] These studies confirm that education helps mothers to process information more effectively, and enable them to use the various social and community services that may be on offer more intensively. Among other things, education appears to impart a degree of self-confidence on a person to avail herself of whatever new facilities that may be on offer. This is invaluable for rural populations living through changing circumstances.[18]

The links between female education, especially secondary education, and reproductive behaviour are varied. (Cochrane 1983 is an illuminating study.) The acquisition of education delays the age of marriage, and this would be expected to reduce fertility. Moreover, at low levels of education and contraceptive prevalence, improvements in literacy and receptiveness to new ideas accompany family planning programmes. Family planning programmes aim at longer birth-spacing and thus to a reduction in infant mortality rates. Furthermore, education increases women's opportunities for work and so their opportunity cost of time. (The cost of child-rearing is higher for educated mothers; see Section 9). Finally, educated mothers would be expected to value education for their children more highly, and so would be more likely to make a conscious trade-off between the quality and number of their children.

Set against these is an effect on fertility which runs the other way. Taboos against post-partum female sexual activity, where they exist, may well be weakened through education. In sub-Saharan Africa, where polygyny is widely practised, post-partum female sexual abstinence can last up to three years after birth. It is also not uncommon for women to practise total abstinence once they have become grandmothers. The evidence is curious: in Latin American and Asia, increased female enrolment in secondary education has had the effect of lowering fertility rates, while in parts of sub-Saharan Africa there is evidence that the effect has been the opposite.[19]

7. THE MOTIVE FOR PROCREATION: CHILDREN AS ENDS AND INSURANCE

Two broad types of reproductive motivations have figured prominently in analyses of population growth in poor countries.[20] The first stems from a regard for children as children. Not only are children desirable in themselves, they carry on the family line or lineage, and they are the clearest avenue open to what one may call "self-transcendence" (Heyd 1992; Dasgupta 1992, 1993). We are genetically programmed to want and to value them. In short: children are an end in themselves.[21] This provides the broadest type of motivation. It comprises a disparate set, ranging from the desire to have children because they are playful and enjoyable, to the dictates of injunctions emanating from the cult of the ancestor, which sees religion as essentially the reproduction of the lineage. This latter motivation has been emphasized by Caldwell and Caldwell (1987, 1990) in explaining why sub-Saharan Africa has, for the most part, proved so resistant to fertility reduction. It is not a good argument. It explains why fertility rates there are high, but it does not explain why they have not responded to declining mortality rates. The cult of the ancestor may prescribe reproduction of the lineage, but it does not stipulate an invariant fertility rate. Even in sub-Saharan Africa, total fertility rates have been less than the maximum possible rate.

The second kind of motivation stems from the old-age security children can provide in an economic environment where capital, or annuity, markets are next to non-existent. In a significant study, Nugent and Gillaspy (1983) used Mexican evidence to show that old-age pension and social security do act as a substitute for children.[22] One way of formalizing this is to assume that parents are interested in household welfare, subject, however, to the condition that the chance of there being an offspring to care for them in old age (i.e. providing sustenance, time, and attention) is no less than a certain amount. In many regions (e.g. the Indian sub-continent) this translates itself to a requirement that the chance of there being a son alive when the parents are old is no less than a certain amount. As a numerical example, we may consider the simulation study by May and Heer (1968), who estimated that an average Indian couple in the 1960s needed to have 6.3 children in order to be 95% sure of having a surviving son when the father reached the age of 65. This is a high figure, about the same as the total fertility rate in India during the decade of the 1950s. The "safety first" model of fertility decision has recently been much explored in a series of articles by Cain (1981, 1982, 1983, 1984).[23]

Old-age security provides a potentially strong motive. In 1980, people aged 65 and over in South Asia formed about 4% of the total population. The sex composition among the aged is far from even, being of the order of 80–85 men for every 100 women among the elderly. In South and South-East Asia, female life expectancy at birth is 59 years, while that of males is about 54 years; at age 60, however, they are approximately 15 and 14 years—not much less than the life expectancy at age 60 in advanced industrial countries (Trease & Logue 1986). In the Indian sub-continent, the proportions of the elderly who live with their children (for the most part, sons) is of the order of 80% or more. (In the United States, the corresponding figure is about 15%). Sons are an absolute necessity in these circumstances. A poor widow with no sons in northern parts of the Indian sub-continent is faced with a near- certain prospect of destitution. In addition, daughters are a net drain on parental resources (dowries can be bankrupting). This goes some way towards explaining the preference parents show for sons there (Sopher 1980; Cain 1984). It also helps explain why daughters in their childhood are expected to work relatively harder for their parents, a matter we come to next.

8. THE MOTIVE FOR PROCREATION: CHILDREN AS INCOME EARNERS

In poor countries, children are also useful as income-earning assets. This provides households in these parts with a third kind of motivation for having children. It has important consequences.

Poor countries for the most part are biomass-based subsistence economies. Rural folk there eke out a living from products obtained directly from plants and animals. Production throughput is low. Households there do not have access to the sources of domestic energy available to households in advanced industrial countries. Nor do they have water on tap. (In the semi-arid and arid regions, water supply is not even close at hand.) This means that the relative prices of alternative sources of energy and water faced by rural households in poor countries are quite different from those faced by households elsewhere. Indirect sources (perhaps tap water nearby) are often prohibitively expensive for the household. As we will see presently, this provides a link between high fertility, degradation of the environmental- resource base of a rural community, and an accentuation of hardship among its members.

From about the age of 6 years, children in poor households in poor countries mind their siblings and domestic animals, fetch water, and collect fuelwood, dung, and fodder. These are complementary to other household activities. They are necessary on a daily basis if the household is to survive. As many as five hours a day may be required for obtaining the bare essential amount of firewood, dung, and fodder. (One should contrast this with the direct time spent by households in acquiring water and fuel in advanced industrial economies, which is nil.) In their study of work allocation among rural households in the foothills of the Himalayas, C.S.E. (1990) recorded that children in the age range 10–15 years work one-and- a-half times the number of hours adult males do, their tasks consisting of collecting fuelwood, dung, and fodder, grazing domestic animals, performing household chores, and marketing.

All this may be expected to relate to the high fertility and low literacy rates in rural areas of the Indian sub-continent and sub-Saharan Africa. Poverty, the sparseness of markets, and an absence of basic amenities make it essential for households to engage in a large number of complementary production activities. Each is time-consuming. Labour productivity is low not only because capital is scarce, but also because environmental resources are scarce.[24] Children are then continually needed as workers by their parents, even when the parents are in their prime. A small household simply is not viable. Each household needs many hands, and it could be that the overall usefulness of each additional hand increases with declining resource availability.[25] A high rate of fertility and population growth further damages the environmental resource base (to the extent that this consists of unprotected common property), which, in turn, provides further (private) incentives for large families in a wide range of circumstances which, in turn, further damages the resource base—and so on, until some countervailing set of factors (whether public policy or falling productivity of additional children) stops the spiralling process. By the time this happens, however, millions of lives may have suffered.[26] Such an explosive process can be set off by any number of factors. Government or private usurpation of resources to which rural communities have had historical access is a potential source of the problem; so is the breakdown of collective agreements among users of common-property resources. Indeed, even a marginal decline in compliance can trigger the process of cumulative causation. Over time, the effect can be large.

As workers, children add so much to household income that they are often costless to rear by the time they reach adolescence. This line of argument has been emphasized by Mueller (1976) and Lindert (1980, 1983). Cain (1977) has studied data from the village Char Gopalpur in Bangladesh. He showed that male children become net producers at as early an age as 12 years, and work as many hours a day as an adult. Using a zero (calorie) rate of interest, he estimated that male children compensate for their own cumulative consumption by the age of 15. This may not be typical in Bangladesh. Nevertheless, I cite it to show the vast difference in the motivation for having children between households in rich countries and poor households in poor countries.

These observations suggest that the transfer of material resources over a life-cycle in poor households in poor countries is from offspring in the aggregate to their parents, a thesis that has been advanced by Caldwell (1976, 1977a,b, 1981, 1982), who has also argued that whether a society has made the demographic transition is related to the direction of the intergenerational flow of resources (Willis 1987). Although intuitively plausible, it is difficult to test the thesis. I have seen no study that includes in the calculation of resource transfers the value of time foregone in the rearing of children, or the risks borne by the mother during the process of reproduction. These amount to resource transfers from parents to their children. In any event, it is not mere poverty that would influence the direction of the flow of resources. If people were mobile (and this was the case in early 19th century England), poor parents would not be able to effect this transfer readily. In these circumstances, much of the motivation for having children would be absent, and even a poor society could display a move towards the demographic transition.[27] However, this is not yet so in the Indian sub-continent and sub-Saharan Africa, and its absence makes for a strong parental motivation for having large families.

9. MODELLING FERTILITY DECISIONS

We have identified three different motives behind procreation. Hybrid accounts of fertility decisions contain all three in varying strengths. They enable us to analyse the population problem in a unified way. For example, should the child mortality rate decline, the fertility rate would be expected to follow suit among households averse to facing risks in the number of children who survive (Sah 1991). Nevertheless, even when mortality rates decline, it takes time for households to recognise this. Demographic transitions would be expected to display sharp declines in fertility rates only some time after steep declines in mortality rates. Even today, rural women in much of sub-Saharan Africa lose something like a third of their offspring by the end of their reproductive years. This provides a strong reason for pro-natalism there.

In noting the effect of a decline of mortality rates on fertility behaviour, I do not, of course, mean that a decline in fertility cannot precede reductions in mortality rates. They can and have (Coale 1969; Knodel & van de Walle 1979; Kertzer & Hogan 1989; Greenhalgh 1990). Indeed, one of the purposes of theorizing on fertility decisions is to identify the several possible reasons why a community may move to a lower fertility regime. In the remainder of this section, I shall put our analysis to work in identifying such reasons.

In Section 6, it was observed that improvements in female education appear to have a salutary effect on household circumstances. It will prove useful now to study the effect of an increase in parental income on fertility. This leads us back to the aggregate data we studied in Section 1.

To begin with, we may trace the increase in parental income to a rise in their labour productivity—as a consequence, say, of rural investment or, more generally, better employment opportunities for men and women in the labour market. A rise in women's labour productivity implies an increase in the opportunity cost of rearing children. At the same time, with increasing parental income, children are needed less as income earners and possibly less also as insurance, since one would imagine that rising income brings in its wake greater access to the capital market. (For an empirical exploration of this last link, see Rosenzweig and Evenson 1977).

Improvements in labour productivity are often associated with urbanization. This accentuates the directional changes we have already identified (Coale & Hoover 1958). Urbanisation tends to break households down into "nuclear" units. This raises the cost that parents have to bear in rearing their children. (The contribution of grandparents, aunts, and other kin is in this situation greatly reduced.) Growing urbanisation in a growing economy also offers children better employment prospects, which improve their bargaining strength relative to their parents. This, in turn, lowers the return on children as investment, since children become less dependable as a source of income to their parents in their old age. (Sundstrum and David 1988 deploy this argument in the context of ante-bellum United States.) Moreover, state legislation on elementary schooling (for example, making it compulsory) and increased private returns to education (arising from general industrialisation) make children less useful as income earners in the immediate future. Compounding all these considerations, we can glimpse those forces at work that relate fertility to household income in an "inverse" way. Increased parental income, especially maternal income, in effect raises the cost of having children. The causal chain is thus roundabout, and the "inverse" relationship between household income and the desired family size holds for a wide range of household motivations.[28]

In societies where the conjugal bond is powerful, as in most of Asia, parents together bear the bulk of the cost of raising their children, even though the sexes typically do so unevenly. The extent of economic dependency of women on men now assumes a central role. This dependency is enormous in the Indian sub-continent, especially in the North (Libbee 1980; Dyson & Moore 1983; Dasgupta 1993). In patriarchal societies, women rightly perceive sons as having especially high value as insurance against personal calamities, such as widowhood and abandonment. We noted this earlier. However, sons cannot be guaranteed. So one has to keep trying. In East and South-East Asia (and also southern India and Sri Lanka), women's economic dependency is less. Among those that were the world's poorest countries in the early 1970s, fertility rates have fallen most dramatically in this part of the world. In a wide-ranging essay on the old-age security hypothesis, Cain (1984) used the median age difference between spouses as an index of female economic dependence in patriarchal societies to demonstrate a remarkably high correlation between this and the total fertility rate in a cross-sectional study of nations.

There are thus forces at work which move the fertility goals of women relative to men in opposite directions, a matter we studied in Section 4. In poor societies marked by gender differences in employment opportunities and power, women's reproductive goals do not differ noticeably from those of men (Mason & Taj 1987). Nevertheless, professed desires are sensitive to the extent to which women are educated; educated women tend to desire smaller families than illiterate ones (although in sub-Saharan Africa the difference appears to be small). A preference for sons is nearly universal in the Indian sub-continent. In sub-Saharan Africa this is not so (Williamson 1976; Dasgupta 1993). Indeed, in parts of Africa for which data on uterine sibling groups have been obtained, there is no evidence of stopping rules that would reveal an implicit sex-preference (Goody *et al.* 1981a,b).[29]

10. HOUSEHOLD VERSUS COMMUNITY BENEFITS FROM NEW BIRTHS

Thus far, we have studied behaviour at the level of the household. In doing so, we have seen that because of differences in the bargaining powers between the principal parties to fertility decisions, there is a sense in which reproductive rates can be overly high; but suppose we were not to peer inside the household and were to regard household choice as sacrosanct. Can there still be a sense in which fertility rates in poor countries are too high?

Some would argue that there is no such sense. For example, Bauer (1981:61,64), in an important essay, says: "The comparatively high fertility and large families in many ldcs (less developed countries) should not be regarded as irrational, abnormal, incomprehensible or unexpected. They accord with the tradition of most cultures and with the precepts of religious and political leaders...allegations or apprehensions of adverse or even disastrous results of population growth are unfounded. They rest on seriously defective analysis of the determinants of economic performance; they misconceive the conduct of the peoples of ldcs; and they employ criteria of welfare so inappropriate that they register as deterioration changes which are, in fact, improvements in the conditions of people."

There are problems with this line of thought. Even when men and women at the household level rationally prefer large numbers of children to small numbers, it does not follow that there is no population problem, a problem they themselves might acknowledge if they were to be asked about it. As in every other field of individual choice, we need here to ask as well if a collection of reasoned decisions at the individual level might be unsatisfactory at the collective level.[30] Putting it in a slightly different way, we need to ask if there can be a resource allocation failure here.

There are two broad reasons for a possible dissonance between household and societal levels of decision-making in the field of procreation. The first is that the relative prices of various goods and services (for example, potable water and fuel sources) that households face may simply be "wrong", for whatever reason. We have studied this in some detail in earlier sections. The second is provided by an ubiquitous phenomenon called *externalities* by economists. In this section, we will study these.[31]

There are, in fact, three sources of externalities in fertility decisions. The first is simple enough: it has to do with the finiteness of space. Increased population size implies greater crowding. No household, acting on its own, would be expected to take into account the inconvenience it would cause others when creating another child.

This is not a precious argument. The human epidemiological environment becomes more and more precarious as communication and population densities rise. Packed centres of population provide a fertile ground for the spread of viruses, and there are always new strains of these in the making. That environmental resources are usually *common property* is also cited as a harbinger of externalities. The point here is that, because households have access to common-property resources, parents (even when regarded as a decision unit) do not fully bear the full cost of rearing children, and so they produce too many.[32]

A second, related source of externalities arises in those soceieties where there is substantial kinship support of one's children. This creates another free-rider problem if parents appropriate a greater proportion of the benefits their children provide than the proportion they incur of the cost of rearing them (Dasgupta 1993). From the collective point of view, households have an incentive to produce too many children in such a social environment. To be sure, the cost of bearing and nursing a child is borne by the mother, but the cost of rearing children is culturally conditioned. In some cultures, as in much of sub-Saharan Africa, children are not raised by their parents; rather, this responsibility is more diffuse within the kinship group, affording a form of insurance protection to be expected in semi-arid regions.[33] In much of West Africa, about a third of the children have been found to live with their kin at any given time. Nephews and nieces have the same rights of accommodation and support as biological offspring. Sub-Saharan Africa has often been characterised by strong descent lineage and by weak conjugal bond. Taken together, these features of the social environment cause an allocation failure in that neither parent bears the full cost of the couple's decision to have a child. For the most part, as in much of the Indian sub-continent, descent is patrilineal and residence is patrilocal. (An important exception are the Akan people of Ghana.) Patriarchy, a weak conjugal bond, and a strong kinship support system of children taken together are a broad characteristic of sub-Saharan Africa. It provides a powerful stimulus to fertility.

Reproductive free-riding has not received attention in what is often called the "new economic demography". Surveying the field, Schultz (1988:417) writes: "Consequences of individual fertility decisions that bear on persons outside of the family have proved difficult to quantify, as in many cases where social external diseconomies are thought to be important." Given the ingenuity economic demographers have displayed in estimating household demand for children, goods and services, it is hard to imagine that reproductive free-riding has been particularly difficult to quantify. One suspects, rather, that quantification has not been attempted.

The third source of externalities lies elsewhere, and is more subtle. It arises from imitative behaviour, and it often lies behind what is often called "traditional practice". Procreation is not only a private matter, it is also a social activity. By this I mean that household decisions about procreation are influenced by the cultural milieu (Easterlin, Pollak & Wachter 1980; Watkins 1990). In many societies, there are practices encouraging high fertility rates which no household desires unilaterally to break. Such practice may well have had a rationale in the past, when mortality rates were high, rural population densities were low, the threat of extermination from outside attack was high, and mobility was restricted. Nevertheless, practices can survive even when their original purpose has disappeared. (Anthropologists call them "dysfunctional social norms".) It can then be that, so long as all others follow the practice and aim at large family sizes, no household on its own will wish to deviate from the practice; however, if all other households were to restrict their fertility rates, each would desire to restrict its fertility rate as well. In such an environment, a society can get stuck at one of several possible self-sustaining modes of behaviour, each being sustained by its own bootstraps, so to speak. Indeed, a society can persist with a mode of behaviour which, while it may have had a collective rationale in the past, does not have one any more.

This does not imply that society will be stuck with it forever. As always, people differ in the extent of their absorption of traditional practice, their readiness to digest new information, and to act upon new information. There are inevitably those who, for one reason or another, experiment, take risks and refrain from joining the crowd. They are the tradition- breakers, and they often lead the way. In the context of fertility, educated women are among the first to make the move towards smaller families (Farooq, Ekanem & Ojelade 1876; Ahmad 1991). Female education is, therefore, a potent force in creating tradition-breakers, as are employment opportunities for women. Special costs are inevitably borne during transitional periods, when established modes of operation are in the process of disintegration without being replaced immediately by new institutions to soften the costs. Demographic transition is possibly a prime example of this. When this is the situation, only a concerted effort (e.g. a massive literacy drive) can dislodge the economy from the rapacious hold of high fertility rates without at the same time inflicting misery on those who alter their mode of behaviour.[34]

In their informative study of fertility behaviour in sub-Saharan Africa, Cochrane and Farid (1989) remark that both the urban and rural, the educated and uneducated in sub-Saharan Africa have more, and want more, children than do their counterparts in other regions. Thus, even the younger women there expressed a desire for an average of 2.6 more children than women in the Middle East, 2.8 more than women in North Africa, and 3.6 to 3.7 more than women in Latin American and Asia.

There are several possible explanations for this. Innate cultural differences is one; differences in the institutional setting is another; multiplicity of social equilibrium arising from imitative behaviour within a community is yet another. The last explanation has the advantage of being parsimonious: we do not need to invoke the thought that folk in sub-

Saharan Africa are intrinsically different from people in other parts of the world, or operate under different institutions, even though they may profess different fertility goals. They could be very similar and could yet find themselves in a different social equilibrium.

11. ALLOCATION FAILURE AND PUBLIC POLICY

In his widely-cited book, Kennedy (1993) writes: "A detailed proposal for dealing with the demographic explosion in developing countries would simply repeat what numerous studies by international agencies have pointed out: that the only practical way to ensure a decrease in fertility rates and, thus, in population growth, is to introduce cheap and reliable forms of birth control."

In this essay we have seen that this is far off the mark. There is a great deal more to the population problem than that. We have also seen why: in the Indian sub-continent and sub-Saharan Africa, children are valuable at the level of the household. If fertility rates are to be reduced, it is not only family planning programmes that need to be improved; public policy needs to be geared toward making children less valuable.

Two motivations behind procreation that we have studied in this essay spring from a general absence of certain basic needs goods in the Indian sub-continent and sub-Saharan Africa: public-health services, old-age security, water, and sources of fuel. Children are born in poverty and they are raised in poverty. A large proportion suffer from undernourishment. They remain illiterate, and are often both stunted and wasted. Undernourishment retards their cognitive (and often motor) development (Dasgupta 1993). Labour productivity is dismally low also because of a lack of infrastructure, such as roads. In this background, it is hard to make sense of the oft-expressed suggestion (Simon 1977, 1981) that there are cumulative benefits to be enjoyed from increases in population size even in poor countries; that human beings are a valuable resource. To be sure, they are potentially valuable as doers of things and originators of ideas, but for this they require inputs of the means for development. Moreover, historical evidence on the way pressure of population led to changes in the organisation of production, property rights, and ways of doing this, which is what Boserup (1965, 1981) studied in her far-reaching work, also does not seem to address the population problem as it exists in sub-Saharan Africa and the Indian sub-continent today. Admittedly, the central message in these writings is that the spectre of the Malthusian trap is not to be taken seriously, but we should be permitted to ask of these modern writers what policy flows from their visions. The Boserup–Simon thesis (if one may be permitted to amalgamate two sets of writings) implies that households confer a benefit to the community when they reproduce. This means that fertility ought to be subsidised. I have not seen this implication advocated by its proponents.

The quality of a child depends on the amount of time and resources devoted to it. It depends as well on the time and effort devoted by the child in acquiring education and skills. Parents thus face a tradeoff between the number of children they rear and the average quality of these children. In this essay, we have identified reasons why poor households in poor countries are forced to give in to the desire for numbers over quality. In what follows, I will collate the various factors that would be expected to influence fertility decisions. I will then use the account we have developed to identify the nature of public policy that should be put into effect.

Children as income earners and as old-age security yield somewhat different implications for public policy. Nevertheless, they do both entail public policy. The provision of such patterns of household infrastructure as we have identified requires resources, and economic analysis informs us why it is the state's obligation in poor countries to make attempts to supply them. The aim should not be to force people to change their reproductive behaviour.[35] Rather, it should be to identify policies that would so change the options men and women face that their reasoned choices would involve a lowering of their fertility rates to replacement levels. The evidence, some of which I have put together here, tells us that poor parents in poor countries *do* calculate when making such decisions as those that bear on household size and assets, even though what emerges at the end is a greater number of yet another cohort of poor, illiterate people. It would certainly be unjust of governments to insist on parents sending their children to schools for so many years if this requirement further impoverished poor households, but it would not be unjust if the complementary household production inputs were made available through the provision of family-planning and public- health services, and infrastructural investment, and for governments then to make free school attendance compulsory.[36] Reasoned choice at the household level would be expected to respond to this through an alteration in fertility goals.

In the absence of such public provisions, the dynamics of a social system can be horrifying. For reasons I have identified, the bulk of the very poor in poor countries have continually to aim at large household sizes, making it, in turn, much more difficult for them to lift themselves out of the grip of poverty: household labour productivity remains abysmally low, investment credit is for the most part unavailable to them, and the avenue of savings is consequently that much constrained for them. The matter is different for those with a greater access to resources. They are, as always, in a position to limit their household size and increase the chance of propelling themselves into still higher income levels. I have not been able to locate published data on the matter, but my impression is that among the urban middle classes in India, the demographic transition has already been achieved. This does not mean there is an inexorable "vicious circle of poverty", however. People from the poorest of backgrounds have been known to lift themselves out of the mire. Nevertheless, there are forces at work which pull rich and poor groups away from one another in terms of the quality of life. The Matthew effect ("For unto everyone that hath shall be given, and he shall have abundance; but from him that hath not shall be taken away even that which he hath") works relentlessly in poor countries.

I am putting matters in stark terms so as to focus only on the idea that men and women would have a different set of fertility goals if the relative prices of environmental and infrastructure goods were different, and if the economic dependency of women on men were less. As regards the latter, female education is now widely suggested as being a key propellent, but increased employment opportunities for females have also been observed to be a route to greater autonomy (Ahmad 1991).

There are, of course, other measures which should be thought about in parallel. Compulsory schooling, for example, makes children prohibitively expensive as assets for generating current income. It therefore reduces their attractiveness as a commodity. Making available alternative sources of basic household needs improves the well-being of poor households via an altered set of fertility goals.

Let me sum up. I have identified three broad categories of policies for alleviating the population problem: (i) increasing the costs of having children; (ii) reducing the benefits of reproduction; and (iii) improving the information base concerning the technology of reproduction, and affecting the locus of household decision-making. Categories (i) and (iii) have found much expression in the demographic literature – unhappily, at the neglect of (ii). It is (ii) that raises the most interesting economic issues: it tells us that among the most potent avenues open for easing the population problem may well be those that involve social coordination, the provision of infrastructural goods, and measures of social security. These services are, however, desirable in themselves and commend themselves even when we do not have the population problem in mind. It seems to me that this consonance among desirable social policies is a most agreeable fact.

Admittedly, in saying all this we are looking at matters wholly from the perspective of the parents. This is limiting.[37] Identifying the right basis for population policies is, however, extremely difficult (Heyd 1992; Dasgupta 1992). What I have tried to argue in this essay is that there is much that we can establish even were we to leave such conceptual difficulties aside. Population policy involves a good deal more than making family-planning centres available to the rural poor. It also involves more than a recognition that poverty is a root cause of high fertility rates in a number of societies. The problem is deeper, but it is identifiable.

ACKNOWLEDGEMENTS:

My greatest debt is to Kerstin Lindahl Kiessling for encouraging me to write the paper and to give it a wider scope than I had originally intended. I am also grateful to Tommy Bengtsson, Henry Bienen, Angus Deaton, Paul Ehrlich, Marc Feldman, Karl-Göran Mäler, James Mirrlees, Sheilagh Ogilvie, and Rolf Ohlsson for their comments on earlier drafts.

REFERENCES

Ahmad, A. 1991 *Women and fertility in Bangladesh*. New Delhi: Sage.
Arrow, K.J. & Fisher, A. 1974 Preservation, uncertainty and irreversibility. *Q. Jl. Econ.* **88**.
Barro, R. 1991 Economic growth in a cross section of countries. *Q. Jl. Econ.*, **106**.
Barro, R. & Becker, G. 1989 Fertility choice in a model of economic growth. *Econometrica,* **57**.
Bauer, P.T. 1981 *Equality, the third world and economic delusion*. London: Weidenfeld & Nicolson.
Becker, G. 1960 An economic analysis of fertility. In *Demographic and economic change in developed countries* (ed. G. Becker). Princeton, NJ: Princeton University Press.
Becker, G. 1981 *A treatise on the family*. Cambridge, MA: Harvard University Press.
Becker, G. & Lewis, H.G. 1973 Interaction between quantity and quality of children. *Jl. Pol. Econ.,* **81**.
Becker, G. & Tomes, N. 1976 Child endowments and the quantity and quality of children. *Jl. Pol. Econ.* (suppl.), **84**.
Behrman, J., Pollak, R.A. & Taubman, P. 1982 Parental preferences and provision for progeny. *Jl. Pol. Econ.,* **90**.
Behrman, J. & Wolfe, B.L. 1984a The socioeconomic impact of schooling in a developing country. *Rev. Econ. Stat.,* **66**.

Behrman, J. & Wolfe, B.L. 1984b More evidence on nutrition demand: income seems overrated and women's schooling underemphasized. *Jl. Dev. Econ.,* **14**.

Birdsall, N. 1977 Analytical approaches to the relationship of population growth anddevelopment. *Pop. Dev. Rev.,* **3**.

Birdsall, N. 1988 Economic approaches to population growth. In *Handbook of development economics* 1 (eds. H. Chenery and T.N. Srinivasan). Amsterdam: North Holland.

Birdsall, N. & Jamison, D. 1983 Income and other factors influencing fertility in China. *Pop. Dev. Rev.,* **9**.

Bledsoe, C. 1990 The politics of children: fosterage and social management of fertility among the Mende. In *Births and power: social change and the politics of reproduction* (ed. P. Handwerker). Boulder, CO: Westview Press.

Bleek, W. 1987 Family and family planning in southern Ghana. In *Sex roles, population and development in West Africa* (ed. C.Oppong). Portsmouth, NH: Heinemann.

Blurton Jones, N.G. & Sibly, R.M. 1978 Testing adaptiveness of culturally determined behaviour: do Bushmen women maximize their reproductive success by spacing births widely and foraging seldom? In *Human behaviour and adaptations* (eds. N.G. Blurton Jones and V. Reynolds). London: Taylor and Francis.

Bongaarts, J. 1978 A framework for analyzing the proximate determinants of fertility. *Popl. Devl. Rev.,* **4**.

Bongaarts, J. 1980 Does malnutrition affect fecundity? A summary of the evidence. *Science,* **208**.

Bongaarts, J. 1991 The KAP-gap and the unmet need for contraception. *Pop. Devl. Rev.,* **17**.

Bongaarts, J. & Cain, M. 1981 *Demographic responses to famine.* New York: Population Council.

Bongaarts, J. & Potter, R.G. 1983 Fertility, biology and behavior: an analysis of the proximate determinants. New York: Academic Press.

Boserup, E. 1965 *The conditions of agricultural growth.* London: George Allen & Unwin.

Boserup, E. 1981 *Population growth and technological change.* Chicago: Chicago University Press.

Bourne, K.C. & Walker G.M. Jr. 1991 The differential effect of mothers' education on mortality of boys and girls in India. *Pop. Stud.,* **45**.

Bulatao, R.A. & Lee, R.D. 1983 (eds) *Determinants of fertility in developing countries,* 2 vols. New York: Academic Press.

Cain, M. 1977 The economic activities of children in a village in Bangladesh. *Pop. Dev. Rev.,* **3**.

Cain, M. 1981 Risk and insurance: perspectives on fertility and agrarian change in India and Bangladesh. *Pop. Dev. Rev.,* **7** .

Cain, M. 1982 Perspectives on family and fertility in developing countries. *Pop. Stud.,* **36**.

Cain, M. 1983 Fertility as an adjustment to risk. *Pop. Dev. Rev.,* **9**.

Cain, M. 1984 Women's status and fertility in developing countries: son preference and economic security. World Bank Staff Working Paper No. 682.

Caldwell, J.C. 1975 (ed.) *Population growth and socioeconomic change in West Africa.* New York: Columbia University Press.

Caldwell, J.C. 1976 Toward a restatement of demographic theory. *Popl. Dev. Rev.,* **2**.

Caldwell, J.C. 1977a The economic rationality of high fertility: an investigation illustrated with Nigerian data. *Pop. Stud.,* **31**.

Caldwell, J.C. 1977b *The persistence of high fertility: population prospects in the third world.* Canberra: Australian National University Press.

Caldwell, J.C. 1979 Education as a factor in mortality decline: an examination of Nigeriandata. *Pop. Stud.,* **35**.

Caldwell, J.C. 1981 The mechanisms of demographic change in historical perspective. *Pop. Stud.,* **35**.

Caldwell, J.C. 1982 *Theory of fertility decline.* New York: Academic Press.

Caldwell, J.C. & Caldwell, P. 1987 The cultural context of high fertility in sub-Saharan Africa.

Pop. Dev. Rev., **13**.

Caldwell, J.C. & Caldwell, P. 1990 High fertility in sub-Saharan Africa. *Scient. Am.*, **262** (May).

Chomitz, K.M. & Birdsall, N. 1991 Incentives for small families: concepts and issues. *Proc. World Bank Annual Conference on Development Economics 1990.*

Christian, P. *et al.* 1988 The role of maternal literacy and nutrition knowledge in determining children's nutritional status. *Food Nutr. Bull.*, **10**.

Cigno, A. 1991 *Economics of the family.* Oxford: Clarendon Press.

Coale, A.J. 1969 The decline of fertility in Europe from the French Revolution to world war II. In *Fertility and family planning: a world view* (eds. S.J. Behrman, L. Corsa & R. Freedman). Ann Arbor, MI: University of Michigan Press.

Coale, A.J. & Hoover, E.M. 1958 *Population growth and economic development in low-income countries.* Princeton, NJ: Princeton University Press.

Coale, A.J. & Trussell, J.T. 1974 Model fertility schedules: variations in the age structure of childbearing in human populations. *Pop. Ind.*, **40**.

Cochrane, S.H. 1979 *Fertility and education: what do we really know?* Baltimore, MD: Johns Hopkins Univerisity Press.

Cochrane, S.H. 1983 Effects of education and urbanization on fertility. In *Determinants offertility in developing countries* (eds. R.A. Bulatao & R.D. Lee), Vol.2. New York: Academic Press.

Cochrane, S.H. *et al.* 1980 Effects of education on health. Washington, DC: World Bank Staff Working Paper No.405.

Cochrane, S.H. & Farid, S.M. 1989 Fertility in sub-Saharan Africa: analysis and explanation. Washington, DC: World Bank Discussion Paper No.43.

Cochrane, S.H., Leslie, J. & O'Hara, D. 1982 Parental education and health: intracountry evidence. *Health Policy and Education*, **2**.

C.S.E. 1990 *Human nature interactions in a central Himalayan village: a case study of village Bemru.* New Delhi: Centre for Science and Environment.

Dasgupta, P. 1969 On the concept of optimum population. *Rev. Econ. Stud.*, **36**.

Dasgupta, P. 1974 On optimum population size. In *Economic theory and planning: essays in honour of A. K. Dasgupta*, (ed. A. Mitra). New Delhi: Oxford University Press.

Dasgupta, P. 1992 Savings and population: normative considerations. *Philosophy and public affairs.* Forthcoming 1994.

Dasgupta, P. 1993 *An inquiry into well-being and destitution.* Oxford: Clarendon Press.

Dasgupta, P. & Mäler K.-G.1991 The environment and emerging development issues. World Bank: Annual Conference on Development Economics 1990.

Dasgupta P, & Mäler, K-G. 1991 (eds.) *The economics of transnational commons.* Oxford: Clarendon Press, forthcoming.

Dasgupta, P. & Mäler, K-G. 1993 Poverty, institutions, and the environmental resource base. In: *Handbook of development economics* **III** (eds. J. Behrman and T.N. Srinivasan). Amsterdam: North Holland, forthcoming 1994.

Dyson, T. & Moore, M. 1983 On kinship structure, female autonomy, and demographic behaviour in India. *Pop. Dev. Rev.*, **9**.

Easterlin, R.A. 1975 An economic framework for fertility analysis. *Stud. Family Planning*, **6**.

Easterlin, R.A. 1978 The economics and sociology of fertility: a synthesis. In *Historical studies of changing fertility* (ed. C. Tilley). Princeton NJ: Princeton University Press.

Easterlin, R.A. 1980 *Population and economic change in developing countries.* University of Chicago Press.

Easterlin, R.A. & Crimmins, E. 1985 *The fertility revolution: a supply–demand analysis.* University of Chicago Press.

Easterlin, R.A., Pollak, R.A. & Wachter, M.L. 1980 Toward a more general model of fertility determination: endogenous preferences and natural fertility. In: *Population and economic change in developing countries* (ed. R.A. Easterlin). University of Chicago Press.

Ehrlich, P. & Ehrlich, A. 1990 *The population explosion.* New York: Simon and Schuster.

Enke, S. 1966 The economic aspects of slowing population growth. *Econ. J.,* **76**.

FAO 1989 *The state of food and agriculture,* Rome: Food and Agricultural Organization.

Farooq, G.M., Ekanem, I.I. & Ojelade, S. 1987 Family size preferences and fertility in south-western Nigeria. In *Sex roles, population and development in West Africa* (ed. C. Oppong). Portsmouth, NH: Heinemann.

Freedman, R. 1979 Theories of fertility decline: a reappraisal. *Social Forces,* **58**.

Goody, J. 1976 *Production and reproduction: a comparative study of the domestic terrain.* Cambridge University Press.

Goody, J. 1990 Futures of the family in rural Africa. *Pop. Dev. Rev.* (Suppl), **16**.

Goody, J. *et al.* 1981a On the absence of implicit sex preference in Ghana. *J. Biosocial Sciences,* **13**.

Goody, J. *et al.* 1981b Implicit sex preference: a comparative study. *J. Biosocial Sciences,* **13**.

Greenhalgh, S. 1990 Toward a political economy of fertility: anthropological contributions. *Pop. Dev. Rev.,* **16**.

Gross, D.R. & Underwood, B.A. 1971 Technological change and caloric costs: sisal agriculture in north-eastern Brazil. *Am. Anthr.,* **73**.

Henry, C. 1974 Investment decisions under uncertainty: the irreversibility effect. *Am. Econ. Rev.,* **64**.

Hess, P.N. 1988 *Population growth and socioeconomic progress in less developed countries.,* New York: Praeger.

Heyd, D. 1991 *Genethics: the morality of procreation.* Los Angeles: University of California Press.

Hill, K. 1992 Fertility and mortality trends in the developing world. *Ambio,* **21**.

Hirschman, C. & Guest, P. 1990 The emerging demographic transition in South-East Asia. *Pop. Dev. Rev.,* **16**.

Hobcraft, J.N., McDonald, J.W. & Rutstein, S.O. 1984 Socio-economic factors in infant and child mortality: a cross-national comparison. *Pop. Stud.,* **38**.

Hull, T.H. 1990 Recent trends in sex ratios in China. *Pop. Dev. Rev.,* **16**.

Jamison, D.T. & Mosley, W.H. 1990 Selecting disease control priorities in developing countries. In: *Evolving health priorities in developing countries* (eds. D.T. Jamison& W.H. Mosley). Washington, DC: World Bank.

Jazairy, I., Alamgir, M. & Panuccio, T. 1992 *The state of world poverty.* New York University Press.

Johnson, D.G. & Lee, R. 1987 (eds.) *Population growth and economic development: issues and evidence.* Madison: University of Wisconsin Press.

Kamarck, A.M. 1988 The special case of Africa. In: *Health, nutrition and economic crises* (eds. D.E. Bell and M.R. Reich). Dover, MA: Auburn House.

Kennedy, E. 1989 *The effects of sugarcane production on food security, health, and nutrition in Kenya: a longitudinal analysis.* Washington, DC: Research Report No.78, International Food Policy Research Institute.

Kennedy, E. & Oniang'o, R. 1990 Health and nutrition effects of sugarcane production in south-western Kenya. *Food and Nutrition Bulletin,* **12**.

Kennedy, P. 1993 *Preparing for the 21st century.* New York: Random House.

Kertzer, D.I. & Hogan, D.P. 1989 *Family, political economy and demographic change: the transformation of life in Casalecchio, Italy, 1861–1921.* Madison: University of Wisconsin Press.

Keyfitz, N. 1991 Population and development within the ecosphere: one view of the literature. *Pop. Ind.,* **57**.

Knodel, J. & van de Walle, E. 1979 Lessons from the past: policy implications of historical fertility studies. *Pop. Dev. Rev.,* **5**.

Lee, R.B. 1972 Population growth and the beginnings of sedentary life among the !Kung bushmen. In: *Population growth: anthropological implications* (ed. B. Spooner). Cambridge, MA:

MIT Press.

Lee, R.B. 1980 Lactation, ovulation, infanticide, and women's work: a study of hunter–gatherer population regulation. In: *Biosocial mechanisms of population regulations* (eds. M.N. Cohen, R.S. Malpass & H.G. Klein). New Haven: Yale University Press.

Lee, R.D. & Miller, T. 1991 Population growth, externalities to childbearing, and fertility policy in developing countries. *Proc. World Bank's Annual Conference on Development Economics 1990.*

Leibenstein, H. 1974 An interpretation of the economic theory of fertility: promising path or blind alley? *J. Econ. Lit.,* **12.**

Libbee, M.J. 1980 Territorial endogamy and the spatial structure of marriage in rural India. In: *An exploration of India: geographical perspectives on society and culture* (ed. D.E. Sopher). Ithaca, NY: Cornell University Press.

Lindert, P. 1980 Child costs and economic development. In *Population and economic change in developing countries* (ed. R.A. Easterlin). University of Chicago Press.

Lindert, P. 1983 The changing economic costs and benefits of having children. In *Determinants of fertility in developing countries* (eds. R.A. Bulatao & R.D. Lee). New York: Academic Press.

Luce, R.D. & Raiffa, H. 1957 *Games and decisions.* New York: John Wiley.

Lutz, E. 1993 (ed.) *Toward improved accounting for the environment.* Washington, DC: World Bank.

Mason, K.O. & Taj, A.M. 1987 Differences between women's and men's reproductive goals in developing countries. *Pop. Dev. Rev.,* **13.**

May, D.A. & Heer, D.M. 1968 Son survivorship motivation and family size in India: a computer simulation. *Pop. Stud.,* **22.**

McGuire, J. & Popkin, B.M. 1989 Beating the zero-sum game: women and nutrition in the third world: Part 1. *Food Nutr. Bull.,* **11.**

Menken, J., Trussel, J. & Watkins, S. 1981 The nutrition fertility link: an evaluation of the evidence. *J. Interdisciplinary History,* **11.**

Mensch B., Lentzner, H. & Preston, S. 1986 *Socio-economic differentials in child mortality in developing countries.* New York: United Nations.

Mirrlees, J.A. 1972 Population policy and the taxation of family size. *J. Pub. Econ.,* **1.**

Mosley, W.H. 1985 Will primary health care reduce infant and child mortality? A critique of some current strategies, with special reference to Africa and Asia. In: *Health policy, social policy and mortality prospects* (eds. J. Vallin & A.D. Lopez). Paris: Institut National d'Etudes Demographiques.

Mueller, E. 1976 The economic value of children in peasant agriculture. In: *Population and development: the search for selective interventions* (R.G. Ridker, ed.). Baltimore, MD: Johns Hopkins University Press.

Neher, P. 1971 Peasants, procreation and pensions. *Am. Econ. Rev.,* **61.**

Nerlove, M. & Meyer, A. 1992 Endogenous fertility and the environment: a parable of firewood. In: *The environment and emerging development issues* (eds. P. Dasgupta & K-G. Mäler). Oxford: Clarendon Press, forthcoming.

Nerlove, M. Razin, A. & Sadka, E. 1987 *Household and economy: welfare economics of endogenous fertility.* New York: Academic Press.

Nugent, J. 1985 The old-age security motive for fertility. *Pop. Dev. Rev.,* **11.**

Nugent, J. & Gillaspy T. 1983 Old age pension and fertility in rural areas of less developed countries: some evidence from Mexico. *Econ. Dev. Cul. Change,* **31.**

Oppong, C. 1987 (ed.) *Sex roles, population and development in West Africa.* Portsmouth, NH: Heinemann.

Page, H.J. & Lesthaeghe, R. 1981 (eds.) *Child-spacing in tropical Africa: tradition and change.* London: Academic Press.

Phillips, J. *et al.* 1988 Determinants of reproductive change in a traditional society: evidence from Matlab, Bangladesh. *Stud. Fam. Planning,* **19.**

Preston, S.H. 1978 (ed.) *The effects of infant and child mortality on fertility.* New York: Academic Press.

Preston, S.H. 1980 Causes and consequences of mortality declines in less developed countries during the 20th century. In *Population and economic change in developing countries* (ed. R.A. Easterlin). University of Chicago Press.

Preston, S.H. 1986 The decline of fertility in non-European industrialized countries. *Pop. Dev. Rev.* (Suppl.), **12**.

Preston, S.H., Keyfitz, N. & Schoen, R. 1972 *Causes of death: life tables for national populations.* New York: Seminar Press.

Preston, S.H. & Nelson, V.E. 1974 Structure and change in causes of death: an international summary. *Pop. Stud.*, **28**.

Pritchett, L. 1993 The determinants of fertility, 1: Fertility desires and the costs of contraception. Washington, DC: World Bank, mimeo.

Rosenzweig, M.R. & Evenson, R. 1977 Fertility, schooling and the economic contribution of children in rural India: an econometric analysis. *Econometrica*, **45**.

Sah, R.K. 1991 The effects of mortality changes on fertility choice and parental welfare. *J. Polit. Econ.*, **99**.

Satahr, Z, & Chigambaram, V. 1984 Differentials in contraceptive use. *World Fertility Survey Studies*, **36**.

Schelling, T. 1978 *Micromotives and macrobehaviour.* New York: W.W. Norton.

Schultz, T.P. 1988 Economic demography and development. In: *The state of development economics* (eds. G. Ranis and T.P. Schultz). Oxford: Basil Blackwell.

Schultz, T.P. 1992 Modern economic growth and fertility: is aggregate evidence credible? Department of Economics, Yale University, mimeo.

Simon, J.L. 1977 *The economics of population growth.* Princeton, NJ: Princeton University Press.

Simon, J.L. 1981 *The ultimate resource.* Princeton, NJ: Princeton University Press.

Simon, J.L. & Kahn, H. 1984 (eds.) *The resourceful earth: a response to Global 1000.* New York: Basil Blackwell.

Sopher, D.E. 1980 (ed.) *An exploration of India: geographical perspectives on society and culture.* Ithaca, NY: Cornell University Press.

Strauss, J. 1990 Households, communities, and preschool children's nutrition outcomes: evidence from rural Cote d'Ivoire. *Econ. Develop. Cultural Change*, **38**.

Sundstrom, W.A. & David, P.A. 1988 Old age security motives, labor markets and farm family fertility in antebellum America. *Expl. Econ. His.*, **25**.

Thomas, D. 1990 Intra-household resource allocation. *J. Hum. Res.*, **25**.

Thomas, D., Strauss, J., Henriques, M-H. 1990 Child survival, height for age, and household characteristics in Brazil. *J. Dev. Econ.*, 33.

Thomas, D., Strauss, J. & Henriques, M.-H. 1991 How does mother's education affect child height? *J. Hum. Res.*, **26**.

Tomich, T.P., Kilby, P. & Johnston, B.F. 1991 *Agriculture and structural transformation: opportunities seized, opportunities missed.* Washington, DC: World Bank.

Trease, J. & Logue, B. 1986 Economic development and the older population. *Pop. Dev. Rev.*, **12**.

Victoria, C.G. *et al.* 1986 Risk factors for malnutrition in Brazilian children: the role of social and environmental variables. *Bulletin WHO*, **64**.

Watkins, S.C. 1990 From local to national communities: the transformation of demographic regions in western Europe 1870–1960. *Pop. Dev. Rev.*, **16**.

Williamson, N.E. 1976 *Sons or daughters? A cross-cultural survey of parental preferences.* Beverley Hills, CA: Sage Publications.

Willis, R. 1973 A new approach to the economic theory of fertility. *J. Polit. Econ.* (Suppl.), **81**.

Willis, R. 1980 The old-age security hypothesis and population growth. In: *Demographic behaviour:*

interdiscipliniary perspectives on decision-making (ed. T. Burch). Boulder, CO: Westview Press.

Willis, R. 1987 Externalities and population. In *Population growth and economic development: issues and evidence* (eds. D. Gale Johnson & R.D. Lee). Madison: University of Wisconsin Press.

Wolfe, B.L. & Behrman, J.R. 1982 Determinants of child mortality, health and nutrition in a developing country. *J. Dev. Econ.*, **11**.

Wolfe, B.L. & Behrman, J.R. 1987 How does mother's schooling affect family health,nutrition, medical care usage and household sanitation? *J. Econometrics*, **16**.

World Bank 1984, 1988, 1990, 1993 *World development report.* New York: Oxford University Press.

World Bank 1991 *The population, agriculture and environment nexus in sub-Saharan Africa.* Washington, DC: World Bank, mimeo.

NOTES

[1]   *Total fertility rate* is the number of live births a woman would expect to give were she to live through her child-bearing years and to bear children at each age in accordance with the prevailing age-specific fertility rates. The measure pertains to the number of live births, not pregnancies. To place international figures in perspective, we should observe that in western industrial countries today, total fertility rates lie between 1.5 and 1.9.

[2]   It is as well to stress that international statistics on national income and other social indicators are unreliable. (See Schultz 1992, for a critical appraisal of such data.) Not only are the methods deployed for estimating them not the same across countries, some of the estimates are not much more than interpolations among those of neighbouring countries. I am referring to them nonetheless because they are much used in public discussions, but I shall not rely on them in the remainder of the essay.

[3]   Preston and Nelson (1974) and Preston (1980, 1986) are illuminating dissections of the evidence bearing on the causes of the decline in mortality rates during the 20th century (see Preston, Keyfitz & Schoen 1972, for world tables). To me, their most striking finding from international data has been that reductions in respiratory diseases (e.g. influenza, pneumonia, and bronchitis) and infectious and parasitic diseases (e.g. tuberculosis, the diarrhoeas, whooping cough, malaria, cholera, diphtheria, measles, and typhoid) have contributed equally (about 25–30%) to this decline. (There are exceptions, of course, such as Sri Lanka.) See Dasgupta (1993) for further discussion of this.

[4]   For fertility analysis in sub-Saharan Africa and the Caribbean, however, the household is not a very useful category. See below.

[5]   However, the concept of net national product, suitably defined, takes the effect of environmental degradation on future consumption possibilities into account. On this, see Dasgupta and Mäler (1991, 1993) and Lutz (1993).

[6]   "The next step is to apply…microeconomic models (of household behaviour) to understand aggregate developments in a general equilibrium framework. But progress

in this field has been slow." (Schultz, 1988:418).

[7] The Prisoners' Dilemma is mentioned so often in the social sciences that it does not require an account here. Luce and Raiffa (1957) have a fine discussion of it.

[8] Hirschman and Guest (1990) provide an illuminating discussion of the factors underlying the demographic transition being experienced in South-East Asia.

[9] In Bangladesh, about 60% of a woman's reproductive life is spent in pregnancy or lactation. The corresponding figure in Pakistan is 50% (McGuire & Popkin 1989).

[10] By way of contrast, we should note that the maternal mortality rate in Scandinavia today is 1 per 20 000 (World Bank 1988).

[11] On this, see Gross & Underwood 1972; Kennedy 1989; Kennedy & Oniang'o 1990; Thomas 1990.

[12] This goes a little way towards explaining why the dowry system is absent.

[13] See Coale and Trussell (1974) for an attempt at constructing a measure of the extent to which members of a society consciously control their fertility.

[14] See also Blurton Jones and Sibly (1978) and Lee (1980). Child-spacing in sub-Saharan Africa is the subject of empirical inquiry in Page and Lesthaeghe (1981).

[15] See World Bank (1984, 1988). However, rather Draconian measures would appear to have been in use, and the cost has not been negligible. Hull (1990) has collated data reflecting the growing increase in the male:female sex ratio at birth in China. The 1987 One Percent Survey in China shows in addition dramatic patterns of high sex ratios for second and higher-order births. There are three possible explanations for this, all of which may be presumed to be operating: female infanticide, gender-specific abortions, and concealments of births. Tomich, Kilby and Johnston (1991) provide a fine discussion of the possibilities.

[16] In a study on international cross-section data, Pritchett (1993) suggests that a society's fertility rate is dependent mostly on household fertility desires, and not on the costs of modern contraceptives.

[17] They have investigated household consumption of nutrients (Behrman & Wolfe 1984a,b), the use of contraceptives (Cochrane 1979; Satahr & Chigambaram 1984), child health in general (Cochrane *et al.* 1980; Cochrane, Leslie & O'Hara 1982; Wolfe & Behrman 1982, 1987; Strauss 1990), infant and child survival rates (Caldwell 1979, 1986; Hobcraft, McDonald & Rutstein 1984; Mosley 1985; Mensch, Lentzner & Preston 1986; Victoria *et al.* 1986; Bourne & Walker Jr. 1991; Thomas, Strauss & Henriques

1991), and children's height (Christian *et al.* 1988; Strauss 1990; Thomas, Strauss & Henriques 1990, 1991). However, not all the studies cited here are methodologically immune to criticism. Indeed, in a few studies, endogenous variables are treated as though exogenous. Strauss (1990) has a good discussion of such failings.

[18] Here is an indication of orders of magnitude. The infant mortality rate in households in Thailand where the mother has had no education (resp. has had primary and secondary education) was found to be 122 per 1000 (resp. 39 and 19 per 1000) (Jamison & Mosley 1990).

[19] How powerful this countervailing force has proved in sub-Saharan Africa is a controversial matter, and it is possible that the increased fertility response to increased education seen in some of the data reflect aggregation biases. However, see Hess (1988) for a time–series analysis which attests to there being such an effect in parts of sub-Saharan Africa. See also Barro (1991), who analyses data from over 100 countries to show that during 1960–85 countries with a higher human capital base (as evidenced by school enrolment figures) had lower fertility rates.

[20] For illuminating empirical analyses of the determinants of fertility, see Leibenstein (1974); Easterlin (1975, 1978); Birdsall (1977, 1988); Bongaarts (1978); Preston (1978); Cochrane (1979); Freedman (1979); Easterlin (1980); Cain (1981, 1982, 1984); Bongaarts & Potter (1983); Bulatao & Lee (1983); Easterlin & Crimmins (1985).

[21] Models with this general motivation have been explored in Becker (1960, 1981); Dasgupta (1969, 1974); Mirrlees (1972); Becker & Lewis (1973); Willis (1973, 1987); Becker & Tomes (1976); Behrman, Pollak & Taubman (1982); Caldwell & Caldwell (1987, 1990); Nerlove, Razin & Sadka (1987); Barro & Becker (1989); Cigno (1991); Lee & Miller (1991); and in a powerful philosophical essay by Heyd (1992).
Note that in evolutionary biology, phenotypic costs and benefits of reproduction are important only to the extent that they are correlated with reproductive measures. Offspring in this theory are valued in terms of the end of increasing fitness. This is not the point of view in economic demography.

[22] See also Neher (1971); Nugent (1985).

[23] Preston (1978) is a useful collection of essays on the effect that have been observed on fertility rates of reductions in rates of infant mortality. We should note here that a preference for sons leads parents to discriminate against higher birth-order girl children, a not-infrequent practice in China and in the northern parts of the Indian sub-continent (Dasgupta 1993).

[24] Cooking in a poor household is a vertically integrated activity: nothing is processed to begin with. It is time-intensive.

[25] This can happen, especially if households discount the future, at a high rate.

[26] For an account of this kind of spiralling process, see Nerlove and Meyer (1991) and Dasgupta and Mäler (1991). In an interesting empirical document, World Bank (1991) has provided partial confirmation of the thesis in the context of sub-Saharan Africa.

[27] I am grateful to Sheilagh Ogilvie for this point.

[28] For the formal model being sketched here, see Becker (1960, 1981); Easterlin, Pollak & Wachter (1980); Nerlove, Razin & Sadka (1987); Cigno (1991). Birdsall (1988) provides a fine discussion of this.

[29] Stopping rules based on sex preference provide a different type of information regarding sex preference than sex ratios within a population. The reason is that in a steady-state, stopping rules have no effect on the sex ratio. To see this, suppose that in a society where sons are preferred parents continue to have children until a son is born, at which point they stop. Assume for simplicity that at each try there is a 50% chance of a son being conceived. Now imagine a large population of parents, all starting from scratch. In the first round, 50% of the parents will have sons and 50% will have daughters. The first group will now stop and the second group will try again. Of this second group, 50% will have sons and 50% will have daughters. The first sub-group will now stop and the second sub-group will have another try—and so on. At each round, however, the number of boys born equals the number of girls. The sex ratio is 1.

[30] The Prisoners' Dilemma game, alluded to in Section 3, is a model of social environment where there is dissonance between the individual and the collective levels.

[31] Instead of defining "externalities" formally, I shall provide the key illustrations directly without recourse to a definition. The reader will be able to infer what the concept amounts to.

[32] In advanced industrial countries, free education and child allowances are the counterparts.

[33] That women are vigorously engaged in agriculture may well have something to do with this.

[34] In applying such ideas about imitative behaviour as we are studying here to urban residential choice, Schelling (1978) refers to constructs such as this as "tipping models".

[35] The draconian measures employed in India during the Emergency period 1975–77

as regards sterilisation are an example of the kinds of activities governments must avoid.

36 The school year in rural United States until the beginning of this century was shorter than in urban areas, and it took account of seasonal labour requirements. I am grateful to Garry Becker for giving me an account of this.

37 Enke (1966) is a notable exploration in the value of prevented births when the worth of additional lives is based entirely on their effect on the current generation. As a simplification, he took the value of a prevented birth to be the discounted sum of the differences between an additional person's consumption and output over the person's lifetime.

Critical Factors affecting Population
Growth in Developing Countries
K. Srinivasan

ABSTRACT

The world's population is currently estimated at 5.57 billion and the last billion has been added in just 12 years. Even under assumptions of continuation of the moderate pace of declines in the fertility levels started since the seventies, in the coming years the population is projected by the UN to reach 6.26 billion by the year 2000 and 8.09 billion by 2020. Over 95% of the future additions will be in the developing countries which are already overcrowded. The recent experiences of sharp declines in the mortality and fertility levels of some of the developing countries, such as China, Thailand, and selected states in India, indicate that extrapolation of past trends into the future in this field is a risky endeavour. However, analysis of the factors associated with recent levels of infant mortality in developing countries indicate that three factors, viz. literacy rates among the females, the economic condition of the people, and the political system, are likely to play major roles, in that order, in shaping mortality trends in the coming years. In the recent past these factors have contributed to over 75% of the variation in the IMR values across the countries. Similarly, analysis of correlates of recent levels of family planning programme, contraceptive acceptance, and fertility levels indicate that the factors of lowered mortality levels, higher literacy among the females, strengthened family planning programme efforts, and the political system are expected to play significant roles in the shaping of future fertility trends in mankind. Political system seems to play a major role in the strengthening or weakening of family planning programme efforts. The Human Development Index recently proposed by the United Nations and the family planning programme efforts come out as the two most significant predictors of fertility levels in a population, explaining over 85% of the variations in recent fertility levels.

1. INTRODUCTION: THE CURRENT DEMOGRAPHIC SCENARIO

The total number of people inhabiting this planet as of July 1993 has been estimated to be 5.57 billion by the United Nations (UNFPA July 1993), with 1.23 billion (or 22.1%) living in the economically more developed countries of Europe, North America, Oceania, former Soviet Union, and Japan, and the remaining 4.34 billion (or 77.9%) living in the less developed countries. The average density of population per square kilometer of land area in 1993 is 55 in the less developed countries compared to 21 in the more developed regions. In 1950, when the total population of the globe was 2.516 billion or only 45% of its present size, the less developed countries had a lower percentage of the world's population, 66.9% or 1.684 billion people. The number of people that were added to the less developed countries since 1950, that inhabit less than 60% of the land area of the globe, is slightly more than the 1950 world's total population. Three people

181

every second or more than 250000 persons every day are added to this planet, and about 95% of this addition is occurring in developing countries. While the annual addition was 93 million at the beginning of this decade, it will increase to 100 million per year by the last year of this decade, 1999–2000, despite a moderate decline in the fertility levels of the population because of large increases in the population base of all the developing countries. There is no doubt that the world is getting to be an extremely crowded planet, getting worse in the already over crowded and less developed regions.

In terms of rates of growth, rather than numbers, presently the world's population is growing at 1.7% per year, being the difference of a birth-rate of 26 and a death rate of 9 per thousand population per year. In the more developed countries, the growth is 0.5% per year, being the difference of a birth-rate of 14 and a death rate of 9, while in the less developed region it is growing four times higher, or 2.0% per year, the difference of a birth rate of 29 and a death rate of 9 in their populations. The peak in the rate of growth of human beings has been crossed during the quinquennium 1965–70 when it was 2.1% per year, and the slow-down in the rate of growth has since commenced with China leading the pace of demographic control. China, with a population of over 1.2 billion at present, reduced her growth rate dramatically from 2.61% per year during 1965–70 to 1.23% during 1980–85. A comparative statement of the trends in the population size, birth, death, and growth rates of different regions of the world from 1950–90 is furnished in Table 1.

The United Nations has classified the nature of changes in the population growth rates in the world since the second world war into three phases: phase 1—from 1950 to 1970 when there was a rapid rise in the population growth rates, from 1.8% during 1950--55 to 2.1% during 1965–70 because of rapid reduction in the death rates of developing countries without equivalent declines in the birth rates; phase 2—from 1970 to 1980 when there was a steep decline in the growth rates because of reductions in the birth rates with a slow down in the reductions in the death rate declines; and, phase 3—from late seventies to the present when there was a stagnation in the growth rate, a trend likely to persist or even contribute to an increase in the growth rate in the future years in the developing world because of changes in the age structure of the population, when even with a decline in the fertility levels the crude birth rates may not show a change because of a proportionate rise in the number of married women in the reproductive ages. The first phase is considered as a period of 'mortality-induced' changes, the second phase as 'fertility-driven,' and the third phase as 'structural adjustment.'

Table 1 reveals that since 1950, while the growth rate in the developed countries has continued to decline from 1.28% in 1950–55 to 0.86% in 1970–75 and to 0.54% in 1985–90, the growth rates in the less developed countries rose from an already high level of 2.04% in 1950–55 to 2.38% during 1970–75 with a moderate decline subsequently to 2.11% during 1985–90. The decline in the global growth rates in the past fifteen years is largely due to sharp reductions in fertility in China. Among the continents, Africa has continued to record a rise in the growth rates since 1950 with a rate of about 3% during 1985–90. Latin America has recorded a moderate but steady decline in her growth rates during the above three periods from 2.73% during 1950–55 to 2.48% in 1970–75 and to 2.06% in 1985–90. Asia, which has 59% of the world's population, has reduced its growth

Table 1. *Trends in population size, growth, birth, and death rates since 1950 by major geographic regions*

regions	population size (in millions)			annual growth rate			crude birth rate			crude death rate		
	1950	1970	1985	1950-55	1970-75	1985-90	1950-55	1970-75	1985-90	1950-55	1970-75	1985-90
world total	2516.4	3697.8	4851.4	1.79	1.96	1.74	37.5	31.5	27.1	19.7	12.1	9.8
more developed countries	832.4	1048.9	1174.3	1.28	0.86	0.54	22.6	16.7	14.5	10.1	9.3	9.8
less developed countries	1684	2648.9	3677.1	2.04	2.38	2.11	44.6	37.1	31	24.3	13.2	9.8
by major regions												
Africa	222	361.8	552.9	2.21	2.66	2.99	49.2	46.6	44.7	26.9	19.2	14.7
eastern Africa	65	108.2	167.8	2.26	2.67	3.19	50.5	49.1	48.5	28.2	20.1	16.4
middle Africa	26.3	39.6	60.2	1.8	2.66	3.03	46.3	46.1	45.9	28.2	20.7	15.9
northern Africa	51.8	83.2	123.3	2.26	2.41	2.61	48.9	43	37	24.7	16.6	10.8
southern Africa	15.7	25.6	36.4	2.28	2.42	2.36	43.7	37.3	33.7	21	14	10.2
western Africa	63.2	105.2	165.1	2.27	2.92	3.19	50.6	49.2	48.3	28.4	21.1	16.5
Latin America	165.9	285.7	404.3	2.73	2.48	2.06	42.5	35.4	28.7	15.4	9.7	7.4
Caribbean	17.1	24.9	31.2	1.78	1.82	1.5	37.5	31.4	25.3	15.5	9.5	8
Central America	37.2	69.7	104.8	2.92	3.1	2.33	47.3	42.7	31.1	17.1	9.5	6.3
South America	111.6	161.1	268.3	2.81	2.34	2.02	41.6	33.2	28.2	14.8	9.7	7.8
North America	166.1	226.5	264.8	1.8	1.06	0.82	24.6	15.7	15	9.4	9	8.7
Asia	1377.3	2101.9	2835.2	1.89	2.27	1.87	42.9	34.8	27.8	24.1	12.4	9
eastern Asia	671.4	987	1248.8	1.75	2.11	1.34	40.8	29.4	20.1	23.3	8.5	6.7
southeastern Asia	182	286.7	401.5	1.92	2.42	2.05	44.1	37.4	29.6	24.4	14.4	8.9
southern Asia	481.4	754.5	1070.3	1.99	2.35	2.3	44.9	40.4	34.8	25.1	16.6	11.8
western Asia	42.4	73.7	114.6	2.7	2.92	2.79	47.6	40.1	36.1	23.4	13.1	8.5
Europe	392.5	459.9	492.2	0.79	0.59	0.25	19.8	15.7	12.9	11	10.4	10.7
eastern Europe	88.5	103	111.7	1.02	0.61	0.27	23.6	16.8	14.6	11.3	10.3	11.3
northern Europe	72.5	80.5	83.2	0.37	0.34	0.25	16.7	14.8	13.4	11.1	11.2	11.5
southern Europe	109	128.3	142.3	0.84	0.77	0.24	21.2	17.8	12	10.4	9.2	9.5
western Europe	122.5	148.1	155	0.83	0.55	0.24	17.6	13.7	12.2	11.4	11.1	11.1
Oceania	12.6	19.3	24.6	2.25	1.81	1.48	27.6	23.9	19.4	12.4	9.8	8.1
Australia/New Zealand	10.1	15.4	19	2.33	1.67	1.28	23.5	19.8	15.2	9.4	8.5	7.6
Melanesia	2.1	3.3	4.7	1.81	2.44	2.26	44.1	39.8	33.7	25.7	15.3	10.5
Micronesia	0.2	0.3	0.4	2.54	2.47	1.61	40.4	36.5	26.7	17.9	10.7	7.1
Polynesia	0.2	0.4	0.5	2.57	1.47	1.53	49.3	40.9	34.1	19.2	10.4	4.9
former USSR	180	242.8	277.6	1.71	0.94	0.78	26.3	18.1	18.4	9.2	8.6	10.6

rate from 2.27% in 1950–55 to 1.87% during 1985–90, which is largely attributable to China. The population growth rate in almost all the developed countries has been reduced by 50% or more since 1950.

According to the medium variant projections of the population into future years carried out by the United Nations, even with moderate declines in fertility levels in the developing countries, the population of the world is expected to be 6.261 billion by year 2000 and 8.092 billion by 2020. Table 2 gives the results of medium variant projections of population size, growth, birth, and death rates in different regions until 2020. The share of the developing countries will increase to 79.8% by 2000 and to 83% by 2020. Because of the persistence of relatively high rates of growth in her population, the share of Africa in the world's population will increase from the existing 12% to 18% in 2020. The populations in Europe, especially in southern and western Europe, will be experiencing negative growth rates by the end of the next decade. Table 2 also reveals that the crude death rates in the developed world are expected to increase in the coming decades because of the ageing of the population and continued declines in their fertility levels. For example, according to UN projections, the crude death rates of Europe and North America are projected to be 11.5 and 9.9 during the period 2020–25 compared to 7 in Africa and Latin America and 7.2 in Asia. While the structural effects will operate in the direction of raising the birth rates in the developing world, they will work in the opposite direction in the developed world. The demographic effects of the structural changes in the age distributions of the population are expected to play a crucial role in the coming decades.

Globally, the annual growth rate is expected to decline to 1.5% and 1.0% per year during 2000–2005 and 2020–2025, with the birth rates declining to 22.9 and 17.5 and the death rates to 8.2 and 7.6 during these two periods. Without any major cataclysmic events pushing up the mortality to very high levels in the world, even in the context of a moderate to substantial reduction in the fertility levels of the population, a continuous further rise in population can be expected and a global size of about 8.5 billion by the year 2025 seems unavoidable. Even to contain the future size to this limit, the total fertility rate of the less developed regions has to be brought down from the present level of 3.7 children per woman to 2.3 during 2020–2025 and the maximum reduction has to occur in Africa from a TFR of 6.1 in 1990–1991 to 3.0 during 2020–2025. In this context, it is worth analysing the factors that have contributed to the substantial reductions in the fertility and mortality levels of the population in developing countries during the past four decades and the lessons they hold for policy and programme implications for the future.

2. MORTALITY TRENDS AND ASSOCIATED FACTORS

Mortality levels have been declining rapidly everywhere in the world during the past four decades, and at an historically unprecedented pace in some countries such as China, Brazil, Mexico, Sri Lanka, and Kerala State in India. Table 3 presents the levels of expectation of life at birth and infant mortality rates in broad geographic regions and countries with over 100 million population, since 1950.

China increased her life expectancy from 40.8 years in 1950–55 to 69.4 in 1985–90, India from 38.7 to 57.9, Indonesia from 37.5 to 60.2 years during the same period. Brazil

Table 2. *Projections in population size, growth, birth, and death rates 1990 to 2020 by major geographic regions, under medium variant assumptions by the UN*

regions	population size (in millions)			annual growth rate			crude birth rate			crude death rate		
	1990	2000	2020	1990-95	2000-05	2020-25	1990-95	2000-05	2020-25	1990-95	2000-05	2020-25
world total	5292	6261	8092	1.73	1.47	0.99	26.4	22.9	17.5	9.2	8.2	7.6
more developed countries	1206	1264	1342	0.48	0.38	0.18	13.9	13.1	11.9	9.6	9.7	10.6
less developed countries	4086	4997	6750	2.08	1.74	1.15	30	25.3	18.6	9.1	7.8	7.1
					by major regions							
Africa	642	867	1452	3.02	2.89	1.9	43.5	39.5	26	13.2	10.6	7
eastern Africa	197	274	488	3.3	3.21	2.12	47.9	43.5	28.3	14.6	11.6	7.1
middle Africa	70	96	172	3.13	3.15	2.2	45.6	43.1	29	14.5	11.6	6.9
northern Africa	141	179	257	2.5	2.16	1.33	34.3	28.9	19.3	9.4	7.3	6
southern Africa	41	51	75	2.32	2.12	1.37	32.2	28.4	19.9	9	7.2	6.2
western Africa	194	267	460	3.21	3.1	1.95	46.9	43.1	26.9	15	12.1	7.5
Latin America	448	538	716	1.91	1.62	1.12	26.8	23.1	18.4	7	6.5	7
Caribbean	34	39	48	1.4	1.2	0.95	24.1	21	18.4	7.7	7.2	7.8
central America	118	145	200	2.19	1.83	1.26	28.8	24.5	19.1	5.8	5.3	6
South America	296	354	468	1.86	1.57	1.07	26.2	22.8	18.2	7.4	6.9	7.4
North America	276	295	326	0.71	0.55	0.34	13.9	12.6	11.7	8.7	8.8	9.9
Asia	3113	3713	4700	1.84	1.43	0.89	26.9	21.7	16.1	8.4	7.4	7.2
eastern Asia	1335	1510	1701	1.31	0.79	0.42	19.8	14.7	12.6	6.6	6.8	8.4
southeastern Asia	445	535	691	1.94	1.51	0.99	27.5	22	16.7	8.1	6.8	6.8
southern Asia	1201	1496	2044	2.28	1.91	1.12	33.5	27.5	18	10.6	8.4	6.7
western Asia	132	172	264	2.75	2.39	1.7	34.4	29.7	22.1	7.4	6	5.1
Europe	498	510	516	0.23	0.15	-0.05	12.8	11.9	10.9	10.6	10.6	11.5
eastern Europe	113	117	122	0.29	0.3	0.12	13.7	13.6	12.1	10.8	10.6	10.8
northern Europe	84	86	88	0.24	0.14	0.03	13.4	11.9	11.4	11.2	10.7	11.2
southern Europe	145	148	149	0.26	0.16	-0.11	12.3	11.8	10.4	9.7	10.2	11.4
western Europe	157	159	157	0.17	0.03	-0.17	12.1	10.7	10.2	10.8	10.9	12.2
Oceania	26	30	37	1.36	1.13	0.76	18.6	16.9	14	8	7.8	8.3
Australia/New Zealand	20	23	26	1.12	0.89	0.59	14.5	13.3	11.9	7.7	8	9.1
Melanesia	5	7	9	2.21	1.91	1.26	32.2	27.4	19.4	9.5	7.8	6.3
Micronesia	0.4	0.4	1	1.51	1.4	0.69	25.1	23.3	16.5	6.5	5.8	6.1
Polynesia	0.6	0.6	1	1.34	1.03	0.48	31.1	26.6	18.8	4.8	4.8	5.2
former USSR	289	308	344	0.68	0.61	0.47	16.7	15.7	14.1	9.9	9.6	9.4

has experienced an increase of about 14 years in her life expectancy in the above period. While in the developed countries as a whole the life expectancy increased from 66 to 74 years, in the developing world it rose from 42.2 to 61.4 years. The differential in the longevity of human beings across the globe has narrowed down considerably during the past four decades.

Similarly, the infant mortality rates have declined sharply in the developing world from a high of 180 during 1950–55 to 78 during 1985–90, while in the developed world the decline was from 56 to 15 in the same period. The reduction in China, again, has been most impressive from 195 to 32 in the same period. The infant mortality rate in the United States of America during 1950–55 was 28, and expectation of life 69 years, levels that are comparable to conditions in China 35 years later with an IMR of 32 and life expectancy of 69.4 years during 1985–90. However, the standard of living as measured by per capita energy consumption in kilograms of oil equivalent was 6500 in 1960 in the USA compared to 598 in China in 1990. China, with less than one tenth of the standard of living in the developed world, has been able to achieve similar levels of life expectancy and infant mortality that prevailed in the developed world. Similar experiences have been recorded within the past three decades in Sri Lanka, Mexico, Republic of Korea, Taiwan, Thailand, the state of Kerala in India, and a number of other smaller countries.

A host of synergistic factors seem to have contributed to such sharp declines in the mortality levels of developing countries in the past three decades. These include: organised programmes of public health and social welfare initiated by many of the governments in the developing countries soon after getting their political independence from the colonial powers in the fifties and early sixties; investments in education making primary education compulsory in many countries; improvements in the status of women through better education, employment opportunities, and their involvement in decision-making processes at all levels; and, most importantly, the concerted efforts of international organisations and bilateral donor agencies in the control of common communicable diseases such as smallpox, cholera, plague, malaria, tetanus, and other infectious diseases. These diseases, that for centuries in the past were taking heavy tolls of human life and suffering in developing countries, were almost eradicated by the combined effects of medical, epidemiological, and organisational interventions.

It has also been hypothesised that the political system by which the country is governed, especially the extent of liberal democracy prevailing in the country, could also contribute to effective welfare and public health measures undertaken by the governments and, hence, on the mortality levels. If the country is governed by a group of leaders elected through a democratic process by the people themselves and are answerable to them through a legislative or elected body of people's representatives, and if there is a viable opposition to the ruling party that can take over control of the government smoothly through an electoral process in case the ruling group is not able to discharge its responsibilities, then in such situations one can expect the governments to be more interested in meeting the basic needs of the people in terms of nutrition, public health and medical services, housing, sanitation—those factors that contribute to lowered infant mortality and increased longevity.

An understanding of the extent to which the three major factors—viz. extent of liberal

Table 3. *Trends in selected mortality measures since 1950 by broad geographic regions and for 10 most populous countries*

region/country	population in millions (1990)	expectation of life at birth			infant mortality rate		
		1950-55	1970-75	1985-90	1950-55	1970-75	1985-90
world total	5292	47.5	58.5	63.9	155	93	70
more developed regions	1206	66	71.1	74	56	22	15
less developed regions	4086	42.2	55.2	61.4	180	105	78
regions							
Africa	642	37.7	45.9	52	188	137	103
Latin America	448	51.9	61.3	66.7	126	81	54
North America	276	69	71.5	75.6	29	18	10
Asia	3113	42	56	62.7	181	99	72
Europe	498	65.8	71.5	74.4	62	24	13
Oceania	26	60.8	66.5	71.3	68	41	26
former USSR	289	64.1	68.6	70	73	26	24
large countries							
China	1139	40.8	63.2	69.4	195	61	32
India	853	38.7	50.3	57.9	190	135	99
former USSR countries	289	64.1	68.6	70	73	26	24
USA	249	69	71.3	75.5	28	18	10
Indonesia	184	37.5	49.3	60.2	160	114	75
Brazil	150	51	59.8	64.9	135	91	63
Japan	123	63.9	73.3	78.3	51	12	5
Pakistan	123	38.9	49	56.5	190	140	109
Bangladesh	116	36.6	44.9	50.7	180	140	119
Nigeria	109	36.5	44.5	50.5	207	135	105

democracy prevalent in the political system governing the country, the standards of living of the people, and the levels of female literacy—have influenced the mortality levels in recent years can be expected to be useful in predicting the course of mortality in the future and in shaping appropriate policies and programmes. Towards this purpose, a cross-national analysis was undertaken with the most recent data available at the country level on the following variables:

2.1.1 A measure of *liberal democracy* recently developed by Bollen (1993) in which he has scored each country from 0 to 100, with 0 assigned for a country with no liberal democracy and 100 representing countries with the maximum level of liberal democracy, as defined by the author. After an extensive analysis of the existing literature on the topic and other scales available for the measurement of liberal democracy, Bollen constructed his score as a simple equally weighted average of three scores: Banks' political opposition variable, Gastil's political rights measure, and Banks' legislative effectiveness measure. This score was available for most of the countries for 1980 and is denoted by variable X_1 in this analysis. (For details on this scoring procedure, see his paper.)

2.1.2 The *standard of living* of people in a country as indicated by the energy consumption (from all sources) per capita, measured in terms of kilograms of oil equivalent. Data were compiled on this variable from the recent publication of the World Bank for 1990 or during 1985–90 (World Development Report 1992) for as many countries for which data were available and denoted by variable X_2.

2.1.3 The percentage of *literate females* in the countries around 1985 as published by the United Nations (Human Development Report 1991), denoted by variable X_3.

2.1.4 The level of *infant mortality* rate during 1985–90 as published by the United Nations, denoted by Y_1 as the dependent variable.

Data on all the above four variables were available for 81 developing countries with a population of a million or more. (The data sheet is not provided here but can be supplied by the author on request.) Among the developing countries, the infant mortality rate varied from a minimum of 8 to a maximum of 172; the liberal democracy score varied from 0 to 100; the energy consumption per capita from close to 0 to 10 874; and the female literacy rate from 9% to 99%. A multiple regression analysis using a linear model relating the IMR with the other three variables yielded the following results:

$$Y = 147.61 - 0.201*(X_1) - 0.008*(X_2) - 1.047*(X_3) \tag{1}$$

$N = 81$ and R-squared = 0.755 and, while the regression coefficient for X_1 is significant at 5% level, the other two are significant at 1% level.

The above equation indicates that even holding constant the political system and the macroeconomic conditions of the population, a 1% increase in female literacy rate reduces the infant mortality rate by one point and all the three factors work in an additive manner in reducing the infant mortality levels. The standardised regression coefficients

Table 4. *Trends in selected fertility measures since 1950 by broad geographic regions and for 10 most populous countries*

region/country	population in millions (1990)	total fertility rate			net reproduction rate		
		1950-55	1970-75	1985-90	1950-55	1970-75	1985-90
world total	5292	5	4.46	3.45	1.65	1.74	1.43
more developed regions	1206	2.84	2.2	1.89	1.27	1.03	0.9
less developed regions	4086	6.19	5.41	3.94	1.86	2.04	1.6
regions							
Africa	642	6.62	6.24	1.91	2.22	2.3	1.58
Latin America	448	5.87	4.99	3.55	2.15	2.09	0.87
North America	276	3.47	1.97	1.81	1.61	0.95	
Asia	3113	5.06	3.48	1.78	1.94	1.44	
Europe	498	2.19	1.72	1.13	1.02	0.82	
Oceania	26	3.21	2.51	1.58	1.41	1.14	
former USSR	289	2.82	2.44	2.38	1.28	1.12	1.11
large countries							
China	1139	4.76	2.45	1.89	2.04	1.11	1.11
India	853	5.43	4.3	1.63	1.85	1.67	
former USSR countries	289	2.82	2.44	2.38	1.28	1.12	
USA	249	1.97	1.83	1.6	0.93	0.88	1.44
Indonesia	184	5.49	5.1	3.48	1.56	1.76	
Brazil	150	4.7	3.46	2.27	1.95	1.52	
Japan	123	2.07	1.68	1.19	0.98	0.81	
Pakistan	123	7	6.5	1.83	2.4	2.5	
Bangladesh	116	6.66	7.02	5.53	1.94	2.27	1.95

that give the relative importance of the three predictor variables in reducing IMR is as follows:

$$Y = -0.142*(X_1) - 0.221*(X_2) - 0.705*(X_3) \tag{2}$$

The standardised regression coefficient of female literacy is the highest among the predictor variables considered, next is energy consumption, and the third is the political system. Thus, female literacy seems to be the cutting edge of reductions in infant mortality levels even after controlling for the political system and the macro-economic conditions.

3. FERTILITY AND FAMILY PLANNING TRENDS AND ASSOCIATED FACTORS

The declines in the fertility levels that have occurred in the population of the developing countries during the past three decade are no less impressive, though the declining trend started a decade or two later depending on the country. Table 4 furnishes data on the trends in total fertility and net reproduction rates for the major regions of the world as well as the large countries with over 100 million people in 1990. In the world as a whole, the TFR has declined from 5 children per woman during 1950–55 to 3.45 during 1985–90 (or 31%) and in developing countries the decline has been higher from 6.19 to 3.94 (or 36%), though starting with a higher base. However, because of equally high reductions in the mortality levels of the population, the percentage decline in the net reproduction rate (NRR) of the population in the developing world is significantly less than in the developed world during the same period, 14% (from 1.86 to 1.6) in the former compared to 29% (from 1.27 in 1950–55 to 0.9 in 1985–90) in the latter. In other words, the long term implications of the small declines in fertility in the developed world are far more significant to these countries than the declines in the developing countries. Among the geographic regions, during this 35-year period there has been practically no decline in the fertility levels in Africa (6%). In other areas the declines in the TFR values have been substantial: 48% in North America; 41% in Asia; 40% in Latin America; 34% in Europe and Oceania; and 16% in the former USSR. In terms of declines in NRR values, North America is experiencing 'below the replacement level' of fertility since 1970, and Europe since 1975. The developing countries are continuing to grow well above replacement levels of fertility.

Among the ten large countries with over 100 million people in 1990, the two developed countries, USA and Japan, are having below replacement levels of fertility since 1970, with TFR values of 1.83 and 1.68 during 1985–90. The declines in the fertility levels of China are unprecedented in history with the TFR declining from 6.24 in 1950–55 to 2.45 in 1985–90 (or 61%). The next in order of percentage decline is Brazil (44%), Indonesia (37%), India (28%), and Bangladesh (17%). There has been no decline in the fertility levels of Pakistan during this 35 year period, and the fertility levels in Nigeria have actually recorded an increase. The fertility levels in the former USSR have declined by about 16%.

One of the major driving forces underlying the fertility decline in the developing countries is the launching by many of these countries of national programmes of family planning during the above period. India was the first country to have an official population policy to curtail its birth rate and launched an official programme of family planning as early as 1952 as a part of its first five year development plan, 1951–56. The sixties witnessed

Table 5. *Government position on population growth and interventions in developing countries with over a million population, circa 1989*

		growth rate too high		growth rate satisfactory	growth rate too low		total
		intervention to lower rate	no direct intervention		intervention to raise rate	no direct intervention	
(1)	sub-Saharan Africa						
	no. of countries	15	7	15	1	1	39
	population (million)	264.6	120.9	169.7	1.3	2.4	558.9
	percentage	47.3	21.6	30.4	0.3	0.4	100
(2)	Latin America/Caribbean						
	no. of countries	11	–	9	1	2	23
	population (million)	162.3	–	253.3	3.1	40.9	459.6
	percentage	35.3	–	55.1	0.7	8.9	100
(3)	Middle East/North Africa						
	no. of countries	5	1	6	4	–	16
	population (million)	174.3	4.3	92.4	39.4	–	310.5
	percentage	56.1	1.4	29.8	12.7	–	100
(4)	Asia						
	no. of countries	8	1	8	3	1	21
	population (million)	2400.8	19.2	451.1	35.7	1.6	2908.4
	percentage	82.5	0.7	15.5	1.2	0.1	100
	total						
	no. of countries	39	9	38	9	4	99
	population (million)	3002.0	144.4	966.5	79.5	44.9	4237.3
	% to all over	70.8	3.4	22.8	1.9	1.1	100

Source: (i) Family Planning and Child Survival Programs-As assessed in 1991 (Ross *et al.* 1992);
(ii) Population as estimated for mid-1992 by the United Nations, Population Division. 1985.

country after country in the developing world formulate population policies and initiate national programmes of family planning.

According to a United Nations survey of governments, as of 1989, out of 99 developing countries each with a population of 1 million or more and with a combined population of 4.24 billion, 48 countries with a total population of 3.15 billion (or 74%) considered their population growth rates to be 'too high,' and 39 of these countries with a total population of 3.00 billion (or 71% of the population of the developing countries) have also initiated family planning programme as public intervention measures to lower their fertility levels. In Asia, out of 21 developing countries with a combined population of 2.91 billion, 9 countries with a total population of 2.42 billion (83% of the population) live under governments that have public intervention programme. These nine countries include the two population giants of the world: China and India. Even some of the countries of Asia such as Indonesia, Philippines, Thailand, and Vietnam, which have very recently (since 1989) considered their population growth rates as satisfactory, have family planning programmes to control their fertility levels. Table 5 provides a distribution of the 99 countries according to their positions on population growth and family planning programme implementation in different regions of the world. It is evident that national programmes of family planning have come to stay as a part of the developmental strategies of the developing countries.

Partly as a consequence of these family planning programmes and partly as a result of the various other developmental efforts initiated by the governments of the developing countries with a view to industrialising and modernising their economies since the sixties, the use of modern methods of contraception have increased dramatically during the past three decades. As of 1990, it has been estimated that over half of the married women in the reproductive ages in the developing world (51%) have been protected by a modern method of contraception compared to less than 15% protected during 1960–65. In terms of actual number of couples using contraception, the increase has been from about 60 million women in the early sixties to 360 million in 1990, a six-fold rise.

The increase in contraceptive use has been the highest in East Asia, from 17% to 70%, followed by Latin America where the increase was from 11% to 60%, and the lowest was in sub-Saharan Africa with a rise from 5% to 9% during 1960–65 to 1990.

3.1 A model of the influence of selected predictors of contraceptive use

A precise assessment of the contribution of various developmental factors and family planning programme efforts towards such sharp increases in contraceptive use and reductions in the fertility levels of the population through a cross national data analysis is a difficult endeavour. The socio-economic, cultural, and political conditions as well as implementation of family planning programmes vary enormously not only from country to country but also within a country, and within country variations are ignored in any cross-national analysis. However, the relative importance of the contribution of selected developmental variables and family planning programme efforts and the manner of their influence on contraceptive use and fertility decline can be investigated through a multiple regression analysis using a path model. The model that we used is given on the following page (Figure 1).

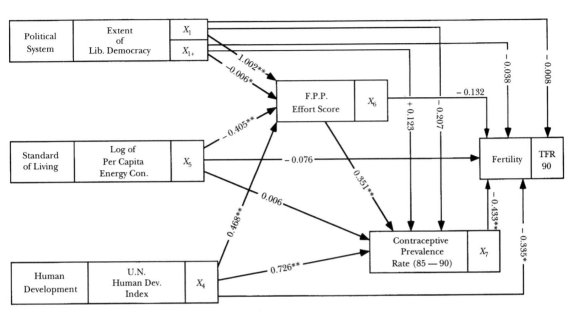

Figure 1. Path diagram relating selected predictors with contraceptive use and fertility (1990).

In the above model we assume that the political system of the country and the level of development of the people will influence the extent and intensity of family planning programme efforts in the country and these will in turn influence the contraceptive use and fertility levels in the population. The operationalisation of the variables was as follows (and see Table 6):

3.1.1 The *political system* was measured by the score on the extent of liberal democracy prevailing in the country (constructed by Bollen, described above in the mortality analysis) by variable (X_1). Since the relationship of this variable with family planning effort was curvilinear, a second degree term of this variable (X_{1+}) was also used. The data available pertains to the year 1980.

3.1.2 The *index of human development*, proposed recently by the United Nations and on which data are published from 1990, is used in this analysis. The HDI developed by the UN attempts to measure the quality of life of people in terms of their longevity, adult literacy levels, school enrolment ratios of children, and per capita income. Among these variables higher weight is given to expectation of life and education than per capita income. Income is considered to contribute to the quality of life only up to a level beyond which there is a diminishing return with regard to its contribution to quality. Scores on the logarithm of per capita income, expectation of life at birth, and education (which combines adult literacy and school enrolment ratios of children) are combined into a single score that ranges from 0 to 1. This index gives a lesser weight to income than to health and education. Since declines in mortality and rises in literacy levels are considered to be important determinants of fertility, the index of HDI captures the essence of development as it influences fertility levels in developing countries. The values published by the UN for 1990, multiplied by 1000, were used in this analysis as variable (X_4).

Another index of development used in our analysis is a pure macro-economic indicator of the standard of living of people in a country measured by the per capita *energy consumption* in kilograms of oil equivalent mentioned earlier. Since the variation across countries in this index was substantial, we used the logarithm of per capita energy consumption for the year 1990 as variable (X_5).

3.1.3 The strength of *family planning effort* in each country was measured by the programme effort scores developed originally by Lapham-Mauldin in 1982 – and using which data were collected by Mauldin and Ross in 1990–91 for assessing the strength of family planning programmes in 93 developing countries around the year 1989. The index is based on opinions about various programme components for each country compiled by the authors through a questionnaire sent to four to six scholars knowledgeable about the country's programme. The questionnaire was structured to compile information on the respondent's opinion on 30 specific programme items, and on each item the scoring was done on a five point scale, 0 to 4, 0 indicating a very low programme strength and 4 the highest among the countries. These 30 items included four aspects of a family planning programme:
   a. policy and stage-setting activities (8 items)
   b. service and service-related activities (13 items)
   c. record keeping and evaluation activities (3 items)
   d. availability and accessibility of fertility control methods (6 items).
The 1989 scores for the available countries expressed as percentage of the total maximum score (120) was used as variable (X_6) in this analysis.

3.1.4 The data on the *contraceptive prevalence rate* (CPR) by any method, traditional or modern, for the latest available year during the period 1985–90 and published by the UNFPA were used as variable (X_7) in this analysis.

3.1.5 The fertility measure used as the ultimate dependant variable in this analysis is the *total fertility rate* for the year 1990 published from the United Nations sources by the Population Reference Bureau in their World Population Data Sheet in 1992. This is denoted by the variable (Z).

Using the path model specified above, the regression equations relating X_6, X_7, and Z with other predictors and using standardised variables are as follows:
$$X_6 = 1.002*(X_1) - 0.006*(X_{1+}) - 0.405*(X_5) + 0.468*(X_4) \qquad (3)$$
$N = 90$; R-squared = 0.374 and all the regression coefficients other than for (X_{1+}) are significant at 1% level and of (X_{1+}) is significant at 5% level. It has to be noted that 63%

Table 6. *Direct and indirect effects of selected variables on contraception and fertility level in 1990*

predictors		programme effort (X₆) DIR	IND	TOT	CPR (all methods) (X₇) DIR	IND	TOT	TFR 1990 (Z) DIR	IND	TOT
(X₇)	CPR	NU	NU	NU	NU	NU	NU	−0.433**	NU	−0.433**
(X₆)	PR.effort	NU	NU	NU	0.351**	NU	0.351	−0.132	−0.152	−0.284
(X₄)	H.D.I.	0.468**	NU	0.468	0.726**	0.164	0.890	−0.335*	−0.447*	−0.782**
(X₅)	LOG.energy	−0.405**	NU	−0.405	0.006	−0.142	−0.136	−0.076	0.112	0.036
(X₁₊)	Sq. Boll. score	−0.576*	NU	−0.576	0.123	−0.202	−0.079	−0.038	0.110	0.072
(X₁)	Boll. score	1.002**	NU	1.002	−0.207	0.352	0.145	−0.008	−0.195	−0.203
	R-squared	0.374			0.856			0.846		

NU: variable not used nor relevant

NOTE: *Indicates significance at 5% level.
         **Indicates significance at 1% level.

of the variance in the programme effort score cannot be explained by the above factors.

$$X_7 = -0.207*(X_1) + 0.123*(X_{1+}) + 0.006*(X_5) + 0.726*(X_4) + 0.351*(X_6) \quad (4)$$

R-squared = 0.856 which is highly significant; only the regression coefficients of family planning effort (X_6) and HDI (X_4) are statistically significant at 1% level, others are not. Similarly,

$$Z = -0.008*(X_1) - 0.038*(X_{1+}) - 0.132*(X_6) - 0.076*(X_5) - 0.335*(X_4) - 0.433*(X_7)$$
$$(5)$$

R-squared = 0.846, highly significant, and only the regression coefficients of contraceptive prevalence (X_7) and HDI (X_5) are statistically significant.

The magnitude and significance of the path coefficients are also indicated in the path diagram above.

3.2 Direct and indirect effects of predictors on contraceptive use and fertility levels

The direct and indirect effects of the various predictors can be computed from the path coefficients and are given in Table 6. From the table the following conclusions can be drawn:

(a) The political system variable, measuring the extent of liberal democracy prevailing in the country, significantly and positively influences the family planning effort score in a curvilinear manner.

(b) The Human Development Index (HDI) significantly and positively influences the programme effort scores.

(c) The macro-economic condition of the country, measured by the log of per capita energy consumption, significantly influences the programme effort score, but negatively. This suggests that under relative economic backwardness of their populations, governments in developing countries are likely to strengthen their efforts in the family planning front.

(d) The variables that have the maximum direct and significant effect on contraceptive use are: family planning effort score and the Human Development Index. Assessed in terms of their standardised regression coefficients, the latter has double the effect as family planning effort score.

(e) The indirect effect of the Human Development Index on contraceptive use through programme effort score is also highly positive and statistically significant.

(f) With regard to their direct effects on fertility, only the level of contraceptive use and the Human Development Index are strongly and negatively significant. All the other predictor variables considered, the family planning programme effort score, the energy consumption per capita, the political system have no statistically significant relationship. It is surprising that the effect of family planning programme on fertility is direct and through the increased use of contraception, while the Human Development Index seems to have strong significant impact on fertility even after controlling for the effects of contraceptive use, implying that its effects on fertility also operate through the other proximate determinants of fertility (for example, rise in age at marriage, induced abortions).

(g) The indirect effect of HDI on fertility is strongly negative and significant

(– 0.447) and is the highest of all the effects, direct as well as indirect, considered in this analysis. Its effect is higher in magnitude than even the direct effects of contraceptive use. This implies that the quality of human life as measured by the components of expectation of life, adult literacy levels, school enrolment ratios of children, and provision of minimum income to people to survive above poverty lines, are the major driving forces behind successful family planning programme efforts, contraceptive use, and fertility levels. Family planning programmes serve mainly as instruments in the realisation of the fertility goals of a population, and the goals seem to be largely determined by the political system and the level of human development in the population. Similarly, the political system also seems to exert a strong influence on fertility indirectly through its ability to strengthen or weaken the family planning programme.

ACKNOWLEDGMENT

The author wishes to record his thanks to Dr. Amy Ong Tsui, Project Director, The EVALUATION Project, Carolina Population Center, The University of North Carolina at Chapel Hill, for making available the Project facilities for the preparation of the paper and acknowledges the excellent assistance in word processing by Mrs. Aline Christenoff.

REFERENCES

Bollen, K. 1993 (Jan.) Liberal democracy: validity and method factors in cross-National measures. University of North Carolina, Chapel Hill: National Science Foundation.

Donaldson, P. J. & Ong Tsui, A. 1990 The international family planning movement. Washington, DC: Population Reference Bureau Vol. 45, No. 3, November.

The Johns Hopkins University 1992 The reproductive revolution: new survey findings. Population Reports Series M, No. 11. Baltimore.

Mauldin, W. P. & Ross, J.A. 1991 Family planning programs: efforts and results, 1982–89. Population Council Working Paper, No. 69. New York: The Population Council.

Population Reference Bureau 1992 Population data sheet 1992. Washington, DC: PRB.

Ross, J. A. *et al.* 1992. Family planning and child survival programs: as assessed in 1991. New York: The Population Council.

United Nations. 1991 World population prospects (Estimates and projections as assessed in 1990). New York: Population Division, United Nations.

United Nations Development Program 1990 Human development report, 1990. New York: Oxford University Press. pp 128–129.

United Nations Population Fund 1993 Population issues: briefing kit 1993. New York: UNFPA.

World Bank 1992 World development report 1992: development and the environment. Oxford University Press.

3/3

The Role of Women
in relation to the Environment
Lydia P. Makhubu

ABSTRACT

Over the centuries, and in all societies, a separation of roles for men and women has existed and formed the basis for social organization and helped foster social stability and cohesion. Women's traditional roles engage them in food production, provision of energy, water and other basic needs for their families and communities. All these activities are heavily dependent on the utilization of the environment. Through their close relationship with children they also play a critical role in social education and consequently in transmitting values and norms from generation to generation. They are key agents for the preservation of culture and promoters of social transformation. These roles constitute a strong potential for women to contribute to all aspects of environmental management and protection, and to the successful implementation of strategies for sustainable development.

This paper attempts to highlight positive aspects of women's roles and makes recommendations for the construction of a plan of action which will take into account women's strengths and pave the way for their greater involvement in environment and development at the leadership and research levels. This is seen as a critical means of strengthening and building capacities in environmental management and protection in developing countries.

1. INTRODUCTION

The environment has become a major global concern following the publication of scientific evidence on the depletion of the ozone layer and consequent global warming, with their potential for hazardous effects on many aspects of human life. The vigorous national and regional preparations preceding the United Nations Conference on Environment and Development, held in Brazil in June 1992, and the subsequent involvement of the nations in that historic conference, reflect the extent of concern and commitment by all nations to changing future approaches to environmental protection and management.

Agenda 21 (United Nations, 1992), the action plan which emanated from the conference, is an international blueprint acknowledging the link between the environment and development, and highlighting the concept of sustainable development as the guideline to be followed by developing and developed countries alike. *Agenda 21* also acknowledges the complexity of environmental issues and emphasizes the need to involve the responses of a wide range of participants: governmental and non-governmental agencies, and the general public from all levels of society.

There is a particular challenge here for universities, scientific academies and learned societies, with their dual obligation of extending the frontiers of knowledge, and imparting this knowledge and a concomitant sense of responsibility in our future leaders.

The management of the environment and natural resources is recognized as an inter-sectoral and inter-disciplinary effort which demands co-operation between those engaged in high-level scientific research and those involved in grassroots activities. It may be concluded, therefore, that because of the multiplicity of actors and the complexity of the drama which engages them, it is essential to analyze carefully each one's role in order to frame appropriate interventions in support of the different actions.

Developed and developing countries share common environmental concerns but have different priorities, reflecting different stages of socio-economic development. While developed countries are mainly preoccupied with environmental protection and the effects of the by-products of industrialization on the biosphere, developing countries are focusing on the use of the environment to provide basic needs for their increasing populations. The common factor however is that development, whether high technology driven or basic needs driven, feeds on the environment. The problems are manifold but whatever they are, people are at the centre as both perpetrators of degradation and as inheritors of the problems. And half of these people are women. In fact the concepts of environment and sustainable development which are now gaining momentum are part of a belated reaction emerging long after serious environmental degradation has already occurred. The challenge to find ways of reducing poverty and protecting the environment is huge but an economist as eminent as the President of the World Bank thinks it is feasible:

> The positive links between promoting income growth, reducing poverty and protecting the environment must be vigorously pursued. Policies which make economic sense as well as environmental sense are the most important positive links. For example ... promoting the role of women, so often the principal managers of resources... (Preston 1992)

This paper addresses the role of Third World women in relation to the environment and focuses on ways to develop their capacities and expertise in education, and in research in environment and sustainable development. This is seen not merely as a matter of equity but as a crucial means of building and strengthening scientific capacities in developing countries by mobilizing a group whose perceptions of the problems may add new dimensions and enhance ongoing efforts to find solutions. The paper will first address the traditional roles of women, and then consider the new roles they should play, and conclude with some suggestions for future action.

2. TRADITIONAL ROLES OF WOMEN

Over the centuries and in all societies, a separation of roles for men and women has existed and formed the basis for social organization and cohesion. Women's traditional roles confine them close to the family and engage them in the provision of food, energy and water and in the general physical sustenance of families and communities.

In this role they are involved in the tillage of the soil, in harvesting fruits and fuel from forests and in the search for and maintenance of water resources. Their role remains critical in the physical usage of the environment to meet society's basic needs and there is no doubt that they have accumulated a wealth of knowledge based on their experience.

By their close association with young children women also play an important role in social education and in transmitting values and norms from generation to generation. They are key agents for the preservation of culture, and, conversely can also be the promoters of social change – an important prerequisite for many aspects of sustainable development.

Women's traditional roles are clearly critical, multifaceted and central. While this is readily acknowledged in all relevant international debates and conferences, most of their recommendations lack sufficient specificity to facilitate activities which would allow women to make an impact. There is also a tendency for such recommendations to make a basic assumption that women are one homogenous group whose activities are anchored at the grassroots levels. In fact, third world women do not all have the same experiences of domesticity and subordination (Afshar 1991). It is important to recognize that women professionals in education, in science and technology, women in politics and in many other spheres, all possess untapped and varied potential which society cannot afford to neglect.

While grassroots activities are very important indeed it is essential to promote women's entry into the higher echelons of decision and policy-making and thus enable them to promote fuller participation of other women in a variety of enterprises. "... the female majority (in all its diversity) should be central, not peripheral, to development theory and practice." (de Groot 1991). There is particularly urgent need for this promotion in the fields of science and technology. Their traditional roles constitute a strong potential for women to contribute to the physical management of the environment and to creating long-term social awareness of environmental and development issues in general. It may be argued that this is a dimension which women are uniquely able to add to the search for answers to the challenges of the environment and sustainable development. It is the translation of their traditional roles into contemporary activities that will enable women to make an effective contribution to environmental protection.

The traditional knowledge of the environment which women have accumulated over centuries is often highlighted as the strongest female potential contribution to the solution of environmental problems. Recently there has been a commendable effort on the part of a few researchers to codify and assess this indigenous system of knowledge (Osunade 1992; Richards 1985). Such work needs to be replicated and extended and the results disseminated to potential users on a large scale. It is also essential that women should take an active part in every aspect of such an exercise. This is highlighted in chapter 24 of *Agenda 21*, which recommends that women researchers should become actively involved in the generation and dissemination of information on the environment (United Nations 1992). The under-representation of women in science and technology is singled out as a serious drawback to women's engagement in action-oriented research. In this context education and training of women become key factors for their empowerment with knowledge and skills to enable them to render an effective contribution to the debate on the environment. The traditional role of women provides a springboard for their entry into modern scientific activities, as the following analysis will indicate.

3. NEW ROLES
3.1 Women in pre-primary and primary education

Women are traditionally educators and this has translated well into modern formal education. Available statistics (Table 1) show that in many countries, developed and developing, women make a substantial contribution to the teaching force and form the majority of teachers at the pre-primary and primary levels of education. As teachers of the young, who will inherit the earth from the present generation, they are strategically placed to cultivate appropriate attitudes towards the environment and its sustainable use. The initial training of pre-primary and primary teachers as well as their continuing in-service training are important means of empowering women teachers to assist in the implementation of concepts of the environment and sustainable development. The

Table 1. *Percentage female representation among teachers at pre-school, primary and secondary levels for selected countries (UNESCO Statistical Yearbook, 1991)*

country	% females among pre-school teachers	% females among primary school teachers	% females among secondary school teachers
Austria	100	81	58
Bangladesh	18	18	10
Bolivia	80	59	48
Botswana	—	78	40
Cameroon	100	30	20
Cuba	90	78	55
Egypt	97	53	40
Ethiopia	—	23	10
France	96	71	—
Iran	100	51	40
Iraq	100	69	55
Italy	—	90	69
Kenya	100	36	30
Korea	86	49	35
Lesotho	—	80	51
Mauritius	98	45	41
Morocco	15	35	29
Niger	100	32	18
Oman	100	46	42
Panama	100	63	54
Senegal	76	26	16
Seychelles	100	82	39
Swaziland	100	78	48
United Kingdom	100	78	52

international scientific community must involve itself with basic education in developing countries and take a lead in making recommendations for the design of appropriate curricula and materials in environmental education for teachers and pupils.

The influence of women as educators goes beyond the concern with the physical environment to issues of social development such as population control, especially in the way these affect their female students. Reports indicate that the mother's education is perhaps the single most important determinant of a family's health and nutrition and that education enhances agricultural productivity and brings about a marked improvement in the management of natural resources. Even a few years of primary education have been shown to lower women's fertility and the rate of infant mortality (World Bank, 1989). This again emphasizes the need for mechanisms to facilitate the translation of women's traditional activities to contemporary formal programmes which address major and complicated subjects such as the environment and population.

Table 2. *Female enrolment as percentage of total enrolment in first degree courses, selected fields and selected countries, in 1989*
(UNESCO Statistical Yearbook, 1991)

country	natural science	maths computer	medical	engineering	agriculture	home economics	education
Austria	38	24	**53**	7	43	**85**	**65**
Bangladesh	17	16	28	3	8	**100**	35
Burkino Faso	14	4	19	–	9	–	7
Cuba	**63**	49	**62**	35	45	–	**67**
Egypt	37	**62**	47	14	33	**80**	48
El Salvador	**58**	–	17	11	6	**98**	**62**
Ethiopia	7	8	8	5	6	†34	9
Ghana	15	12	22	2	11	‡**80**	21
Iran	35	28	**61**	6	7	–	42
Jordan	48	–	**55**	24	44	–	**53**
Kenya	15	–	22	4	23	**99**	44
Korea	30	28	35	3	20	**96**	57
Madagascar	41	17	45	15	35	–	36
Mexico	**54**	40	**53**	15	21	–	**64**
Niger	6	–	26	4	6	–	28
Sweden	**50**	22	**61**	20	**52**	**94**	**74**
Zambia	14	–	28	1	7	–	23
Zimbabwe	18	–	25	1	15	–	19

Bold type denotes the cases (27 out of 110) where female enrolment equals or exceeds that for male students.

† denotes diploma level students

‡ denotes diploma and degree level students combined

3.2 Women in science education

Around the world, from Norway to Australia to Botswana (Sjøberg & Imsen 1988; Kahle 1988; Duncan 1989) and for several decades writers have been lamenting the under- representation of women in science and technology – the "missing half" as one researcher puts it (Kelly 1981). In many developing countries the situation is particularly serious. This is attributed to socio-cultural factors which hinder their participation at the lower levels of education and consequently at the university level. From the data in Table 2 it is clear that female enrolment in university science courses is much too low in developing countries. Women lag behind and yet science education is a prerequisite for involvement in scientific activities, including the wise management of the environment. It must be added that it is not just science education which is of concern. Other statistics show that women are behind generally in access to education and training in many developing countries (Haddad 1990). This combined with high illiteracy rates among women, a common feature of many countries (op. cit.), places women at a serious disadvantage with respect to the application of modern techniques to the solution of environmental and other developmental problems.

A close examination of Table 2 shows interesting trends in the selection of disciplines by female students at the undergraduate level. An almost 100% female enrolment in Home Economics in all institutions offering this subject is recorded, with Ethiopia being a stunning exception. As might be expected, Education is another female stronghold. Women have made notable inroads into the medical fields in many parts of the world and they are also quite well represented in Agriculture, a development of their traditional roles as providers and carers. There is need for research to establish the trends of female enrolments in the new areas of biotechnology and computer science. Women engineers remain a very rare breed but when the overwhelming problems of the third world are considered, it would seem that women are showing strengths in fields of close relevance to these problems, including the environment.

3.3 Third world women in science

The Third World Organization for Women in Science (TWOWS) was formed in 1989 under the auspices of the Third World Academy of Sciences (TWAS). Its overall objective is to promote the participation of Third World women scientists in the scientific development of their countries. One of TWOWS achievements has been the compilation of an inventory of its members indicating their areas of specializations and their current research interests. Information from this inventory has been used to compile Table 3 and Figure 1. Women's disciplinary choices are clear, the bio-medical sciences and chemical sciences predominate, with a fair representation from Agriculture. The data in Tables 2 and 3 indicate a possibility for developing activities on environmental management and protection based on women's disciplinary inclinations and research skills. This could be designed to link grassroots activities and high-level research and to combine the natural sciences and other disciplines relevant to environmental issues. The TWOWS proposed programme for 1993–1997 has made this a particular focus, laying emphasis on interdisciplinary research teams.

Table 3. *TWOWS Membership by Geographical Region and Discipline (TWOWS Inventory of Members, 1992)*

region and number of countries represented		agriculture	biological & medical	chemistry	engineering	earth sciences	mathematics	physics	totals
Caribbean	(6)	3	18	4	3	0	6	5	39
Near & Middle East	(8)	3	17	7	19	0	2	13	61
Africa – North	(4)	29	34	37	11	3	1	9	124
Africa – Southern & Eastern	(14)	5	42	12	6	4	5	5	79
Africa – West	(11)	11	128	23	5	6	5	7	185
Latin America	(13)	7	74	11	11	4	10	31	148
South Asia & Pacific	(14)	15	140	44	14	5	17	64	299
Totals: 70 countries		73	453	138	69	22	46	134	935

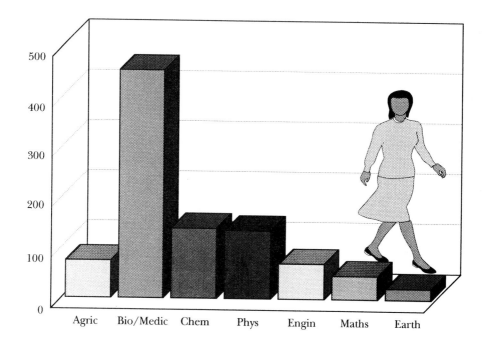

Figure 1. Female scientists by discipline (TWOWS Membership).

3.4 Women in leadership roles

The improvement in female enrolment in science may be small but it is to be welcomed and must be supported. There remains, however, the problem of the very poor representation of women in the upper echelons of international science and technology. Data on women in university faculties of science (Table 4 and Figure 2) show the grim situation around the world. There is clearly a need for programmes designed to assist the promotion of women in science. Some are already in progress in many parts of the developing world; they target women in education, science and technology, some of which are highlighted in the suggestions for future action outlined below.

4. SUGGESTIONS FOR FUTURE ACTION
4.1 Support for basic education

The basic education of girls deserves special attention since it is a prerequisite for their progress to higher levels and is also important in building a population that is receptive to new ideas and amenable to social change. Scientific societies and learned societies have a special role to play in the design of materials, on subjects such as the environment, for teacher training colleges and schools. The complexity of issues and interrelationships in environmental management and protection call for informed interventions in the education of children and the young inheritors of the earth.

Table 4. *University staff (expatriate and local), in science-related faculties, by rank and gender (Commonwealth Universities Yearbook, 1992)*

university/faculty		professors		senior lecturers		lecturers	
		male	female	male	female	male	female
Dar-es-Salaam	medicine	34	0	30	11	39	3
	engineering	14	0	11	0	27	1
	all science	16	3	27	4	28	2
Ghana (Legon)	medicine	16	1	20	2	34	14
(Kumasi)	engineering	3	0	10	0	49	2
(Legon)	all science	17	0	20	3	31	8
Hong Kong	medicine	18	4	49	12	58	24
	engineering	8	0	28	1	53	0
	all science	10	0	29	1	47	2
Ibadan	medicine	33	4	45	16	44	18
	engineering	4	0	17	0	18	1
	all science	39	1	23	5	37	5
Malaya	medicine	15	3	54	21	86	50
	engineering	4	0	23	2	35	0
	all science	14	0	86	9	60	21
Nairobi	medicine	39	2	49	11	94	27
	engineering	7	0	18	0	42	0
	all science	27	0	25	4	47	6
Singapore	medicine	84	15	56	11	56	15
	engineering	45	0	90	3	45	2
	all science	61	5	59	6	71	10
Sri Lanka	medicine	10	3	23	11	5	4
(Peradeniya)	engineering	6	0	21	0	26	3
	all science	23	3	29	9	18	5
Swaziland	medicine	–	–	–	–	–	–
	engineering	–	–	–	–	–	–
	all science	2	1	12	0	13	7
West Indies	medicine	13	2	25	6	30	24
	engineering	10	0	17	0	30	4
	all science	4	0	24	3	23	6
Zimbabwe	medicine	10	2	22	4	51	19
	engineering	8	0	10	0	31	4
	all science	7	0	21	2	58	10

all sciences = biological sciences, chemistry, computer science, geography, geology, mathematics & physics

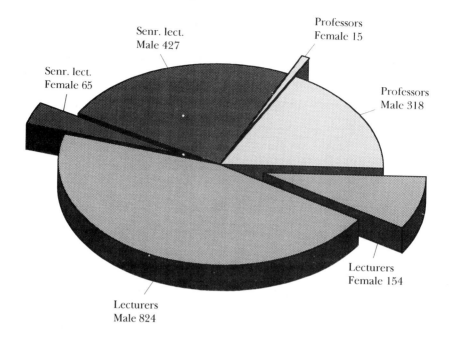

Figure 2. Science staff by rank and gender in ten African universities (Botswana, Ghana, Ibadan, Lesotho, Malawi, Nairobi, Swaziland, Tanzania, Zambia, Zimbabwe).

4.2 Support for girls in science education

The poor enrolment of girls in science at the lower levels of education lays the foundation for their under-representation in university faculties of science and thus in scientific research and leadership. There is need to support programmes that target female education, such as the African Academy of Sciences (AAS) programme on Research Priorities for the Education of Girls and Women in Africa. Such a programme should be supported and strengthened to provide special focus on science education for girls.

4.3 Supporting women in scientific research and leadership

The formation of special programmes and organizations for women always elicits lively debate on the wisdom of such action in view of the expressed desire to bring women into the mainstream of international scientific activities. This is a valid concern but when the poor involvement of women in such activities is examined, special action is clearly justified.

The Third World Organization for Women in Science (TWOWS), as already mentioned above, was formed to address this problem and to promote women in scientific research and decision-making. Scientific academies might consider undertaking collaborative ventures with TWOWS and thus directly supporting women scientists in the third world. There is wide scope for involving women scientists in research on the environment and in the dissemination of information to all levels of society.

For example, research into women's traditional knowledge of the environment and its compilation could constitute an important project for TWOWS to undertake, linking women practitioners and scientists. Women scientists of the Third World are already involved in environment-related disciplines, and research in this area could become a major programme.

Many women scientists work in isolation and sometimes have to interrupt their work for family responsibilities; in an endeavour to counteract this, TWOWS is encouraging the formation of research teams among its members. This approach lends itself to collaboration between the natural and social sciences, an essential ingredient in research which touches upon the human condition; environmental research is clearly in this category. This initiative deserves support as a good example of the multifaceted dimension which women are able to bring to the debate on the environment.

In conclusion, it must be emphasized that although the above discussion has focused on ways to enhance the participation of professional women, the important contribution of all women is acknowledged. The creation of scientific leadership and research capability among women, however is a priority and is seen as a means to facilitate their entry into the mainstream of international efforts to address environmental concerns.

The place we are prepared to accord to women affects not only the society in which we live but also the one we are trying to build.

REFERENCES

Afshar, H. (ed.) 1991 *Women, development and survival in the third world.* London, UK: Longman.

Commonwealth Universities Year Book, 1992.

De Groot, J. 1991 Conceptions and misconceptions: the historical and cultural context of discussion on women and development. In *Women, development and survival in the third world* (ed. H. Afshar). London, UK: Longman, pp. 107-138.

Duncan, W.A. 1989 *Engendering school learning: science, attitudes and achievement among girls and boys in Botswana.* Institute of International Education, University of Stockholm.

Haddad, W.D., Colletta, N.J., Fisher, N. *et al.* 1990 *Meeting basic learning needs: a vision for the 1990s.* World Conference on Education for All, pp. 124-135.

Kahle, J.B. 1988 Gender and science education II. In *Development and dilemmas in science education* (ed. P. Fensham). London, UK: Falmer Press, pp. 249-256.

Kelly, A. (ed.) 1981 *The missing half,* Manchester University Press.

Osunade, M.A.A. 1992 Soils and the small farmers of Swaziland. *UNISWA Res. J.,* **6**, 71-82.

Preston, L.T. 1992 Reducing poverty and protecting the environment. Address to United Nations Conference on Environment and Development. Washington, DC: World Bank.

Richards, P. 1985 *Indigenous Agricultural Revolution.* London, UK: Hutchinson.

Sjøberg, S. & Imsen, G. 1988 Gender and science education I. In *Development and dilemmas in science education* (ed. P. Fensham). London, UK: Falmer Press, pp. 218-248.

United Nations 1992 *Agenda 21* Report of the UN Conference on Environment and Development, Rio de Janeiro, 3-14 June 1992.

TWOWS Inventory of Members, 1992 (membership < 1000).

UNESCO Statistical Year Book, 1991.

World Bank 1989 *Sub-Saharan Africa: from crisis to sustainable growth.* Washington, DC: World Bank, p. 79.

3/4

Population Policy and Family Planning Programmes: Contributions from a Focus on Women
Mayra Buvinić

ABSTRACT

In 1970, Ester Boserup, a noted population and development scholar, provided the conceptual and empirical framework for women's issues in development (WID). Despite this genesis from population and development studies, only recently have these two fields been 'reunited' after having gone their separate ways during the 1970s and 1980s. Today, a dialogue between researchers of women's issues in development—as well as those doing advocacy on behalf of women—and the population community is being re-established.

This paper adds to the dialogue by focusing on women in the understanding of population dynamics and the design of family planning programmes. It uses recent findings regarding women's poverty and work in developing countries to shed light on the appropriateness of two contradictory population policies: one that promotes employment opportunities for women to reduce fertility versus one that keeps women at home to ensure child welfare. The increasing feminisation of both poverty and low-paid work supports the argument for increasing economic opportunities for poor women.

Evidence indicates that women invest in their children's welfare even when resources are meagre. Social and economic factors that increase poor women's work and economic responsibilities can foster the perpetuation of poverty from mothers to their children, in the absence of effective development policies targeted specifically at poor women. These factors include changes in fathers' traditional responsibilities towards children, and declining household incomes during economic crisis, as well as the unintended consequences of social and economic policies such as structural adjustment programmes and child-centred policies.

The paper concludes by recommending complementary policies that 'protect' poor women by increasing their productivity in home and market production and their earnings. It also suggests that the findings on women's poverty offer additional insights to the design of population policies and family planning programmes.

1. TWO CONTRADICTORY POLICIES

Population and family planning researchers were among the first to study women in the context of social and economic development. They preceded the scholarship on women in development studies (WID) by at least a decade, and focused on women because of the growing awareness of a world population problem in the 1960s. The objective was to identify the determinants of fertility in developing countries and understand the factors that led to the use of modern contraception. A series of studies were launched on the relationship between women's labour force participation and fertility, as well as on women's knowledge, attitudes and practices regarding modern contraception (the KAP studies on family planning programmes). Two contradictory policy recommendations emerged from these studies: the first, based on a presumed inverse work—fertility relationship, was to promote employment and income-earning opportunities for women in developing countries in order to reduce fertility. An opposite recommendation emerged as a result of a corollary inverse work–child welfare relationship; this was to keep women at home in order to promote child welfare and reduce child mortality.

These two contradictory policies have coexisted side by side in policymaking pronouncements regarding women in development and in project interventions. For instance, the first time the World Bank made an explicit reference to women was in the context of a 1977 population speech, which called for expanding poor women's earning options in order to 'delay marriage, increase intervals between childbearing episodes, and foster sensible decisions about childbearing' (World Bank 1981). Since the 1960s, this affirmative (although not widely-implemented) policy statement has coexisted alongside child-centred policies promoted by the Bank and other international agencies— policies which require intensive maternal time inputs at home and, in theory at least, preclude women from devoting time to market work. Evidence from WID research helps to address the dilemma created by these contradictory policies.

The population research community's interest in studying women was an important genesis for women in development (WID) studies. In 1970, Ester Boserup, a noted development and population scholar, published *Woman's Role in Economic Development*, widely recognised as providing the conceptual framework and the analytical tools to study women's participation in development. The WID framework is different from the one used in population studies in two fundamental ways. First, it balances a heavy emphasis on women's traditional reproductive and motherhood roles with an appreciation of women's functions as economic producers and contributors, both in terms of home and market production. Second, the WID framework considers women's well-being as a development objective. The awareness that women's welfare can be separated from children's welfare, and that policies should strive to maximise women's welfare, can substantially alter the content of development and population studies and policies and their implementation.

The emphasis on women's individual rights and well-being has re-oriented the studies on family planning. The early KAP studies were designed to find out how much women knew about, liked or practised family planning. The new studies centre on the reproductive health needs of women including, but not limited to, contraception; how family planning programmes respond to women's needs and rights; and their consequences in women's lives (Dixon-Mueller 1993). Although perhaps less articulate, the WID emphasis on women's economic roles has made substantial contributions to the understanding of population policies and the design of family planning programmes. This paper reviews these latter WID contributions and highlights knowledge from research on women's poverty in developing countries. Throughout, the paper uses the term women in development (WID) studies in recognition that the main focus of research to date has been to document the conditions of women. However, because these studies analyse sex and gender differences WID knowledge is progressively generating information regarding men's roles in development. This information is helping to re-orient family planning studies and programmes to include men's roles in parenting and family planning.

2. AN INVERSE EMPLOYMENT–FERTILITY RELATIONSHIP?

Based on factors associated with the demographic transition in industrialised countries, population researchers focused their early studies in developing countries on investigating a presumed inverse relationship between female labour force participation and fertility behaviour. A predominant sociological explanation for this inverse relationship is role incompatibility, where employment and child-rearing take place in separate locations and compete directly for women's limited resources of time and energy (Mason & Palan 1981). A complementary explanation from the economic theories of fertility is that as a woman's potential wages increase, the higher the costs of raising children become because women forego more money when time is devoted to childbearing. The maternal role incompatibility hypothesis highlighted the critical interrelationships between women's productive and reproductive lives. These economic theories of fertility provide valuable insights and analytical tools for the study of the value of women's economic contributions in home production and the opportunity costs of women's time. The economic model of the rational household provides a framework in which to examine the trade-offs between time spent on child care, time spent in the labour force, and other uses of women's time (DaVanzo & Lee 1983; Mueller 1982).

The WID-guided empirical research has demonstrated that the relationship between women's work outside the home and fertility is much more complex than originally anticipated, and that a number of variables mediate the relationship, alter the hypotheses and modify the outcomes. Key intervening factors are the structure of economic opportunities for women and households, as well as poor women's lack of access to family planning services (Mason 1987; Lloyd 1991). This empirical research has implicitly underscored the importance of a poverty-oriented focus when studying women's productive and reproductive lives in developing countries.

In industrialised countries it is well established that women's employment is positively correlated with lower birth rates, especially when women in low income groups are excluded (Blake 1965; Oppenheimer 1970). In developing countries, however, the situation is ambiguous and often contradictory, in part because there is less conflict between women's roles as workers and mothers (Standing 1978; Youssef 1982). Research in Malaysia has shown that role incompatibility is often normatively rather than spatially or temporally based, and that the opportunity structure available to households is an important mediating factor in the work—fertility relationship (Mason & Palan 1981). The household's dependence on individual earnings versus joint ventures, on women's versus children's earnings, as well as the importance households assign to children's formal schooling, mediate and alter the work–fertility relationship. This study also yields contradictory evidence in the form of a positive employment–fertility relationship among Indian wives in the rubber estates of Malaysia, who work when additional income is needed as a result of a birth. A recent review of World Fertility Survey (WFS) data, that includes information on women's work before and after marriage, points out that the variability in findings among countries and within countries is a function of the opportunity structures available to women within and without households. Few women are in modern sector employment and, for the majority of women in mixed, transitional and traditional occupations, the work–fertility relationship varies over the life cycle, and with the type of occupation and earnings (Lloyd1991).

The explanations provided by both models—maternal role incompatibility and the rising costs of children models—are based on the assumptions that mothers always take care of children; that fathers economically support children; and that parents live together over the life cycle of the family. Research has shown, instead, that the social arrangements of families in developing countries are highly variable and often opposite to these assumptions. Parents often live separately, and even when they live together, child fostering can occur (Lloyd & Gage-Brandon 1992; Lloyd 1993). Fathers' support of children is variable; the burden of childrearing outside marriage may be shared with siblings, family members, co-residential members, and/or hired help (Lloyd 1993; Buvinić & Gupta 1994; Desai & Jain 1992).

The empirical findings, therefore, highlight the importance of a focus both on the structure of opportunities for women and on family and residential arrangements in explaining the work–fertility relationship; they also show that, under certain circumstances, the cause–effect relationship hypothesised by the early population studies can be reversed: that is, women may need to work to support their children rather than needing to stop work in order to have children (Anker *et al.* 1982). Unfortunately, the cross-sectional surveys that have been used to gather information on population variables, such as the WFS, are ill-equipped to disentangle the direction of causation. A further contribution from a focus on WID is the utilisation of longitudinal methods that can provide a narrative for events in women's lives and determine cause–effect relationships.

Because more reliable and valid measures of women's work and wage rates are required, because there is a need for longitudinal studies to track causality, and because there are so many intervening individual, family and community/institutional factors in the work–fertility relationship, some scholars have questioned the utility of pursuing further work in this area (Schultz 1988; Cleland *et al.* 1987). Continuing to invest in research in this area can yield valuable information about women and how they balance responsibilities in their lives. From a policy perspective, however, further research investments seem less justified, and this is because of independent evidence on women's poverty and the intergenerational transmission of poverty in mother–child pairs. This evidence makes a case for *targeted* policies which increase the economic opportunities of poor women, *regardless* of their impact on fertility behaviour.

3. THE FEMINISATION OF POVERTY

The feminisation of poverty, linked closely to the rise of poor households headed by women, is a well-documented trend in the USA (Ross & Sawhill 1976; Garfinkel & McLanahan 1986). A similar trend in developing countries is neither well-recognised nor accurately documented. For instance, the *World Development Report* on poverty is sympathetic to the plight of poor women, but concludes that there is not enough evidence to assert changes in the composition of poverty groups by sex, and only mentions in passing the large numbers of single-mother households among the poor (World Bank

1990). There is still a reluctance to acknowledge that women may be worse-off than men among the poor in developing countries, linked to a resistance in recognising variability in family forms and in parental responsibility for children. However, two indicators suggest that women's share of poverty in developing countries has increased to a greater extent than men's; they are IFAD's estimates of rural poverty and evidence on the economic situation of women who head households.

3.1 The poverty of rural women

The last decade has not been kind to the poor. The economic crisis of the early 1980s wiped out gains the developing countries had achieved in the 1970s in terms of improvements in living conditions. The recovery from the crisis has been slow at best. According to World Bank estimates, the head count index of poverty (that is, the estimated proportion of the population consuming less than $32 per person per month at 1985 purchasing prices) increased between 1985 and 1990 in sub-Saharan Africa, the Middle East, northern Africa, Latin America and the Caribbean (World Bank 1993). A recent IFAD study of the extent of rural poverty in developing countries, calculated on the basis of 41 countries with data which account for 84% of the total rural population of 114 developing countries, shows that since the mid-1960s the absolute number and proportion of women among the rural poor have increased. Table 1 shows calculations (based on the IFAD estimates) which establish the percentage growth in the number of the rural poor by sex. The table shows that the total number of rural women living below the poverty line in developing countries increased between 1965 and 1988 by 47%, while the total number of rural men living below the poverty line increased by only 30%. That is, while in 1965–1970 women comprised 57% of the rural poor, by 1988 they formed 60% of the rural poor (Jazairy *et al.* 1992). IFAD explains the worsening of poverty among rural women: first, the explicit gender biases in the allocation of productive services and resources, such as rural credit and land allocations; second, the drop in agricultural production and the increased degradation of the environment (related to population pressures) that result in increases in women's work burdens; and third, family disintegration, male desertion and male migration and an increase in single motherhood that result in a rise in households headed by women (Jazairy *et al.* 1992).

Table 1. *Total number of rural people living below poverty line[1] Source: Jaiziry, I., Alamgir, M. & Panuccio, T. 1992* The state of world rural poverty: an inquiry into its causes and consequences, *pp. 405,422–423 New York University Press.*

	1965–70	1988	% change
women	383,673	564,000	47.0
men	288,832	375,481	30.0
total	672,505	939,481	39.7

[1]Calculated on the basis of 41 countries with data which account for 84% of the total rural population of 114 developing countries. Estimates are in millions.

3.2 The poverty of woman-headed households

While comparable statistics for various countries over time are not available, it is widely agreed that the percentage of households headed by women and of families maintained by women has risen in both developing and industrialised countries (Folbre 1991). The percentage of households headed by women varies from 10–20% in some South and South-East Asian countries to about 40% in some African and Caribbean countries. Table 2 compiles recent statistics on the percentage of households headed by women in a selection of countries. Additional evidence shows that these households are overrepresented among the poor. In a recent review of 61 empirical studies that examined the relationship of female headship to poverty, 38 established that woman-headed households were poorer than male-headed households. Fifteen other studies found that poverty was associated with certain types of female heads, or that the association emerged for certain poverty indicators (Buvinić & Gupta 1994). Figure 1 presents data gathered in the mid-1980s for five cities in Latin America. The figure shows that, with the exception of Bogota—where there was a greater proportion of woman-headed households in the total population than among the lower income groups—woman-headed households were over-represented in the lower income groups in the other four cities examined.

The evidence suggests three sets of factors that determine the greater poverty of woman-headed households.

First, woman-headed households, despite their smaller size in comparison to other types of households, often carry a higher dependency burden—a higher ratio of non-workers to workers—than do other households. This type of household composition would not necessarily lead to poverty if the household received child support payments from absent fathers. The poverty of woman-headed households thus reflects a disruption of traditional systems of family governance that used to enforce income transfers from fathers to children (Folbre 1991).

Second, the main earners of woman-headed families are, by definition, women who have lower average earnings than men, fewer assets and less access to remunerative jobs and productive resources such as land, capital and technology. For example, an analysis of the earnings of household heads in Belo Horizonte, Brazil revealed that the less remunerative jobs open to women in the labour market (rather than sex disparities in education) explained most of the differentials in earnings between male and female heads. Of the female heads, 53% held low-paid jobs in the informal sector, but only 30% of the male heads did so (Merrick & Schmink 1983). In rural areas of Botswana, the mean yearly income including transfers is 903 Rand for men-headed households and only 433 Rand for female-headed ones. These rural households headed by women in Botswana are poorer than those headed by men because they have less land, fewer oxen to use for ploughing and less access to other productive resources, such as farm technology and agricultural extension (Koussudji & Mueller 1983).

Third, there may be an independent effect of female headship on household economic vulnerability that cannot be reduced to the characteristics of women or of the household. Women who are heads of households also have to fulfil home production and domestic roles. Therefore, they face greater time and mobility constraints than male heads, which can result in an apparent 'preference' for working fewer hours for pay, for choosing

Table 2. *Percentage of households headed by women in 1980s in selected countries. Sources: United Nations (1, 2, 4, 6, 8, 12) 1991* The world's women: trends and statistics 1970–1990, *pp. 26–29. New York: United Nations.*

1.	Botswana	45
2.	Barbados	45
3.	Jamaica	42
4.	Malawi	29
5.	Cuba	28
6.	Ghana	27
7.	Venezuela	22
8.	Honduras	22
9.	Chile	20
10.	Bangladesh	17
11.	S. Korea	15
12.	Indonesia	14

Folbre, N. (5, 7, 10, 11) 1990 Mothers on their own: policy issues for developing countries, pp.48-49. Paper prepared for the joint ICRW/Population Council series on the Determinants and Consequences of Female-Headed Households.

CASEN (9) 1990 A survey of national socioeconomic characteristics conducted by the Ministry of Planning in collaboration with the Department of Economics, University of Chile.

Louat, F., Grosh, M.E. & van der Gaag, J. (3) 1992 Welfare implications of female headship in Jamaican households, p.7. Paper presented at International Food Policy Research Institute workshop on intrahousehold resource allocation: Policy issues and research methods. Washington, DC, Feb 12-14, 1992.

lower paying jobs that are more compatible with child care, and for spending more for certain services such as water and housing, because they cannot contribute time to offset transaction costs. Women who head households may also encounter discrimination in access to jobs or resources beyond that which they encounter because of their sex, or may make inappropriate choices that affect the household's economic welfare because of social or economic pressures. Female heads may also have a history of premature parenthood and family instability that tends to perpetuate poverty in succeeding generations. Premature lone parenthood is an increasing phenomenon in developing countries, especially in Latin America and in sub-Saharan Africa (Singh & Wulf 1990; PRB 1992). There is emerging evidence in some developing countries and a plethora of studies in the USA that show that early sexual experience and early childbearing, as well as low educational attainment and remaining unmarried, are key links in the intergenerational transmission of poverty between mothers and their children (Furstenberg *et al.* 1987; Buvinić *et al.* 1992).

4. THE FEMINISATION OF LOW-PAID WORK

The factors associated both with the poverty of rural women and the poverty of woman-

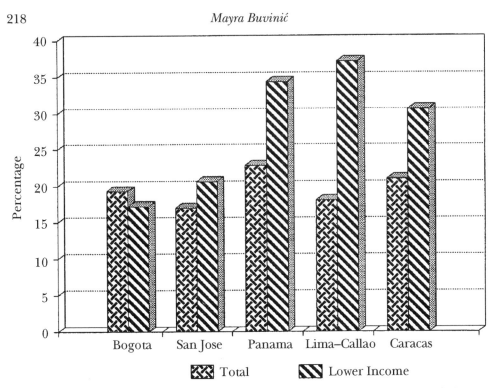

Figure 1. Percentage of woman-headed households among all households in selected cities, by class. Source: United Nations 1984 *La Mujer en el sector Popular Urbano: América Latine y el Carike*, p. 246. Santiago, Chile: UN.

headed households underscore poor women's work burdens and economic responsibilities. The feminisation of poverty goes hand-in-hand with increased work burdens for women that exacerbate women's and children's deprivation and poverty. The characteristics of women's poverty argue for targeted interventions rather than universal programmes to help all women.

4.1 Gender differences in the allocation of work

Time-use analyses explore the trade-offs women make between childcare, labour force participation and leisure (Ho 1979). These poverty-oriented studies have yielded valuable evidence on the invisible economic contributions of poor women to home production as well as on gender differences in the way poor families allocate labour and respond or adjust to external demands:

1. Poor women tend to work longer hours and have less leisure time than poor men (Leslie 1988).
2. When these working hours are assigned an economic value and added to the household's cash income, the contribution of women and children to the income of a poor household can be greater than that of men (King & Evenson 1983).
3. Unlike the evidence from industrialised societies which shows a trade-off

between market work and childcare, evidence from developing countries indicates that when poor women enter the workforce, it is leisure time rather than home production time that is reduced (Popkin 1983).

4. As in industrialised countries, women and children in developing countries must adapt to increasing household burdens such as additional children or declining household income, but men's roles tend to resist change, for example in their allocation of time between home and market production and leisure (King & Evenson 1983).

In summary, the evidence shows that poor women in developing countries have both home and market production roles, and that the poorer the household, the more burdensome both roles become. WID studies have included the time women spend in unpaid community management work as a separate category (Moser 1993; Commonwealth Secretariat 1991). It has been found that women's community work increased in order to compensate for the decreasing provision of governmental services in poor communities, associated with structural adjustment programmes (SAPs). Documentation of this female 'added worker' effect include the community kitchens in Peru that were set up and run by poor women (Francke 1992) and the volunteer work of women who provided community services in Guayaquil, Ecuador in the early 1980s (Moser 1993). The Guayaquil study followed women over a decade and revealed that the allocation, rather than the amount, of women's work time changed as the result of the cut-backs in government services associated with SAP: women increased time allocated to productive and community activities at the expense of home activities, with costs for themselves and their children. It can be further assumed that women have compensated for the reduction in government health service delivery by increasing their time in the provision of primary health care activities (Leslie *et al.* 1988). A recent analysis of the anticipated impact of SAPs in African agriculture argues that the shift from non-tradeables to tradeables in agriculture imposes more work on women, who have to provide free labour in men's farms, without having control over the returns of their labour (Palmer 1991).

This flexibility in the allocation of women's time to the multiple roles of home, market, community and health worker in response to external demands on the family, such as SAPs, is a unique gender feature in poor families, one that differentiates poor women from their better-off counterparts, and one that suggests key mechanisms and points for intervention in the transmission of poverty from mothers to children. The Guayaquil study reveals that women who are 'coping' or 'hanging on' in response to the additional work burdens imposed by SAP are in stable partner relations or have female sources of support in the family. Women who instead are 'burnt out' and unable to cope are most likely to be heads of household and have handed over reproductive responsibilities to older daughters who, therefore, have to drop out of school, insuring the perpetuation of poverty from one generation of women to another (Moser 1993). The analysis of African agriculture under SAPs predicts that the increased work burdens of women could lead to a new crisis of poverty, keeping poor households in a high-mortality and high-fertility frame while agricultural incomes rise (Palmer 1991).

The evidence on women's work patterns also suggests that, especially for the poorest women, additional children can be associated with high costs in time as well as in health, and questions the conventional wisdom of the value of children for poor families. While it has been argued that the more arduous women's work is, the greater the economic value of children to mothers (Oppong 1983), it is also possible that the demand for additional children is a consequence of men imposing their preferences on women, the less powerful members of the family, who bear the burden or assume most of the costs for additional children because of their disadvantaged position in the home (Sen 1992). Divergent views by men and women on the demand for children have been mentioned in the recent literature, although the evidence to support contrasting views is still lacking (Bruce 1989b).

Lastly, data on time allocation indicate that increasing the productivity of poor women's work is central to reducing the vulnerability of women and families to external shocks. An evaluation study in Quito, Ecuador, on the effects of a credit programme on microentrepreneurs illustrates gender differences in the value of time for the poor. One of the major impacts of credit was to raise the productivity of women-owned firms by increasing earnings and reducing the amount of time women spent in the business, from an average of about ten hours a day, six days a week, to an average of about nine and one-half hours daily. This credit effect happened only for women-owned and not for men-owned firms (men increased earnings but did not reduce time spent at work), stressing the importance that women themselves assign to reducing their long market work hours (Buvinić, Berger & Jaramillo 1990).

4.2 Women's participation in low-wage work

While the true economic contribution made by women in developing countries may be the same, the pattern of women's work has certainly changed over time. A number of social and economic forces have motivated greater numbers of women everywhere to seek paid work or engage in income generation activities in formal or informal labour markets. The proportion of women officially recorded as being part of the paid labour force in developing countries grew from 28% in 1950 to 32% in 1985 (Sivard 1985). The real numbers are probably much higher. Two recent trends help to explain women's growing participation in low-paid, unprotected and often undocumented work in developing countries. The world-wide economic crisis of the early 1980s motivated low-income women to seek paid work in order to compensate for real declines in household income, and the export promotion policies that have been in vogue since the mid 1980s in a majority of countries in the south—as part or independent of SAPs—have increased the demand for low-paid women workers.

There are historical precedents for families' increased reliance on women's wages during economic recessions. During the Great Depression of 1929–32 in the USA, women secondary workers took up available marginal and part-time jobs available while unemployed men searched for higher-wage jobs. The proportion of gainfully employed women rose, while the unemployment rate among women decreased and that of men increased during the height of the depression (Humphries 1988). A similar change was observed in industrialised countries during the 1974–75 world recession: female labour force participation rates increased in 11 out of 15 OECD countries and female

Table 3. *Feminization of work in developing countries in the 1980s. Source: Standing, G. 1989 Global feminization through flexible labor. In* World development *17(7), pp. 1082.*

	activity rates	
	type of change	%
women	increased	69
	decreased	8
	no change	22
	total	99
men	increased	36
	decreased	33
	no change	31
	total	100

unemployment declined (OECD 1976). Data on this 'added worker' effect—that is, the voluntary entrance of females into the paid work force to increase family income—is available for a number of Latin American countries in the 1970s and the 1980s. A common problem with the data is the separation of cyclical effects related to economic downturns from the secular rise in female labour participation rates that may confound the effects or prevent the rising trend from reverting back to its pre-recession stage at the end of the cycle. Data for Chile during the 1974–75 economic crisis is perhaps the most clear in illustrating the 'added worker' effect of the recession without a confounding rising secular female participation trend: despite a trend toward long-term declines in women's labour force participation, women's activity rates in the lowest quintiles of the household income distribution increased sharply, from 18% to 22.4%. The reverse happened with women in the upper quintiles of the household income distribution, and both trends reverted back to their pre-crisis levels with the end of the recession (Rosales 1979). Added worker effects for women in response to the economic downturns of the early 1980s have been documented for Argentina, Brazil, Costa Rica, Mexico and Uruguay (ICRW 1992; Moser *et al.* 1993).

The economic downturns of the early 1980s increased the supply of women workers, and the outward-oriented economic policies that followed the recession increased the demand for female labour in unregulated manufacturing and agribusiness jobs that pay individual rather than family wages, often include subcontracting arrangements, and offer few or no benefits and no employment security. Table 3 shows the feminisation of work in the 1980s, indicated by variations in activity rates for women and men in different developing countries, as a percentage of countries. The table shows many more cases of countries where the activity rates of women have increased rather than decreased in the 1980s as compared to the activity rates of men (Standing 1989). Table 4 illustrates the percentage of women in selected countries in self-employment, which includes subcontracting and piece work for export promotion industries as well as traditional, small-scale commercial and production activities linked to local rather than international markets. As the table reveals, women comprise almost half of the self-employed in a number of developing countries and there is plenty of individual country evidence of growing female participation in self-employment.

The conclusion of this analysis on the growing work responsibilities of low-income women at home and in the low-wage work force in recent decades highlight important questions for consideration when policies are formulated. Is it good or bad for poor families? Is it effective or not in terms of increasing family welfare in developing countries? A corollary to the original population hypothesis of the inverse women's work–fertility relationship is the hypothesis that women's labour force participation is directly related to reductions in time spent in breastfeeding and childcare, which, in turn, have negative consequences for child well-being (Nerlove 1974; Popkin 1978).

Table 4. Percentage of women in self-employed/unprotected work (selected countries)

Africa				
	1.	Congo	(1984)	39
	2.	Gambia	(1983)	25
	3.	Zambia	(1986)	53
Latin America				
	4.	Ecuador (Quito)	(1985)	50
	5.	Mexico (urban)*	(1981)	35
	6.	Bolivia (La Paz)	(1983)	48
Asia				
	7.	India	(1981)	49
	8.	Indonesia	(1980)	43
	9.	Malaysia	(1986)	43

*excludes domestics

Sources:

United Nations (1,2,3,8 & 9) 1991 *The world's women 1970-1990: trends and statistics*, p. 93. New York: United Nations.

Buvinic, M., Berger, M. & Jaramillo, C. (4) 1989 The impact of a credit project for women and men microentrepreneurs in Quito, Ecuador. In *Women's ventures: assistance to the informal sector in Latin America*, p. 223. West Hartford, Connecticut: Kumarian Press.

PREALC (5) (Programa regional del empleo para America Latina y el Caribe) 1981 *Sector informal: funcionamiento y politicas.* Santiago: PREALC, Oficina Internacional del Trabajo.

Casanovas, R., et al. (6) 1985 Los trabajadores por cuenta propia en el mercado de trabajo: El caso de la cuidad de La Paz. In *El sector informal urbano en los paises andinos*, p.217. Quito and Guayaquil, Ecuador: Instituto Latinoamericano de Investigaciones Sociales (ILDIS) y Centro de Formacion y Empleo para el sector informal urbano (CEPESIU).

Mitra, A. (7) 1981 Participation of women in socio-economic development. In *Women and Development.* Paris: UNESCO.

5. AN INVERSE EMPLOYMENT–CHILD WELFARE RELATIONSHIP?

Until fairly recently, the assumption among those concerned with child health was that any positive income effect of women's employment on children's health and well-being would be offset by the negative effects of reduced child care time by working mothers or by the substitution of older siblings in child care. Leslie's (1988) review of the findings of 21 studies that looked at the relationship between women's work and infant feeding practices and of 22 others that related women's work to child nutritional status found that the empirical evidence from the studies does not support the conclusion that women's work will have a negative effect on child nutrition. As far as women's work and infant feeding practices are concerned, most of the reported negative effects are not on initiation of breastfeeding but on duration, particularly on duration of exclusive breastfeeding. Several studies found that the only significant difference between working and non-working mothers was that mothers who worked away from the home began mixed (bottle and breast) feeding earlier. Some studies indicated that certain categories of working mothers, such as self-employed women or women farmers, actually were more likely to breastfeed or to breastfeed longer than non-working mothers, suggesting that cultural factors are at play in breastfeeding behaviour. Leslie's review of the studies that focused specifically on the relationship between women's work and child nutrition, using multivariate analysis and disaggregating both independent and dependent variables, points to the importance of the productivity of women's work and the level of women's wages in ensuring child nutrition. There is a negative effect of women's employment on child nutrition only if mothers work very long hours at substandard wages. Otherwise, there is no effect or, as the evidence below points out, a positive effect of women's work for pay on child nutrition.

That women are highly motivated by nature or nurture to ensure child survival is well accepted (Mason 1987; Fuchs 1989). Recent studies that use female headship, the proportion of household income women earn, or women's unearned income as proxies for women's control over income find significant positive effects of income in women's hands on measures of child well-being, especially in the case of poor households. In Brazil, for instance, income in the hands of the mother has an effect on child health that is almost 20 times greater than income that is controlled by the father (Thomas 1990). In Guatemala it takes 15 times more expenditure in child nutrition when income is earned by the father than when it is earned by the mother (Engle forthcoming). Similar results have been reported for Chile (Buvinić *et al.* 1992), Kenya and Malawi (Kennedy 1992). The preference that women have to invest in child well-being appears in poorer families rather than in better-off ones, either because investments in children yield greater returns at lower levels of income or because there are fewer competing alternative investments than in higher income households (Kennedy 1992). These gender differences in expenditure patterns within households and families suggest that the income poor women earn can yield higher health or social benefits than the income men earn (World Bank 1993).

There are also studies that report negative effects of female headship on child well-being. For instance, Wood (1989) found that the survival probabilities of children in woman-headed households in Brazil were significantly lower than those of children in male-headed households. Similar findings have been reported for Zambia (Kumar 1991) and the Philippines (García 1991). A likely hypothesis to reconcile positive and negative findings is that women need a minimum level of earnings or income to act on their preferences to invest scarce resources on child well-being. Below a minimum threshold, the economic deprivation that poor women who work in the market suffer is readily transmitted to the next generation.

6. POLICY AND PROGRAMME IMPLICATIONS

A critical implication of the WID findings reviewed here is the need to implement policies and projects that reinforce the virtuous cycle between women's and children's well-being in poor families when women have increased income and/or control of income, and avoid those that instead can trigger a vicious cycle of deprivation between mothers and children. Winikoff (1988) has documented the intergenerational perpetuation of ill-health that can occur between mothers and daughters in poor countries. This review has shown how social and economic factors that increase poor women's work and economic responsibilities can foster the perpetuation of poverty between mothers and children. These factors include alterations in fathers' traditional responsibilities towards children and the effects of declining household incomes during economic downturns, as well as the unintended consequences of social and economic policy—such as the effects of the promotion of tradeables in African agriculture, the decrease in service provision by the state that accompanies SAPs, and standard child-centred policies and projects that rely heavily on women's time for their successful implementation. The implementation of these policies *without* complementary policies that 'protect' poor women in their multiple roles as economic producers and reproducers is likely to set in motion the vicious cycle of poverty.

Perhaps the most effective way to 'protect' poor women is to implement policies that increase women's productivity in home production as well as their productivity and earnings in market production. Suggestions of specific policies and projects to increase women's productivity, as well as examples and lessons from project interventions, are many and are contained in the WID literature. However, these suggestions have seldom been implemented in any significant or major way. Anti-poverty policies that are directed to increasing the productivity of the poor, many of which are part of compensatory SAP packages, target only poor men, implicitly or explicitly. The same can be said about labour-intensive employment policies. Until this situation changes, and until the time that poor women are seen as economic producers and responsible for family economic maintenance, well-intentioned social sector policies and interventions will do little to break the cycle of poverty in mother–child pairs.

Aside from increasing women's productivity and income, 'empowering' women in other ways so that they can have control over family income, or a say about how it is allocated, could also help transform the vicious cycle of poverty into a virtuous one. Female education increases women's autonomy, but the returns are delayed. The mobilisation of women into women's groups and collectives can be a powerful complementary measure and may 'empower' women, but it does not address the central issue of women's work. The most straightforward vehicle to 'empower' poor women is to increase their productivity in home and market production and the income they obtain from work. This may or may not have an effect on fertility behaviour, but failure to enact policies whose objective is to assist poor women economically will certainly increase women's and children's poverty. In most instances, these policies will need to be targeted at poor women, in response to the unique conditions of women in poverty. Universal policies, unless they include elements of self-targeting by the poor, are likely to be less effective in reaching poor women.

Quality of care or user perspectives in family planning programmes have implicitly recognised the situation of poor women in their recommendations to expand and modify service delivery (Bruce 1989a; Kabeer 1992). A more explicit recognition of the factors linked to poverty that constrain women's demand for family planning and reproductive health services can help to explain the success of interventions and fine tune the design of services to meet the needs of the poor. The success of projects that integrate family planning with mother–child health services, for instance, is readily explained by the increased affordability of integrated services that reduce time costs to poor women. A focus on women in poverty should highlight the need to design appropriate reproductive health and family planning services for women who head families, have no stable partners and experience both time and income constraints, and for the growing numbers of poor women in the low-wage work force. It is not difficult to visualise modifications of existing service delivery mechanisms to increase these women's needs for reproductive health and family planning services. In conclusion, population policies and family planning services will be more effective and responsive to women's needs if they are crafted on the basis of understanding the interactions between gender and poverty in developing countries.

REFERENCES

Anker, R., Buvinić, M. & Youssef, N.H., eds. 1982 *Women's roles and population trends in the Third World.* London: Croom Helm Ltd.

Blake, J. 1965 Demographic science and the redirection of population policy. *J. Chron. Dis.* **18.**

Boserup, E. 1970 *Woman's role in economic development.* London: George Allen and Unwin.

Bruce, J. 1989a Fundamental elements of the quality of care: A simple framework. The Population Council Programs Division Working Paper No. 1. New York: The Population Council.

Bruce, J. 1989b Homes divided. *World development,* **17**(7), 979–991.

Buvinić, M., Berger, M. & Jaramillo, C. 1990 The impact of a credit project for women and men microentrepreneurs in Quito, Ecuador. In *Women's ventures: assistance to the informal sector in Latin America* (eds. M. Berger & M. Buvinić). West Hartford, CT: Kumarian Press, Inc., pp. 222-246.

Buvinić, M., Valenzuela, J.P., Molina, T. & Gonzalez, E. 1992 The fortunes of adolescent mothers and their children: a case study on the transmission of poverty in Santiago, Chile. *Pop. Dev. Rev.* **18**(2), 269–297.

Buvinić, M. & Gupta, G.R. 1994 Targeting poor woman-headed households and woman-maintained families in developing countries: views on a policy dilemma. Prepared for the Population Council/ICRW Joint Program on Female Headship and Poverty in Developing Countries.

Cleland, J., Johnson-Acsadi, G. & Merckwardt, A.M. 1987 The core questions. In *The world fertility survey: an assessment* (eds. J. Cleland & C. Schott). Oxford, UK: Oxford University Press.

Commonwealth Secretariat. 1991 *Women and structural adjustment: selected case studies commissioned for a Commonwealth group of experts.* Commonwealth Economic Papers No. 22. London: The Commonwealth Secretariat.

DaVanzo, J. & Lee, D.L.P. 1983 The compatibility of work and child care: preliminary evidence from Malaysia data. In *Women and poverty in the third world* (eds. M Buvinić, M. Lycette & W.P. McGreevey). Baltimore, Maryland: The Johns Hopkins University Press, pp. 62–91.

Desai, S. & Jain, D. 1992 Maternal employment and changes in family dynamics: the social context of women's work in rural south India. Population Council Research Division Working Paper No. 39. New York: The Population Council.

Dixon-Mueller, R. 1993 *Population policy and women's rights.* Westport, CT: Praeger.

Engle, P. (forthcoming) Influences of mother's and father's income on children's nutritional status in Guatemala. *Soc. Science & Med.*

Folbre, N. 1991 Mothers on their own: policy issues for developing countries. Paper prepared for the Joint Population Council/ICRW series on The Determinants and Consequences of Female-Headed Households. Washington, DC: ICRW.

Francke, M. 1992 Women and the labor market in Lima, Peru: Weathering economic crises. Paper prepared for the ICRW Seminar on Weathering economic crises: Women's responses to recession in Latin America, August 11, 1992, Washington, D.C.

Fuchs, V.R. 1989 Women's quest for economic equality. *J. Econ. Persp.* **3**(1), 25–41.

Furstenberg, F., Brooks-Gunn, S. & Morgan, P. 1987 *Adolescent mothers in later life.* Cambridge, MA: Cambridge University Press.

Garcia, M. 1991 Income sources of the malnourished rural poor in the provinces of Abra, Antique, and South Cotabato in the Philippines. Working Paper. Washington, DC: International Food Policy Research Institute.

Garfinkel, I. & McLanahan, S.S. 1986 *Single mothers and their children.* Washington, DC: The Urban Institute Press.

Ho, T. 1979 Time costs of child-rearing in the Philippines. *Pop. Dev. Rev.* **5**(4), 643–662.

Humphries, J. 1988 Women and work. In *The new Palgrave: a dictionary of economics* (eds. J. Eatwell, M. Milgate & P. Newman). New York: Stockton Press.

ICRW (International Center for Research on Women) 1992 Weathering economic crises: women's responses to the recession in Latin America and the Caribbean. Selected country studies. Washington, DC: ICRW.

Jazairy, I., Alamgir, M. & Panuccio, T. 1992 *The state of world rural poverty: an inquiry into its causes and consequences,* 365. New York University Press, pp. 273–298.

Kabeer, N. 1992 From fertility reduction to reproductive choice: gender perspectives on family planning. Institute of Development Studies Discussion Paper No. 299. Brighton, NJ: Institute of Development Studies.

Kennedy, E.T. 1992 Effects of gender of head of household on women's and children's nutritional status. Working paper. International Food Policy Research Institute workshop on The Effects of Policies and Programs on Women, Washington, DC.

King, E. & Evenson R.E. 1983 Time allocation and home production in Philippine rural households. In *Women and poverty in the third world* (eds. M. Buvinić, M. Lycette & W.P. McGreevey). Baltimore, MD: Johns Hopkins University Press, pp. 35–61.

Koussoudji, S. & Mueller, E. 1983 The economic and demographic status of female-headed households in rural Botswana. *Econ. Dev. Cult. Change* **31**(4), 831–859.

Kumar, S.K. 1991 Income sources of the malnourished poor in rural Zambia. Working Paper. Washington, DC: International Food Policy Research Institute.

Leslie, J. 1988 Women's work and child nutrition in the third world. *World Development* **16**(11), 1341–1362.

Leslie, J., Lycette, M. & Buvinić, M. 1988 Weathering economic crises: the crucial role of women in health. In *Health, nutrition and economic crises* (eds. D.E. Bell & M.R. Reich). Dover, MA: Auburn House, pp. 307–348.

Lloyd, C. 1993 Family and gender issues for population policy. Population Council Research Division Working Paper No. 48. New York: The Population Council.

Lloyd, C. 1991 The contribution of the world fertility surveys to an understanding of the relationship between women's work and fertility. *Stud. Fam. Planning* **22**(3), 144–161.

Lloyd, C. & Gage-Brandon, A.J. 1992 Does sibsize matter? The implications of family size for children's education in Ghana. Population Council Research Division Working Paper No. 45. New York: The Population Council.

Mason, K.O. 1987 The impact of women's social position on fertility in developing countries. *Soc. Forum* **2**(4), 718–745.

Mason, K.O. & Palan, V.T. 1981 Female employment and fertility in peninsular Malaysia: the maternal role incompatibility hypothesis reconsidered. *Demography* **18**(4), 549–575.

Merrick, T.W. & Schmink, M. 1983 Households headed by women and urban poverty in Brazil. In *Women and poverty in the Third World* (eds. M. Buvinic, M. Lycette & W. McGreevey). Baltimore, MD: Johns Hopkins University Press, pp. 244–271.

Moser, C.O.N. 1993 Adjustment from below: Low-income women, time and the triple role in Guayaquil, Ecuador. In *Viva: women and population protest in Latin America* (eds. S.A. Radcliffe & S. Westwood). London: Routledge, pp. 173–196.

Moser, C.O.N., Herbert, A.J., & Makonnen, R.E. 1993 Urban poverty in the context of structural adjustment, recent evidence and policy responses. Transportation, Water, and Urban Development Department Discussion Paper No. 4. Washington, DC: The World Bank.

Mueller, E. 1982 The allocation of women's time and its relation to fertility. In *Women's roles and population trends in the third world* (eds. R. Anker, M. Buvinić & N.H. Youssef). London: Croom Helm, pp. 85–86.

Nerlove, S.B. 1974 Women's workload and infant feeding practices: a relationship with demographic implications. *Ethnology* **13**, 207–214.

OECD (Organisation for Economic Cooperation and Development) 1976 *The 1974–1975 recession and the employment of women*. Paris: OECD.

Oppenheimer, V.K. 1970 *The female labor force in the United States*. Berkeley, California:University of California, Institute of International Studies.

Oppong, C. 1983 Women's roles, opportunity costs, and fertility. In *Determinants of fertility in developing countries* (eds. R.A. Bulatao & R.D. Lee). Washington, DC: National Academy Press, pp. 439–473.

Palmer, I. 1991 *Gender and population in the adjustment of African economies: planning for change.* Geneva: International Labour Office, p. 146.

Popkin, B.M. 1983 Rural women, work, and child welfare in the Philippines. In *Women and poverty in the third world* (eds. M. Buvinić, M. Lycette & W.P. McGreevey). Baltimore, MD: Johns Hopkins University Press, pp. 157–176.

Popkin, B.M. 1978 Economic determinants of breast-feeding behavior: the case of rural households in Laguna, Philippines. *Nutrition and human reproduction* (ed. W.H. Mosely). New York: Plenum Press, pp. 461–496.

PRB (Population Reference Bureau). 1992 *Chartbook: Africa demographic and health surveys.* Washington, DC: Population Reference Bureau.

Rosales, O.V. 1979 La mujer Chilena en la fuerza de trabajo: participacion, empleo, y desempleo (1957–1977). Santiago, Chile: Universidad de Chile.

Ross, H. & Sawhill, I. 1976 *Families in transition: the growth of households headed by women.* Washington, DC: The Urban Institute.

Schultz, T.P. 1988 Economic demography and development: new directions in an old field. In

The state of development economics: progress and perspectives (eds. G. Ranis & T.P. Schultz). Oxford: Basil Blackwell.

Sen, G. 1992 Women, poverty and population—issues for the concerned environmentalist.Paper prepared for collaborative project of the International Social Sciences Association, the Social Science Research Council, and Development Alternatives with Women for a New Era (DAWN) on 'Rethinking Population and the Environment.'

Singh, S. & Wulf, D. 1990 *Today's adolescents, tomorrow's parents: a portrait of the Americas.* New York: The Alan Guttmacher Institute.

Sivard, R.L. 1985 *Women ... a world survey.* Washington, DC: World Priorities.

Standing, G. 1989 Global feminization through flexible labor. *World development* **17**(7), 1077–1095.

Standing, G. 1978 Migration, labour force absorption and morbidity: women in Kingston, Jamaica. Population and Employment Working Paper No. 68, World Employment Programme. Geneva: International Labour Office.

Thomas, D. 1990 Intra-household resource allocation: an inferential approach. *J. Human Resources* **XXV**(4), 635–664.

Winikoff, B. 1988 Women's health: an alternative perspective for choosing interventions. *Stud. Fam. Planning* **19**(4), 197–214.

Wood, C.H. 1989 Women-headed households and child mortality in Brazil, 1960–1980. Draft presented at joint ICRW/Population Council Seminar II February 27–28: Consequences of Female Headship and Female Maintenance. Washington, DC: ICRW.

World Bank. 1981 To the Massachusetts Institute of Technology: An address on the population problem – April 28, 1977. In *The McNamara years at the World Bank: major policy addresses,* pp. 415–416. Baltimore, MD: Johns Hopkins University Press.

World Bank. 1990 *World development report 1990: poverty.* Washington, DC: The World Bank.

World Bank. 1993 *World development report 1993: investing in health.* Washington, DC: The World Bank.

Youssef, N.H. 1982 The interrelationship between the division of labour in the household, women's roles and their impact on fertility. In *Women's roles and population trends in the third world* (eds. R. Anker, M. Buvinić & N.H. Youssef). London: Croom Helm, pp. 173–201.

Different Pathways to Demographic Transition
John Cleland

ABSTRACT

The main aim of this paper is to identify the conditions that have facilitated or impeded demographic transition in developing countries. The emphasis will be on fertility rather than mortality, although the relationships between these two components of transition will be discussed. Before entering the arena of determinants, or pathways, it will be helpful to present a brief statistical overview of fertility trends in the last 30 years. Outside the narrow confines of technical demography, there is much confusion about what has actually happened. The fact that the annual rate of global population growth remains high, and indeed has not declined much in the last decade, is often interpreted to mean that stable, high levels of human reproduction remain entrenched in most developing regions. As will be shown, this perspective is largely false. Fertility has declined and still is declining in most developing countries, though important exceptions remain. The reason for the apparent contradiction between global population growth and declining fertility has much to do with the age structure of populations; as a result of past high fertility, the proportion of population in the reproductive age span is increasing in most developing countries and this factor acts to sustain high crude birth rates, even in the context of falling rates per woman. Mortality decline further contributes to the persistence of high growth rates.

1. THE COURSE OF FERTILITY TRANSITION IN DEVELOPING REGIONS

The striking feature of fertility transition over the past 30 years is the divergent pathways that different regions and countries have followed (Figure 1). In the early 1960s, the level of fertility in major developing regions of the world fell within a narrow span of six to seven births per woman. This level may be slightly higher than historical levels in traditional societies. There is fragmentary evidence that fertility may have risen in the first half of the present century for a variety of reasons: declines in pathological sterility; erosion of customary restraints, such as sexual abstinence and prolonged breastfeeding; and, in Latin America, earlier marriage ages for women.

While the magnitude of any rise in the rate of childbearing prior to 1960 is uncertain, the levels in the early 1960s certainly represent what demographers call 'natural' fertility: fertility in the absence of conscious attempts by married couples to limit family size. The fertility trajectories since that time, shown in Figure 1, are largely the outcome of increased birth control, though rising ages at marriage have also made an appreciable contribution.

Fertility declines have been steepest in East Asia, numerically dominated by China. The staggering success of the 'later, longer, fewer' Chinese family planning programme in the 1970s is clearly evident in Figure 1; equally clear is the relative failure of the one-child policy of the 1980s.

Fertility declines elsewhere cannot match that in East Asia. Falls in fertility in Latin

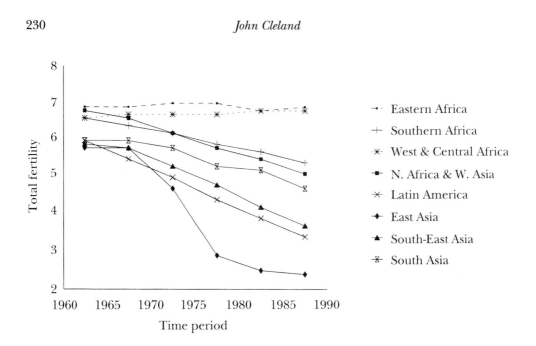

Figure 1. Trends in total fertility: major developing regions: 1960–1990

America, however, started earlier, in the 1960s, and have proceeded steadily ever since to reach a level of under 3.5 births per woman in the late 1980s. Closely paralleling the Latin American trend, is that of South-East Asia, where recent fertility is a little above 3.5 births. Thus for three regions, which together comprise over half of the total population of the developing world, fertility transition is well advanced. In Latin America and South-East Asia, there is no sign yet of any abatement in the decline, and even in China, where fertility plateaued for much of the 1980s, there is evidence of a further recent fall in response to an unexpected tightening of state population policies (China Population Today 1993). However, the continuation of declines in these regions does not necessarily imply that replacement level fertility (at a little above two births per woman) is inevitable in the near future. In Latin America, for instance, there are signs of incipient stabilisation for certain more demographically advanced countries at fertility levels appreciably above the two birth mark; for instance, in Argentina, family sizes have been more or less constant at three children for the past 30 years.

From these relatively low fertility regions, we turn to a further three regions where appreciable fertility declines of some 25% or thereabouts have been registered and where recent levels lie in the range of 4.5 to 5.5 births per woman. Southern Africa, south Asia and the predominantly Arab states of northern Africa and western Asia comprise this group. The trend for southern Africa is largely a reflection of the longstanding fertility decline among the black population of the Republic of South Africa, though smaller falls are also apparent in neighbouring countries of the sub-region. The south Asian figures are a composite of divergent trends. In some countries, such as Pakistan, Afghanistan and Iran, there is little convincing evidence of decline. In north India and Nepal, the drop in fertility has been very modest. By contrast, fertility is now very low in south India and Sri Lanka and has fallen remarkably in Bangladesh.

North Africa and western Asia is an equally heterogeneous region, with sustained declines in Egypt and Tunisia, more recent and modest falls in Morocco and Jordan but a persistence of high fertility in other countries, including the indigenous populations of most of the wealthy Gulf states.

We come lastly to two sub-regions—eastern Africa and central and west Africa—where, according to UN estimates, the level of fertility has remained constant at about 7.0 births per woman over the last 30 years. For central and west Africa, the verdict of stable fertility is correct, through there are signs of incipient decline among younger women in Senegal and parts of Nigeria. For eastern Africa, the regional estimate is rather misleading. Upwards adjustments by UN of fertility in Ethiopia and Uganda have masked unmistakable declines in Kenya and Zimbabwe.

Several general points can be made on the basis of these regional trends. Firstly, the level of childbearing has fallen in most of the developing world, though there still remain important areas of unchanging high fertility, mainly in Africa and south Asia. The ubiquity and speed of decline have exceeded the expectations of most population experts. Until about the mid-1970s, the tone of most discussions about the prospects for third world fertility decline was pessimistic (Davis 1969). In particular, it was doubted that couples would reduce voluntarily their family sizes, unless compensation in some form was offered. In the event, the fertility transition has been fuelled largely by voluntary adoption of contraception, though, in some Asian countries, government pressure and the use of financial payments no doubt have played a part. Furthermore, it is clear from Figure 1 that the economic crisis of the 1980s has not resulted in any obvious retardation of decline; declines in family sizes do not appear to be dependent upon steady improvements in living standards. Finally, there is now a mass of recent empirical evidence with which to address the conditions that influence transition. As we shall see, the picture that emerges is fascinating, complex and ultimately destructive of the most widely held beliefs and theories.

2. THE THEORY OF DEMOGRAPHIC TRANSITION AND MORTALITY— FERTILITY RELATIONSHIPS

The concept of demographic transition has dominated theorising about population and provides a unifying framework in which mortality, fertility and to a lesser extent migration can be accommodated. Paul Demeny (1972) succinctly captures its essence: 'In traditional societies, fertility and mortality are high. In modern societies, fertility and mortality are low. In between there is demographic transition'. It is thus appropriate to start analytic discussion by considering the nature of the relationship between mortality and fertility, with the particular aim of identifying any policy implications.

The sequence of events in classic formulations of demographic transition theory is displayed in Figure 2. In traditional societies, vital rates are high and in balance. The oscillation of mortality reflects the ravages of periodic famine, disease and war: Malthus's famous 'positive' checks on population growth. Mortality declines first, followed, after a lag, by fertility. Eventually, equilibrium is restored. Population growth accelerates at point (a), the start of mortality decline and growth continues for a further 30 to 40 years

Vital Rates

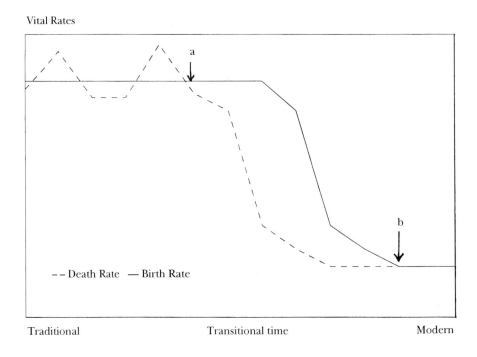

Traditional   Transitional time   Modern

Figure 2. The classical view of the Demographic Transition

beyond point (b) when fertility and mortality are again in balance. This extension of population growth beyond the achievement of low fertility is known as population momentum and reflects the crucial role of age-structure in determining the annual numbers of births and deaths and the growth rate.

One of the first exponents of demographic transition theory was Thompson (1929) and important contributions were made by Davis (1945) and Notestein (1945). The theory was both a description of supposed trends in Europe, North America and overseas European colonies and a causal model that attempted to explain the sequence of events. Two major types of causal relationship between mortality and fertility decline were proposed. The first, and dominant one, may be termed the 'common cause' hypothesis. The essential idea here is that economic and social development initially induce a decline in mortality and only later bring about a similar decline in fertility.

In the 'common cause' version of transition theory, the time lag between mortality and fertility decline is usually explained in cultural terms. In the case of mortality, there is no cultural resistance to change. No society embraces premature death or disease and improvements are unreservedly welcomed. In the case of fertility, however, cultural resistance to change may be strong. All human societies have evolved institutions and values that support (and, at the same time, moderate) reproduction. The idea of deliberately limiting childbearing within marriage may be alien and even repugnant. But economic and social development erodes the need for large families and increases the costs of childbearing in a multitude of ways. Sooner or later, the cultural props to high fertility wither under this onslaught and fertility declines.

The second type of causal relationships between mortality and fertility decline, the 'child survival' hypothesis, is more simple and direct. High fertility as seen as a functional adaptation to high mortality. In pre-transitional societies, couples bear many children, simply because they know that many will die. As survival improves, this reproductive imperative is progressively removed and, as a result, the rate of childbearing is reduced. There are many formalised expressions of this 'child survival' hypothesis and much empirical attention has been devoted to *replacement* and *insurance* strategies of family formation. Replacement in this context denotes the extent to which couples consciously replace dead children by additional births, while insurance refers to the possibility that couples bear children in excess of their desires, because they anticipate possible future deaths. Declining child mortality not only reduces the number of `replacement' and `insurance' births but may erode fatalism and thus encourage fertility planning. In addition it may give parents the confidence to invest more in children and thereby engender a switch from quantity to quality in matters of family size (Lloyd & Ivanov 1988).

Finally, a purely physiological link between enhanced child survival and fertility should be noted. In societies such as Bangladesh, where prolonged breastfeeding is almost universal, early death of an infant implies curtailment of post-partum amenorrhoea and thus a shortening of intervals between births. A reduction of the infant death rate tends to widen intervals between births thereby reducing fertility. This mechanism can be powerful. For instance, Chowdhury *et al.* (1978) estimate for Bangladesh that infant death reduces the length of lactational protection against conception by 13 months.

There is no contradiction between what we have called the 'common cause' and 'child survival' variants of demographic transition theory. Indeed most accounts invoke both types of causal link and the sequence of events depicted in figure 2 is consistent with either explanation.

In contrast to its relatively rich and plausible causal underpinning, demographic transition theory has always been imprecise as a descriptive or predictive tool. The extent of mortality decline that is necessary to provoke a fertility response is unspecified as is the time lag between the onset of mortality change and the drop in fertility. As no population can grow indefinitely, transition theory in its most general form amounts to little more than an assertion that balance will be restored eventually by a drop in fertility rather than by a resurgence in mortality.

As mentioned earlier, demographic transition theory was originally formulated in response to the presumed sequence of events in the West. Since that time, our knowledge of European transition has been transformed, largely by a coordinated programme of research, the Princeton European Fertility Project. Demographic transition theory has been damaged fatally by this detailed empirical scrutiny. It is now clear that the temporal relationship between declines in childhood mortality and fertility took a bewildering variety of forms in Europe (F. van de Walle 1986). A few examples will illustrate this point. In Sweden, the onset of decline in infant mortality preceded the decline in marital fertility by 100 years. In Germany, infant mortality declined first in 36 administrative areas, but marital fertility decline came first in 34 other areas. In England, the big declines in childhood mortality started in about 1900, some 20 years after the onset of marital fertility decline. Moreover, mortality in Europe was still high when the fertility transition started, with infant death rates well above 100 in most countries. For Europe at least, the 'child survival' variant of transition is untenable. Nor has there been much success in the many attempts to identify development factors that could account for both mortality and fertility decline. Between 1880 and 1930, the era in which most of Europe experienced substantial fertility decline, there was a huge variation between countries in terms of social and economic development. There is a growing body of evidence that ill-understood cultural factors must have played a key role in determining fertility decline (Knodel & E. van de Walle 1986) and that mortality was responding to a broad range of influences, such as public health measures, breastfeeding customs and maternal education, that were not adequately captured by crude economic indicators such as income and urbanisation.

Demographic transition theory has fared rather better in relation to trends in developing countries over the last 40 years. In contrast to Europe, mortality decline has preceded fertility decline. There is probably no exception to this generalisation, which reflects the fact that a world-wide improvement in life expectancy occurred in the 1950s and 1960s. The major causes of this transformation, which is the origin of the current phase of rapid world population growth, are not clearly understood. Mass application of new medical technologies, favourable terms of trade for producers of food and raw materials, and the growth of communications may all have contributed, but their relative importance is still a matter of controversy. It is also true that there is a strong correlation between levels of childhood mortality and fertility. In other words, countries that have succeeded most in reducing childhood mortality also tend to record earlier and sharper declines in fertility, than countries where childhood mortality remains relatively high. China, Cuba, Sri Lanka and Costa Rica are often cited examples of countries with modest living standards but whose governments made exceptionally determined efforts to improve health and reduce mortality. All four have experienced steep fertility declines. This relationship is well illustrated in UNICEF's State of the Children report for 1991.

In other regards, however, the relationship between mortality and fertility response has proved to be highly variable. Casterline (1993) and Guzman (1993) have recently calculated the life expectancy and infant mortality that prevailed at the time when fertility started to decline, for a large number of Asian and Latin American countries. In both regions, there is a wide span in mortality conditions at the onset of fertility decline. In Asia, infant mortality ranges from 80 to 145 and in Latin America from 62 to 151. Indeed in ten of the sixteen countries examined by Guzman, infant mortality was over 100 at the onset of fertility transition. There is similar variability in the time lag between onsets of mortality and fertility decline.

To sum up, it is apparent that demographic transition theory has proved largely inadequate for purposes of description, explanation or prediction. The experience of historical Europe demonstrates that there is no inviolate rule that substantial mortality decline must precede fertility decline. In that region, the mass use of birth control and fertility reduction quite often preceded declines in childhood mortality. In developing regions of the world, the expected sequence depicted in Figure 2 holds true and it is also true that early, large declines in mortality are usually associated, after a lag, with early, large declines in fertility. At the same time, there is considerable variation in mortality - fertility links. Over the last 30 years, fertility had declined in a wide range of mortality regimes. Such diversity has profound implications. It is, for instance, misleading to claim that mortality must be reduced to any specified level before fertility reduction will occur. Furthermore, the levels of mortality that now prevail in the remaining high fertility countries of the world, mostly in Africa and south Asia, are little different from the levels found in Latin America and elsewhere at the time of their fertility transition. There is thus little empirical support for the widely held view that child mortality is still too high in Africa or in parts of south Asia to expect fertility declines. Similarly it would be false to assert that a certain proportionate decline in mortality will engender a predictable fertility response. The world is far too complex for such simple functional relationships. Even if exceptional efforts were made to reduce child mortality by, say, a further 20 to 30% in a short time period in Africa, it is uncertain whether this change would impinge upon parental perceptions about risks of death and thus trigger a fertility response. A host of factors—economic, political, cultural and programmatic—intervene to obfuscate clear mortality–fertility links.

These negative policy conclusions are not intended to imply that child survival initiatives should receive lower priority, but merely to suggest that they have to be justified in their own right rather than an indirect way to achieve demographic equilibrium. Nor should they blind us to the fact that mortality should be viewed as a chronologically remote but nevertheless fundamental cause of fertility decline. No human population can grow indefinitely. Sooner or later balance must be restored, either by a resurgence of mortality or by fertility reduction. Nearly all the evidence to date suggests that the benign latter pathway will be followed. However welcome rapid population growth may be initially to governments and however welcome large numbers of surviving children may be to families, the disadvantages — indeed the impossibility — of large long term divergencies between births and deaths eventually become apparent and corrective initiatives are taken either by governments, or spontaneously by citizens, or by both acting in concert. The United Nation Population Division has monitored the changing attitudes of governments in Africa. In 1980, for instance, few governments saw population growth as a problem or thus felt no need for the promotion of birth control as a solution. Less than ten years later, 27 out of 45 governments considered fertility to be too high and Nigeria, Rwanda and Senegal had joined Ghana and Kenya in formulating policies with explicit demographic objectives (UN 1989). Of course, they were under considerable international pressure to do so, but there is undoubtedly a genuine, indigenous shift in outlook.

At this juncture it is appropriate to state an obvious truth, which is nevertheless usually ignored. Throughout many centuries of the human species, the average woman can have seen no more than two children survive to maturity, giving a net reproduction rate of close to unity and stable population size. While there was no doubt considerable variation between families around this average, because of the vagaries of natural fertility and the unpredictable ravages of high childhood mortality, it is clear that all traditional human societies must have been adapted to low net fertility: an adaptation in terms of land usage, inheritance, organisation, old age security, use of familial labour and so on. This perspective undermines the position of those who argue that there is some social or economic imperative for large family sizes in poor countries and that radical structural transformation of economies is a necessary precondition for demographic change. It also supports the suggestion made earlier that, sooner or later, the disadvantages and disruptions caused by the combination of high fertility and high child survival will become apparent and adaptation will occur.

3. FERTILITY TRANSITION PATHWAYS: CASE STUDIES

The attempts by population scientists to identify the determinants of fertility transition typically take one of two forms. The first comprises statistical analyses where the unit of study is nation states, the dependent variable is fertility level or trend (or sometimes the prevalence of contraceptive practice) and the explanatory or predictor variables typically include measures of mortality, indicators of socio-economic development and of strength of family planning programmes. The results from numerous such analyses may be summarised succinctly. Measures of social development (particularly adult education and life expectancy) are more closely associated with fertility decline than measures of economic development such as income per head, energy consumption per head (e.g. Cutright 1983). The strength of family planning programmes, measured by summing scores on a large number of components is itself closely related to development. In other words, 'good' programmes are more typically found in relatively developed countries than in poorer, largely illiterate societies. Notwithstanding this degree of confounding, programme strength is related to fertility change, though its effect is less than, and subordinate to the effect of development (Mauldin & Berelson 1978; Mauldin & Ross 1991). These findings have been immensely influential, but suffer from a fatal defect particularly with regard to the influence of family planning programmes. Population policies and provision of family planning services do not arise by chance or in a vacuum. It is reasonable to argue that they often arise in response to a clear need, as evidenced for instance by high rates of illegal abortion. To the extent that this sequence of events is valid, programme strength may be as much a consequence of actual or incipient fertility decline as a cause.

The second common approach to elucidate fertility determinants is to analyse fertility at the micro or family level. By relating the level of childbearing to the position of individuals or families within the socio-economic structure, insights into the underlying causes of decline may be obtained. This type of research has a long pedigree and it is less easy to encapsulate the main findings. Parental education again emerges as a key influence on reproductive decisions, and fertility is nearly always lower in urban than in rural areas (UN 1987a). In other regards, however, the findings are more surprising. Participation by women in the labour force does not appear to be a decisive factor (UN 1987a) and there is no fertility difference between families where the household head runs a family business, or farm, from those where the head is an employee (Rodrigues & Cleland 1981). Thus the erosion of the role of families in economic production does not appear to be of major importance. Furthermore, cultural identity, as indicated by religion, ethnicity or language, is often found to be a major predictor of reproductive patterns, even after controlling for socio-economic factors.

The great weakness of these cross-sectional studies of fertility differentials is that they fail to distinguish deep-seated causes from what may be transitory divergencies of little consequence. During the course of fertility transition, very large differences between socio-economic strata in childbearing may arise, because more advanced sectors are in the vanguard of change. But as transition progresses, there is a re-convergence as the rural and less educated follow the behavioural pathway of the urban middle classes. This process of diffusion has been documented most adequately in Latin America (Rodrigues & Avavena 1991).

In this paper, a different approach to the elucidation of demographic pathways is taken. The mode of analysis is essentially a case study approach, though pairs or groups of countries are considered. The analysis serves to emphasise the diversity of conditions under which fertility has declined and to warn against simple mono-causal explanations. However, there are some general lessons to be learnt and these will be summarised in the final section.

3.1 North and South Korea

It is rare that a single country splits with two sovereign states, which then pursue radically different population (and economic) policies. Such, however, is the case of Korea. At the time of partition, most of the heavy industry was in the North but, over recent decades, development in the South has far outstripped that in the North.

Since the mid-1960s, successive governments in South Korea have pursued vigorous policies to reduce population growth. A network of family planning fieldworkers was created and couples have been offered financial inducements to become sterilised. Fertility decline began in the early 1960s amidst conditions of considerable poverty (Kwon Tai-Hwan 1993). It has proceeded at a fast pace and in recent years has fallen below replacement level, causing new concerns about population ageing and shrinkage of the labour force. By contrast, North Korean policies towards family planning provision have vacillated between hostility and neutrality, and population growth rates have been regarded as too low rather than too high (UN 1987b).

The demographic consequences of this divergence in government policies may be seen in Figure 3. Fertility in the South began to decline much earlier than in the North, and, by the late 1960s, a very large gap between rates of childbearing in the North and South had opened up. However, fertility transition started in the North in the 1970s and since then there has been a convergence in natality. In the late 1980s, total fertility in the South was slightly under two births per woman: in the North, it was estimated to be about 2.5.

The main lesson to be drawn from this comparison is that, in settings that are favourable for fertility decline, state interventions may hasten the onset and accelerate the rapidity of change but do not necessarily affect the medium term outcome. North Korea is not an isolated example. For example, appreciable fertility decline has almost certainly occurred in Myanmar, despite explicit opposition to family planning by the Government (UN 1987b). It is also true that spontaneous declines in many Latin American countries started before widespread services for contraception were created in the public sector or by large non-government organisations.

The Korean experience also suggests that state provision of security in old age, sickness or adversity is not an essential precondition of fertility decline. The South Korea government, for instance, did not introduce a state pension scheme until 1988, by which time family sizes had already fallen to replacement level. This sequence is the dominant one, both in Europe and in developing countries; welfare measures follow rather than precede declines in the birth rate.

Finally the example of Korea demonstrates that fertility can fall to very low levels despite a strong parental preference for sons over daughters. Thirty years ago, many Korean couples ideally wanted a family of two sons and one daughter, and many observers thought that such desires would act to sustain fertility at a level of about four births per woman. Over recent decades, a shift has occurred not towards greater gender equality, but towards a contentment with only one son, thus permitting very low fertility. The growing practice of sex-selective abortion further erodes the residual incompatibility between a persisting desire for a son and an equally strong desire for a small family.

Does Korea represent a pathway that other son-preferring societies (for example, North India, and Pakistan) will follow? Of course, no-one can be certain but Korea's transition does demonstrate that a societal bias towards sons does not necessarily act as an absolute barrier to low fertility.

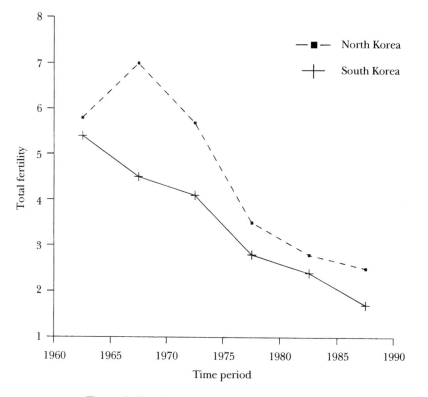

Figure 3. Fertility trends in North and South Korea

3.2 Philippines and Indonesia

The demographic histories of Philippines and Indonesia demonstrate that high educational levels and reasonably high status of women, factors normally thought to be particularly conducive to low fertility, do not always have this effect. In 1960, Philippines was one of the wealthiest countries of South-East Asia. The level of adult literacy was 72%, compared to only 39% in Indonesia. Income per head was almost double the Indonesian level at that time, life expectancy was ten years longer and infant mortality correspondingly lower. It comes as no surprise, therefore, that fertility decline started earlier in Philippines than in Indonesia. However, since the mid-1970s, the pace of decline has been much greater in Indonesia; the level of fertility in 1985–1990 was estimated to be 3.5 births and it has fallen further since that time. In Philippines, by contrast, fertility decline since the mid-1970s has been rather modest; the level of contraceptive practice even appears to have fallen between 1978 and 1983 (Perez & Cabigon 1985). For the quinquennium 1985–1990, the UN estimate of fertility is 4.3, nearly one birth higher than in Indonesia.

The explanation for this unexpected outcome lies well beyond the realm of statistical evidence, but almost certainly involves the intertwined factors of religion and government policy. The Indonesian government skilfully evaded the potential danger of opposition from Islamic leaders by eschewing abortion and contraceptive sterilisation. It mounted a very forceful family planning programme with considerable community pressure on couples to adopt birth control (Warwick 1986). In the mid-1970s, fertility in Java was actually lower among the less educated rural population than among the urban, more educated sectors: a highly unusual situation that undoubtedly reflected the impact of the programme (Freedman *et al* 1981).

In Philippines, no compact between Church and State has been reached and Roman Catholic leaders remain strongly and openly opposed to modern birth control (Aslam 1993). This opposition has both inhibited the evolution of comprehensive family planning services and no doubt has influenced the climate in which reproductive decisions are taken (Hull 1991).

The persistence of rather high fertility in Philippines is made even more surprising in view of the relatively high status of women in that country. Educational levels for women are exceptionally high, as is labour force participation. However, the example of Philippines is consistent with a large body of evidence that the status of women—if defined in terms of participation in public life, including paid employment—is not an important precondition for sustained fertility decline. Indeed it is probably more a consequence of decline than a cause. However, participation in public life is only one dimension of the status of women. Their domestic autonomy—that is, their influence on decisions about household expenditure, children's schooling and matters of reproductive control—possibly may be a more important factor. In patriarchal societies with large age differences between spouses, limited inter-spousal communication and male hegemony in domestic affairs, it is likely that effective reproductive decision making will be difficult. Unfortunately there is very little research evidence with which to address this issue.

It should be stressed again that, as for North Korea, Philippines is not a maverick example, of curiosity value but holding no wider significance. In nearby Malaysia, it is

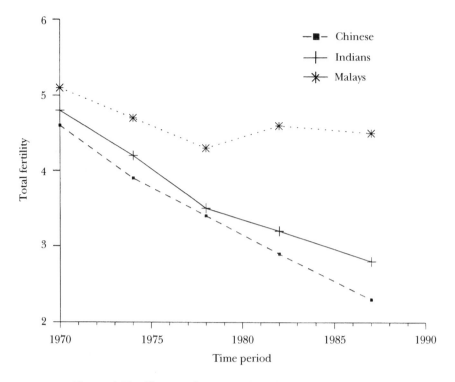

Figure 4. Fertility trends among the ethnic groups of Malaysia

difficult to explain puzzling fertility trends without invoking both religious and political influences. Like Philippines, Malaysia has long been one of the more affluent and better educated societies of South-East Asia, but has a much more enviable recent record of economic and social progress than Philippines. Also like Philippines, fertility transition began relatively early. Among the Chinese and Indian communities, the decline has been unchecked and the level of childbearing is now approaching replacement level (Figure 4). Among the Malays, on the other hand, the decline was actually reversed in the late 1970s and early 1980s; the practice of modern contraception fell and fertility aspirations rose (Leete & Tan Boon An 1993). Leete and Tan Boon An point out that this period coincides with a distinct movement toward traditional Islamic values among some sectors of the Malay community. Moreover in 1984, the government announced a new population policy, that was widely interpreted as a radical shift from antinatalism to pronatalism. While cause and effect cannot be established with any scientific rigour, it appears probable that family formation trends among Malays were responding to, and part of, the changing religious and political climate in that country.

3.3 Arab states

The Arab states provide numerous further examples to support the argument that there is no straightforward relationship between socioeconomic development and fertility. While fertility rates have fallen in nearly all Arab states—albeit from exceptionally high levels—they remain high (at six births or more per woman) among the indigenous populations of some of the richest, mostly highly urbanised and increasingly educated countries, such as the United Arab Emirates, Kuwait and Saudi Arabia (Farid 1993). Conversely fertility transition is most advanced in countries with moderate living standards but whose governments have made a serious commitment to the promotion of family planning (Egypt, Tunisia, Morocco).

Consider the example of Jordan, where trends in fertility and contraceptive practice are well documented in repeated surveys. The country is highly urbanised; standards of living are reasonable; and levels of adult education are high. According to the most recent survey in 1990, 54% of ever-married women in the reproductive age span had received secondary or higher schooling, an impressive achievement (Jordan, Ministry of Health 1992). The national level of fertility has declined from about 7.5 births in the mid-1970s but still remains high at 5.6 births. There is a large divergence in fertility according to the educational status of women. Women with no schooling record a level of nearly seven births; the largest group, those with secondary schooling, have 5.4 births; while those with tertiary schooling have about four births.

Despite the inevitable strains associated with very rapid population growth, estimated to be 3.7% per annum in the period 1980–1985, the Jordanian government regards the level of fertility as satisfactory and does not promote the use of contraception (UN 1987b).

It is well nigh impossible to account for the persistence of high fertility in Jordan, or the population policies of the government, in narrow economic terms. No satisfactory interpretation of Jordan's demography can evade the political dimension, involving perceptions that population numbers, territorial rights and nationhood are inextricably linked. Here again there is indirect, but compelling, evidence that cultural and political factors can exert a major influence on reproductive behaviour.

3.4 Colombia and Mexico

Colombia and Mexico represent a fascinating contrast in the development of their respective population policies. The popularisation of contraception was initiated in Colombia in the mid-1960s largely by progressive medical doctors and non-government organisations, against a background of government permissive neutrality (Mundigo 1990). In 1969, the organisation, Profamilia, began its first public information campaigns to promote its services and, some five years later, started its well-known community-based distribution programme. The government did not become officially involved until fertility decline was well underway and non-government services already widely available.

In Mexico, perhaps the most centralised state of the region, the government was firmly opposed to family planning throughout the 1960s. The main reason was not religious in nature but economic. Population growth was considered as an essential ingredient in attempts to accelerate industrial development. In 1972, however, this opposition was reversed and family planning services and education were made rapidly available through a very well developed public health infrastructure.

The demographic imprint of these two different policy sequences can be seen in Figure 5. Fertility decline began a decade earlier in Colombia than in Mexico. Indeed, in the early 1970s, Mexico was one of the very few Central or South American countries

John Cleland

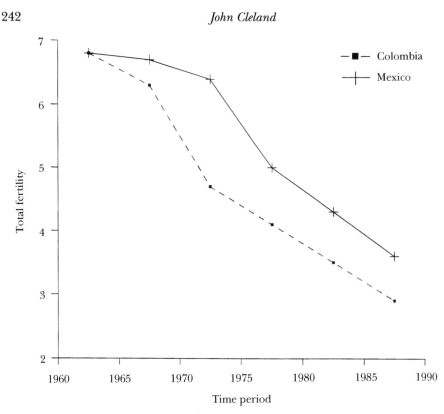

Figure 5. Fertility trends in Colombia and Mexico

without clear evidence of falls in fertility. A low level of social or economic development cannot provide a plausible explanation for the late onset of decline in Mexico. Incomes were higher there than in Colombia, for instance. The almost irresistible interpretation is that firm government opposition delayed reproductive change, by denying legitimacy to the idea of birth control and by imposing severe restrictions on the means of birth control. When official government policy changed, there was an immediate response; in the next five years, fertility fell sharply and has continued to fall since that time.

There are two general lessons to be drawn from this comparison. Firstly, many governments, like those in Colombia, have been reluctant to take a firm lead in matters of birth control until convinced that their actions will be successful and non-controversial. The role of non-government organisations and university researchers can be vital in demonstrating to political leaders the acceptability of and need for family planning. Secondly, the case of Mexico suggest that governments, at least in more centralised states, can postpone reproductive change by opposition to fertility regulation, even in settings where conditions are otherwise conducive to smaller families. Far too little attention has been paid to government actions, or inactions, that retard demographic transition.

3.5 Bangladesh and Pakistan

This case study, like the Korean one, concerns two countries that were once united. In the 1960s, before partition, Bangladesh and Pakistan shared the experience of President

Ayub's crash family planning programme that collapsed in the late 1960s as an almost complete failure. Since then, population policies have diverged radically. Pakistan, it could be argued, has not yet fully recovered from that first disastrous attempt to moderate the birth rate. Successive governments have paid lip service to the provision of family planning services but have never, until perhaps very recently, committed their funds or their prestige. Moreover, throughout the 1980s, the climate of opinion and public debate became in some ways more hostile to the idea of family planning, with a partial reversion to traditional Islamic values and laws.

In contrast, Bangladesh governments, faced with a highly visible population problem, had little choice but to address it as a top priority. Starting in 1975, a comprehensive family planning service was gradually created. Facilities for contraceptive sterilisation were made available at district level and financial compensation offered to couples seeking this method. A cadre of literate female workers was recruited to counsel women and distribute contraceptive supplies at the doorstep. Incessant publicity about family planning was disseminated through radio and other media. In all those endeavours, governments encountered very little political or religious opposition, unlike Pakistan.

Fertility trends in the two countries are shown in Figure 6. In Pakistan, there has been little change in fertility since the early 1960s. The most recent national survey showed the level of contraceptive practice to be a mere 12%. In Bangladesh, on the other hand,

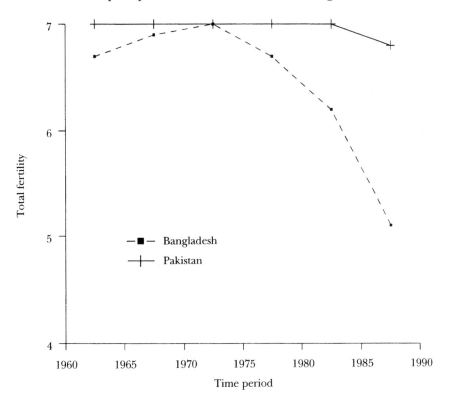

Figure 6. Fertility trends in Bangladesh and Pakistan

a steep decline has occurred. By the late 1980s, fertility had fallen from traditional levels of about 7.0 births per woman to about 5.0. The 1991 contraceptive prevalence survey showed that 40% of Bangladeshi couples were practising some form of contraception and fertility is now probably well below five births.

It is totally implausible to seek an explanation for this marked divergence in terms of differential development. Though levels of literacy and life expectancy are similar, Pakistan is a more urbanised country, with much higher incomes per head. Some have argued that fertility decline in Bangladesh may be driven by deepening poverty and economic desperation (Freedman & Freedman 1986). But detailed analysis has shown that reproductive change has been just as pronounced among the relatively affluent land owners as among landless labourers (Cleland *et al.* 1992). Thus there does not appear to be any strong link between extreme poverty and falling family sizes.

It is also implausible to argue that Pakistani couples want or need larger families than couples in Bangladesh. When both countries were surveyed in the mid-1970s, an almost identical profile of reproductive preferences were revealed. Subsequent surveys in Pakistan have attested to a huge latent demand for fertility regulation.

The experience of Bangladesh and Pakistan suggests that determined government action can hasten fertility transition, even in societies where conditions appear unfavourable. Bangladesh is one of the poorest countries in the world, has relatively high mortality, low literacy and very low levels of female employment. Such highly constrained circumstances, it appears, do not act as an absolute barrier to fertility decline. However, they may imply that exceptional efforts have to be made to present modern contraception in an acceptable manner. One of the keys to the success of the Bangladesh programme has been the widespread deployment of female workers who can overcome the severe barriers imposed by purdah, or female seclusion, by offering a doorstep service.

4. CONCLUDING COMMENTS

Several lessons can be drawn from the review of fertility trends in the period 1960 to 1990 and the case studies. Most importantly, there are grounds for optimism on the part of demographers about the economic and environmental future of the planet. During the past 30 years, fertility transition has spread throughout the developing world with a speed that has dazzled demographers and confounded many experts. It is easy to forget the profound pessimism about the prospects for fertility decline that prevailed in the 1960s and much of the 1970s. The turning point came in the mid-1970s with convincing signs that fertility decline was underway in Thailand and Indonesia, both largely agricultural countries with low incomes at that time. Hitherto, fertility decline had been confined to countries with a typically favourable conditions: rapid economic transformation in the case of Taiwan and South Korea; a metropolitan environment as in Hong Kong and Singapore; and the idiosyncrasies of an insular status such as Fiji, Mauritius and parts of the Caribbean.

As has been shown, fertility decline in the third world is now the norm rather than the exception. In Asia, the main exceptions are Pakistan, Afghanistan and some of the small countries of Indo-China. In Central and South America, fertility decline is already well advanced or still underway in all countries. Among the Arab states of north Africa and the Middle East, most countries have experienced falls in fertility though decline is not yet ubiquitous. Finally in sub-Saharan Africa, fertility transition is clearly starting in east and southern parts of the sub-continent, leaving central and western Africa as the main areas where fertility remains largely unchanged. The existence of such widespread transformations of reproductive behaviour is not yet fully appreciated outside the specialist domain of demography.

One of the major generalisations of demographic transition theory is that once fertility decline, fuelled by birth control within marriage, is underway, the trend is irreversible and sustained until fertility reaches replacement level or thereabouts. Like most simple generalisations, this one has to be qualified. Reversals have occurred, most notably the post second world war baby boom in western Europe and North America. More commonly, fertility may plateau before resuming a downward path, as has been the case in Egypt and Malaysia. Moreover, the speed of decline has varied from the near-precipitous drops in China and Mexico to a slow pace of change, as, for instance, in Philippines or Jordan. A much more profound uncertainty exists about the proposition that fertility will continue to fall until the replacement level of a little over two births per woman is reached. In the aggregate, there is a logic in this ultimate destination for levels of human reproduction because it implies long term stability of population sizes. But, at the level of families and individuals, such aggregate considerations may hold little force. It has already been noted that family sizes appear to have stabilised in some Latin American countries at a level that is well above replacement. In other regions, most notably sub-Saharan Africa and the Arab states, it is difficult to imagine the achievement of replacement level fertility under existing socioeconomic and cultural conditions. Fertility aspirations, as recorded in surveys, remain much higher. In Zimbabwe, for instance, which is at the forefront of fertility transition in Africa, the 1988 Demographic and Health Survey indicates a mean ideal family size of 5.4 children among currently married women; and nearly half of women who already have 4 or more living children want additional children.

Of course, societal conditions do not remain stable. Indeed one of the biggest mistakes of demographers has been to underestimate the rapidity with which societies change. Kenya provides a good example of the pace of change. A national survey conducted in the late 1970s depicted a highly pronatalist society. Total fertility amounted to about eight births per woman; mean desired family size was about seven children; only 16% of married women wanted to cease childbearing; and only 7% were practising contraception. Ten years later, a repeat survey showed a sharp decline in fertility and a rise in contraceptive practice to 27%. In addition, average desired family size had dropped to 4.4 children and 49% wanted to have no more.

A second major lesson is that the relationship between socioeconomic modernisation and fertility transition is neither strong nor straightforward. In the last 30 years, fertility has fallen sharply in condition of poverty and widespread illiteracy. As has also been shown, it can remain high, even in urbanised, reasonably educated populations. Perhaps the biggest mistake of many population scientists has been their belief that poverty and illiteracy inevitably imply a demand, or need for large numbers of children.

Of course, reproductive change is unlikely to occur in static societies, where traditional values and forms of social organisation are still unchallenged. But here again there are grounds for optimism. Countries of the world are increasingly interconnected by mass media, migration and transport networks. People are progressively exposed to new models of behaviour and new aspirations. Such trends no doubt facilitate the acceptance of new ideas about family size and reproductive control.

Finally, the evidence presented in this paper emphasises the crucial role that political leaders and other leaders can play in determining the timing and speed of fertility decline. The future course of fertility in countries where it is still high depends to a large extent on the actions of political leaders.

REFERENCES

Aslam, A. 1993 Beyond the Holy War. *Populi* **20**, 7–9.

Casterline, J. (1993). Fertility transition in Asia. In *The onset of fertility transition in sub-Saharan Africa* (eds. T. Locoh & V. Hertrich). Liège: Ordina.

China Population Today 1993 Vol. **10**. Beijing: China Population Information and Research Centre.

Chowdhury, A.K., Alauddin, M., Khan, A.R. & Chen, L.C. 1978 Experience in Pakistan and Bangladesh. In *The effect of infant and child survival on fertility* (ed. S.H. Preston). New York: Academic Press.

Cleland, J., Phillips, J., Amin, S. & Kamal, G.M. 1992 *The determinants of reproductive change in Bangladesh*. World Bank, South Asia Region, report No. 10389–BD.

Cutright, P. 1983 The ingredients of recent fertility decline in developing countries. *Int. Fam. Plann. Persp.* **9**, 101–109.

Davis, K. 1945 The world demographic transition. *Ann. Am. Acad. Pol. Soc. Sci.* **273**:1–11.

Demeny, P. 1972 Early fertility decline in Austria–Hungary: a lesson in demographic transition. In *Population and Social Change* (eds. D.V. Glass & R. Revelle). London: Edward Arnold.

Farid, S. 1993 Family planning, health and family well-being in the Arab world. Paper presented at Arab Population Conference, Amman, 1993.

Freedman, D. & Freedman, R. 1986 *Adding demand-side variables to the intersection between demand and supply in Bangladesh*. The World Bank: Population, Health and Nutrition Note 86–128.

Freedman, R., Khoo, S-E. & Supraptilah, B. 1981 Use of modern contraceptives in Indonesia: a challenge to conventional wisdoms. *Int. Fam. Plann. Persp.* **7**: 3–15.

Guzman, J.M. 1993 The onset of fertility decline in Latin America. In *The onset of fertility transition in sub-Saharan Africa* (eds. T. Locoh & V. Hertrich). Liège: Ordina.

Hull, T. 1991 Government and society in South-East Asian family planning programmes: the case of Indonesia, Vietnam and the Philippines. Paper presented at the 1991 annual meeting of the Population Association of America, Washington DC, 21–23 March.

Jordan Ministry of Public Health 1992 *Jordan Population and Family Health Survey*. Amman, Dept. of Statistics.

Knodel, J. & Van de Walle, E. 1986 Lessons from the past: policy implications of historical fertility studies. In *The decline of fertility in Europe* (eds. A. Coale & S.Watkins). Princeton: Princeton University Press.

Kwon, T-H. 1993 Exploring socio-cultural explanations of fertility transition in South Korea. In *The revolution in Asian fertility* (eds. R. Leete & I. Alam). Oxford: Oxford University Press.

Leete, R. 1989 Dual fertility trends in Malaysia's multi-ethnic society. *Int. Fam. Plann. Persp.* **15**, 58-65.

Leete R. & Tan, B.A. 1992 Contrasting fertility trends among ethnic groups in Malaysia. In *The revolution in Asian fertility* (eds. R. Leete & I. Alam). Oxford: Oxford University Press.

Lloyd, C.B. & Ivanov, S. 1988 The effects of improved child survival on family planning practice and fertility. *Stud. Fam. Plann.* **19**, 141–161.

Mauldin, W.P. & Berelson, B. 1978 Conditions of fertility decline in developing countries, 1965–75. *Stud. Fam. Plann.* **9**, 90–146.

Mauldin, W.P. & Ross, J. 1991 Family planning programs: efforts and results, 1982–1989. *Stud. Fam. Plann.* **22**, 350–367.

Mundigo, A. 1990 The role of family planning programmes in the fertility transition of Latin America. Paper presented at seminar on fertility transition in Latin America. Buenos Aires, 3–6 April, 1990.

Notestein, F. (1945) Population: the long view. In *Food for the world* (ed. T.W. Shultz). Chicago: University of Chicago Press.

Perez, A. & Cabigon, J. 1989 Contraceptive practice in the Philippines: a synthesis. *Philipp. Pop. J.* **1**, 36–57.

Rodrigues, G. & Avavena, R. 1991 Socio-economic factors and the transition to low fertility in less developed countries. In *Proceedings of the Demographic and Health Surveys World Conference.* Maryland, CO: IRD, Macro International Inc. vol. 1, 39–72.

Rodrigues, G. & Cleland, J. 1991 Socio-economic determinants of marital fertility in twenty countries: a multivariate analysis. In International Statistical Institute, *World Fertility Survey Conference Record of Proceedings Vol. 2.* Netherlands: Voorburg.

Thompson, W. 1929 Population. *Am. J. Soc.* **9**: 54–70.

United Nations 1987a *Fertility behaviour in the context of development.* New York: Dept. of International Economic and Social Affairs, Pop. Stud. No. 100.

United Nations 1987b *World population policies.* New York: Department of International Economic and Social Affairs, Pop. Stud. No. 102.

United Nations 1989 *Trends in Population Policies.* New York: Department of International Economic and Social Affairs, Pop. Stud. No. 114.

Van de Walle, F. 1986 Infant mortality in Europe during the demographic transition. In *The decline of fertility in Europe* (eds. A.J. Coale & S.C. Watkins). Princeton: Princeton University Press.

Warwick, D.P. 1986 The Indonesian family planning programme: Government influence and client choice. *Pop. Dev. Rev* **12**, 453–490.

Introduction to Session 4:

FAMILY PLANNING AND REPRODUCTIVE HEALTH
P.N. Tandon

In the next session, 'Family Planning and Reproductive Health', Dr Mahmoud Fathalla provided a global overview of the subject. Based on his vast experience, he commented, 'Planet Earth is sending signals of distress, loud and clear. Science, however, can detect few messages of hope. One such message is the success story of family planning. During the past 25 years the number of contraceptive users has increased from an estimate of 31 to 381 million. Women are increasingly looking beyond a domestic and reproductive role, into playing a productive role in their societies. He reiterated the observations of Dr Sadik that there was a major unmet need for contraception in developing countries. About 400 million couples in the developing countries do not have access to family planning services and at least 100-120 million would use it, if available. Dr Kerstin Hagenfeldt's presentation on the current status of contraceptive research and development acquires an added significance in the light of Dr Fathalla's observations. She pointed out that in the face of increasing demand for contraceptives only a few new methods have been added during the past decade or are likely to be added in the near future; there is a reduction in financial resources for research and development, and global expenditure on contraceptive research and development from all sources is less than 3% of annual global sales. There were identified needs for research to develop new generations of fertility regulation methods, with special emphasis on incorporating protection against AIDS and other sexually transmitted diseases. It was necessary to involve women's health advocates and potential users in all decison making and advisory bodies concerned with research in this area. Research on male contraceptives has not received due attention.

Professor G.P. Talwar summarized the current status and future prospects for immunological approaches to fertility control both for women and men. These may provide alternative methods, which demand periodic intake, can be administered by semi-skilled personnel, are reversible and do not disturb menstrual regularity.

Dr Fred Sai discussed the various hinderances to universal availability, accessibility and acceptability of family planning programmes in different parts of the world. He referred to the developmental, political, religious and cultural as well as the legal, technical and financial constraints. Suggestions were made for overcoming these. Based on the information available from countries like Bangladesh, Indonesia, Brazil and Italy, he concluded that religious beliefs do not necessarily constitute a hinderance to achieving demographic transition.

Dr Soledad Díaz described her experience of a very successful programme in Chile which included integrated maternal child care, contraception and breast feeding.

Treatment of women with respect and as responsible people, provision of information, education and support, and tailoring the programmes to facilitate their participation were some of the factors responsibile for success.

Professor Roger Short, discussing the contraceptive strategies for the future, pointed out that we already have a wide range of safe and effective contraceptives. It was not necessary to wait for newer and better ones, even though existing contraception was required to work when taking into consideration the additional needs for AIDS control. He exhorted the developed world to provide the funding for supporting programmes in the developing countries by allocating 1% of their defence budget. Dr Sadik had earlier suggested that the overseas development aid for family planning should be raised from 1.5 to 4% to provide resources for meeting the demands.

4/1

Family Planning and Reproductive Health
– a Global Overview
Mahmoud F. Fathalla

ABSTRACT

Total Fertility Rate in developing countries, as a whole, has declined from 6.1 in 1965–1970 to 3.9 in 1985–1990, more than halfway to the fertility level needed to keep population size constant. During the same period, the number of contraceptive users in all developing countries has increased from an estimated 31 million to 381 million, and the prevalence of contraceptive use has increased from 9% to 51%. A scientific revolution in contraceptive technology has helped hundreds of millions of women, living in the most diverse circumstances, to achieve their aspirations in fertility regulation.

The past few decades have witnessed a major interest among governments in the rates of fertility of their populations. As of 1990, only 28.8% of world population lived in countries with 'satisfactory' rates of fertility, according to government appraisal, and in the less developed regions, 13.9%. Government perceptions of fertility levels and their interventions vary and fall within a wide spectrum, from the desirable to the acceptable to the objectionable. Family planning is a dignified behaviour and services should be provided with respect and dignity. Women should not be coerced into family planning; nor should they be coerced into motherhood by denying them access to family planning or by denying them any choice in life beyond childbearing and child rearing.

The ability to regulate and control fertility is a basic ingredient of reproductive health. Family planning saves lives. An unwanted or unplanned pregnancy can have serious physical, mental and social consequences for the woman. Pregnancies that are too early, too late or too many carry extra hazards not only for the health of the woman, but also for the child.

The World Health Organization (WHO)'s minimal estimate for the yearly incidence of bacterial and viral sexually-transmitted diseases, excluding HIV infection, is 130 million. For the year 2000, WHO projects a cumulative total of 30–40 million HIV infections and 10 million adult AIDS cases, of which nearly 90% will be in developing countries. The implications for family planning and contraceptive technology need to be considered.

Unsafe abortion is one of the great neglected problems of health care in developing countries. It is estimated that out of the 500,000 maternal deaths that occur each year throughout the world, as many as one-quarter to one-third may be a consequence of complications of unsafe abortion procedures.

Major challenges still face family planning today, one being the need to create a common ground between proponents of the demographic, health and human rights rationales for family planning. Recent data suggests that the total number of cases of unmet need for contraception in developing countries could be in excess of 100 million. There is an urgent need to expand the access and improve the quality of family planning services. Science must be mobilised for a Contraception-21 initiative to launch a second contraceptive technology revolution—surely a collective responsibility of the international community.

1. INTRODUCTION

The pessimists may shake their heads, but it is too early to despair of the future of humanity ... Some day, let us be sure, the world will recognise all that it owes to those noble pioneers who, at the risk of obloquy, had the vision to see the fate that threatens Man and the courage to face it with hope (Havelock Ellis 1931).

Spaceship Earth is sending signals of distress, loud and clear. The globe is warming; the ozone-layer is being depleted; and degradation of natural resources, soil erosion, water stress, deforestation and loss of biological diversity are threatening the quality of life. As the 20th century draws to a close, the world is confronted by a daunting challenge: to bring growing human numbers and their increasing needs into balance with the natural resource base that underpins any development. Panic and apportioning of blame is unhelpful at a time for scientific objectivity and for international cooperation.

There are grounds for hope and guarded optimism. A revolution in reproductive behaviour has been taking place in developing countries in the past few decades. Family planning has been a great success story. The optimism, however, is guarded because there are still major challenges ahead.

2. FAMILY PLANNING TRENDS IN DEVELOPING COUNTRIES

The past few decades have witnessed a major change in reproductive behaviour in developing countries. The Total Fertility Rate (the average number of children that would be born per woman if all women lived to the end of their child-bearing years and bore children at prevailing levels of fertility) in developing countries, as a whole, has declined from 6.1 in 1965–1970 to 3.9 in 1985–1990 (Ross *et al.* 1992). Remarkably, the developing world, in just a few decades, has come over half way to the replacement fertility level (the level needed to keep population size constant) of 2.1 children per woman. With a further decline of 1.8 children per woman, fertility in developing countries would reach the replacement level.

Table 1. *Trends in fertility in the developing world by region. (Ross* et al. *1992).*

	births per woman	
	1960–65	1985–90
East Asia	5.9	2.4
South Asia	6.0	4.4
Middle East and North Africa	6.9	5.1
sub-Saharan Africa	6.7	6.6
Latin America	6.0	3.6
mean fertility	6.1	3.9

The adoption of a smaller family norm, with consequent decline in total fertility, should not be viewed only in demographic terms. It means that people, and particularly women, are empowered to take control of their fertility and to plan their lives; it means that more children are born by choice, not by chance, and that births can be planned to take place at optimal times for childbearing to ensure better health for women and children; and it means that families are able to invest relatively more in a smaller number of beloved children while trying to prepare them for a better future.

Family planning should not be looked upon in a narrow perspective as a measure to ease the world population problem. Family planning will be a permanent feature of the way of life of all succeeding generations on this planet. Our reproductive function is being voluntarily adapted to dramatic new realities. What we are witnessing is a major evolutionary jump that is science-mediated, rather than brutally imposed by Nature.

To put the rate of fertility decline in developing countries in perspective, a recent study compared the time taken for fertility to decline from 6.5 to 3.5 in different countries. What took 58 years in the USA took 27 years in Indonesia, 15 years in Colombia, 8 years in Thailand, and merely 7 years in China (UNFPA 1991a).

In developing countries, the prevalence of contraceptive use—defined as the percentage of married women of reproductive age (or their husbands) using any form of contraception—rose from 9% in 1965–1970 to 51% in 1985–1990. The total number of contraceptive users in developing countries is estimated to have risen, during this period, from 31 million to 381 million (UNFPA 1991a).

Between the mid-1960s and the present, 17 countries have had fertility declines of more than 50%, and an additional 31 countries have had declines exceeding 25% (Ross *et al. 1992*). Declines are widespread in East Asia and Latin America, are moderately widespread in South and South-East Asia and in North Africa and the Middle East, and have just begun in sub-Saharan Africa (Table 1). This reflects variations in the trends for contraceptive prevalence in the different regions (Table 2).

Three major factors have contributed to this revolution in reproductive behaviour. Women are looking beyond a domestic reproductive role, to more productive roles, helped by socioeconomic progress and change. A technological revolution has introduced a range of effective contraceptive methods that are convenient to use. Governments and

Table 2. *Trends in contraceptive prevalence in the developing world by region.*
(United Nations Population Fund 1991a)

	percentage use	
	1960–65	1990
East Asia	13	70
South Asia	7	40
Africa	5	17
Latin America	14	60
All developing countries	9	51

the international community realised that enabling women to control their fertility requires information and services.

3. THE CONTRACEPTIVE TECHNOLOGY REVOLUTION

In the past, contraceptive choice was limited to coitally-related methods which lacked in effectiveness, or to permanent methods. Contraceptive choices have now been broadened. Contraception was moved outside the bedroom by the development of systemic methods such as the pill. People no longer had to make the choice between a method to be used at every coitus or a permanent method; long-acting reversible methods now offer protection ranging from one month to several years. Also, highly effective but reversible methods became an available option. Technical developments have allowed sterilisation to be performed as out-patient procedure and without the need for general anaesthesia.

Perhaps the most significant development brought about by the contraceptive technology revolution has been the empowerment of women. For the first time, women had access to effective methods for regulation of their own fertility.

4. PREVALENCE OF VARIOUS CONTRACEPTIVE METHODS

The most striking feature about the prevalence of contraceptive methods worldwide is the diversity of method mix between different countries and regions (Table 3). The general tendency is for modern methods to prevail, although there are no signs that varying patterns of use are converging to a single typical method distribution. This illustrates the need for a broad range of methods to meet the widely diverse needs and perceptions of people. There is not, and there probably will never be, an ideal method of contraception for all users, but there can be a variety of 'ideal methods' for the needs of different users (Fathalla 1990a).

The second striking feature is the prevalence of modern methods of contraception in some developing countries, where there has been a dramatic decline in fertility in the past few decades.

Table 3. *Prevalence of different contraceptive methods in developing and developed regions of the world (%). (UN 1989)*

	more developed regions	less developed regions	world
female sterilization	10	33	26
male sterilization	5	12	10
intrauterine device	8	24	19
oral contraception	20	12	15
condom	19	6	10
injectables	–	2	1
vaginal barrier methods	3	1	2
rhythm	13	5	7
withdrawal	20	3	8
other methods	2	3	2

Clinic and supply methods account for approximately 80% of contraceptive use worldwide. These methods, which include male and female sterilisation, intrauterine devices, the pill, injectable hormonal contraceptives, condoms and female barrier methods (diaphragm, cervical cap, spermicidal foams, creams, jellies and sponges) make up a larger fraction of contraceptive use in developing than in developed countries— about 90% and 65%, respectively (United Nations 1989), The prevalence of traditional methods is more in developed than in developing countries, 24% and 6% respectively. This group includes rhythm or periodic abstinence, withdrawal (coitus interruptus), abstinence, douching and various folk methods.

The heavy reliance on modern methods of contraception in developing countries may reflect their more recent adoption. Whereas in most developed countries marital fertility reached low levels well before modern contraceptives were invented, in most developing countries contraception did not become widespread until modern methods became available (United Nations 1989). There is also another rationale for this difference. Modern methods, particularly clinic-based methods are very effective but can be associated with side-effects. Where safe pregnancy termination services are widely available, and where the health risks of continuing with the pregnancy are negligible, a relatively lower efficacy is an acceptable trade-off for freedom from side-effects. The situation in most developing countries, on the other hand, is such that contraceptive failure can be a major health hazard—hence the trend to use more effective methods.

The prevalence of modern methods of contraception in developing countries has been helped by government support of family planning programmes. A recent United Nations survey on access to modern methods of fertility regulation gave these results (United Nations Secretariat 1990):

Access restricted	5
Access unrestricted	
no governmental support	10
indirect support	13
direct support	103
Total	131 countries

4.1 Sterilisation

Sterilisation accounts for over one third of world fertility regulation. In most countries where trends can be traced, sterilisation has increased in prevalence more rapidly than other methods. The prevalence of sterilisation is highest in Eastern Asia and Northern America, while this method is uncommon in sub-Saharan Africa, Western Asia and Eastern and Southern Europe. Sterilisation use is remarkably concentrated geographically. Twenty countries contain over 95% of all users in the developing world; China has over half of that total, and India a fourth (Ross 1992). In general, female sterilisation is far more common than male sterilisation and the gap between the two continues to widen.

4.2 Intrauterine devices (IUDs)

In the majority of countries, IUDs account for less than 10% of contraceptive use.

However, because of its high prevalence in China (more than 40% of all contraceptive used, the IUD has more users worldwide than the pill. In most countries with information about trends, the IUD has increased its share or has retained approximately the same share of total use.

4.3 Oral contraceptives

The 'pill' makes up an important fraction of contraceptive use in the most countries, although not in the two most populous, China and India. The pill is especially uncommon in Japan, where it is not yet approved for use as a contraceptive. Globally, it comprises approximately 15% of contraceptive use, with estimates of 12% and 20% for the developing and developed countries, respectively.

By region, the share of the pill in total contraceptive practice is highest in Africa, Latin America and Northern and Western Europe (28–41% of total use). For countries with trend information, the share of the pill in total contraceptive practice has more often decreased than increased in recent years. Increases in the proportion are common in Europe, however, and they also appear in several developing countries. In other countries where the share of use has declined, this decline often merely means that the number of women using the pill did not increase as rapidly as did the number using other methods. In some countries where the overall prevalence of the pill has decreased, such as the USA and the Netherlands, the more recent data show a renewed growth in use of this method (United Nations 1989).

4.4 Condom

Globally, 10% of contraceptive users use the condom within marriage. The condom tends to be more popular in developed than in developing countries. In addition to Japan, where in 1986, 69% of contraceptive users employed the condom, regions where this method is relatively important include Europe, Northern America and the Caribbean. It is less frequently used in Africa, Central America and tropical South America. In Asia, the condom attracts a substantial share of contraceptive users in several countries.

In most countries, there is little change in the proportion of total contraceptive use attributable to the condom. This, however, may not apply to the use of the condom outside stable unions. In the US, use of the condom among sexually active single women increased from 8% to 14% between 1982 and 1988, while remaining stable among married women (Mosher & Pratt 1990).

4.5 Other methods

Injectable hormonal contraceptives account globally for an estimated 1% of total contraceptive use.

Vaginal barrier methods have a similar number of users. In most countries, their use has either decreased in relation to other methods or has maintained a roughly constant low share of current practice.

Rhythm, or periodic abstinence, and withdrawal are employed by 7% and 8%, respectively, of contraceptive users. Withdrawal is the more common of the two in most European countries, while rhythm is more common in most non-European countries, In most countries, rhythm and withdrawal have been declining in use in relation to other methods.

Table 4. *Governments' overall appraisal of fertility rates, 1990. (UN 1992)*

	more developed regions	less developed regions	world
rates too low			
countries	11	9	20
population (%)	20.8	1.1	5.5
rates satisfactory			
countries	27	48	75
population (%)	79.2	13.9	28.8
rates too high			
countries	0	74	74
population (%)	0	85.0	65.6

5. FAMILY PLANNING AND THE STATE

The basic objective of the State is to promote the economic and social development of the country and to ensure the maximum well-being of its citizens. The objective applies to the future as well as to the present... Avoiding a long term weakening of a country brought about by a dangerously low birth rate and, inversely, avoiding excessive population growth when it becomes and obstacle to economic development and to the well-being of the population must certainly be among the basic goals of all governments (Veil 1978).

No society, primitive or advanced, no culture, no religion, and no legal code has been neutral about reproductive life, and governments have begun to appraise rates of fertility of their populations and, where appropriate, to develop policies of intervention to increase or decrease fertility (Table 4).

As of 1990, only 28.8% of world population lived in countries with 'satisfactory' rates of fertility, according to government appraisal (United Nations 1992), and only 13.9% in the less developed regions.

An analysis derived from a comparison between government's perceptions concerning the rate of fertility and the actual fertility rates suggests that fertility perceptions tend to be influenced but are not determined simply by the prevailing demographic situation (Table 5). In countries with the same total fertility rates, the assessments vary from too low, to satisfactory to too high.

Governments' perceptions of fertility levels are often translated into policies of intervention, to lower, maintain or increase fertility (Table 6). As of 1990, 76.2% of world population live in countries with policies of intervention in the rate of fertility, with 64.6% aiming to lower fertility, 7.3% to maintain and 4.3% to raise it (United Nations 1992). For 83.8% of the population in developing countries, governments have policies of intervention to lower fertility.

Table 5. *Comparison of total fertility rate, 1985–1990, and governments' perception of the rate (number of countries). (UN 1992)*

	perception of fertility		
	too low	satisfactory	too high
total fertility rate (TFT)			
fewer than 2.0	10	17	0
2.0 – 4.0	4	21	11
4.0 – 6.0	3	7	25
more than 6.0	2	17	29
number of countries	19	62	65

The concern of governments is legitimate. But government interventions vary, can sometimes be clumsy and may raise ethical concerns (Fathalla 1984). Measures taken by governments to influence fertility behaviour may be direct or indirect.

Indirect measures intended to lower fertility include improving the education and status of women, enhancing child survival so that people will not need to over-reproduce in anticipation of expected child losses, and providing care and protection for the aged to make children less needed for old age security. These indirect measures, apart from any intended effect on fertility, are 'good' on their own, serving worthy social causes; however, social policies specifically directed at changing fertility fall within a wide spectrum, from the desirable to the acceptable to the objectionable.

Provision of family planning services, including education and information, is a desirable social measure on its own. Maternity or paternity benefits and family allowances, as measures intended to increase fertility, can also be justified as desirable social policies on their own. Promotion of public awareness is acceptable, whether it is intended to

Table 6. *Governments with policies of intervention to influence rates of fertility, 1990. (UN 1992)*

	more developed regions	less developed regions	world
rates too low			
countries	10	10	20
population (%)	14.4	1.3	4.3
rates satisfactory			
countries	7	10	17
population (%)	27.8	1.3	7.3
rates too high			
countries	0	66	66
population (%)	0	83.8	64.6

decrease or increase fertility. It is, however, at the borderline. It can slip into the potentially objectionable if it results in undue psychological pressure on individuals.

In another category are a range of measures including incentives, disincentives and coercion (to decrease fertility), and restriction of access to family planning and abortion (to increase it). These strong-handed measures by governments may impact adversely on the health of women whether they are meant to decrease or increase a woman's fertility. As far as health and human rights are concerned, there is little to choose between coerced contraception, sterilisation or abortion because society does not want the child, and coerced motherhood because society wants the child. From a health point of view, coerced motherhood may be more serious. It can cost the woman her life.

In 1976, the national population policy of India permitted state legislatures to enact laws for compulsory sterilisation. During the following national emergency period, it was reported that several million forced sterilisations were performed (Andorka 1990). The opposite side of the same coin was the declaration of Nicolae Ceaucescu that 'the fetus is the socialist property of the whole society. Giving birth is a patriotic duty... Those who refuse to have children are deserters, escaping the law of natural continuity' (Hord *et al.* 1991). In October 1966, Romania severely restricted the availability of abortion and prohibited the import of contraceptives. The birth rate, 15.6 per 1000 population in 1965, after a transient rise, was down to 14.3 in 1983. Meanwhile, the maternal mortality rate increased from 86 maternal deaths per 100000 live births in 1966 to 150 in 1984, with 86% of these deaths being attributed to induced abortion. In 1988, 505 maternal deaths were linked to abortion. On 25 December 1989, abortion was legalised again.

Romania under Ceaucescu may have been an extreme example of coerced motherhood, but coerced motherhood or compulsory childbearing, broadly defined, is still a problem in the world today. Women are coerced into childbearing when they are denied the choice, when they are denied the means to avoid unwanted pregnancy, and when society makes children the only goods a woman can deliver and is expected to deliver. In many societies in the world today, women are left with no choice in life except to pursue a reproductive career (United Nations 1990).

6. FAMILY PLANNING AND REPRODUCTIVE HEALTH

In the constitution of the World Health Organization, health is defined as a state of complete physical, mental and social well-being. While this ideal may not be readily attainable, it serves to remind us that health is not merely the absence of disease or infirmity.

Family planning and reproductive health should be viewed in this broad context of the definition of health (Fathalla 1991a, 1992a). The ability to regulate and control fertility is a basic ingredient in the positive definition of health, particularly for women. A woman who is unable to regulate and control her fertility cannot be considered in a state of complete physical, mental and social well-being. She cannot have the mental joy of a pregnancy that is wanted, avoid the mental distress of a pregnancy that is unwanted, plan her life, pursue her education, and enjoy both a productive and reproductive career (Fathalla 1993a).

The ability of a man and woman to engage in a mutually fulfilling sexual relationship is an important element in reproductive health. Freedom from the risk of unwanted pregnancy helps a woman to fulfil her sexuality and to better enjoy sexual relationship.

6.1 Family planning saves lives

An unwanted or unplanned pregnancy can have serious physical, mental and social consequences for the woman. These consequences vary widely for different women in different societies, but they account for much avoidable suffering and deaths in the world today.

The extent of the physical hazards of unwanted pregnancies depends largely on two factors: the availability of efficient and accessible maternity services to deal with complications of pregnancy and childbirth, and the availability of safe pregnancy termination services.

Although maternal deaths have become rare events in industrialised countries, they are still a major cause of death for women of childbearing age in developing countries. The World Health Organization has recently estimated that over 500000 women continue to die each year from causes related to pregnancy and childbirth (World Health Organization 1991). The maternal mortality ratio in developing countries is estimated to be on average 450 per 100000 births, approximately one maternal death for every 220 births (World Health Organization 1991). Worldwide, and particularly in developing countries, prevention of unwanted pregnancy is making an impact on safe motherhood (Fathalla 1992c).

Pregnancies that are too early, too close, too late or too many carry extra hazards not only for the health of the woman but also for the child. Evidence implying that family planning does indeed help save children's lives is beginning to become more clearly available. A recent study analysed the impact of fertility patterns upon child survival for 18 countries, based on data from the Demographic and Health Surveys (Hobcraft 1992). Results were also contrasted with those from earlier World Fertility Surveys. The findings confirmed that children born to teenage mothers, especially those under age 18, experience considerable excess mortality before the age of five. More important at the population level is the deleterious effect of short birth intervals for child survival. The study showed that the overall impact of poor timing of births on child survival is substantial in many countries, but has been improving over time, probably as a result of increased use of family planning.

6.2 Family planning and sexually transmitted diseases (STDs)

One of the most disappointing aspects of medicine during the past 25 years has been the great increase in the incidence of infections caused by sexually transmitted agents. STDs are now the most common group of notifiable infectious diseases in most countries. The World Health Organization's minimum estimate for the yearly incidence of bacterial and viral STDs (excluding HIV infection) is 130 million (World Health Organization 1992).

It may be postulated that the availability of contraception can encourage casual sexual relations. Although the postulate has never been proven, it has been used to justify the restrictive attitudes in some societies toward contraceptive availability to adolescents. It may be that the availability of the more convenient systemic methods of contraception has decreased reliance on the coitus-related barrier methods that offer protection against STDs. In developed countries, there was an apparent time coincidence between the contraceptive revolution, the sexual revolution, and the explosive epidemic of STDs. This may have been a reason for postulating a link. In developing countries, on the other hand, there is no such clear correlation. African countries with high incidence of STDs have the lowest prevalence of contraceptive use. The People's Republic of China, with a very high contraceptive prevalence, does not seem so far to have STDs as a major public health problem.

6.3 Family planning and the AIDS pandemic

The pandemic of human immunodeficiency virus (HIV) infection, which appears to have commenced in the late 1970s or early 1980s, has been a major set-back for efforts to improve reproductive health. The World Health Organization has estimated, as of early 1992, that some two million AIDS cases may have occurred worldwide since the beginning of the pandemic and at least 10–12 million HIV infections (World Health Organization 1992). For the year 2000, WHO projects a cumulative total of 30–40 million HIV infections and 10 million adult AIDS cases, of which nearly 90% will be in developing countries.

The outbreak of the AIDS pandemic, and particularly its potentially devastating impact in Africa, does not in any way decrease the future need for family planning in that continent. Women in Africa and in other parts of the world deserve to have access to services to plan their families and their lives, irrespective of the AIDS situation and the level of population growth. To put the impact of AIDS in perspective, it should be noted that the upwardly revised projections for AIDS deaths for men, women and children in the decade of the 1990s is equivalent to only about one month of global population growth (Potts & Rosenfield 1990). Also, the number of women who die each year as a result of unsafe abortion is higher than the number known to have died from AIDS through the decade of the 1980s.

On the other hand, the AIDS pandemic has implications for contraceptive technology (Fathalla 1990b). Contraceptive choices, at the individual and programme level, will have to take the risk and prevalence of HIV infection into consideration. The need for dual protection against unwanted pregnancy and against STDs/HIV poses a challenge to the field of contraceptive research and development.

6.4 Contraceptive safety

In view of the major worldwide expansion in the use of modern methods of contraception by healthy women over prolonged periods of time, contraceptive safety has become an important issue in reproductive health (Fathalla 1991b). The past two decades have witnessed a major global research effort on the safety of contraceptives. In fact, no other drugs or devices in the history of medicine have ever been subjected and continue to be subjected to such scrutiny. As a testimony to this scrutiny, no significant public health problem has yet emerged in spite of contraceptive use by hundreds of millions of women.

7. FAMILY PLANNING AND ABORTION

Governments are urged to take appropriate steps to help women avoid abortion, which in no case should be promoted as a method of family planning, and, wherever possible, provide for the humane treatment and counselling of women who have had recourse to abortion [International Conference on Population 1984 (United Nations 1984)].

It is estimated that 36–53 million induced abortions are performed in the world each year, an annual rate of 32–46 abortions per 1000 women of reproductive age (Henshaw, 1990),

The performing of abortions, which in many countries was prohibited or regulated by strict legal constraints, underwent substantial liberalisation in the past few decades. A review of current abortion laws shows that some 52 countries, with about 25% of the world's population, fall into the most restrictive category, where abortions are prohibited except when the woman's life would be endangered if the pregnancy were carried to term (Henshaw 1990). Forty-two countries, comprising 12% of the world's population, have statutes authorising abortion on broader medical grounds—for example, to avert a threat to the woman's general health and sometimes for genetic or judicial indications such as incest or rape—but not for social indications alone. Some 23% of the world's population live in 13 countries which allow abortion for social or socio–medical indications. The least restrictive category includes the 25 countries (about 40% of the world's population) where abortion is permitted up to a certain point in gestation without requiring that specific indications be present.

It should be pointed out that abortion rates do not necessarily correlate with the degree of liberalisation of the abortion law. For example, the Netherlands, with a liberal abortion law, has one of the lowest abortion rates. Restrictive laws also do not necessarily mean that safe abortion services are unavailable. Services may exist despite legal constraints because laws are either interpreted with flexibility or are not vigorously enforced. On the other hand, absence of restrictions does not guarantee that safe services are available to all.

Information on clandestine abortions is difficult to document. Combining various estimates yields a total of 15 million clandestine abortions. However, since these figures cannot be fully relied upon, the actual number may be as low as ten million or as high as 22 million (Henshaw 1990).

It is estimated that out of the 500,000 maternal deaths that occur each year throughout the world, as many as one-quarter to one-third may be a consequence of complications of unsafe abortion procedures (World Health Organization 1990). Unsafe abortion is one of the great neglected problems of health care in developing countries and a serious concern to women during their reproductive lives. Contrary to common belief, most women seeking abortion are married or living in stable unions and already have several children. However, in all parts of the world, a small but increasing proportion of abortion seekers are unmarried adolescents; in some urban centres in Africa, they represent the majority. WHO estimates that more than half of the deaths caused by induced abortion occur in South and South-East Asia, followed by sub-Saharan Africa.

The magnitude of the problem of unsafe abortion in the world today is a striking testimony to the magnitude of the problem of unwanted pregnancy.

8. THE CHALLENGES AHEAD

Significant progress has been made in the field of family planning. Compared to progress in other fields of human development, the achievements have been spectacular. There is, however, no room for complacency. There are still major tasks ahead and major challenges to be faced. The penalties for our failure to act responsibly and collectively as a world community will exempt no-one on this planet and will be passed to all future generations.

8.1 Creating a common ground

Family planning could bring more benefits to more people at less cost than any other single 'technology' now available to the human race. But it is not appreciated widely enough that this would still be true even if there were no such thing as a population problem. [UNICEF (Grant 1992)].

A major challenge facing the family planning movement is the need to create a common ground for all advocates of family planning. There are three major *rationales* for the organised family planning movement: *demographic, health*, and *human rights* rationales. They have evolved separately, at different times and for different objectives. Although most people are willing to embrace all three, each rationale has strong advocates who sometimes find themselves in conflict with enthusiastic supporters of another rationale.

Whatever one's concern for family planning may be, be it demographic and development driven, be it health or human rights, the ultimate objective is human welfare. If there is a lesson learnt from the past few decades, it is that there is more common ground between the three rationales for family planning than some people realise (Fathalla 1987).

The family planning movement started as a movement by women for women. Dr Marie Stopes, who wrote *Wise Parenthood* in 1918 and opened the first clinic in London in March 1921, was not a demographer and was not a physician. She had a doctorate degree in palaeobotany (McLaren 1990). When Margaret Sanger, her sister Ethel, and a social worker Fania, opened the first clinic in Brooklyn, the clinic was soon raided and the three women arrested. Released on bail, they promptly reopened the clinic and were arrested and charged with maintaining a public nuisance (Suitters 1973).

Demographic concerns, serious as they are, should not override the human rights and health rationale of contraception. A reproductive rights and health approach, with women at its centre, can only help to achieve long-term demographic objectives. Some demographers have clung to the belief that programmes and policies based on voluntary family planning would not bring about substantial reductions in fertility in the foreseeable future. They have argued that the demand for family planning would not be nearly sufficient to produce stabilisation of the population in time to avert catastrophic outcomes, including famine and ecological collapse. The very success of voluntary family planning programmes over the past 25 years attests to a high (if not geographically uniform) demand for contraception. The ideational change for a small family norm has permeated even the least developed countries. Bangladesh is a case in point.

Demographers have often used Bangladesh as an example of a society that was unlikely to initiate a transition from higher to lower fertility in the foreseeable future, in contrast to several Asian and Latin American countries that were experiencing spectacular family planning programme successes and rapid fertility declines (Demeny 1975; Arthur & McNicoll 1978). It was considered that Bangladesh's social and economic institutions perpetuate high fertility; natural calamities, political upheaval and economic adversity exacerbate these institutional constraints to the modernisation of reproductive behaviour. However, the results of two recent independent national surveys show that Bangladesh has achieved a moderate level of contraceptive use. Among currently married women aged under 50 years, 31% use a contraceptive method and, of these, almost 25% use a modern method. In addition, 44% of ever-married women younger than 50 have used a method at some time (Larson & Mitra 1992). Reflecting the increase in contraceptive prevalence, the total fertility rate declined from seven during the mid-1970s to about five by the end of the 1980s. Mean desired family size in 1989 was three children, indicating that there may still be considerable unmet need for family planning services.

A recent analysis of data derived from Demographic and Health Surveys, using conservative estimates for the unmet need for limiting fertility and for spacing births, estimated the unmet need to be 24% in sub-Saharan Africa, 13% in Asia and North Africa, and 16% in Latin America. The same study concluded that the total unmet need for contraception could be close to or in excess of 100 million (Bongaarts 1991).

Meeting the unmet need for family planning will in most cases achieve the desired demographic goals. Seventeen developing countries included in recent Demographic and Health Surveys have quantitative demographic targets. A recent study estimated that in 13 of the 17 countries, satisfying the unmet need would exceed the government targets by 1-31 percentage points (Sinding *et al*, 1992). The same study concluded that satisfying an unmet need of 17% of married women of reproductive age would result in a decline in total fertility in developing countries from 3.9 to 3.11.

It should be a responsibility of the whole international community to ensure that women, wherever they are, are given a choice in their lives and are given the means to implement their choice. Even the poorest people in the world should make these choices. There is no justification in denying poor people access to family planning.

8.2 Expanding access and improving quality of family planning services

A recent study tried to measure access to family planning in 124 developed and developing countries, representing 95% of the world population (Population Crisis Committee 1992). Countries were scored from 0 to 100 on the basis of ten indicators which cover the range of birth control choices available in the country, the competence of those providing family planning services, the convenience of services and the amount of information available to contraceptive users through various outreach and education efforts. Countries were ranked as having good, fair, poor or very poor access to family planning.

The study assessed access to family planning in 1992 as 'good' for 39% of the world population, 'fair' for 36%, 'poor' for 16%, 'very poor' for 5% and 'not studied' in the remaining 5%. Some 56 of the 95 developing countries studied and 2 of the 29 developed countries (Japan and Ireland) fell into the poor or very poor category with scores below

50. In the 22 countries in the very poor category, couples still have virtually no access to birth control information or services through either the public or private sector.

Adolescents have special problems in having adequate access to contraception. Providing adolescents with reproductive health services is one of the major challenges.

Demographic concerns have tended to emphasise quantity. Experience of family planning programmes has shown that there is no question of quality versus quantity; on the contrary, quantity will not be achieved and sustained without quality. If family planning services are perceived as of high quality, couples will be more likely to accept contraception and to continue its use; there will be fewer contraceptive failures; resources are more likely to be forthcoming; and opposition can be countered more convincingly (IPPF 1993).

Quality does not necessarily mean sophisticated facilities. Quality means satisfied customers. A crucial element in quality is proper attention to users' perspectives, especially women's (Bruce 1990). Another crucial element in the quality of a family planning service is the freedom to know, the freedom to choose and the freedom to decide. Family planning is a dignified behaviour, and services should be provided with full respect to human dignity.

8.3 A Contraception-21 initiative to launch a second contraceptive technology revolution

In the early days of the contraceptive technology revolution, the scientific community envisaged the 'ideal' contraceptive for everyone, everywhere, every time—a 'magic bullet'. There is a need for a wide range of contraceptives tailored to various human needs: for people who are different, for circumstances which are different and for the same individual at different phases of life with different needs (Fathalla 1990a). Broadening contraceptive choice is a key to quality of family planning services. It influences contraceptive prevalence (Ross *et al.* 1989). It also benefits reproductive health (Fathalla 1989).

The contraceptive technology revolution has stalled and still has an unfinished agenda. Choices need to be broadened to meet the vast expanding and diverse needs for fertility regulation. Moreover, with all its benefits to the quality of life of women, the currently available contraceptive technology has left women with some genuine concerns as well as unmet needs. The qualities of convenience, effectiveness and use by women in modern contraception were not without trade-offs. The modern contraceptive revolution has been largely demographic-driven. Women have benefited in the process but were not in the centre of the process. As far as policymakers are concerned, women were often means to an end, objects and not subjects. This has accentuated the suspicions of women's groups and resulted in a feminist critique of the medicalised contraceptive technology (Dixon-Mueller 1993). Whether justified or not, the critique must be heard because the concerns are genuine.

To complete the agenda for contraceptive research and development, and to provide the contraceptives of the 21st century, there is a need for a second contraceptive technology revolution, driven by women's needs and women's perspectives. This requires a clear *mission*, a reinvigorated *science* and sustainable *resources* (Fathalla 1993b).

The first contraceptive technology revolution was goal-driven, with emphasis on methods that could have a demographic impact. When the revolution stalled, the poorly funded field became driven by scientific opportunity. For the second contraceptive technology revolution, the field must again be goal-driven, and the goal should be set right. The field should focus on contraceptive approaches where the needs of women are still unmet by existing methods. The message for all who are concerned about population growth, should be clear: *What women want for themselves is what the world needs for survival.*

Particular emphasis and priority should be given to methods that coincide with the women's perceived needs and priorities, including methods that are under the user's control; that protect against STDs; post-ovulatory methods; and safe male methods that enable men to share responsibility for fertility regulation and disease prevention (World Health Organization 1993).

The agenda for contraceptives of the 21st century will have to be based on the application to fertility regulation of new advances in cell and molecular biology and biotechnology. While these advances have opened new frontiers for medical and biological sciences, the field of contraceptive research and development is yet to benefit from the opportunities provided by these new advances. New frontiers now opening up in science can provide a broader choice of better and safer state-of-the-art contraceptives. For this, there is a need for a major and sustained investment in human capital to build up a critical mass of scientists active in the field—it was the major investment in the field of reproductive endocrinology which gave most of the leads for the first contraceptive technology revolution. Now, the field is ripe for another major initiative.

It may be noted that the global expenditure on contraceptive research and development, from all sources, is less than 3% of the global contraceptive sales, estimated to be between $2.6 billion and $2.9 billion (PATH 1993). The funding of public sector programmes involved in contraceptive research and development represents about 3% to 4% of the international assistance for population and family planning, estimated in 1990 to be $802 million (UNFPA 1992). Another figure to note in these budgetary considerations is that an estimated $230 million is required to bring a new chemical entity from research to the market.

Any major infusion of resources in the contraceptive research and development field will have to come from industry. The limited resources available for family planning and reproductive health are badly needed for expanding the access and improving the quality of services (Fathalla 1992b). The potential of industry, in terms of finance and expertise, is great compared with other resources. The pharmaceutical industry in the developed world invests a substantial amount of money (about 16% to 19% of revenues) in research and development of new products (Pharmaceutical Business News 1992). With US and European companies reporting total revenues of over $90 billion per year and a projected annual growth of 9% to 10% over the next five years, there are significant resources for research activities. The constraints that led to the retrenchment of industry must be addressed, if the vast resources of industry are to be mobilised (Mastroianni *et al.* 1990; PATH 1993).

8.4 Mobilisation of resources

The rhetoric about population and family planning is not matched by allocation of resources.

Some developing country governments are not foresighted enough to invest in the future of their population. When they have the will, they also often lack the wallet. It should be clear, however, that of today's total expenditure on population and family planning, about two thirds is provided by the developing countries themselves (UNFPA 1991a). India and China pay for over 85% of their population programme activities, Indonesia pays 73%, Zimbabwe pays 67% and five other developing countries contribute more than 50% of their national population programme budgets.

As to the international donor community, 1.18% of official development assistance in 1990 was allocated for population assistance, of which family planning is only a part (UNFPA 1992). The total population assistance has remained remarkably stable in constant dollar terms since 1972, hovering around $US 500 million, in spite of the greatly expanding demand for family planning. Grants for international population assistance reached an all time high of US$ 801.8 million in 1990. In constant 1985 dollars, this amounts to US$ 549 million.

Using the United Nations medium-variant population projection of 6.2 billion by the year 2000, it was estimated that about 567 million couples will be using some contraceptive at the end of the century (UNFPA 1991b). Based on patterns of contraceptive method mix, these couples will need 151 million surgical procedures for male or female sterilisation, 8.76 billion cycles of oral pills, 633 million doses of injectables, 310 million IUDs and 44 billion condoms (not taking into consideration condom requirements for prevention of HIV infection). From an annual cost of $US 416 million in 1991, the bill for contraceptives will rise to $US 627 million by the year 2000.

The total costs of contraceptive commodity requirements in developing countries are currently shared among developing country governments (61%), the private commercial sector (17%), and the international donor community (22%). In 27 developing countries, production of oral pills, IUDs, condoms and injectables is now going on, or under serious consideration, by local affiliates of multinational companies or by government-owned and private local companies.

The costs of contraceptive commodities are only one component of the total need for family planning services. The total national and international expenditures for this in all developing counties in 1987 amounted to about US$ 4.5 billion. An additional US$ 4.5 billion will be needed annually by the year 2000 to meet the expanding needs in family planning (UNFPA 1989). How to mobilise the additional resources is, according to the Amsterdam Declaration of the International Forum on Population in the 21st century, *a central challenge facing all of us today, both as members of the international community and as individuals seeking to realise the vision of sustainable development throughout the world* (UNFPA 1989).

This is what it takes. It should not be a question of whether we can afford to do it, but can we afford *not* to do it.

REFERENCES

Andorka, R. 1990 The use of direct incentives and disincentives and of indirect social economic measures in fertility policy and human rights. In *Population and human rights*. New York: United Nations, pp. 132–147.

Arthur, B. & McNicoll, G. 1978 An analytical survey of population and development in Bangladesh. *Pop. Dev. Rev.* **4**, 23–80.

Bongaarts, J. 1991 The KAP gap and the unmet need for contraception. *Pop. Dev. Rev.* **17**, 293–313.

Bruce, J. 1990 Fundamental elements of the quality of care: a simple framework. *Stud. Fam. Planning* **21**, 61–91.

Demeny, P. 1975 Observations on population policy and population programs in Bangladesh. *Pop. Dev. Rev.* **1**, 307–321

Dixon-Mueller, R. 1993 *Population policy & women's rights*. Westport, CN: Praeger, pp. 47–50.

Ellis, H. 1931, *More essays of love and virtue*. New York: Doubleday, Doran & Company, p. 175.

Fathalla, M.F. 1984 The ethics of family planning. *World Health*, June 1984, pp. 27–29.

Fathalla, M.F. 1987 Health and family planning issues: a global perspective. In *Better health for women and children through family planning*. Report on an international conference held in Nairobi, Kenya, October 1987 (ed. M.Black). New York: The Population Council, pp. 11–13.

Fathalla, M.F. 1989 New contraceptive methods and reproductive health. In *Demographic and programmatic consequences of contraceptive innovations* (eds. S.J.Segal, A.O. Tsui & S.M.Rogers). New York: Plenum Press, pp. 153–176.

Fathalla, M.F. 1990a Tailoring contraceptives to human needs. *People* **17**, 3–5.

Fathalla, M.F. l990b Relationship between contraceptive technology and HIV transmission: an overview. In *Heterosexual transmission of AIDS* (eds. N.J. Alexander, H. L.Gabelnick & J.M. Spieler). New York: Wiley-Liss, pp. 225–238.

Fathalla, M.F. l991a Reproductive health: a global overview. *Ann. New York Acad. of Sci.* **626**, 1–9.

Fathalla, M.F. l991b Contraceptive technology and safety. *Pop. Sci.* **10**, 7–26.

Fathalla, M.F. 1992a Reproductive health in the world: two decades of progress and the challenge ahead. In *Reproductive health: a key to a brighter future* (eds. J. Khanna, P.F.A. Van Look & P.D.Griffin). Geneva: World Health Organization, pp. 3–31.

Fathalla, M.F. 1992b Family planning: Future needs. *AMBIO* **21**, 84–87.

Fathalla, M.F. 1992c Safe motherhood and child survival: the importance of family planning and the interdependence of services. Background paper to the *Expert Group Meeting on Family Planning, Health and Family Well-being*. Bangalore, 26–30 October 1992. United Nations.

Fathalla, M.F. 1993a Contraception and women's health. *Brit. Med. Bull.* **49**, 245–251.

Fathalla, M.F. 1993b Mobilization of resources for a second contraceptive technology revolution. In *Proceedings of the International Symposium on 'Contraceptive Research and development for the Year 2000 and beyond'* Mexico City, 8–10 March, 1993. Geneva: World Health Organization. (In press)

Grant, J.P. 1992 *The state of the world's children 1992*. New York: Oxford University Press, p. 58.

Henshaw, S.K. 1990 Induced abortion: a world review, 1990. *Fam. Planning Persp.* **22**, 76–89.

Hobcraft, J. 1992 Fertility patterns and child survival. *Pop. Bull. UN* **33**, 1–31.

Hord, C., David, H.P., Donnay, F. & Wolf, M. 1991 Reproductive health in Romania; reversing the Ceausescu legacy. *Stud. Fam. Planning* **22**, 231–240.

IPPF (International Planned Parenthood Federation) 1993. *Meeting challenges: promoting choices*. A report on the 40th anniversary- IPPF family planning congress, New Delhi, India. Lancs, UK: Parthenon, p. 13.

Larson, A. & Mitra, S.N. 1992 Family planning in Bangladesh: an unlikely success story. *Int. Fam. Planning Persp.* **18**, 123–129.

Mastroianni, L.J.R., Donaldson, P.J., Kane, T.T. (eds.). 1990. *Developing new contraceptives: obstacles and opportunities.* Washington DC: National Academy Press, pp. 1–5.

McLaren, A. 1990. *A history of contraception—from antiquity to the present day.* UK, USA: Basil Blackwell, p. 217.

Mosher, W.D. & Pratt, W.F. 1990. *Contraceptive use in the United States, 1973–88.* Advance data from vital and health statistics o£ the National Center for Health Statistics. 182,12. United States Department of Health and Human Services. Hyattsville, MD.

PATH (Program for Appropriate Technology in Health). 1993. Enhancing the private sector's role in contraceptive research and development. In *Proceedings of the International Symposium on 'Contraceptive Research and Development for the year 2000 and beyond'.* Mexico City, 8–10 March 1993. WHO, Geneva. (In press)

Population Crisis Committee (Population Action International). 1992. *World access to birth control.* Report on world progress towards population stabilization. B.P. 28 ISSN: 0199-9761. Washington DC: Population Action Committee.

Potts, M.& Rosenfield, A. 1990 The fifth freedom revisited: II, The way forward. *Lancet* **336**, 1293–1295.

Ross, J.A., Rich, M. & Molzan, J.P. 1989 *Management strategies, for family planning programs.* Centre for Population and Family Health, School of Public Health, Columbia University, New York, p. 34.

Ross, J.A. 1992 Sterilization: past, present, future. *Stud. Fam. Planning* **23**, 187–198.

Ross. J.A., Mauldin. W.P.. Green, S. R. & Cooke E.R. 1992 *Family planning and child survival programs as assessed in 1991.* New York: The Population Council, p. 1.

Sinding, S.W., Ross, J.A. & Rosenfield, A.G. 1994 Seeking common ground: unmet need and demographic goals. *Int. Fam. Planning Persp.* **20**. 23–27.

Suitters, B. 1973 *Be brave and angry.* London: International Planned Parenthood Federation, p.5.

UNFPA (United Nations Population Fund). 1989 *Report of the International Forum on population in the twenty first century.* New York: UNFPA (ISBN-0-89714-072-9), p. 8.

UNFPA (United Nations Population Fund). 1991a *The state of world population.* New York: UNFPA.

UNFPA (United Nations Population Fund). 1991b *Contraceptive requirements and demand for contraceptive demand for contraceptive commodities in developing countries in the 1990s.* A background document submitted to the UNFPA Consultative Meeting on Contraceptive Requirements in Developing Countries by the year 2000, 25–26 February, 1991. New York: UNFPA.

UNFPA (United Nations Population Fund). 1992 *Global population assistance report 1982–1990.* New York: UNFPA, p. 1.

United Nations. 1984 *Report of the International Conference on Population 1984.* New York: United Nations Department of Technical Cooperation for Development (E/CONF.76/19), p. 21.

United Nations. 1989 *Levels and trends of contraceptive use as assessed in 1988.* Sales No. E.89.X111.4, New York: UN.

United Nations. 1990 *The world's women, 1970-1990: Trends and statistics.* New York: UN, pp. 1–9.

United Nations. 1992 *World Population Monitoring 1991.* Population Studies No. 126. p.75. Department of International Economic and Social Affairs. New York: UN.

United Nations Secretariat. 1990 Population trends and policies in the 1980s. In *Population and human rights.* United Nations Department of Economic and Social Affairs. ST/ESA/SER.R/107. New York: UN. p. 43.

Veil, S. 1978 Human rights, ideologies and population policies. *Pop. Dev. Rev.* **4**, 313–321.

World Health Organization, Division of Family Health. 1990 *Abortion: a tabulation of available data on the frequency and mortality of unsafe abortion.* WHO/MCH/90.14. Geneva: WHO, pp. 2–3.

World Health Organization. 1991 New estimates of maternal mortality. *Weekly Epidemiological Record* **66**, 345–348.

World Health Organization. 1992 *Global health situation and projections.* Division of
    Epidemiological Surveillance and Health Situation and Trend Assessment. WHO/HST/92.1.
    Geneva: WHO, pp. 41–44.
World Health Organization. 1993. *Declaration of the International Symposium on 'Contraceptive
    research and Development for the year 2000 and Beyond'.* Mexico City, 8–10 March 1993. Geneva:
    WHO.

Current Status of Contraceptive Research and Development
Kerstin Hagenfeldt

ABSTRACT

Financial resources for contraceptive research and development have decreased during the last two decades, mainly due to the diminished contributions to the field by the pharmaceutical industry. The main contributors today are the international public sector programmes. Through their collaboration and the building of resources and training of scientists in developing regions, substantial progress has been made both in biotechnology and social science. These achievements have increased the safety and efficacy of existing methods, developed new methods for both women and men and promoted the importance of sexual and reproductive health aspects in the field of fertility control. In the future the research needs to concentrate on the methods that coincide with women's perceived needs and priorities, methods that are under the user's control and that also protect against STD including AIDS, and on safe male methods. Efforts must be made to increase the involvement of the industry, including the industry in developing countries, and women's health advocates and potential users need to be represented in all decision-making bodies to guide the research process.

1. FINANCIAL RESOURCES FOR CONTRACEPTIVE RESEARCH AND DEVELOPMENT

Financial resources for the field of contraceptive research and development are provided by governments, philanthropic foundations and private industry. Government support is provided directly to the traditional research groups of universities and other national research institutions and directly or indirectly through UN agencies. The 1970s witnessed the emergence of international public sector research programmes that focus on contraceptive research and development. These include the WHO Special Programme of Research, Development and Research Training in Human Reproduction (WHO/HRP), the Population Council's International Committee for Contraceptive Research (Population Council), and the largely US AID supported agencies: Family Health International (FHI) and the Contraceptive Research and Development Programme (CONRAD).

In a report on the status of global reproductive sciences and contraceptive development, sponsored by the Ford Foundation (Greep *et al.* 1976), it was shown that governments played an increasing role in funding the whole field of reproductive research, contributing to 69% during 1974, the last year of the study.

During the review period 1965–74 the share coming from private philanthropy declined from 22% to 14%, while the proportion contributed by the pharmaceutical industry was cut by more than half, from 34% to 16%, apparently as a result of the revised assessments of the potential profitability of new contraceptive methods. Most of the funds (57%) went to fundamental research in reproductive sciences. Contraceptive research and development declined from 35% to 30% while training declined from 7% to 5%.

In a recent report from the Institute of Medicine, U.S. Academy of Sciences, the situation in the U.S.A. was analysed, stating that although government funding for basic research and reproductive biology had remained virtually unchanged or maybe increased since the 1970s, the funding of contraceptive research and development had actually decreased mainly because of a decline in the support from the pharmaceutical industry and from private foundations. Training opportunities for young scientists were fewer, and in the U.S.A., as in many other countries, there had been a decline in the number of researchers entering the contraceptive field (Mastroianni *et al.* 1990). Expanding any science requires a regularly replenished and expanding pool of trained scientists. There is a genuine concern about the ageing of the scientists active in contraceptive development. Dr C.W. Bardin of the Population Council estimates that within U.S. Obstetric/Gynaecological departments fewer than 5% of the researchers are currently working on research related to new contraceptives (PATH 1993).

This development has partly been counteracted by the activity of up-building of resources in developing countries. Through the WHO/HRP Programme for 20 years, one third of its budget has been set aside for resource development and training of scientists from developing countries. UNFPA has greatly contributed to the strengthening of reproductive research in China and in several other countries. The decrease in training opportunities in developed countries could, however, have a negative impact on the possibility to train Third World scientists. Another important factor is that new advances in cell and molecular biology and biotechnology have not yet been exploited for contraceptive research and development; these are costly research areas which need more funding (Mastroianni 1990).

The most important factor contributing to the decrease in contraceptive research and development is probably the retrenchment of industry from the field. Many large pharmaceutical firms that in the 1960s and 1970s played an active and essential role in developing contraceptive products have stopped their activities in this area in the past decade. Only four major companies, one in the U.S.A., are still active in research today compared with 12–15 twenty years ago. A study funded by WHO/HRP and the Rockefeller Foundation has been done to assess the changing role of industry in contraceptive research and development, and to propose mechanisms by which public sector agencies can encourage the private sector to take a larger role in contraceptive development. Some traditional reasons cited for the diminishing role of industry include: the present existence of highly effective methods, saturated and/or difficult markets, limited product profit potential, product liability, regulatory requirements, intellectual property law and political climate, i.e. the anti-abortion and anti-contraceptive movement in the U.S.A. (PATH 1993).

While public sector agencies have played the major role in the research and development of contraceptive products during the past two decades, it is difficult, if not impossible, for public sector agencies to implement all of the steps necessary to research, develop, register, and market a contraceptive product. This process is long and costly: about U.S. $230 million is generally estimated to be required to bring a new chemical entity from the basic science research pool, through applied basic research, phased animal and clinical testing, up to final development, registration, manufacturing and finally marketing (PATH 1993).

A recent rough assessment puts the annual worldwide funding for contraceptive research and development at about U.S. $57 million, with the U. S. government providing 43%, the non-profit sector 18% and private industry 39%. It may be noted that global expenditure on contraceptive research and development from all sources is less than 3% of annual global contraceptive sales, estimated to be between U.S. $2.6 billion and U.S. $2.9 billion, and is well below the pharmaceutical industry norm of investing 16–19% of sales revenues in research and development. The funding of public sector programmes involved in contraceptive research and development represents about 3–4% of the international assistance for population and family planning, estimated in 1990 to be U.S. $802 million. The total budget for the WHO/HRP Programme in 1992 was U.S. $24 million, and for the three most important non-profit U. S. organizations, the Population Council, the Family Health International and CONRAD a total of U.S. $16 million in 1988. The funding for the Contraceptive Research and Development branch on NIH represents only 0.07% of the NIH budget (Sinding 1993).

The WHO/HRP-Rockefeller Foundation study made the following recommendations to encourage industries participating in contraceptive research and development:

- Offering incentives to industry such as a special fund for the development of contraceptives, longer patent lives on contraceptive products or negotiated guaranteed purchase agreements;
- Providing detailed descriptions of the contraceptive markets in developing countries by performing market analyses, identifying key product features required, and defining strategies for entry into developing country markets;
- Coordinating regular conferences on contraceptive research and development where public and private sector researchers share information and set priorities (PATH 1993).

2. PROGRESS WITHIN THE BIOMEDICAL FIELD

Although the financial resources for contraceptive research and development have decreased during the last decade, collaboration between national and international government agencies and non-governmental organisations and the few pharmaceutical industries still active in research have made substantial progress. An important part of this progress is the evaluation and improvement of the safety and efficacy of existing contraceptive methods as well as the development of new methods for both women and men. A few areas will be highlighted, stressing their importance for reproductive health.

2.1 Hormonal methods and neoplasia

Steroidal hormonal contraceptives used by women presently include oral pills (OCs), injectables and implants. Ever since OCs first became available, there has been a concern that their use might be associated with an increased risk of cancer, especially in the reproductive organs. WHO/HRP in 1979 launched a major multinational case-control study to investigate the possible relation between the use of hormonal contraceptive methods and cancer. This study took place in 11 countries, 8 of them in the developing world. The results showed that the use of OCs has a protective effect against cancer of the ovary and the endometrium. OCs reduce the woman's risk of developing ovarian cancer by about 40% and endometrial cancer by about 50%. With regard to cancer of the breast, the WHO study indicated that women who have ever used OCs had an overall and relative risk of 1.15 of developing breast cancer as compared to women who had never used OCs. Breast cancer risk was not significantly different in developing as compared to developed countries, nor was the risk significantly different among women under the age of 35 years as compared to over 35. The relation between OCs and cervical neoplasia is not conclusive; some of the recent studies provide evidence for a positive relationship, particularly for long-term use. The results, however, are difficult to interpret because of a variety of methodological problems of the observational, epidemiological studies addressing this relationship. Nevertheless, if an increased risk of cancer of the cervix exists, it is small (WHO 1992a).

Concern has also been expressed about the most commonly used injectable contraceptive, depot medroxyprogesterone acetate (DMPA) and cancer of the reproductive organs. Another WHO/HRP multinational case-control study did not find any significant relationship between the use of DMPA and breast cancer in women. The study also showed that DMPA dramatically lowers the risk of endometrial cancer for at least eight years following its discontinuation. Neither ovarian nor liver cancer have been found with increased frequency among women who have used DMPA. The study found that DMPA did not alter the risk of cervical cancer (WHO 1993).

The results of the above-mentioned studies are of importance for the reproductive health of some 65 million in the world using OCs and some 12 million in the world using injectable contraceptives.

2.2 Hormonal contraceptives and cardiovascular diseases

Cardiovascular diseases (CVD), namely venous thrombosis, ischaemic heart disease and cerebrovascular disease, are still the main safety concerns associated with OC use. There is evidence that the modern low-dose pills have a lesser degree of CVD risk; however, more research is needed in this area as not enough information has been accumulated as yet among different ethnic groups in developing countries, where the prevalence of risk factors and incidence rates of CVD are very different from those found in developed countries. WHO/HRP is conducting a study in 17 centres in Africa, Latin America, Asia and Europe. The main phase of the study started in 1989 and data will be collected until mid-1993 for stroke and venous embolism and until 1995 for acute myocardial infarction (WHO 1993).

2.3 Injectables

The large clinical experience accumulated over the last years indicates that available progestin-only formulations, DMPA and norethisterone enanthate (NET-EN) are highly effective, long-lasting, safe and reversible agents for fertility regulation. However, their continuation rates are low, menstrual irregularities being the most frequent reason for their discontinuation. It has been realised that the addition of a short- or medium-acting oestrogen to progestin preparations could result in an improvement of endometrial bleeding pattern, thus enabling the development of once-a-month injectable contraceptives of high efficacy that cause bleeding patterns resembling those of a normal menstrual cycle. Recently, two progestogen–oestrogen injectable combinations have completed world-wide clinical testing and introductory trials have been conducted under the WHO/HRP Programme. One formulation, Cyclofem, contains low doses of medroxyprogesterone acetate (25 mg) and oestradiol cypionate (5 mg) while the other, Mesigyna, contains low doses of NET-EN (50 mg) and oestradiol valerate (5 mg). Both preparations have proved their high efficacy in large multicentre studies and are at the point of registration and inclusion into national family planning programmes (WHO 1993).

During the next decade new approaches to sustained hormone release such as the recent development of monolytic microspheres could fulfil the requirement of safety, high efficacy, reversibility and privacy and further improve both long-acting and once-a-month injectable preparations known today. Following the multinational synthetic efforts of WHO/HRP undertaken in collaboration with the Center for Population Research, National Institute of Child Health and Human Development, USA (CPR/NICHD), new steroid compounds have been identified and tested in humans. The studies have resulted in the selection of a simple levonorgestrel ester, levonorgestrel butanoate (HRP-002) for further evaluation. The drug has completed Phase I and Phase II comparative clinical trials and a multinational study will be undertaken to assess metabolic effects (WHO 1992b).

2.4 Hormonal implants

The development of subdermal contraceptive implants was made possible by the introduction of silicone rubber in the late 1940s. Silicone capsules containing a progestin or silicone tubing surrounding a steroid–silicone rod allowed the compound to be delivered at a constant rate for a duration of several years. Based on this technology, the Population Council has developed the implant system Norplant which has been approved for sale and distribution in 24 countries, including the USA. The Population Council has devoted more than 20 years to develop and introduce the six-capsule Norplant system which releases the progestin levonorgestrel over a period of five years. In the process, the Council not only developed a new form of reversible, long-acting contraception but also pioneered the introduction of a new contraceptive method—with attention to training, counselling and consumer information. These research and development efforts were supported by several government agencies, foundations and individuals. During the past 10 years efforts have been made to develop additional implant systems that are expected to fulfil the needs of special user groups. Norplant II is a two-implant system which releases the same amount of levonorgestrel as Norplant but from two instead of six implants making insertion and removal easier. Norplant II has reached the stage of Phase III trials and is likely to become available commercially before the turn of the century. The Population Council has also developed a single implant to release the progestin ST 1435 with an expected duration of effectiveness of at least one year. Prototype devices are undergoing clinical trials. The initial results are very promising: no pregnancies have occurred in any of the women using the implant (Population Council 1992). FHI is doing studies on a NET-implant (Annulle). This biodegradable implant developed by an US pharmaceutical company is designed to provide a high level of continuous contraceptive protection for about a year through implantation of NET pellets. A Phase II clinical trial comparing the pharmacokinetics of two sets of the pellets is currently ongoing (FHI 1992). CPR/NICHD has continued its interest in developing biodegradable implants. The concept behind this approach is to develop a drug-releasing device which can be degraded in the body after the drug has been released. The research has resulted in the development of implants made from a biodegradable polymer, Caprolactone, which releases approximately 40 µg levonorgestrel. The initial studies have shown that a single device, Capronor I™, was easy to implant and remove and that women in general were satisfied with it. A newer version of the device, Capronor II™, is now ready for initial clinical evaluation. Further development of the co-polymer device, Capronor III™, is essentially a joint venture between NICHD and a pharmaceutical company (CPR 1993).

Other implants under development are one releasing 3-keto-desogestrel (by the pharmaceutical company Organon) and the nomegestrol acetate-releasing Uniplant (by the South-to-South Cooperation in Population Science and Reproductive Health). The WHO/HRP considers that within the next five years as the number of users of new injectables and new implants increases, epidemiological studies need to be initiated in the form of post-marketing surveillance, reporting of adverse events and, possibly, cohort studies. Casecontrol studies on neoplasia, as those performed with OCs and DMPA, will be feasible only at a later stage when the number of users has grown sufficiently large (WHO 1993).

2.5 Vaginal rings

Vaginal rings represent an entirely new approach to contraception; the only long-acting method which is under the control of the user. The woman can insert or remove the ring at will without help from a health care provider. The ring has some other advantages as well. It releases a very small amount of hormones at a constant rate; conversely, the hormone level in the blood falls rapidly when the ring is removed, an advantage in the case of an accidental pregnancy or if the woman wishes to regain her fertility. Vaginal rings are of two types. One delivers a single hormone, a progestogen, and is worn continuously for three months. This ring acts by thickening the cervical mucus, making it impenetrable to sperm; in some women it also inhibits ovulation. WHO/HRP has developed a ring which releases levonorgestrel continuously at a rate of 20 µg/day. Extensive testing in 19 centres world-wide confirms its efficacy and acceptability. This ring is now produced on an industrial scale and pre-introductory trials have started. Unfortunately, during these trials it has been revealed that women using the ring are found to have vaginal lesions of an unclear nature. Studies are in progress to reveal if these lesions depend on the stiffness of the ring or on the steroid released (WHO 1993).

The other type of ring developed by Population Council is releasing two hormones, noretindrone acetate and ethinyl oestradiol, and can be used by women who wish to use combined hormonal contraception to block ovulation. Rings releasing various doses of the two hormones are currently under investigation to determine the optimal formulation.

The Population Council has also developed a vaginal ring releasing the natural hormone progesterone to be used by lactating mothers, an important development as methods to be used during lactation are few. This ring has undergone a multicentre comparative Phase III clinical trial in which the period of lactational amenorrhoea was extended and effective contraception for nursing women was provided. The Population Council is also developing a ring releasing a new gestagen, ST 1435 (which is poorly absorbed from the gastrointesinal tract), and thus also can be ideally used by post-partum women. The advantage with this ring will be that women can continue the method even after they stop nursing. This is not possible with the progestogen ring which does not perform well in menstruating women. Ortho Pharmaceutical Co. is developing a combination ring releasing 3-ketodesogestrel and ethinyl oestradiol (Population Council 1992).

The delivery of contraceptive hormones by vaginal administration is a promising addition to the list of available antifertility methods. Since ring use is both simple and entirely under the user's control, many women find a ring to be an attractive option.

2.6 Antihormones

Contraception is the first line of defence against unwanted pregnancy. However, abortion rates are highest in those countries where information and services of family planning are weakest and where the greatest restraints on the autonomy of women exist. At least 40–60 million induced abortions are estimated to take place annually throughout the world; half of them are performed by unskilled persons usually where abortion is legally restricted. It is estimated that out of 500000 maternal deaths that occur each year throughout the world, as many as one-quarter to one-third may be a consequence of complications of unsafe abortion procedures. Research on safe methods for the interruption of early pregnancy is therefore an important integral part of research programmes concerned with fertility regulation. Progesterone is indispensable for normal reproductive function. Because progesterone plays such a key role in the reproductive process, any approach that affects the hormone's availability to its target cells in the reproductive organs and other tissues would thus have antifertility effects. An effective way of achieving this is through using antiprogestogens (Puri & Van Look 1991).

Although several hundreds of antiprogestogens have been synthesised to date by various pharmaceutical companies and private investigators, only one of them, i.e. mifepristone (RU 486), developed by Roussel Uclaf (Paris, France) has been studied extensively in humans. Mifepristone is also the only antiprogestogen which is presently registered for clinical use in China, France, UK and Sweden. In all four countries the drug is licensed for use in medical termination of pregnancy with the recommendation that it be administered in conjunction with a uterotonic prostaglandin analogue (WHO 1992b). WHO/HRP is the only international organisation which has pursued research with the antiprogestogen mifepristone since 1983. The various possible clinical applications of the drug have constituted the main activities of the Task Force on Post-ovulatory Methods for Fertility Regulation of the HRP Programme. Combined regimens of mifepristone and prostaglandin analogues have proved to be an effective alternative to conventional surgical methods for the termination of early pregnancy. There are still, however, some unresolved issues, such as the minimally effective dose of mifepristone, the most appropriate type and dose of prostaglandin, and the maximum duration of pregnancy for which the treatment remains effective and safe. Apart from these biomedical issues, there is a need to address questions relating to user acceptability and the service facilities that should be available to women choosing this non-surgical method of pregnancy termination.

Clinical trials have also been completed on the use of mifepristone plus prostaglandin for menses induction and on the use of mifepristone alone for emergency contraception. With regard to the latter, it was shown that the antiprogestogen was more effective, and caused significantly less nausea, vomiting and other side- effects than the currently most often used, so-called Yuzpe regimen. Other potential uses of mifepristone include suppression of ovulation when the drug is given in low continuous doses during the cycle, and this line of research is also supported by HRP (WHO 1993). The development of a safe medical method for early pregnancy termination and for emergency contraception will have immense implications for the reproductive health of women both in developed and developing countries.

2.7 Intrauterine devices (IUDs)

The IUD is one of the most commonly used methods for fertility regulation, especially in developing country programmes. It is estimated that there are more than 80 million users with some 74 million in China alone (WHO 1992c). The copper- and hormone-releasing IUDs combine high continuation rates with low pregnancy rates. The Population Council has during the last 20 years developed several new models of the copper-IUD, the most recent being Copper-T 380A, which now serves as a bench mark for IUD use. The Population Council and WHO/HRP have both conducted large multicentre studies in developed and developing countries on the Copper-T 380A, and its failure rate, after many years of use, is of the same level as surgical sterilisation. As far as effectiveness, these modern IUDs have probably reached the maximum level which is possible to obtain in terms of pregnancy protection. Data recently submitted by the Population Council to the United States Food and Drug Administration (USFDA) in support of an extension of the US FDA's approval of the IUD indicates that the ten-year cumulative (net) pregnancy rate for the Copper-T 380A is the astonishing low level of 2.1/100 woman years. The IUD has also been shown to protect against ectopic pregnancy, a complication of pregnancy with serious outcome for many women in the developing world (WHO 1993).

The health importance of an effective IUD is indicated by recent Chinese developments. Here, with the highest number of IUD users in the world, the most commonly used IUD is the stainless steel ring, with a high pregnancy rate of 20% and an expulsion rate of the same order. In China, the women born during the 1960s baby boom are causing a secondary baby boom in the 1990s and will be causing an IUD boom during this decade. A combined UNFPA/HRP study in China has projected what will happen during the next decade. If China, beginning this year 1993, would instead of the stainless steel ring insert a Copper-T 380A, it is estimated that during the next decade the following events could be averted; 55.6 million pregnancies resulting in 18.5 million live births and 35.6 million induced abortions, 16300 maternal deaths, 365000 infant deaths and 28000 child deaths. The decision recently taken by the Chinese government to follow this road will thus have a tremendous reproductive health impact in China (WHO 1993).

One of the side-effects of the IUD identified early in its history was the increase in menstrual blood loss following the insertion of the device. Although healthy women do not experience serious health effects of the menstrual blood loss, it could be a problem in women with anaemia or bad nutritional status. The Population Council has sponsored the development and clinical testing of an IUD which releases 20 μg levonorgestrel per day. This device has been reported in randomised studies as having a pregnancy rate at 5 years of 1.1/100 woman years. The IUD also markedly reduces the risk of ectopic pregnancy. Studies on menstrual blood loss have shown a decrease but also a high removal rate for amenorrhoea of nearly 20%.

Only modest technical improvements in IUDs should be expected in the next decade. Improved guidelines for IUD use together with improved counselling and training programmes for health care providers will have a greater impact on IUD prevalence than will further development in IUD technology (Sivin 1993).

2.8 Barrier methods and spermicides

The global spread of sexually transmitted diseases (STDs) including the HIV virus has made it more important than ever to create effective barrier methods that also provide protection against infection.

According to the WHO, male condom use amounts to 19% of all contraceptive methods in the developed part of the world, but only to 6% in less developed regions (WHO 1992c). Ongoing research has concentrated on efficacy of the condom method and on condom acceptability. Policy recommendations from the studies done so far underscore the need for condoms to be promoted as an alternative family planning method to improve the image of the condom as a legitimate and acceptable barrier methods for stable couples (WHO 1992c).

Until recently, advances in the development of new barrier methods—condoms, diaphragms, cervical caps and spermicides—have been minimal. The CPR/NICHD has initiated a wide ranging programme of research, development and clinical testing of new barrier methods. While historically these methods have had high failure rates, the causes of which could be traced to a variety of personal dislikes for these methods, a new variety of condoms made from polyurethane are entering a phase of extensive clinical testing. Preliminary data indicates that many men prefer these plastic condoms to the latex rubber condoms. Studies on hyperextensible elastomeric male condoms are near in completion and studies are also current on the development of a modified latex condom (CPR 1993).

The female condom, or vaginal sheet, is a barrier method for prevention of transmission of sexually transmitted diseases (including the HIV virus) from men to women and vice versa. The device is under the woman's control and can be inserted some time prior to coitus. CONRAD and FHI are evaluating the female condom and focus on acceptability and contraceptive efficacy. The data from this investigation has been used to get the approval of the USFDA for the device. CONRAD is also supporting

Phase II clinical studies of Lea's shield, a vaginal barrier device which is being tested for efficacy with and without a spermicide. Other barrier methods are in Phase I safety and postcoital evaluations within the CONRAD programme. They include the Fem Cap™ cervical cap and two contraceptive films (Gabelnick 1993).

CPR/NICHD is involved in the development of new spermicides and new delivery systems for the well known spermicide nonoxynol-9 (CPR 1993).

The whole field of barrier contraceptives has been given an enhanced awareness due to the STD/HIV pandemic. There is, however, a great deal of basic research to be pursued in this area before the development of an ideal barrier method can be reached. Among these needs are:

- basic research on the genital transmission of STD pathogens
- a greater knowledge on the physical and biological properties of the vaginal and cervical environment
- development of good *in vitro* and animal models for genital pathogen transmission to be used to evaluate the effects of existing or potential contraceptive products
- research on the effect of contraceptive and other steroid hormones on disease transmission
- research on inflammation and trauma of the reproductive tissues related to the use of other contraceptive products (Claypool 1993).

2.9 Male methods

For more than 100 years, the single reversible contraceptive method to be used by men has been the condom. All of the funding agencies have through the years expressed interest to develop male methods and a lot of basic research has been performed during the last two decades. There is now a greater promise for the development of new male fertility-regulating methods. The introduction of simple, less traumatic methods of vas occlusion such as nonscalpel vasectomy and the percutaneous injection of vas-occluding materials have improved acceptability and reduced the adverse effects. A multicentre study conducted by WHO/HRP Programme has demonstrated that once spermatogenesis is suppressed to azoospermia by a hormonal method, high contraceptive efficacy is achieved and maintained for the duration of drug administration (12 months). Upon drug withdrawal, the suppressive effect is completely reversible. A Phase II study to evaluate the likelihood that hormonally induced severe oligozoospermia (<5 million sperms/ ml) is associated with an acceptable level of contraceptive efficacy is ongoing. Progress to date has been good.

Clearly, no method based on weekly hormone injections as used in the trials would be acceptable and practical for family planning programmes. WHO/HRP in collaboration with CPR/NICHD has therefore developed new long-acting androgen preparations, (testosterone buciclate, testosterone microcapsules, testosterone implants), which have been shown to provide stable physiological levels of androgen replacement in hypogonadal men. These drugs are now being studied in normal men for the suppression of spermatogenesis. These agents alone or together with long-acting progestogen preparations (levonorgestrel butanoate, levonorgestrel or desogestrel implants) may provide adequate suppression of spermatogenesis for effective contraception in the majority of men from some Asian countries. In the studies performed by WHO/HRP it was shown that men in the Asian centres achieved azoospermia more frequently than in the Caucasian centres. For men of Caucasian origin, the possibility of induction of azoospermia with short periods of gonadotrophin-releasing hormone (GnRh)-antagonist administration followed by androgens alone or androgen and progestogens is being considered (WHO 1993).

During the last few years, the question of long-term health effects of vasectomy has received considerable attention. None of the numerous epidemiological studies have found any increase in cardiovascular disease in vasectomised men (WHO 1992c). Other studies suggested an increase in risk of cancer of the testis and prostate following vasectomy (WHO 1992b, WHO 1993). In the event that the recently reported association between prostate cancer and vasectomy should be shown to be of a true causal nature, the public health importance would be great in developed countries where vasectomy has been used as a method of contraception and where prostate cancer incidence is high. In developing countries, the age-specific incidence rates of prostate cancer are far lower than in developed countries and the public health implications would be of lesser significance. It is therefore important to undertake independent epidemiological studies to obtain a firm basis for advice to family planning programmes in developing countries on the long-term safety of vasectomy. WHO/HRP is planning studies on the relationship between vasectomy and prostate cancer in countries where vasectomy has been widely used such as China (Chengdu province), India, the Republic of Korea and Nepal. WHO/HRP is also supporting an ongoing historical cohort study in Denmark on the association between vasectomy and testicular cancer (WHO 1993).

2.10 Antifertility vaccines

It has been proposed that one method of fertility regulation that would be attractive for both the users and the providers of family planning services, particularly in developing countries, would be a preparation which is taken once every 12–24 months and which is free from side-effects and the use and disposal problems that are associated with some of the currently available methods. WHO and a number of national and international agencies are funding research on antifertility vaccines (Ada & Griffin 1991). WHO has concentrated the research efforts on the development of vaccines that would work after fertilisation has occurred but before pregnancy becomes established and has developed a prototype antifertility vaccine consisting of a synthetic fragment of the hCG-molecule. Phase I trials were performed between 1986 and 1988 in sterilised women and WHO/HRP is now in the process of starting clinical Phase II trials in Sweden to assess the effectiveness of the vaccine (WHO 1993). NICHD is supporting two cooperative contraceptive development centres in the USA working on the development of antifertility vaccines. Until recently, progress in the field has been slow, partly because the antigens defined in experimental animals have sometimes been irrelevant outside a particular species, or their human counterparts have proved difficult to isolate and characterise (CPR/NICHD 1993). In the development of antifertility vaccines, safety and effectiveness would be extremely important. The vaccines would be administered to healthy individuals and the safety requirements would be expected to be more stringent than those used for preparing a vaccine against a pathogen (Cook & Dickens 1991).

3. PROGRESS IN SOCIAL SCIENCE RESEARCH

The response of governments and non-governmental institutions to excessive population growth has mostly emphasised the provision of contraceptives and public education to encourage people to use family planning services. Such efforts have contributed to the decline in family size in most developing countries. During the last decade it has, however, become clear that the research efforts in contraceptive development cannot only be focused on biomechanical problems. The social dimensions of reproductive health have become of utmost importance. In many parts of the world, the last decade has witnessed a growing concern for what is often called 'the quality of life'. This concern focuses on reducing inequity and discrimination and on promoting observance of ethics and human rights. While women's health advocates have a long history of pointing out the need for more comprehensive approaches to reproductive health care, only in recent years has the population community begun to understand that addressing the broader needs for women and their families will also contribute to encouraging smaller family norms.

The WHO/HRP has, during the last decade, expanded its research to address several important topics including sexual behaviour and its impact on reproductive health. In this regard it is of particular concern to study the sexual activity of adolescents. Also the situation among married women often bound by culturally determined gender roles including their status and decision-making power within the household. These roles influence the degree to which women can exercise control over sexual practice and contraceptive choice.

The situation of unsafe abortion in many developing countries has prompted new studies to explore the social and behavioural factors associated with abortion. These studies aim to help policy makers in developing countries to improve reproductive health policies. At the present time, a large number of projects are under way in all world regions with two main aspects of induced abortion in focus. Firstly, the determinants of factors that explain why women resort to abortion with emphasis on whether the decision to terminate the pregnancy is the result of ignorance of contraception, method failure or lack of services or whether it results from a risk-taking behaviour. Secondly, the consequences of induced abortion, i.e. the effect on the woman, her family, her partner as well as on society in general, in terms of health and of increased strain on health services.

Studies are also performed on the role of the male in reproductive choices identifying cultural barriers to the use of contraceptives. Acceptability of contraceptive methods is especially important before introduction of new methods in family planning programmes. Realising that in some developing countries breast feeding prevents more unwanted pregnancies than all other contraceptive methods combined, the prevalence and duration of breast feeding and the social dimensions of maternal health are also under investigation. An important integral part of the social science research of WHO/HRP is the strengthening of research capacity in developing countries by support to centres and training of scientists (WHO 1993).

The Ford Foundation, an organisation which strongly supported reproductive endocrinology and contraceptive research during the 1960s and 1970s has responded to the need for increased social science research and since 1990 developed a programme focused on the social, economic and cultural factors that affect reproductive health. Three main strategic lines have been defined:

- support of social science research to develop knowledge about factors influencing reproductive health behaviour
- empowering women in particular, but also men and the larger community, to participate in improving their reproductive health
- promoting a public dialogue to facilitate the definition of ethical and legal frameworks for reproductive health and rights that are appropriate to each society.

In the same way as the WHO/HRP efforts, an important component of the Ford Foundation strategy has been to identify and strengthen social science research and training centres in developing countries. Support has been provided for research on sexuality and abortion and several countries have examples of effective programmes on adolescent issues. Efforts to promote a dialogue on ethical and legal aspects of reproductive health are starting to take place in virtually all of the offices (Barzelatto 1993).

The CPR/NICHD through its Demographic and Behavioural Sciences Branch supports a large research and research training programme in the USA. Although this programme is not directed to or support developing countries, it is of importance because it gives training possibilities to scientists from third world countries (CPR 1993).

4. THE FUTURE

To review the progress made in the field of contraceptive research and development and to identify the challenges ahead, an international symposium on *Contraceptive Research and Development for the Year 2000 and Beyond* was organised jointly by the government of Mexico and the WHO/HRP Programme in March 1993. The symposium brought together senior managers of all the international and some national public sector agencies that undertake contraceptive research, along with programme directors and senior staff of some 12 international and national agencies that support or are otherwise involved in the field of fertility regulation research. The symposium identified 11 priority actions that, if taken in a timely and concerted manner, would produce a new generation of fertility regulation methods and improve services that would greatly enhance human well-being now and in the decades to follow.

In their discussions and presentations, the participants affirmed that in developing new methods of fertility regulation special priority should be given to methods that will also protect against STDs as well as to male methods. They also stressed the need to ensure that women have access to safe abortion. In spite of major financial constraints, increased collaboration and coordination among agencies in the field have produced significant advances in the development of new and improved fertility regulation methods, important scientific findings on the safety of existing methods, the initiation of efforts to improve the quality of services, and recognition of the concurrent need to address interrelated sexual and reproductive health issues.

The conference held the view that there is no doubt that higher levels of funding, especially for research, from both the public and private sectors, would considerably hasten progress towards reducing the enormous sexual and reproductive health problems that cause unnecessary death and untold suffering, as well as undermining human rights and dignity, especially for women. Human sexual behaviour is complex and has a bearing on the selection and use of fertility regulation methods; moreover, fertility regulation needs of women and men evolve during the course of their lives and people need different methods at different stages. Research is required not only to develop methods suitable for use by different people at different stages of their lives, but also to understand the social and behavioural issues related, for example, to sexuality and gender relations and acceptance and use of fertility regulation. Depending on the nature of problems to be studied, some research will have an immediate pay-off, while for certain problems solutions will take a longer time to emerge. It was also stressed that women's health advocates and potential users should be represented in all decision making mechanisms and advisory bodies that are established to guide the research process (Declaration of the International Symposium on Contraceptive Research and Development for the Year 2000 and Beyond, 1993).

REFERENCES

Ada, G.L. & Griffins, P.D. 1991 Report of the symposium. In *Vaccines for fertility regulation* (eds. G.L. Ada & D. Griffin). Cambridge, UK: Cambridge University Press, pp. 251–298.

Barzelatto, J. 1993 Personal communication. The Ford Foundation.

Center for Population Research, National Institute of Child Health and Human Development. 1992 Progress Report. Washington, DC: US Department of Health and Human Services.

Claypool, L.E. 1993 The challenges ahead. Implications of STD/AIDs for contraceptive research. In *Proceedings, symposium on contraceptive research and development for the year 2000 and beyond*. Mexico City, March 8–10.

Cook, R.J. & Dickens, B.M. 1991 Legal and ethical aspects of development and use of fertility-regulating vaccines. In *Vaccines for fertility regulation* (ed. G.L. Ada & D. Griffin). Cambridge, UK: Cambridge University Press, pp. 201–232.

Declaration of the International Symposium on Contraceptive Research and Development for the Year 2000 and Beyond. 1993 Geneva, Switzerland: WHO/HRP.

Family Health International. 1992 Contraceptive technology and family planning research. Semiannual Report October 1991—March 1992. Durham, NC: Family Health International.

Gabelnick, H. 1993 Personal communication. Contraceptive Research and Development Program (CONRAD).

Greep, R.O., Koblinsky, M.A., & Jaffe, F.S. 1976 *Reproduction and human welfare: A challenge to research*, Cambridge, Massachusetts and London, England, MTP Press, pp. 16–25

Mastroianni, L.J., Donaldson, P.J. & Kane, T.D. (eds.) 1990 *Developing new contraceptives: obstacles and opportunities*. Washington, DC: National Academy Press, pp. 75–88.

PATH (Program for Appropriate Technology in Health) 1993 Enhancing the private sector's role in contraceptive research and development. In *Proceedings, symposium on contraceptive research and development for the year 2000 and beyond*. Mexico City, March 8–10.

Population Council. 1992 Annual report 1991, Center for Biomedical Research. New York, NY: The Population Council.

Puri, C.P. & Van Look, F.P.A. 1991 Newly developed contraceptive progesterone antagonists for fertility control. In *Antihormones in health and disease* (ed. M.K. Agarwal). Frontiers of Hormone Research **19**. Basel, Switzerland: Karger AG, pp. 127–167.

Sinding, S. 1993 Personal communication. The Rockefeller Foundation.

Sivin, S. 1993 IUDs — A look to the future. In *Proceedings, symposium on contraceptive research and development for the year 2000 and beyond.* Mexico City, March 8–10.

WHO 1992a Oral contraceptives and neoplasia. WHO Technical Report Series No. 817, Geneva, Switzerland: WHO.

WHO 1992b Annual technical report 1991. Special Programme of Research, Development and Research Training in Human Reproduction. Geneva, Switzerland: WHO.

WHO 1992c Reproductive health: A key to a brighter future. WHO Biennial Report 1990–1991. Special 20th anniversary issue. Geneva, Switzerland: WHO.

WHO 1993 Annual technical report 1992. Special Programme of Research, Development and Research Training in Human Reproduction. Geneva, Switzerland: WHO.

4/3

Current Status and Future of
Immunological Approaches to Fertility Control
G.P. Talwar, Rahul Pal, Suman Dhawan, Om Singh
and Chandrima Shaha

ABSTRACT

Progress on various birth control vaccines, in particular those in clinical trials, is reviewed. Six vaccines have reached the Phase I clinical trials, and one, the HSD-hCG vaccine, has completed Phase II efficacy trials, demonstrating the feasibility of preventing pregnancy by a birth control vaccine at or above 50 ng/ml antibody titres without undesirable side effects. The effect of the vaccine is fully reversible and fertility is regained when antibody titres decline in absence of booster injections; the resulting offspring are normal in every respect.

A new category of vaccines are on the horizon that act by *local* stimulation of cell mediated immunity and one such vaccine, Praneem VILCI, has completed Phase I clinical trials in women. This vaccine may also provide a novel approach for reversible male fertility control; it induces aspermatogenesis without decline in testosterone. A vaccine against FSH for male fertility control is in Phase I clinical trials.

LHRH vaccines, though usable for both male and female fertility control (with depot supplements of sex steroids), are currently in clinical trials in prostate carcinoma patients.

It will be logistically desirable to have multiple doses of the vaccine delivered at a single contact point. Biodegradable microspheres encapsulating the vaccine are being evaluated in experimental animals for a six-month or a one-year antibody response. A low cost live recombinant vaccine has also been developed that generates protective antibodies in non-human primates for two years.

1. THE NEED FOR BIRTH CONTROL VACCINES

There is a continuing need to have additional options of methods for couples desiring contraception. Birth control vaccines (BCVs) have attractive characteristics. They require periodic intake, are reversible, can be used at either the early, middle or the late stages of reproductive life and do not block ovulation nor change menstrual regularity and bleeding patterns. The current status of BCVs is reviewed with particular focus on those which have reached the stage of clinical trials and may be available for family planning in the not distant future.

2. PRINCIPLES OF ACTION AND THE RANGE OF BIRTH CONTROL VACCINES

Birth control vaccines seek to induce antibody and/or cell mediated immune (CMI) responses against reproductive hormones or gamete antigens crucial to the success of reproduction. The reproductive processes are regulated by a cascade of hormones. The sperm carry several auto and isoantigens. The egg has a layer of zona glycoproteins with

Table 1 *Vaccines under development*

	target	antigen	current status
1.	hCG	HSD vaccine	Phase I and Phase II clinical trials completed in India. clinical trials approved in Mexico in patients with hCG-producing lung cancer.
		ßhCG-TT vaccine	Phase I clinical trials completed in India, Finland, Chile, Dominican Republic
		CTP-ßhCG vaccine	Phase I clinical trials completed in Australia
2.	sperm	Praneem VILCI (CMI vaccine) female	Phase I clinical trials completed in India
		Praneem VILCI male	under test in rodents and monkeys
3.	FSH	oFSH	Phase I clinical trials in progress in India in male subjects
4.	LHRH	LHRH-Dlys^6-DT	clinical trials in carcinoma prostate patients in India and Austria
		female fertility control	toxicology studies completed for extension of lactational amenorrhoea
		LHRH-1-TT	clinical trials in carcinoma prostate in USA
		male fertility control	in experimental animals with androgen supplements
5.	sperm antigens	a number of promising antigens identified by MoAbs and infertile couple sera	molecular characterisation
			gene cloning and expression
			efficacy testing in experimental animals
6.	zona pellucida antigens	glycoproteins involved in sperm– egg interaction identified	genes cloning and expression
			peptides with B and T cell epitopes
			efficacy testing in experimental animals
			molecular characterisation, epitope analysis
7.	riboflavin carrier protein	chicken riboflavin carrier protein	efficacy testing in experimental animals

References and description given in the text.

receptors for sperm attachment and for species discrimination. There are numerous sites at which reproductive processes can be intercepted. Consequently *several* vaccines are conceivable for control of fertility. Table 1 gives the vaccines currently under development. Six vaccines, all directed against hormones, are in clinical trials, albeit at different stages. Three of these are directed against human chorionic gonadotropin (hCG), two against luteinising hormone releasing hormone (LHRH) and one against follicle stimulating hormone (FSH). In each case, the vaccine is designed to generate antibodies that can inactivate the bioactivity of the hormone. A vaccine, Praneem VILCI (PV), which activates locally cell-mediated immune (CMI) reactions at the site of application has completed Phase I trials in India and will be entering Phase II trials this year. The CMI vaccines have *unique* properties. Their action is highly localised. No antibodies or other systemic effects are detectable. PV has also promise for control of male fertility.

A number of tissue-specific antigens have been identified on the sperm and these are being evaluated for their potential for fertility regulation in experimental animals, including subhuman primates. Progress has also been made in molecular dissection of the family of glycoproteins constituting the zona pellucida which surrounds the mammalian egg. Vaccines inducing immune response against sperm or egg antigens that prevent sperm–egg interaction are foreseeable. A vaccine is being developed (Adiga *et al.* 1991), which seeks to intervene in the transport of riboflavin to the embryo and thereby abrogate pregnancy at an early stage.

Table 2 *Characteristics of the antibodies generated by the hCG vaccines during Phase I clinical trials in women*

vaccine	CTP-37-DT[a]	ßhCG-TT[b]	HSD-TT/DT[c]
adjuvant & vehicle	squalene, MDP Arlacel A	alum	alum + SPLPS
titre (ng/ml)	36–127	120–1800	222–6000
aviditiy (M^{-1})	10^8	10^{10}	10^{10}
B/I index*	?	52	61
crossreaction with:			
hTSH, hFSH	–	–	–
hLH	–	+	+
pancreatic cells	+**	–	–

a: Jones *et al.* 1988
b: Thau *et al.* 1989
c: Om Singh *et al.* 1989
B/I Index: Talwar *et al.* 1988
*: % bioneutralisation capacity per unit radioimmunoassay titre.
**: Rose *et al.* 1988
Avidity data from collaborative studies.

2.1 The HCG vaccines

Vaccines against hCG are the most advanced of the fertility-regulating vaccines. HCG as a target molecule for immuno-contraception was the choice of three groups of investigators and three vaccines have completed Phase I trials. Table 2 gives the characteristics of these vaccines. An important consideration in choosing hCG was the expectation that, in contrast to steroidal contraceptives, the vaccine would not block the pituitary–ovarian axis and that the women will keep ovulating and have regular menstrual cycles. This expectation has been fulfilled by all hCG vaccines.

Two different strategies were adopted in making the hCG vaccines. One approach envisaged the utilisation of the 37-aminoacid carboxy terminal peptide (CTP) (Stevens *et al.* 1981), which is not present in ßhLH, as the immunogen. In the other approach, the entire ß-subunit was considered necessary (Talwar *et al.* 1976). The CTPs were poor immunogens and had a limited number of determinants, with the result that the antibodies generated by them were of low affinity and low bioneutralisation capacity (Ramakrishnan *et al.* 1979).

Women are immunologically tolerant to hCG (or its subparts). ßhCG was therefore linked to an immunogenic carrier which could provide T cell help. Tetanus toxoid (TT) was chosen initially for this purpose so as to confer also immunoprophylactic benefit to the recipients against tetanus. The ßhCG-TT conjugate was indeed successful in inducing antibodies against both hCG and TT (Talwar *et al.* 1976).

2.1.1 Safety studies

Extensive toxicology studies were conducted on the hCG vaccines as per the guidelines set by WHO and the Indian Council of Medical Research (ICMR). All the vaccines were free of side effects in rodents and primates.

2.1.2 Reversibility, regain of fertility and normalcy of progeny

On immunisation with the entire ßhCG vaccines, sub-human primates become infertile (Hearn 1976; Stevens 1976; Talwar *et al.* 1980, 1986). The efficacy is related to the ability of the antibodies to inactivate the species CG (Rao *et al.* 1988). On decline of antibodies, the monkeys (and the baboons) regain fertility and engender progeny which are normal in every respect. It was pertinent to enquire whether the progeny of previously immunised animals can reproduce normally. This has been observed in six bonnet monkeys and two baboons. Thus, reproductive capabilities are unaffected and these animals can engender normal second generation progeny.

2.1.3 Clinical trials of the first prototype vaccine, ßhCG-TT

The first vaccine, ßhCG-TT, was approved for Phase I clinical trials in women of reproductive age, who had undergone elective tubal ligations, in India as well as in Finland, Sweden, Chile and Brazil. The vaccine did succeed in generating anti-hCG antibodies in women (Talwar *et al.* 1976; Nash *et al.* 1980). The response was reversible and the titres declined to zero levels in course of time. Menstrual regularity was maintained. Luteal progesterone values and endometrial biopsies indicated that ovulation was not impaired. The antibodies recognised and bound to exogenously administered hCG. This, however, did not act as booster. The titres were replenished to levels approximating those prevailing at the time of challenge within four weeks, which implied that the subject can meet successive challenge of pregnancy in two consecutive cycles.

While the ßhCG-TT vaccine fulfilled many essential requirements, the vaccine produced widely variable titres of antibodies (Talwar 1984) and those with low titres were prone to become pregnant.

2.1.4 Improved vaccine–heterospecies dimer (HSD)–TT/DT

To augment immunogenicity, an adjuvant, sodium phthalyl derivative of lipopolysaccharide (SPLPS) was included in the first injection (Om Singh *et al.* 1982). This doubled, on an average, the antibody titres obtained with alum alone. It was also considered important to enhance the intrinsic immunogenicity of ßhCG. This was done by associating it to the α-subunit of ovine gonadotropin (Talwar & Om Singh 1988). The ability of α and ß-subunits to associate with each other to generate a conformation that recognises target tissue receptors and exercise hormonal action is conserved across species. Thus the human ß-subunit can associate with α-subunit of ovine origin. The heterospecies dimer (HSD) thus created, a man-made hormone, is superior to hCG in steroidogenic capacity (Talwar *et al.* 1988). It is more immunogenic than ßhCG and antibodies have better hCG bioneutralisation capacity (Talwar *et al.* 1988, Pal *et al.* 1990).

2.1.5 The CTP vaccine

The vaccine consists of a synthetic 37-amino acid (109-145) ßhCG carboxy terminal peptide conjugated to diphtheria toxoid (Stevens *et al.* 1981). N-acetyl-glucosamine-3yl-acetyl-L-alanyl-D-isoglutamine and a saline–oil emulsion vehicle with an oil phase consisting of four parts squalene to one part Arlacel A have been employed as vehicle and adjuvant. The vaccine has undergone Phase I clinical trials in 20 women in Australia. Ten additional women, immunised with just the vehicle, served as controls. Over a six month follow-up, no side effects of any significance were observed. All immunised women generated antibody titres against hCG, the titres varying from 0.95–3.368 nmol/L (36–127 ng/ml) (Jones *et al.* 1988). Phase II clinical trials are planned.

2.1.6 Clinical studies with the HSD-hCG vaccine

After due toxicology, drug regulatory and ethical approvals, Phase I studies with this vaccine were conducted in women to confirm its reversibility and lack of side effects (Talwar *et al.* 1990; Om Singh *et al.* 1989). The crucial studies of determining whether the vaccine is efficacious in preventing pregnancy started thereafter. Phase II clinical trials were conducted in three major institutes of India: 148 women of proven fertility who were sexually active and had at least 2 children were enrolled. Two pre-immunisation cycles were studied for evidence of menstrual regularity and ovulation (luteal progesterone 11–56 nmol/L). A presumptive threshold for efficacy of 50 ng/ml of hCG bioneutralisation capacity of antibody titres was fixed; the objective of the trials was to investigate whether pregnancy was prevented at these or higher titres. Observations had to be made over 750 cycles for 95% confidence. The women were asked to use IUDs or condoms during the period of antibody titre build-up following initial immunisation.

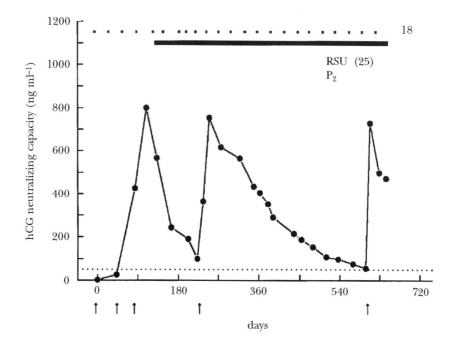

Figure 1. Efficacy of HSD-hCG vaccine to prevent pregnancy: Phase II clinical trials were conducted in 148 women. Figure shows the antibody response in a subject (RSU), 25 years old with 2 children and active sex life. She received 3 doses of the HSD vaccine for primary immunisation and a booster to generate an antibody response above the threshold of 50 ng for 561 days. The rectangles at the top abcissa mark the menstruation events. The solid horizontal bar denotes the period (18 months) during which she had unprotected intercourse without becoming pregnant.

Alternative contraceptives were withdrawn once titres above 50 ng/ml were attained and subjects were exposed to unprotected intercourse during the period that the antibodies stayed above this limit. In the declining phase of antibody titres, the women had the option of either receiving a booster immunisation or opting out of the study. Follow-up was continued on those desiring a child to confirm reversibility. The results show that only one pregnancy took place above 50 ng/ml in the first 750 cycles recorded. Figure 1 is a representative illustration of the antibody response in a subject immunised with the HSD–hCG vaccine. With the fulfillment of the Phase II objectives, enrolment of new subjects was stopped. However, those with circulating antibodies were followed up. Boosters were also administered to women on *specific* request in recognition of their participation in the study. Another 400 cycles have been recorded with no new pregnancy having taken place.

The data suggest that the vaccine indeed protects women from becoming pregnant. The efficacy has been further confirmed by post-coital tests on eight women with circulating anti-hCG antibodies, who volunteered for the study. In spite of high cervical mucous scores and good quality and number of sperm, none of them became pregnant. Menstrual regularity was maintained. No significant change in number of bleeding days and amount was noted. Progesterone values in the single bleed taken in mid-luteal stage were in the ovulatory range in 80% of cycles. Women became pregnant with decline of antibody titres. Some pregnancies were carried to term; normal healthy children have been born to five women who were previously immunised with the vaccine.

2.1.7 Further developments required for use of HSD vaccine on a large scale

The HSD vaccine is safe, reversible and can prevent pregnancy at and above 50 ng/ml titres. Before it is taken up for Phase III, the following points have to be addressed:

(i) Coverage of the lag period: The primary immunisation requires three injections of the vaccine given at six weeks interval. It takes about three months for the antibody titres to build up. This "vulnerable" period requires to be covered by a compatible companion approach so that a woman is protected right from the day she opts for the vaccine. This may be achievable by the use of Praneem VILCI described later, which has now reached the stage of clinical testing.

(ii) Another desirable requirement would be the delivery of multiple doses of the vaccine at a single contact point, so as to obviate the need of return visits. This may again be possible. Biodegradable microspheres encapsulating multiple doses of the vaccine have been made. These generate the requisite type and degree of immune response in experimental animals (Stevens *et al.* 1990; Singh *et al.* 1992). These should be ready for clinical trials in the near future.

(iii) The effective agent for prevention of pregnancy is the antibodies that the vaccine induces. It would be necessary to have a simple self-administered test, which the woman can perform that can provide information on the adequacy (or otherwise) of the antibodies. For this purpose a number of monoclonal antibodies (MoAbs) have been developed. It has been observed that almost all women protected in the Phase II study made antibodies to certain determinants recognised by two MoAbs (Deshmukh *et al.* 1993). Using these MoAbs, a prototype test has been made. This would be taken up for validation in the next series of clinical trials and refined for sensitivity and specificity.

A live recombinant vaccine with insert of ßhCG gene co-expressed with a transmembrane fragment (Srinivasan *et al.* 1993) induces a long-lasting protective response in bonnet monkeys. The vaccinia recombinant version of the vaccine would be cheap and producible in large quantities. With the spread of HIV infection and thereby the possibly larger number of immunosuppressed subjects, it may be prudent to use an alternative pox vector, totally devoid of possible neurovirulence in immunosuppressed subjects. Avian pox viruses have the property of expressing inserted genes, while they do not replicate in mammals. Our colleagues Chandrasekhar and Anushree Gupta are making an hCG vaccine in fowl pox virus.

3. PRANEEM VILCI

Neem (*Azadirachta indica*), a tree that grows in most parts of the subcontinent, is known for its many medicinal properties. Extracts of neem seeds have compounds with potent immunomodulatory properties. A purified fraction (Praneem) administered in the uterus in small amounts (0.1 ml) prevents rodents of proven fertility becoming pregnant (Upadhyay *et al.* 1990). The effect lasts for several months and is reversible. The treatment does not impair ovarian functions: the animals ovulate, have normal libido and reproductive hormone levels. The uterus remains normally responsive to oestradiol and progesterone. The action is exercised by local activation of cell-mediated immune (CMI) reactions. The phagocytic cells are activated; a higher density of MHC class II antigens is noticeable with immuno markers. Immune cells from Praneem-treated animals react to challenge with sperm, with substantially higher transformation of lymphocytes and production of an array of cytokines (Upadhyay *et al.* 1992). These in turn kill the sperm and/or the developing embryo, imposing a pre-implantation block to fertility. It is an elegant mechanism, operating by CMI. No antibodies are generated. The effect is highly localised: even the contralateral horn in the rat, if untreated, is not affected and can bear a normal pregnancy (Fig. 2). Praneem VILCI has undergone Phase I clinical trials. No side effects were observed. Phase II trials are due to start to determine the efficacy of VILCI alone and the ability of VILCI and hCG vaccine in combination to protect the women from pregnancy right from the day of enrolment.

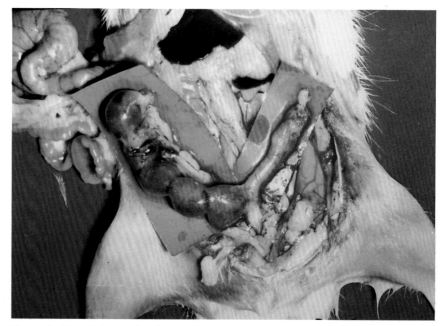

Figure 2. The right uterine horn of the rat was administered 100 µl of Praneem VILCI (PV); whereas the contralateral horn received the same volume of peanut oil. The animal mated normally; no implantation sites are visible in the treated horn inspite of ovulation having taken place in the right ovary. The action is highly localised without influencing even the contralateral horn. The effect is reversible, and fertility is regained after several months. The action is exercised by stimulation of cell mediated immunity at the site of application.

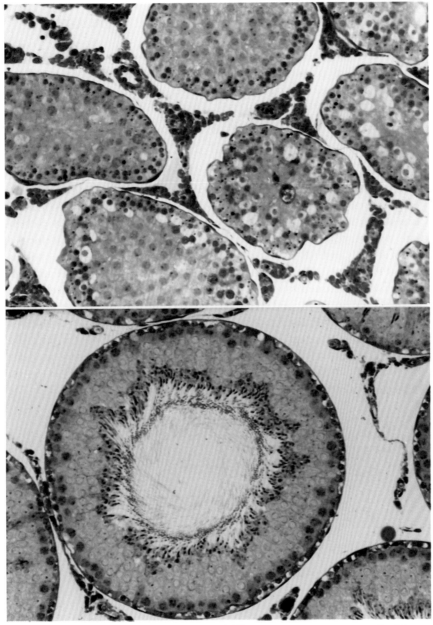

Figure 3. The ability of Praneem VILCI (PV) to arrest spermatogenesis: The rat was injected 50 µl of PV intra-vas; the contralateral vas received an equal volume of peanut oil. Fig. 3a is a photomicrograph of testis 4 week after intra vas administration of PV. Spermatogenesis was arrested, in contrast to normal spermatogenesis visible in the contralateral testis in Fig. 3b. Note the presence of spermatogonia in Fig. 3a which indicates the reversibility of the effect.Animals administered bilaterally with PV become infertile but regain fertility after several months (From Upadhyay, Dhawan & Talwar 1993).

4. MALE FERTILITY CONTROL BY IMMUNOLOGICAL APPROACHES

4.1 The FSH vaccine

Moudgal *et al.* (1992) have developed a vaccine that employs ovine FSH to induce antibodies reactive with primate and human FSH. Their earlier studies had shown the requirement of FSH for spermatogenesis in primates. The inactivation of FSH by passive or active immunisation led to oligospermia. The fertilising capacity of the sperm was also impaired. The vaccine has completed toxicology studies and has entered Phase I clinical trials in men.

4.2 The LHRH vaccines

Two vaccines are in clinical trials. The Population Council vaccine links the carrier TT at the N-terminal amino acid. Male rats immunised with this vaccine become infertile. Libido is restored by depot injection of testosterone-17-trans-4-n-butyl cyclohexane carboxylate, without restoring spermatogenesis (Ladd *et al.* 1989). The vaccine is also in Phase I clinical trials in USA in four orchiectomised prostate carcinoma patients. The vaccine was well tolerated. The subjects responded by making anti-LHRH antibodies on repeat boosters. It is planned to extend the study to 20 non-orchiectomised patients.

The LHRH vaccine developed by us has utilised the amino acid at position 6 for creating a functional group for covalent linkage; Gly-6 was replaced by D-lysine. This is in turn linked to aminocaproic acid, a spacer molecule to which the carrier diphtheria toxoid (DT) is attached via its ε-amino group. This vaccine design has several advantages. Gly-6 is the point of metabolic cleavage in LHRH and its replacement by a D-amino acid has a stabilising effect on the molecule. Modeling of the structure of LHRH on the basis

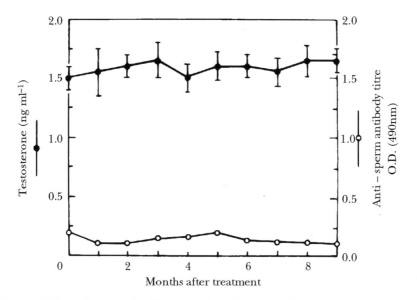

Figure 4. Rats of proven fertility were given intra-vas PV bilaterally. They became infertile over 9 months of observation period. The treatment did not produce any decline in the testosterone levels and no anti-sperm antibodies were detectable.

of conformational preferences of homologous sequence stretches in the protein data banks and the known data on structure–activity relationships suggests that the LHRH molecule is folded through a ß-turn defined through a weak hydrogen bond between the backbone carboxylate of Trp-3 and the amide of Gly-6 (Gupta *et al.* 1993). Carrier conjugation at position 6 does not disturb this site.

Immunisation of male and female rats and monkeys with this vaccine leads to a block of fertility (Talwar *et al.* 1984). The prostate undergoes a *marked* atrophy (Jayashankar *et al.* 1989; Giri *et al.* 1990). Clinical trials in patients at an advanced stage of carcinoma of the prostate in two centres in India and one centre in Salzburg indicate that the vaccine is well tolerated. With the production of anti-LHRH antibodies, LH and FSH and testosterone levels decline. Acid phosphatase and prostatic specific antigen (PSA) also register a marked decline from the high levels obtained in these carcinoma patients. Ultrascans revealed that in several cases, immunisation caused a shrinkage in the prostate size. Nephrestograms showed clearance of urinary passages. The effect was seen in many but not all patients.

Although the emphasis on the use of this vaccine has been for immunotherapeutic purposes in clinical disorders, the vaccine has the potential for use in women for extending the period of lactational amenorrhoea and inter-child interval. An expected and perhaps undesirable side effect of such intervention would be the decreased levels of oestrogens, possibly leading to osteoporosis. This, however, has not been observed in trials with an LHRH agonist; ovulation remained suppressed for 11 months in women given the agonist Buserelin, with no residual side effects of any significance (Fraser *et al.* 1989).

4.3 Cell-mediated immunity approaches for male fertility control

The male reproductive system offers unique possibilities. While the cytoarchitecture of the tubules, and the germinal cells are laid during fetal life, the ontogenesis of spermatogenesis takes place in pubertal years, with the result that some proteins unique to sperm are made only at this stage. These are 'foreign' to the host immune system and can be selectively reacted against if the barrier separating the immune system in the testes is labilised and local suppressor mechanisms overcome. The immune reaction should not occur against Leydig cells that make testosterone, as these cells are present and functional during fetal life and are recognised as 'self' by the immune system. Following this logic we conducted a conceptual experiment in 1979. BCG (Bacillus Calmette and Guerin) was injected intratesticularly. It led to mononuclear infiltration in interstitial spaces causing a cessation of spermatogenesis. Testosterone levels remained normal. The testicular origin of testosterone (and not adrenal) was confirmed by its rise with hCG and not by ACTH stimulus (Talwar *et al.* 1979). The process was reversible (Naz and Talwar 1986). The effect was manifest in rodents, monkeys, dogs and rams, the species investigated. Repeat immunisations render monkeys infertile with regain of fertility after nine months. No anti-sperm antibodies were detectable in circulation.

The above studies laid the basis for developing a CMI vaccine for male fertility control. More recently, the potential of PV to induce azoospermia was investigated. PV (50μl) was given in vas of rats. Within four to six weeks, spermatogenesis was completely arrested (Fig 3). The effect took place without inflammatory reaction or occlusion in the vas or epididymis. The testosterone levels remained normal (Fig 4). Animals caged with females mated (as evidenced by pseudo pregnancy and prolonged dioestrous) without siring a litter, while the control rats given the same amounts of peanut oil in vas were fertile (Upadhayay et al. 1993). Infertility persisted over eight months of observation period.

4.4 Sperm and zona antigens

In many clinical cases of infertility due to immunological factors, antibodies immobilising or agglutinating sperm have been recognised. Sperm carry several auto and isoantigens. A large number of monoclonal antibodies were generated by investigators all over the world (Anderson *et al.* 1987) to identify the immuno-dominant epitopes that are specific to sperm, and antibodies which can prevent sperm–egg interaction.

Another track followed was the search through antisera of well-characterised infertile patients. A handful of promising antigens are being actively explored as possible candidates for contraceptive vaccines (Primakoff *et al.* 1988; Herr *et al.* 1990; Shaha *et al.* 1990; Goldberg 1991; Naz 1993; Suri *et al.* 1993). In spite of their great interest, these will not be reviewed in this article in detail, as these approaches are currently in experimental stages and their clinical applications are distant. For the same reasons, readers are referred to the scientific literature for the exciting work in progress on zona antigens (Henderson *et al.* 1988; Millar *et al.* 1989; Sehgal *et al.* 1989; Sacco *et al.* 1991; Bagvant *et al.* 1993).

5. CONCLUDING COMMENTS

Immunocontraception is an area of active research. The HSD–hCG vaccine is the first vaccine at present whose efficacy in preventing pregnancy has been determined. The immune response generated by the vaccine is fully reversible and immunisation does not disturb menstrual cyclicity and ovulation, nor other body functions. This vaccine has thus the potential for use on a wider scale. However, it requires three ancillary developments before it is suitable for wider use: (1) a biodegradable delivery system by which multiple doses can be administered at a single contact point. Delivery systems currently under evaluation stimulate antibody levels above the efficacy threshold for six months to one year in experimental animals after a single injection. (2) Coverage of the lag period of about three months in antibody titre build up at the time of primary immunisation. Praneem VILCI may be able to do so. (3) A simple self-administered test for assessing the adequacy of antibody titres. A prototype test is under development which will undergo validation trials.

It will be desirable to have a low cost vaccine. This would demand the making of the gonadotropin subunits by DNA recombinant methods. Live recombinant vaccines may also offer effective cheap options. Vaccinia virus with the ßhCG gene co-expressed with a transmembrane fragment generates a high antibody response of long duration in monkeys. Efforts are being made to transfer this cassette to avian pox viruses, which can express the cloned proteins in a mammalian host without replication of the virus, thereby minimising the chances of side effects.

A relatively new and promising approach to immunocontraception will be the use of vaccines which act by stimulating local cell-mediated immunity. Purified Neem seed extracts (Praneem) have provided fractions that block fertility in rodents and monkeys without disturbance of ovulation or alteration in hormone levels and libido. The effect is highly localised. The action is exercised by activation in the uterus of CMI with an enhanced immune reactivity to sperm challenge, which is accompanied by local production of cytokines, noxious to the sperm and/or the pre-implantation embryo. No sperm-reactive antibodies are detected. VILCI has gone through toxicology studies and is currently in clinical trials.

Praneem VILCI may also provide an elegant approach to male fertility control. A single injection in the vas deferens causes an arrest of spermatogenesis without decline in testosterone.

Another vaccine for male fertility control eliciting antibodies against FSH is in Phase I clinical trials in India.

Vaccines have been developed against LHRH which can induce the formation of bioeffective antibodies and can be used for fertility regulation in both sexes. However, steroid hormone supplements would have to be provided by depot formulations or transdermal delivery systems. An important use of the LHRH vaccine may be for immunotherapy of reproductive health disorders such as precocious puberty and hormone-dependent prostate cancers as an alternative to the use of LHRH agonists and antagonists, which are expensive.

Vaccines directed against the sperm and egg are attractive propositions, but are at present at the experimental stage.

ACKNOWLEDGEMENTS

Our work on Fertility Regulating Vaccines is supported by S & T Project of the Department of Biotechnology, Govt. of India, the International Development Research Centre (IDRC) of Canada and the Rockefeller Foundation. It has benefited from cooperative interaction with the International Committee for Contraception Research (ICCR) of the Population Council, New York.

REFERENCES

Adiga, P.R., Kakrande, A.A., Visweswaraiah, S. & Seshagiri, P.B. 1991 Carrier protein mediated transplacental riboflavin transport in the primate. In *Prospectives in primate reproductive biology* (ed. N.R. Moudgal, K. Yoshinaga, A.J. Rao & P.R. Adiga). New Delhi: Wiley Eastern, pp. 129–140.

Anderson, D.J., Johnson, P.M., Alexander, N.J., Jones, W.R. & Griffin, P.D. 1987 Monoclonal antibodies to human trophoblast and sperm antigens: Report on two WHO-sponsored workshops. *J. Reprod. Immunol.* **10**, 231–257.

Bagvant, H., Yurewicz, E.C., Sacco, A.G., Talwar, G.P. & Gupta, S.K. 1993 Delineation of epitopes on porcine zona pellucida relevant for binding of sperm to oocyte using monoclonal antibodies. *J. Reprod. Immunol.* **23**, 265–279.

Deshmukh, U., Pal, R., Talwar, G.P. & Gupta, S.K. 1993 Antibody response against epitopes on hCG mapped by monoclonal antibodies in women immunized with an anti-hCG vaccine and its implications for bioneutralization. *J. Reprod. Immunol.* **25**, 103–117.

Fraser, H.M., Dewart, P.J., Smith, S.K., Cowen, G.M., Sandow, J. & McNeilly, A.S. 1989 LHRH agonist in contraception in breast feeding women. *J. Clin. Endocrinol. Metab.* **69**, 996–1002.

Giri, D.K., Chaudhuri, M.K., Jayashankar, R., Neelaram, G., Jayaraman, S. & Talwar, G.P. 1990 Histopathological changes in reproductive organs of male Wistar rats following active immunization against LHRH. *Exp. Mol. Pathol.* **52**, 54–62.

Goldberg, E. 1991 Lactate dehydrogenase C₄ as an immunocontraceptive model. In *Gamete interaction: prospects for immunocontraception* (ed. N.J. Alexander, D. Griffin, J.M. Spieler & G.M.H. Waites). New York: Wiley Liss Inc. pp. 63–73.

Gupta, H.M., Talwar, G.P. & Salunke, D.M. 1993 Novel molecular modelling approach to the structures of small bioactive peptides: the structure of gonadotropin releasing hormone. *Proteins* **16**, 48–56.

Hearn, J.P. 1976 Immunization against pregnancy. *Proc. R. Soc. Lond.* **B** 195, 149–161.

Henderson, C.J., Hulme, M.J. & Aitken, R.J. 1988 Contraceptive potential of antibodies to the zona pellucida. *J. Reprod. Fertil.* **83**, 325–343.

Herr, J.C., Flickinger, C.J., Homyk, M., Klotz, K. & John E. 1990 Biochemical and morphological characterization of the intra-acrosomal antigen SP-10 from human sperm. *Biol. Reprod.* **42**, 181–193.

Jayashankar, R., Chaudhuri, M.K., Om Singh, Alam, A. & Talwar, G.P. 1989 Semisynthetic vaccine causing atrophy of the prostate. *Prostate* **14**, 3–11.

Jones, W.R., Bradley, J., Judd, S.J. *et al.* 1988 Phase I clinical trial of a World Health Organization birth control vaccine. *Lancet* **i**, 1295–1298.

Ladd, A., Tsong, Y.Y., Prabhu, G. & Thau, R. 1989 Effects of long-term immunization against LHRH and androgen treatment on gonadal function. *J. Reprod. Immunol.* **15**, 85–101.

Millar, S.E., Chamow, S.M., Baur, A.W., Oliver, C., Robey, F. & Dean, J. 1989 Vaccination with a synthetic zona pellucida peptide produces long-term contraception in female mice. *Science (Wash.)* **246**, 935–938.

Moudgal, N.R., Ravindranath, N., Murthy, G.S., Dighe, R.R. Aravindan, G.R. & Martin F. 1992 Long term efficacy of vaccine of ovine follicle stimulating hormone in male bonnet monkeys (*Macaca radiata*) *J. Reprod. Fert.* **96**, 91–102.

Nash, H., Talwar, G.P., Segal, S. *et al.* 1980 Observations on the antigenicity and clinical effects of a candidate anti-pregnancy vaccine: ß-subunit of human chorionic gonadotropin linked to tetanus toxoid. *Fertil. Steril.* **34**, 328–335.

Naz, R.K. 1993 Development of contraceptive vaccine for humans using sperm antigens. In *Immunology of reproduction* (ed. R.K. Naz). Boca Raton: CRC Press, pp. 279–291.

Naz, R.K. & Talwar, G.P. 1986 Reversibility of azoospermia induced by Bacillus Calmette Guerin (BCG). *J. Androl.* **7**, 264–269.

Om Singh, Rao, L.V., Gaur, A., Sharma, N.C., Alam, A. & Talwar, G.P. 1989 Antibody response and characteristics of antibodies in women immunized with three contraceptive vaccines inducing antibodies against human chorionic gonadotropin. *Fertil. Steril.* **52**, 739–744.

Om Singh, Shastri, N., Narang, B.S. & Talwar, G.P. 1982 Immuno-prophylaxis: search for an adjuvant acceptable in humans. In *Cellular and humoral mechanism in immune response*. New Delhi: Department of Atomic Energy, pp. 114–118.

Pal, R., Om Singh, Rao, L.V. & Talwar, G.P. 1990 Bioneutralization capacity of the antibodies generated in women by the beta subunit of human chorionic gonadotropin (ßhCG) and ßhCG associated with alpha subunit of ovine luteinizing hormone linked to carriers. *Am. J. Reprod. Immunol.* **22**, 124–126.

Primakoff, P., Lathrop, W., Woolman, L., Cowan, A. & Myles, D. 1988 Fully effective contraception in male and female guinea pigs immunized with sperm protein PH-20. *Nature* **335**, 543-546.

Ramakrishnan, S., Das, C., Dubey, S.K., Salahuddin, M. & Talwar, G.P. 1979 Immunogenicity of three C-terminal synthetic peptides of the beta subunit of human chorionic gonadotropin and properties of the antibodies raised against 45-amino acid C-terminal peptide. *J. Reprod. Immunol.* **1**, 249–261.

Rao, L.V., Om Singh & Talwar, G.P. 1988 Immunological cross-reactivity of antibodies with species chorionic gonadotropin is a critical requirement for efficacy testing of human chorionic gonadotropin vaccines in sub-human primates. *J. Reprod. Immunol.* **13**, 53–63.

Rose, N.R., Burek, C.L. & Smith, J.P. 1988 Safety evaluation of HCG vaccine in primates: auto antibody production. In *Contraception research for today and the nineties* (ed. G.P. Talwar). New York: Springer-Verlag, pp. 231–239.

Sacco, A.G., Yurewicz, E.C., Subramanian, M.G., Lian, L. & Dukelow, W.R. 1991 Immunological response and ovarian histology of squirrel monkeys (*Saimiri sciureus*) immunized with porcine zona pellucida ZP3 (Mr = 55,000) macromolecules. *Am. J. Primatol.* **24**, 15–28.

Sehgal, S., Gupta, S.K. & Bhatnagar, P. 1989 Long term effects of immunization with porcine zona pellucida on rabbit ovaries. *Pathol.* **21**, 105-110.

Shaha, C., Suri, A. & Talwar, G.P. 1990 Induction of infertility in female rats after active immunization with 24kD antigens from rat testes. *Int. J. Androl.* **13**, 17–25.

Singh, M., Om Singh, Singh, A. & Talwar, G.P. 1992 Immunogenicity studies on diphtheria toxoid loaded biodegradable microspheres. *Int. J. Pharm.* **85**: R5-R8.

Srinivasan, J., Om Singh, Pal, R., Lall, L., Chakrabarti, S. & Talwar, G.P. 1993 A recombinant anti-fertility vaccine. In *Local immunity in reproductive tract tissues* (ed. P.D. Griffin & P.M. Johnson). Delhi: Oxford University Press, pp. 477–481.

Stevens, V.C. 1976 Perspectives of development of a fertility control vaccine from hormonal antigens of the trophoblast. In *Development of vaccines for fertility regulation*. Copenhagen: Scriptor, pp. 93–110.

Stevens, V.C., Cinader, B., Powell, J.E., Lee, A.C. & Koh, S.W. 1981 Preparation and formulation of a hCG antifertility vaccine. Selection of peptide immunogen. *Am. J. Reprod. Immunol. Microbiol.* **6**, 307-314.

Stevens, V.C., Powell, J.E., Rickey, M., Lee, A.C. & Lewis, D.H. 1990 Studies of various delivery systems for a human chorionic gonadotropin vaccine. In *Gamete interaction: prospects for immunocontraception* (eds. N.J. Alexander, D. Griffin, J.M. Spieler & G.M.H. Waites). New York: Wiley Liss Inc., pp. 549-563.

Suri, A., Chabra, S., Seshadri, T. & Shaha, C. 1994 Identification of sperm antigens: use of immuno-infertile sera and polyclonal sera. In *Recombinant and synthetic vaccines* (eds. G.P. Talwar & K.V.S. Rao). New Delhi: Narosa Publishing House (in press).

Talwar, G.P. 1984 Structured vaccines for control of fertility and communicable diseases. In *Critical review in tropical medicine, vol 2* (ed. P. Chandra). New York: Plenum Press, pp. 245–269.

Talwar, G.P., Das, C., Tandon, A., Sharma, M.G., Salahuddin, M. & Dubey, S.K. 1980 Immunization against hCG: efficacy and teratological studies in baboons. In *Non-human primate models for study of human reproduction* (ed. T.C. Anand Kumar). Basel: Karger, pp. 190–201.

Talwar, G.P., Hingorani, V., Kumar, S. *et al.* 1990 Phase I clinical trials with three formulations of anti-human chorionic gonadotropin vaccine. *Contraception* **41**,301–316.

Talwar, G.P., Naz, R.K., Das, C. & Das, R.P. 1979 A practicable immunological approach to block spermatogenesis without loss of androgens. *Proc. Natl. Acad. Sci.* USA **76**, 5882–5885.

Talwar, G.P, Om Singh, Singh V. *et al.* 1986 Enhancement of anti-gonadotropin response to the ß-subunit of ovine luteinizing hormone by carrier conjugation and combination with the ß-subunit of human chorionic gonadotropin. *Fertil. Steril.* **46**, 120–126.

Talwar, G.P, Sharma, N.C, Dubey, S.K. *et al.* 1976 Isoimmunization against human chorionic gonadotropin with conjugates of processed ß-subunit of the hormone and tetanus toxoid. *Proc. Natl. Acad. Sci. USA* **73**, 218–222.

Talwar, G.P., Singh, V., Om Singh, Das, C., Gupta, S.K. & Singh, G. 1984 Pituitary and extra-pituitary sites of action of gonadotropin-releasing hormone: potential uses of active and passive immunization against gonadotropin-releasing hormone. In *Hormone receptors in growth and reproduction* (ed. B.B. Saxena, K.J. Catt, L. Birnbaumer & L. Martini). New York: Raven Press, pp. 351–359.

Talwar, G.P. & Om Singh. 1988 Birth control vaccines inducing antibodies against chorionic gonadotropin. In *Contraception research for today and the nineties* (ed. G.P. Talwar). New York: Springer-Verlag, pp. 183–199.

Talwar, G.P., Om Singh & Rao, L.V. 1988 An improved immunogen for anti-human chorionic gonadotropin vaccine eliciting antibodies reactive with a conformation native to the hormone without crossreaction with human follicle stimulating hormone and human thyroid stimulating hormone. *J. Reprod. Immunol.* **14**, 203–212.

Thau, R.B., Croxatto, H., Luukkainen, T. *et al.* 1989 Advances in the development of an antifertility vaccine. In *Reproductive immunology 1989* (eds. L. Mettler & B.D. Billington). Amsterdam: Elsevier, pp.237–244.

Upadhyay, S.N., Dhawan, S., Garg, S. & Talwar, G.P. 1992 Immunomodulatory effects of neem (*Azadirachta indica*). *Int. J. Immunopharmac.* **14**, 1187–1193.

Upadhyay, S.N., Dhawan, S. & Talwar, G.P. 1993 Antifertility effects of neem (*Azadirachta indica*) oil in male rats by single intra-vas administration: An alternate approach to vasectomy. *J. Androl.* **14**, 275-281.

Upadhyay, S.N., Kaushic, C. & Talwar, G.P. 1990 Antifertility effects of neem (*Azadirachta indica*) oil by a single intrauterine administration: a novel method for contraception. *Proc. R. Soc. Lond.* B **242**, 175–179.

4/4

Obstacles to Family Planning
Fred T Sai

ABSTRACT

Despite evidence that family planning programmes have been successful in reducing fertility and in improving the health of women and children, there are still many obstacles to the universal availability of quality contraception. The removal of these obstacles has an important role to play in the achievement of global population stabilisation. The paper deals in turn with the developmental, political, religious and cultural, legal, technical and financial constraints to the wider availability of family planning, and reviews the approaches which hold out the best hope of overcoming these obstacles.

1. INTRODUCTION

The family planning movement has had an extraordinary success over the last 30 years in spreading the use of contraception. At least 51% of couples in developing countries were using contraceptives in 1990 (Ross 1992), as against the average of only 9% 30 years earlier (Keller 1989). At the same time, fertility has fallen in most countries of the world: in each region of the developing world except sub-Saharan Africa, fertility has fallen by at least one child per woman in the past 20 years. In some countries the decline has been very rapid: in the Republic of Korea total fertility began to fall around 1960 and dropped from 6.1 to 2.1 children per woman in 25 years, essentially within one generation (World Bank 1993). Today, South Korean fertility is 1.69, well below replacement level.

Without family planning programmes, it has been estimated that total fertility for developing countries in 1980–85 would have been 5.4 instead of 4.2 children per woman (Bongaarts 1990), and there would have been 400 million more births.

This increased use of contraception clearly reflects the removal of many of the obstacles to the distribution and acceptance of contraceptives at the political, local and personal levels. Nevertheless, many obstacles still exist, as is reflected in the estimates of the unmet need for family planning, which range from 100 million couples upwards. Sinding has calculated that satisfaction of a 'very conservative' measure of current unmet need of 12% of couples in developing countries would result in a decline from the present developing country total fertility rate of 3.90 to 3.03. This would represent a reduction of 50% between current fertility and replacement-level fertility. What is more, 'in terms of demographic outcomes there is no significant difference between programmes designed to achieve demographic targets and those designed to respond to the individual reproductive needs and aspirations of women and couples.' So concerted efforts to extend the provision of family planning and reproductive health services to meet the expressed needs of the people, and especially of women, 'would carry the world a very long way towards replacement-level fertility' (Sinding 1993).

Clearly, the removal of obstacles to family planning has a major, perhaps paramount, role to play in the achievement of global population stabilisation. Those obstacles fall into a number of categories, which will be dealt with in turn below: developmental, political, religious, legal, technical and financial constraints.

2. DEVELOPMENTAL CONSTRAINTS

Obviously, family planning programmes cannot expect to be successful in the absence of a comprehensive development strategy: one that includes lowering infant mortality, raising female literacy, improving maternal and child health and nutrition, providing clean water and sanitation. The most important element is probably, as the World Bank has pointed out, ensuring that girls receive a good education, because from this will result better child care and nutrition, a better understanding of the benefits of smaller families, and an improvement in women's status. Even in situations where household income is low, family planning is accepted and better family health is found where women are educated and have better status: an example is the Indian states of Kerala and Tamil Nadu. Demographic and Health Surveys have confirmed the close association of education and desired family size: in Liberia, for example, those with no education wanted an average of 6.8 children, those with primary 5.3 and those with secondary or higher 4.5.

Another major constraint is the location of health services in most developing countries, through which contraceptive services are largely distributed. In countries where maternal and child health services reach only 20–30% of the population, family planning programmes, even if they were fully integrated, would still only reach the same percentage.

Culture and tradition may act as constraints in many societies, especially in Africa. A widespread belief in the rebirth of ancestors and a desire for sons, whether to help in the fields, to perform rites at the father's funeral, or as an insurance for old age, are both powerful pro-natalist factors. In some societies they are being counterbalanced by the high cost of bringing up children in today's world, but they are still a force to be reckoned with.

Some traditional families and fundamentalist religious leaders discourage the education of girls and women and the employment of women outside the home: they are thus less likely to understand the benefits of family planning or to have easy access to it. The patriarchal systems that prevail in rural Bangladesh, Pakistan and in Hindu communities in India as well as in parts of the Middle East certainly make the delivery of family planning services more difficult. The system of purdah results in the effective seclusion of women, which requires intensive outreach programmes, using female healthworkers, to deliver services at or near the client's household. Low levels of female education restrict this type of delivery: in Bangladesh, outreach workers need to have at least 10 years of schooling, but only 16% of women are literate and a much smaller percentage went to school for 10 years. Other constraints are the potential harassment of outreach workers, perceived as violating norms of female behaviour, and transport difficulties in a society where women bicycling is considered immodest (Koenig 1992).

3. POLITICAL OBSTACLES

At the global level, the major political influences for the contraceptive revolution have been international agencies through various conferences, notably the 1965 UN Debate on the Population Problem and the 1968 Tehran Declaration on the human right to family planning. It is only since the Bucharest World Population Conference in 1974 that we have had a real international consensus on family planning: one of the most important advances in this field was the agreement on Article 14(f) which stated:

> All couples and individuals have the basic right to decide freely and responsibly the number and spacing of their children and to have the information, education and means to do so...

This particular article was reconfirmed and expanded in the 1984 conference as follows:

> Governments should, as a matter of urgency, make universally available information, education and the means to assist couples and individuals to achieve their desired number of children. Family planning information, education and means should include all medically approved and appropriate methods of family planning including natural family planning, to ensure a voluntary and free choice in accordance with changing individual and cultural values. Particular attention should be given to those segments of the population which are most vulnerable and difficult to reach (ICPRec.25).

However, there are still some important international organisations, such as the Organization of African Unity and, until recently, the European Community, which are lukewarm about population and family planning programmes, and some wealthy countries, such as France and Italy, which, because of national political constraints, make little contribution to international family planning efforts.

Government policies—sometimes devised to meet religious or traditional objections, sometimes in a misguided attempt to increase national numbers—may influence the availability of family planning. An extreme case was that of Romania under the Communist dictator Ceausescu, who obsessively pursued the ever-receding target of a higher national birth rate through a draconian ban on contraceptives and abortion: the demographic influence was slight, but the maternal mortality rate soared as more and more women, unable to obtain family planning, submitted themselves to unsafe clandestine abortions to dispose of unwanted pregnancies.

The number of countries overtly opposed to the provision of family planning services has fallen sharply over the past two decades: in 1989 governments in 125 developing countries provided support for contraception for demographic, health and human rights reasons and as part of poverty alleviation efforts (World Bank 1993). Only 16 of the 131 countries that responded to a UN questionnaire still provide no support for family planning. However, policies alone are not enough: my own country, Ghana, published a population policy in 1969, yet by 1988 the contraceptive prevalence rate was only 10–12%—and half of this was accounted for by traditional methods.

For programmes to succeed, national policies must be ratified and supported. Elected national-level politicians should be prepared to be identified with their population and family planning programmes. The leaders themselves ought to understand what the programmes are and then to speak for them. Tunisia's family planning programme could never have been as successful as it has been without the commitment and interest of the late President Bourguiba, and, more recently, Zimbabwe's programmes have benefited strongly from the leadership shown by President Robert Mugabe. That country's contraceptive prevalence rate rose from 17% when Mugabe came to power to 43% in 1991.

Leadership by formal or official politicians is not enough, however. Their efforts can be thwarted by lower-level echelons in the political and social administrative systems. There is also the possible social backlash that can be created at the peripheral level if the political leaders feel that contraception is being used in a discriminatory manner. The reverse is also true. With good local-level support and national-level approval, much can be achieved, as is shown by the experience of Indonesia, which developed its own family planning programme managed by a separate organisation, BKKBN. This organisation has the support and leadership of the President himself and it operates through the politico-administrative structure which at the most peripheral level is headed by the local mayors. These mayors are active proponents in the communities. The programmes themselves are combined with some mother and child care and are therefore seen by the people as answering some of their politically expressed needs. Indonesian family planning activities and mother and child care are operated in largely integrated health stations called *Posyandus*, which also provide services in immunisation.

The Indonesian programme has operated in a staunchly Muslim country without any substantial religious opposition, but this is by no means the case in all countries.

4. RELIGIOUS AND CULTURAL OPPOSITION

Although the widespread use of modern contraception has certainly reduced the number of abortions which would otherwise have occurred, it has also produced tensions in society and for religion, because it helps to separate the act of sexual intercourse from reproduction. Many traditional societies would hold that the prime purpose of sexual intercourse is for procreation, and that contraception is wrong because it frustrates that natural function. These tensions express themselves both politically and socially.

Contraception officially sanctioned and supported by governments has flown in the face of many entrenched beliefs, particularly the beliefs of the Roman Catholic Church, religious fundamentalists, and moralists and traditionalists in many societies. Sex, according to Catholicism, is for conception, and using artificial means to prevent this end constitutes a sin, a position strongly reinforced by the publication of the Encyclical *Humanae Vitae* by Pope Paul VI in 1968. It is held by some moralists that tolerance to contraception leads to moral degeneration in human society (Barnes 1977). According to this school of thought, the very act of sex is immoral, and so society becomes more immoral when there is more sexual activity. It is also argued that so long as contraception removes the fear of pregnancy, a vital force that restrains the individual from sex, no inner discipline or personal code of ethics can prevail in society. Some extreme moralists claim that increasing indiscriminate sexual behaviour, coupled with early sexual activity among adolescents, are the natural concomitants of the wide availability of contraceptives in society (Senanayake 1985). Traditionalists also fear the freedom that contraception could give women.

It seems likely that the attitude of the Roman Catholic Church has been the most important obstacle to the wider use of contraception worldwide, and its effect has indeed been felt worldwide, and not just in the predominantly Catholic countries. One hears it said that the influence of the Vatican does not often extend to the bedroom or the village hut: after all, nearly 70% of US Catholics favour the use of 'artificial' contraception (Kissling 1986), against the strictures of their bishops, and many third world Catholic priests are known to turn a blind eye to couples in difficult circumstances using contraceptives. While this may be true, it is also true that the political influence of the Vatican is tremendous and extends to the very highest realms of secular power.

The change in the US Government's attitude to family planning, for instance, culminating in the notorious 'Mexico City Policy' in 1984 which cut off funds to the International Planned Parenthood Federation (IPPF) and Family Planning International Assistance (FPIA), has recently been shown to have been engineered by the Catholic Church. Quoted in *Time* magazine, William Wilson, President Reagan's first Ambassador to the Holy See, said flatly: 'American policy was changed as a result of the Vatican's not agreeing with our policy... American aid programmes round the world did not meet the criteria the Vatican had for family planning.' He went on to explain that USAID emissaries were flown to Rome to be 'briefed' by the president of the Pontifical Council of the Family until 'they finally got the message' (Swomley 1992).

The hand of the Vatican can also be seen behind the decision of the US Government, at the same time as they cut off funds to IPPF, to provide increasingly large sums for 'natural' family planning (NFP) programmes, although many studies have shown the unsuitability and high failure rates (11–35%) of these methods for many people in third world settings (Hermann 1986).

The tragedy is that the funding cuts to international family planning and encouragement of the use of less efficient methods of contraception must undoubtedly have resulted in an increase in the number of unwanted pregnancies and, inevitably, in the number of abortions. This is an outcome that we in the family planning movement deplore. Believing that some common ground might be found between family planners and the Roman Catholic Church in a desire to prevent abortions, I wrote an Open Letter to the Pope urging the opening of a sensitive dialogue between the Church and those who believe that 'voluntary family planning is the best protection against abortion' (IPPF 1991), but the challenge remained unanswered.

The other Christian churches are on the whole supportive of family planning. And no other religion has the same dogmatic opposition to contraception as the Roman Church. In Muslim countries, family planning is sometimes opposed at the local level for pro-natalist reasons, or because it is perceived as an alien imposition. However, most senior Muslim clerics and scholars agree that there is nothing in Islam which prevents the use of temporary contraceptive methods, or indeed early abortion, although most forbid permanent contraceptive sterilisation (Omran 1992).

Religious influences on family planning are greatest in communities where literacy is low and the need for family planning greatest.

5. LEGAL OBSTACLES

Lip service is not enough if family planning programmes are to reach all those in need. Obsolete laws and regulations can act as major obstacles, even if politicians and lawyers regard them as a dead letter. Generally, the law has not kept pace with the changing social attitudes towards fertility regulation, and with recent developments in contraceptive technology and the expansion of family planning services beyond the confines of formal clinics. Until the 1980s, a French law of 1920, designed to boost the domestic birth rate after French manpower losses in the 1st World War, still outlawed the promotion, distribution and sale of contraceptives in former French colonies in West Africa, and a similar Belgian colonial law was still in force in Zaire. Although family planning services were nevertheless set up in many of these countries, the existence of the law on the statute book created bureaucratic problems and provided a tool for opposition elements to attack the programme. Governments of this region repealed these laws when policy makers realised that family planning programmes had an important role to play in improving maternal and child health and that rapid population growths were undermining national development aspirations.

Laws and regulations have a symbolic value in reinforcing a country's commitment to family planning, but, more than this, regulations and red-tape can be an important hindrance to the distribution of contraceptives in many countries. Import licences for contraceptives are required in most developing countries, and import duties are imposed in 40% of countries; in some countries, import duties are levied as high as 77% (in Guinea) and 57% (in Colombia), and even a country with a serious AIDS problem, Thailand, was levying a 50% duty on condoms in 1989. South Korea only abolished duties in 1989, although import licences are still needed and, in some countries, even the Ministry of Health must pay duty to another ministry on contraceptives it imports (Ross 1992). Personal taxes as well as direct charges on contraceptive supplies, often meant to generate revenue for local-level leaders, add to this problem.

Regulatory bodies, especially those in the developed world, impose heavy financial burdens and often delays on the wide distribution of new contraceptives. The prime example was the refusal of the US Food and Drug Administration (FDA) to license the injectable contraceptive Depo-Provera, although recommended to do so by its scientific committees. Because developing countries often refuse to authorise a drug unless it is distributed in the donor country, this decision had the effect of restricting the distribution of this contraceptive in many other countries apart from the United States, a situation only reversed in 1992 when the FDA finally issued a licence.

6. MEDICAL AND TECHNICAL CONSTRAINTS

Outdated regulations, as well as the attitude of the medical profession, often hinder the expansion of the role of health personnel and the extension of service delivery outlets. In many countries, especially in Africa, regulations limit the right to prescribe oral contraceptives and to insert IUDs to certified medical doctors, few of whom practise in rural areas. As early as the mid-1970s, the IPPF Central Medical Committee stated that 'the limitation of oral contraceptive distribution to a doctor's prescription makes the method geographically, economically and sometimes culturally inaccessible to many women'. Some countries, such as Bangladesh, Egypt, Nepal and Pakistan now allow the distribution of contraceptives without prescription. Other countries authorise trained health personnel (midwives, nurses and health workers) to issue prescriptions for oral contraceptives and/or to insert IUDs. In Zaire, specially trained nurses are allowed to perform Caesarean operations and female sterilisations in rural areas (Bouzidi 1990).

In many developing countries, regulations still require drugs (including contraceptives) to be supplied in pharmacies or medical centres, under the supervision of licensed pharmacists. These two conditions represent a major obstacle to the extension of service delivery outlets, especially in rural areas. In countries where regulations have been liberalised, for example Morocco and Zimbabwe, effective outreach and community-based distribution projects have been established, resulting in a much higher use of contraceptives among rural populations.

The effects of such obstacles, added to shortcomings in the health care infrastructure, are reflected in the percentage of a country's population with access to family planning services, meaning that 'the recipient spends no more than an average of two hours per month to obtain contraceptive supplies and services' and pays less than 1% of a month's wages for a one-month supply of contraceptives. A 1989 survey suggested that wild fluctuations still exist between developing countries in ease of access: while most methods were available to 95% of the population in Botswana, less than 10% of the population in Côte d'Ivoire, Madagascar and Zaire had such easy access (Ross 1992).

Service regulations often impose obstacles in the form of the requirement of spousal consent and the denial of services to adolescents and the unmarried. The explosion of adolescent pregnancies and teenage abortions in many parts of the world shows the shortsightedness of the latter approach. However, even where services are available to the unmarried, adolescents are often put off by the usual family planning or maternal and child health clinic: they really need specially designed services, with an informal approach and counsellors drawn from their own age group, who understand their problems.

Where family planning is only available through maternal and child health clinics, this may make it impossible for men, and difficult for women with no children, to use the service.

Finally, the technologies used could themselves be an obstacle to the successful implementation of family planning programmes. When the industrialised countries went through their fertility transition, the major methods of birth control were withdrawal and, later, the condom: both were under the influence of men, and it was therefore the man and his ability that helped women to control their fertility. With the Pill, IUD and injectable, methods of fertility control passed to women, and some of the family and social conflict over contraception arises from this fact, and from men's unhappiness, in many societies, to women controlling their own fertility without male intervention. These methods also depend for their success on good health service back-up, and where this is not consistently available, problems and a high drop-out rate are inevitable.

7. QUALITY OF SERVICES

During the 1980s, there was a shift in focus of many family planning programmes away from demographic targets to meeting unmet needs and improving quality of care, and the result, in many cases, was better acceptance figures. Indeed, many recent reports have stressed that programmes of high quality are, not surprisingly, likely to lead to better uptake, fewer contraceptive failures and fewer drop-outs. As a result, resources are more likely to be forthcoming, and opposition can be countered more convincingly.

Demographic and Health Surveys in 12 countries suggested that over half of all women were unsuccessful or dissatisfied with the contraceptive methods they had been using, which is a measure of just how far contraceptive technology and family planning delivery programmes are falling short of what developing country women want and need (IPPF 1992). Recently, IPPF has published its Medical and Service Delivery Guidelines, which cover training, methods of contraception, counselling, and the rights of the client. Family planning associations and other non-governmental organisations are well placed to focus attention on the deficiencies of programmes and to work side-by-side with governments in making their programmes more client-friendly.

Community involvement in devising and running family planning programmes is increasingly seen as being essential to success. The top-down imposition of family planning, complete with targets and official visits, can never be a long-term success. But once the community has become convinced of the value of family planning, it will take the decision-making role, and the programme will flourish.

8. FINANCIAL CONSTRAINTS

The United Nations Population Fund (UNFPA) has estimated that, in order to meet the cost of contraceptive supplies and other programme needs that are required to hold population levels to the UN medium variant projection, total spending on family planning and population activities in the developing world should reach a minimum of $9 billion per year by the year 2000—about double what was spent in 1990. The developing countries themselves would raise more than half this sum, with the international community having to provide about $4 billion.

While total population assistance in the 1960s and 1970s probably exceeded the absorptive capacity of developing country governments, this changed in the 1980s and is certainly not the case today. Between 1975 and 1987 there was a 50 million increase in the number of women worldwide who wanted no more children (not counting those who wanted contraception for spacing), yet over the 12-year period the donor resources available remained virtually stagnant in real terms (Sinding 1993). As for the future, many programmes, especially in Africa, are new and will need substantial funding as they expand. The numbers of women in the reproductive age groups are increasing and the proportion of those women who want to use contraception is also increasing: by the year 2000, there will be nearly 1 billion women of reproductive age in the third world (rising to over 1.2 billion by 2010), and UNFPA's target is that 567 million couples—59%—should have access to quality family planning by that time. On the supply side, only about half of the 10 leading donors are enthusiastic about increasing population assistance: most of them give less than 2% of their overseas development assistance to family planning, whereas they should probably be following Norway in giving over 4% if the needs are to be met.

Users of family planning face financial constraints as well. Contraceptives supplied by government clinics or family planning associations are usually free or heavily subsidised, and the prices charged by social marketing or community-based distribution projects are usually nominal, although even these may be a deterrent to the poor. However, if for any reason commercial sources are used, users are faced with costs of up to 10% of annual income for a supply of pills or condoms. This is particularly a constraint to the wider distribution of condoms, which men may prefer to purchase when needed rather than obtain from a clinical source: the cost of condoms bought from a pharmacy is a considerable expense, especially in Africa. Even when contraceptives are free, their accessibility may be a problem: loss of wages, transport costs, and excessive waiting time at clinics may all militate against contraceptive use.

9. CONCLUSIONS

Obstacles still exist at many levels to the wider distribution and use of family planning, even though there remains a substantial unmet need for such services. Among the approaches which hold out the best hope of overcoming these constraints are: overt policy commitment, internationally and nationally, to supplying family planning information and services to all who need them; the involvement of all levels of administration, down to the community level, in programme planning and management; and quality programmes, oriented to meet client needs, with user involvement and real choice.

REFERENCES

Barnes, A.C. 1977 In *Risks, benefits and controversies in fertility control* (eds. J.J.Sciarra, G.I. Zatuchni, J.J. Speidel). Maryland: Harper & Row: pp. 7–11.

Bongaarts, J., Mauldin, W.P., & Phillips, J.F. 1990 The demographic impact of family planning programmes. *Studies in Family Planning*, **21** (6): 299–310.

Bouzidi, M. 1990 Legal requirements relating to extension of services. In *Family planning for life: papers presented at the Conference on the Management of Family Planning Programmes* (eds. M. Bouzidi, R. Korte). Harare, Zimbabwe, 1–7 October 1989. London: IPPF.

Hermann, C.B. *et al.* 1986 *Periodic abstinence in developing countries: update and policy options.* Columbia, MD: Institute for Resource Development at Westinghouse.

IPPF (International Planned Parenthood Federation) 1991 Open letter to Pope John Paul II from Dr Fred T Sai, President.

IPPF (International Planned Parenthood Federation) 1992 *IPPF Annual Report 1991–92.* London: IPPF.

Keller, A., Severyns, P., Khan, A., Dodd, N. 1989 Toward family planning in the 1990s: a review and assessment. *International Family Planning Perspectives*, **15**: 127–135.

Kissling, F. 1986 *A Church Divided: Catholics' attitudes about family planning, abortion and teenage sexuality.* Washington DC: Catholics for a Free Choice.

Koenig, M. A., & Simmons, R. 1992 Constraints on supply and demand for family planning: evidence from rural Bangladesh. In *Family planning programmes and fertility* (eds. J.F. Phillips, J.A. Ross). Oxford: Clarendon Press, pp. 259–275.

Omran, A.R. 1992 *Family planning in the legacy of Islam.* London and New York: Routledge.

Ross, J.A., Parker Mauldin, W., Green, S. R., Romana Cooke, E. 1992 *Family planning and child survival programs as assessed in 1991.* New York: The Population Council.

Senanayake, P. 1985 The politics of contraception. In *Future aspects in contraception. Part 2 Female contraception* (eds. B. Runnebaum, *et al.*). Lancaster: MTP Press.

Sinding, S. W. 1993 Getting to replacement: bridging the gap between individual rights and demographic goals. In *Meeting challenges, promoting choices. Proceedings of the 40th anniversary IPPF Family Planning Congress, New Delhi, October 1992* (eds. R. Kleinman, P. Senanayake). Carnforth, Lancs., UK and New York: Parthenon.

Swomley, J. M. 1992 Political power of Roman Catholic Bishops. In *The Human Quest* May–June 1992.

World Bank, 1993. *Effective family planning programs.* Washington DC: World Bank.

Scientific Aspects in Family Planning Services
Soledad Díaz and Horacio B. Croxatto

ABSTRACT

Contraception implies a woman or a couple using a method and reacting to the benefits and inconveniences perceived. Services have a crucial role in facilitating and supporting this process. Personal success involves satisfaction with the method chosen and prevention of pregnancy for as long as desired. Clinic and programme success means reaching those who need the service, good acceptability and continuation rates and good demographic and reproductive health indicators at the lowest cost possible.

Scientists can contribute to better family planning services by helping providers and managers to understand the biomedical and psychosocial background of the clients so that the services suit their specific needs. They can help to evaluate the outcome in terms of biomedical indicators and users' satisfaction, and stimulate the imagination needed to find new solutions or to overcome bureaucratic constraints.

These assumptions led us to develop and evaluate a contraceptive *post partum* programme, in view of the physiology of this period. This is a transitional stage in which the breast replaces the nutritional, immunological and endocrine functions of the placenta and the mother reshapes her roles in the family and her sexual and reproductive life. The programme was tested in a research clinic, the Consultorio de Planificacion Familiar, ICMER, and in a community-based clinic, the Consultorio San Luis de Huechuraba.

The services provided include integrated maternal–child care, contraception and breastfeeding management. Information and counselling are most important components. Methods offered are those which do not interfere with lactation or infant growth. The programme promotes exclusive breastfeeding on demand during the first six months, mother's responsibility for her own health care and reproductive decisions, including the selection of contraceptive methods, and for the care of the child. Providers are trained to support women in these tasks. The quantitative and qualitative outcomes of the programme are assessed, including contraceptive performance, breastfeeding duration, infant growth and health, and women's and staff satisfaction. Continuation rates at the end of the first year were above 96% for long-term methods and 'lost to follow-up' ranged from 1% to 6%. Breastfeeding duration was significantly higher (91% and 58% at 6 months and 12 months) than in the general population (around 50% at 6 months). There was one infant death in 5500 cases and the rate of severe illness was 0.02 x 100 infant-months. Women appreciated being treated as respected and responsible persons. The staff are highly motivated by the success of the programme and the positive feedback from the users.

1. INTRODUCTION

Contraception implies that a woman, a man or a couple uses a method, and reacts to the benefits and inconveniences perceived. Family planning services have a crucial role in facilitating and supporting this process. Personal success means the postponement of pregnancy for as long as desired. To achieve this, the choice of contraceptive method should be in accordance with biomedical criteria and lifestyle of the clients and they should have the freedom to change method when the experience is not satisfactory or needs are different. The success of a family planning clinic can be gauged by its ability to reach everyone who needs the service, and by the acceptability and continuation rates of the methods offered. Programme success implies good indicators in terms of fertility regulation and reproductive health at the lowest cost possible. Therefore, we need to look at the users, the services, the methods and the interaction among them when we search for the contribution that science can and should make to family planning. The quality of this interaction is what will determine the success or failure of family planning, both at the personal and population levels.

Research conducted in the last two decades focused initially on the development and evaluation of a variety of contraceptive methods. The basic assumption was that a wide range of options would help women to find an adequate method and that this was the best strategy to ensure widespread use of contraception. Eventually, it became evident that this biomedical and technologic approach was not sufficient to attain the level of contraceptive use required to improve reproductive health status and population goals. This gap is particularly evident in some developing countries.

The methods are only one aspect of family planning. Research is required to understand the perspective of the users and the ways to expand and improve family planning services. Psychosocial research and service research increased their contribution to the field in the last decade, but there is still a long way to go in the understanding of the interactions between users, methods and services and how to make them successful.

These assumptions led us to develop a *post partum* contraceptive and health care programme based on the physiologic and psychosocial background of this period. From the biologic perspective, we understand the *post partum* period as a transitional stage from pregnancy to a period of relative autonomy for both the mother and the child. In this transition, the breast replaces the placenta in its nutritional functions and in the transference of immunological and endocrine factors. The neuroendocrine changes occurring during the early *post partum* period allow the establishment of lactation and the bonding between the mother and the child. The suckling stimulus keeps maternal physiology tuned to the needs of the child and suppresses ovarian function and the recovery of fertility. The interaction between the nursing mother and the infant changes with time as the suckling frequency diminishes and other food is given to the child. The decrease of suckling influence upon maternal endocrine functions allows anatomic and functional changes in the mother until she recovers a reproductive condition similar to the one she had before pregnancy. From the psychosocial perspective, the *post partum* period is a difficult experience for women because of the demands of the child, the desire to fulfil the maternal roles which compete with other roles they have at home or outside, the uncertainties about how to perform the task and the emotional stress related to the changes in physiology, interpersonal relationships and life situation. This stress is aggravated when a woman has little support from her spouse, her family or the health services.

Such perception of the *post partum* period has programmatic implications which are described below. They were first tested in the Consultorio de Planificacion Familiar, ICMER, a clinic devoted to research in contraception. Later on, they were tested at the Consultorio San Luis de Huechuraba (CSLH), a community-based clinic run by a NGO involved in health care.

2. CHARACTERISTICS OF *POST PARTUM* SERVICES AT ICMER

The family planning services provided include health care for both the mother and the child. The main message conveyed to the mother is that she is responsible for her own health care and reproductive decisions, including the selection of contraceptive methods, and for the care of the child. The role of the staff of the clinic is to provide her with the information and the technical means she needs and to support her in these tasks.

Women who come to the clinic participate in research protocols that determine the admission requirements. They are healthy and had a normal pregnancy and term delivery of a healthy child. They are regularly cohabiting, willing to breastfeed and do not work outside home. They have no medical contraindications for the use of contraceptive methods. They belong to the low middle and low socioeconomic groups and all of them are literate, which is in accordance with the high literacy index in the country. The features of the services provided include:

2.1 Integrated maternal–child care

Mother and child are seen at the same day visit and have the same number of follow-up visits in the first *post partum* year. This is convenient to the woman, who saves time and money by a single visit to the clinic. It reinforces the message that mother and child are still a biologic unit and that both are equally important. This differs from the approach of the local health services where the child receives more attention than the mother as well as from the contraceptive services in which the child is ignored. They share a common clinical record which allows the paediatric and gynaecologic team to be informed of what is happening with both. This is important to the providers since the decisions regarding the mother affect the child and *vice versa*.

2.2 Admission and follow-up

Women are contacted at the maternity ward and invited to attend the clinic. Visits are scheduled at 8, 20, 30, 40, 55 and 70 days *post partum* and at monthly intervals thereafter. Contraceptive methods are initiated around 55 days *post partum* in fully nursing women. Women are encouraged to attend the clinic at any other time if they have problems or doubts regarding nursing, contraceptive use or health. An alternative schedule tried involves the same visits in the first three months and later visits at three months intervals, to evaluate the results of a less demanding follow-up schedule.

2.3 Information and counselling

This is one of the most important components of the *post partum* programme in the clinic. The educational process starts at the maternity ward where women receive information about the advantages of breastfeeding, the mechanisms underlying milk production and practical advice regarding nursing and infant care in the first *post partum* days. The two additional visits scheduled during the first *post partum* month are to reinforce breastfeeding, to educate women in her own health and nutritional care and to support the mother through this more difficult period. At the end of the first month, women receive information and counselling on the contraceptive choices available for lactating women.

The education and counselling activities are maintained through the whole interval in which the women attend the clinic. The content is tailored to the needs of each case, as perceived by the providers, and include contraceptive, health and nutritional matters.

2.4 Contraceptive management

Methods offered are those considered adequate for lactating women in the sense that they do not interfere with lactation or infant growth. Choices have varied along the years according to the research projects ongoing at the clinic. They have been copper IUDs (T Cu), devices that release progesterone, Norplant® implants, progestin-only pills (POPs) and barrier methods. Contraceptives were prescribed according to the woman's choice.

At each visit, women are interviewed to evaluate their health and their experience with the methods. Counselling on side effects is provided. Subjects keep a menstrual record that allows an objective assessment of their bleeding problems. They may discontinue the method chosen for any reason and contraceptive alternatives are available.

2.5 Breastfeeding management

Exclusive breastfeeding on demand is promoted during the first six months. The nutritional and health benefits and the influence of breastfeeding upon fertility, are explained to the mothers. Basic physiologic concepts and the importance of suckling frequency are also explained. Mothers are asked to keep a daily record of the number of day and night feeds (and they do it!). The use of water and pacifiers are discouraged. The first month visits are considered particularly important for the establishment of lactation.

Milk supplements are prescribed by the paediatrician or the nurses when the infant growth curve is altered. Non-dairy meals are introduced after six months. Mothers are encouraged to follow these instructions but they are free to do otherwise if they decide so.

2.6 Health management

General health services are provided for the women and their children, including screening for cervical cancer, anaemia, blood pressure and gynaecologic infections, infant growth monitoring and paediatric examination in case of illness.

2.7 Providers work as a team

All the health workers have been trained in breastfeeding and contraceptive management in the same way. Therefore, they provide consistent information to the women. Each professional knows and reinforces the messages that other members of the team provide. This is facilitated by the joint mother–child clinical record and staff meetings.

The different members of the team are available to each other to discuss and find solutions for special cases or unexpected problems. The health team also meets on weekly basis to coordinate the ongoing activities, review procedures or plan new activities.

3. OUTCOME OF THE HEALTH CARE PROGRAMME AT ICMER

The programme was initiated at the end of 1977 and more than 5500 mothers have participated. The quantitative and qualitative aspects of the model have been assessed. Quantitative parameters have been used to evaluate contraceptive performance, breastfeeding duration and infant growth and health. Qualitative aspects have been evaluated through in-depth interviews and focus groups involving a sample of the mothers attending the clinic. The perception of the staff about the programme was also assessed through interviews. This qualitative assessment was performed by an external team formed by a sociologist and four psychologists.

3.1 Contraceptive performance

The results are in part related to the method chosen and the demands of the research protocols. All women attending the clinic choose to use a contraceptive method but this is not considered an achievement because they know from the first interview that this clinic conducts clinical trials of contraceptives for lactating women. Women are free to switch methods and are advised to change from POPs to combined pills at the time of weaning. Pregnancy rates range from less than 1% (long term methods) to less than 2% (POPs). 'Lost to follow-up' ranges from less than 1% (implants) to around 6% (POPs). In general, continuation rates at the end of the first year are above 96% for long term methods such as T Cu or NORPLANT® implants. Since women may switch methods, the overall contraceptive continuation rate is around 98% in clients who reach the end of the year within the programme.

3.2 Breastfeeding performance

The proportion of women who are breastfeeding at six months (91%) and at 12 months (58%) has remained stable throughout the 15 years of this programme. The same has happened with the proportion of cases in exclusive breastfeeding at six months that ranges from 55% to 60%. This breastfeeding performance differs significantly from the one reported for the general population in Santiago where no cases are fully nursing and 40% to 50% have weaned at six months.

The breastfeeding performance was also significantly better than the pattern found in a cohort of women who delivered at the same maternity ward and met all the biomedical criteria used for selection of participants but who did not attend the ICMER clinic. Therefore, the difference cannot be explained by the *post partum* health or nutritional condition of the cases.

3.3 Infant growth and health

Growth and health of the breastfed infants has been an extremely positive outcome of the programme. There is one infant death in around 5500 cases and the rate (x100 infant-months) of illness considered severe was 0.02. The rate for diarrhoea was 1.7% in fully nursed infants and increased to 7.9% after weaning. The rate for respiratory diseases increased from 18% during full nursing to 35% after weaning. Nutritional problem rates were 0.6%, 2.2% and 6.2% during full nursing, partial nursing and after weaning, respectively.

3.4 Qualitative assessment

The women attached importance to the quality of the interactions with the staff, particularly the perception of being treated with respect and considered responsible persons (Vera H., 1993). They appreciated the information, education and support regarding infant care and contraceptive choice. They also appreciated the professional and friendly attitude of the staff, the cleanliness of the clinic, the time saving implied in the joint visits, the sharing of experiences with other women in the waiting room and the knowledge that they may come for unscheduled visits for any reason and with no restrictions. The following quotes from the interviews express how the women feel:

> You are treated totally different here, you are treated as an equal. In other places...they want to demean us.

> Here I learned things of my body that I never knew I had. Here I have been told...what things can hurt me, what things are good for me.

> They explain everything...For me it is something like pride because I never knew anything...Then everything that I have learned, I have learned here.

> I learned how to be a mother...I have learned why his belly aches or why he cries too much...how to treat him well.

> I have learned...that one is valued more.

> I am valuing myself more...I am a person and I should take care of myself...I can protect myself.

> One also talks to the other women and one learns.

> It is good here...you are controlled well, you are not afraid that you will get sick, that you will get cancer...or infections, everything is clean.

> Here the midwifes are all good, they all take my side...they never say a bad word.

3.5 Alternative follow-up schedule

Preliminary results suggest that the contraceptive and breastfeeding performance is similar to that of the more intensive schedule. This is not surprising since both schedules are similar in the first three *post partum* months, period in which contraceptive decisions are taken and breastfeeding behaviour is established.

4. *POST PARTUM* PROGRAMME AT CSLH

The success of the programme led us to test it in a different setting where the biomedical research conditions would be absent. The place chosen was the Consultorio San Luis de Huechuraba, located in a very poor neighbourhood in Santiago. This clinic is part of an NGO involved in community health work.

In this project, all pregnant women in the catchment area were contacted by a community health worker and invited to the Consultorio, regardless of their biomedical or socioeconomic characteristics. Education was initiated during this first contact. *post partum* visits were scheduled as described for the ICMER model. Health care and breastfeeding management were the same.

The time at which contraceptive methods were initiated was left at women's choice and the alternatives were the second month *post partum* or when any of the three markers of fertility recovery occurred: the first menses, when women introduce supplements to the child, or the sixth month, whichever came first. The choice of methods included T-Cu, POP barriers and the lactational amenorrhoea method LAM. Out of 200 women enrolled, 139 (69.5%) initiated a method within the first two months *post partum*, which is the time when the state system provides *post partum* contraception. At the end of six and 12 months, 169 (85%) and 179 (89.5%) of the women had initiated contraception. (Those who did not were separated or single mothers who said they have no exposure to the risk of pregnancy.) Women were concerned about the risk of a new pregnancy and the first options were IUDs (41%) and POPs (51%). Women had the freedom to change methods according to their experience with the first choice. At the end of the year, 135 (75.4%) continued with the initial contraceptive, 39 (21.8%) had changed method, and the overall contraceptive continuation rate was 97%.

The results of the intervention were compared with those of a state health clinic located close to the study area, which provides *post partum* care to women living in a similar neighbourhood. Preliminary results show significant differences between the CSLH and the state clinic in terms of breastfeeding behaviour and infant's health (Alvarado & Rivero 1993).

The percentage of women in exclusive breastfeeding at three and six months *post partum* was 87% and 38% in the CSLH and 20% and 0% in the state clinic, respectively. The percentage of women who had weaned at 6 months was 2% at the CSLH and 38% at the state clinic, respectively. Mean weight of the infants at birth, six months and 12 months was 3.3±0.5 kg, 8.0±0.8 kg and 10.1±0.9 kg in the CSLH and 3.3±0.4 kg, 7.8±0.8kg and 9.6±0.9 kg in the state clinic, respectively. The rate of diarrhoea (per 100 infant-months) was 0.1 in the CSLH and 1.5 in the state clinic. The percentage of infants who required hospitalisation was 2.6 and 8.5 in the CSLH and the state clinic, respectively. Except for birth weight, these differences were statistically significant (p values < 0.01).

An assessment of women's perception of the *post partum* period, their needs and the demands towards the health services was done by two independent social scientists. The report regarding the service characteristics led to similar conclusions as the one done at ICMER. Women particularly appreciated the education, the freedom of choice, the technical support and the quality of interpersonal relationships. This programme included adolescent mothers (n=22) who expressed the trust they had in the staff, how much they had learned and how their experience had been easier because of the support received (Rico & López 1993).

5. CONCLUSIONS

According to the criteria listed at the start, the *post partum* family planning programme described has been acceptable and appreciated from the clients' perspective. It is also successful according to the biomedical indicators used to evaluate the health service. We have attempted to identify the elements that contributed to this result and, inevitably, reached to the conclusion that the initial research component was a very significant ingredient.

We had planned to do research on *post partum* contraception. Our biological background had taught us that the *post partum* period was peculiar since it involved two individuals in close interaction and that breastfeeding was affected by many bio–psycho–socioeconomic variables. To control these variables, we started a comprehensive health programme where we could do our planned research and multivariate analysis of the results. At the end, we found that the women and children involved received the benefit of this holistic approach. And we learned something about the contribution of science to services which can be summarised in the following methodologic and personal issues:

Scientists can contribute to better family planning services by helping providers and managers to understand the biomedical and psychosocial background of the clients so that the services suit their specific needs. They can help to identify the variables involved in services, as they have to be identified in any research protocol. They can contribute to the assessment of the relative importance of these variables and help design the service accordingly. Scientist can also help to evaluate the outcome in terms of biomedical indicators, users' satisfaction and providers' fulfilment with the work done.

Above all, they can stimulate the analytic mind of providers to achieve a growing insight of their task and the imagination needed to find new solutions or to overcome bureaucratic constraints. In this way, a scientist's contribution is not limited to the dissemination of research results. Beyond that, the direct interaction with the providers and their input in the design of the services may greatly contribute to their success. Scientists may also benefit in this process by achieving a wider perspective than the one provided by the academic world.

ACKNOWLEDGEMENTS

We are grateful to the WHO Special Programme of Research Development and Research Training in Human Reproduction, the Population Council, the Contraceptive Research and Development Programme (CONRAD) and the International Development Research Center (IDRC), for the support provided to the research that originated this programme.

REFERENCES

Alvarado, R. & Rivero, S. 1993 Improvement of the quality of life in the first year postpartum through coordinated management of breastfeeding and family planning. Progress Report to The Population Council, Santiago, Chile.

Vera, H. 1993 The clients' view of high-quality care in Santiago, Chile. *Stud. Fam. Plann* **24**: 40–49.

Rico, N. & Lopez, S. 1993 Maternidad y Postparto en Mujeres de Sectores Populares. Final Report to The Population Council, Santiago, Chile.

Contraceptive Strategies for the Future
R. V. Short

ABSTRACT

Scientifically, it is well within our power to bring human population growth to a halt in the foreseeable future. This is essential if we are to save the fragile ecosystems of planet Earth, and prevent mankind from becoming his own executioner. With the population of the world currently increasing by a quarter of a million people each day, we have not a moment to lose.

The first priority for the future must be to satisfy without delay the large unmet demand that already exists for contraception. We need to treble contraceptive expenditure in order to ensure that the contraceptives we have already developed are made freely available to all. This additional money represents a mere 1% of global expenditure on defence.

The second priority is to educate the women of the world, so that they become fully informed about the contraceptive choices that are already available to them. We must ensure that they become at least equal partners with men in any decisions about family size. This will do much to increase the future demand for contraception.

The third priority is to design strategies to overcome the enormous inequalities in reproductive health that currently exist between developed and developing countries. Improved access to modern contraceptives and abortion facilities can save the lives of many millions of women.

The fourth priority is to develop new, more acceptable and more cost-effective contraceptives, and new ways of reducing the spread of sexually transmitted diseases. The human immunodeficiency virus is currently spreading at an alarming rate, especially in developing countries, and AIDS will account for almost two million deaths per year by the end of this century.

In order to achieve these objectives, we need to develop an integrated approach to family planning, maternal and child health, sexually transmitted diseases, and AIDS prevention. If we fail to convince governments of the urgency and the gravity of the human population problem, then we must regard ourselves as scientific failures, and future generations will live to condemn us.

1. INTRODUCTION

The most recent United Nations population projections for the 21st century give a 'medium' estimate of 6.3 billion people in the year 2000, rising to 10 billion by 2050, 11.2 billion by 2100, and plateauing at 11.6 billion by 2150 (United Nations 1991a). These projections have already had to be revised upwards by 1.4 billion from the 1980 estimates.

In order to bring these figures into sharper focus, it is as well to remember that many of us attending this conference were alive in 1930, when the world's population was a mere 2 billion.

If this medium projection is to be realised, the total fertility rate must decline throughout the world to a replacement level of no more than 2.1–2.2 children per couple within the next 1–2 generations. Although 34 developed countries and one developing country, Cuba, have already achieved this objective (World Bank 1993), most developing countries still have a long way to go (Population Reports 1992; see Figure 1). It will come as no surprise that the Total Fertility Rate is strongly influenced by the prevalence of modern contraceptives.

If Total Fertility Rates fail to reach replacement level throughout the world within the next two generations, the population could reach 6.4 billion in the year 2000, 12.5 billion by 2050, 17.6 billion by 2100 and 20.8 billion by 2150, when it would still not have plateaued. Who would want to live in such a world? Indeed, would it be a world in which we could live?

Any actions that we take now, in the dying days of the 20th century, to increase contraceptive prevalence are critically important in determining which of these future scenarios is ultimately realised. Already there is a vast unmet demand for contraceptives in developing countries; it is estimated that as many as 100 million couples who would wish to use contraceptives are currently denied access to them (Bongaarts 1991).

We now have available a wide range of safe and effective contraceptives that have enabled the developed countries voluntarily to bring their Total Fertility Rates to replacement level or below. It would have been difficult, if not impossible, for any western nation to have achieved its present level of development without access to these modern contraceptives, since a rapidly expanding population places heavy economic demands on the community.

2. THE FIRST PRIORITY FOR THE FUTURE

The first priority for the future must be to ensure that these same methods are made freely available to all those in developing countries that want to use them, so that they do not become caught forever in the poverty trap. This will cost money. To achieve the 'medium' projection of 10 billion people by 2050, we must increase contraceptive use from the present 390 million couples to 500 million by the year 2000, 650 million by the year 2010 and 900 million by the year 2025 (United Nations 1989).

In 1986, global contraceptive expenditure was only $US 4.5 billion, two-thirds of which was provided by the governments of the developing countries themselves; this must eventually rise to $US 11.1 billion by the year 2000 (Population Reports 1991). In 1986, the total global expenditure on defence was in excess of $US 800 billion (World Bank 1988; Sadik 1990). If we were to turn a mere 1% of our metaphorical swords into ploughshares, of our weapons into contraceptives, the funding problem would be solved.

There is a certain hypocrisy in the attitude of those of us who have the good fortune to live in the developed world towards those in the developing world. The use of the word 'developing' implies that if they try hard enough, they too can become developed like us. And yet we know in our heart of hearts that there are simply not enough natural resources to enable the whole world to enjoy our standards of living. Therefore we must realise that we have a price to pay for our affluence; we must strive to achieve ecologically

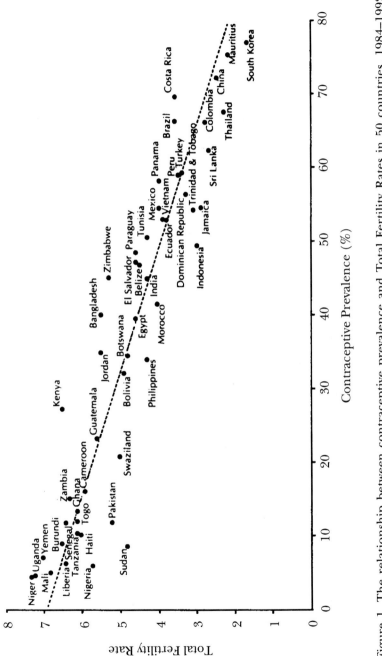

Figure 1. The relationship between contraceptive prevalence and Total Fertility Rates in 50 countries, 1984–1992. (From Population Reports 1992.)

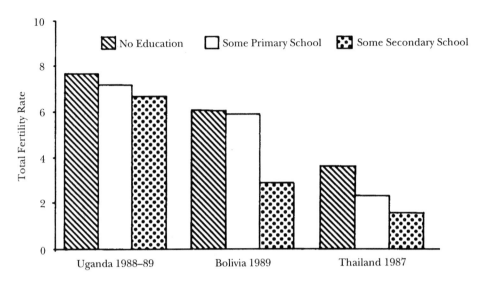

Figure 2. Total Fertility Rates in three countries by women's level of education. Before fertility rates start to fall, fertility is high in all groups (Uganda). As educated women are first to reduce their fertility, differences widen amongst groups (Bolivia). Eventually, fertility is low in all groups (Thailand). (From Population Reports 1992.)

sustainable development in the future, and we must be prepared to foot the bill for containing rates of population growth in countries less fortunate that ourselves. Nor is this a purely altruistic act, since an increasing polarisation between the living standards of the rich and the poor, of the few 'haves' and the increasing number of 'have nots', sows seeds of discontent that could ultimately grow into conflict. Of all forms of population control, warfare is surely the most costly, the most destructive and the least defensible.

When we write the epitaph for the 20th century, we must record the sorry fact that we have fought more than 200 wars and killed almost 90 million people and yet the world's population has still increased by over 4 billion. The result is that today, over 1 billion people live in absolute poverty and 600 million are on the borders of starvation (World Bank 1990/1991).

3. THE SECOND PRIORITY FOR THE FUTURE

The second priority for the future must be education, and especially the education of women and children. Studies show that educated women are much more likely to use contraception that those with little or no education (Population Reports 1992; see Figure 2). Education also transforms children from being an economic asset to becoming an economic liability. Parents will therefore be increasingly motivated to restrict family size; this motivation will be increased still further if the parents know that the children they do have are likely to survive to adulthood.

Women in particular need to be informed about the contraceptive choices that are available to them, and they need to be empowered to use them. Although women constitute only a third of the world's labour force, they are nonetheless responsible for two-thirds of the hours worked, whilst receiving only 10% of the world's income and owning less than 1% of the world's property (WHO 1987). We must therefore ensure that women become at least equal partners with men in any decisions about family size. In a world of almost total male domination of politics, economics, religion and the law, it will not be easy to bring about these changes—and men in all these professions can be expected to fight a strong rearguard action to retain their dominance.

4. THE THIRD PRIORITY FOR THE FUTURE

The third priority for the future must be to improve the reproductive health of the world. Table 1 summarises the ills that now beset us (WHO 1992b). There are many more acts of intercourse than there are conceptions, and this situation is unlikely to change. It reflects the fact that the human species, unlike the vast majority of animals, has always enjoyed sex for non-reproductive reasons, and will continue to do so. It is surely no accident that we euphemistically refer to copulation as 'making love'. To revert to a Malthusian solution of abstinence as the best way of reducing our fertility is as unrealistic as it is unphysiological.

Of the 910000 conceptions that occur each day, it is estimated that at least half are unplanned and a quarter are frankly unwanted. Surely contraceptive education and the provision of contraceptive services could bring us nearer to achieving the goal of making every pregnancy a wanted pregnancy?

Of the 150000 abortions that are performed each day, a third are carried out in countries where abortion is still illegal. This denies women access to the safe, efficient and humane procedures that have been developed in recent years. It seems that no developed country has been able to bring its fertility down to replacement level without some recourse to abortion for those inevitable contraceptive failures. The lowest incidence of abortion anywhere in the world is in the Netherlands, thanks to excellent sex education

Table 1. *A day in the life of the world 1993*

100 000 000	acts of intercourse will take place
910 000	conceptions will occur
150 000	abortions will be performed
500	mothers will die as a result of abortion
384 000	babies will be born
1 370	mothers will die of pregnancy-related causes
25 000	infants in the first year of life will die
14 000	children aged 1-4 will die
356 000	adults will become infected with a sexually transmitted disease
250 000	is the net increase in population of the world

programs in the schools. Is there not a lesson to learn from the fact that abortion is now legal in most developed countries, and yet illegal in almost all developing ones? And how is it that we have allowed male politicians, theologians and lawyers to dominate this debate?

Five hundred women a day will die as a result of having had an abortion. Most of these deaths will occur in developing countries, for the reasons outlined above. If women are prepared to go to such desperate lengths as drinking petrol, or pushing a wire coathanger through the cervix, or persuading another woman to knead the uterine contents into a pulp with her fists, should we not be listening to these women's silent screams for help?

The health statistic that shows the greatest difference between developed and developing countries is the pregnancy-associated maternal mortality rate. In a developed country, the lifetime risk of dying from pregnancy-related causes is 1 in 1750; in a developing country it may be as high as 1 in 24 (WHO 1987). The five major causes of this mortality are haemorrhage, infection, unsafe abortion, hypertension and obstructed labour. With appropriate training and technology, doctors or nurse-midwives could prevent the vast majority of these deaths.

For the 25000 infants that die each day whilst under one year old, diarrhoea is the commonest cause of death. The most effective way of preventing diarrhoea in the first year of life is breastfeeding for at least the first 4–6 months and to continue to breastfeed after the baby has started to take supplements. It is sad that Nature's protective mechanism against diarrhoea, which is in the gift of every newly delivered mother, is still being undermined in developing countries by the inappropriate use of milk formula preparations exported by the developed countries.

Lactational amenorrhoea, followed by the use of modern contraceptives once menstruation has returned, also has a major role to play in increasing the spacing between births, which in turn lowers the infant and childhood mortality rate (Short 1992). A child that is born less than two years after its older sibling is twice as likely to die as one born after more than two years.

Unfortunately, the increasing incidence of HIV (human immunodeficiency virus) infection in women in developing countries, where there tend to be as many women infected as men, means that more and more infected children are being born, and they will all die within the first five years of life. Already this is beginning to increase infant and child mortality rates in sub-Saharan Africa. An added complication is the number of AIDS orphans that are being produced; these are children born to infected mothers who have themselves escaped infection, but their mothers will die from AIDS during their childhood. It is estimated that there will be 10 million of these AIDS orphans in sub-Saharan Africa by the end of this century, and many of them are destined to die a lingering death from starvation and neglect (WHO 1992a).

One of the most surprising statistics is that 356000 adults will become infected each day with a sexually transmitted disease (STD). Table 2 gives some indication of the nature of these infections (WHO 1992b). Although numerically the least important, HIV infection is the most serious, since it is lethal and we have as yet no effective treatment. HIV infection is increasing at an alarming rate, especially in the developing countries of

Table 2. *Minimum yearly number of new cases of sexually transmitted diseases (millions)*

trichomoniasis	120
chlamydia	50
papilloma virus	30
gonorrhoea	25
genital herpes	20
syphilis	3.5
chancroid	2
human immunodeficiency virus	1

sub-Saharan Africa, South-East Asia and South America. WHO now predicts that in the year 2000, 26 million individuals will be infected with the virus and 1.8 million a year will die of AIDS (Merson 1993). In that same year, there may be more infected people in India than in the whole of the rest of the world combined. Since an individual's susceptibility to HIV infection may be increased up to five-fold by the presence of some of these other STDs, which produce lesions in the male or female genital tract through which HIV may gain entry more easily (Wasserheit 1992), reducing the prevalence of all STDs will help contain the spread of HIV infection.

We know that many people first become infected with STDs and/or HIV during their teens or twenties. Teenagers in the United States experience higher rates of sexually transmitted diseases, including HIV, than heterosexuals of any other age group. Nearly 25% of all cases of sexually transmitted diseases in the United States occur in adolescents, with 2.5 million new cases a year, or 1 in 7 of all 15 to 19 year olds. In 1980, about 1 in every 100 women in the United States aged 15–19 who had ever had sex was hospitalised for pelvic inflammatory disease, a relatively common consequence of STDs. But teenagers the world over are blissfully unaware of the risks that they run. They have a sense of personal invulnerability, and a propensity for risk seeking and risk taking (Widdus, Meheus & Short 1990).

The reason for this early age of STD infection is that teenagers are the group most likely to have multiple sexual partners before they settle into a long-lasting relationship, and frequent partner change places them at greater risk of acquiring STDs including HIV. The earlier that they start sexual activity, the more sexual partners they are likely to have; anything that reduces the number of sexual partners will significantly reduce the spread of STDs and HIV. After all, if everybody was monogamous, all sexually transmitted diseases would become extinct in one generation.

Since the majority of STD infections are asymptomatic, it is difficult to persuade all infected people to present for treatment. The first priority must therefore be prevention. Failing celibacy, or lifelong monogamy of both partners, both rather rare types of behaviour, the only prophylactic that we have at the moment is the condom. The World

Health Organisation has therefore recommended that the condom should become the contraceptive of first choice for all young couples starting sexual activity (WHO 1990). The only trouble is that condoms are not particularly popular, especially in areas such as sub-Saharan Africa, and they have a rather high contraceptive failure rate, which may pose problems in those countries where abortion is not freely available as a backup.

5. THE FOURTH PRIORITY FOR THE FUTURE

Although we could certainly solve the world's population problem by deploying the contraceptives we have already developed, there is no doubt that, by taking thought for the morrow, we could easily develop far more acceptable and cost-effective methods that would hasten the decline in the Total Fertility Rate. We must also develop new contraceptives that will help to reduce the spread of STDs and HIV infection.

Table 3 summarises the current percentage use of different forms of modern contraceptives (UN1991b), and it is worth considering each of these methods in turn to see how they could be improved.

5.1 Female sterilisation

This is currently performed surgically, by ligating, cauterising or clamping the fallopian tubes. It requires the presence of a skilled anaesthetist, a gynaecologist trained in laparoscopy, a laparoscope, and a hospital environment. This makes it a relatively expensive procedure with restricted availability. The fact that it is nevertheless the most widely used modern form of contraception gives some indication of the lengths to which

Table 3. *Percentage use of contraceptive methods worldwide (1987)*

Currently, 390 million couples are using modern contraceptives, about 51% of the total

female sterilisation	29
intrauterine devices	20
oral contraceptives	14
condoms	9
male sterilisation	8
coitus interruptus	8
rhythm	7
injectables	2
other methods	2
barrier methods	1

Note. Methods with lowest failure rates predominate in developing countries.
Methods with highest failure rates predominate in developed countries.

a woman will go to protect herself from 'the tyranny of excessive fertility'. If female sterilisation could be converted from a surgical to a medical procedure, that could be performed by suitably trained paramedical personnel in a rural setting, it would greatly reduce costs and increase the availability of the method.

This may now be possible. In 1970, Dr Jaime Zipper in Santiago, Chile, first demonstrated that the intra-uterine application of the cheap antimalarial drug quinacrine to women would cause occlusion and fibrosis of the fallopian tubes (Zipper, Stachetti & Medels 1970). After more than two decades of research and development, a large scale field trial of this method in over 31000 women volunteers was recently completed in Vietnam (Hieu, Tran, Tan, Nguyet, Than & Vinh 1993). Seven 36mg pellets of quinacrine hydrochloride, costing less than one US dollar, were placed in the lumen of the uterus during the proliferative phase of the menstrual cycle on two occasions one month apart, using a standard Copper T intra-uterine device inserter to deliver the pellets at the uterine fundus. The subsequent pregnancy rate per 100 woman-years of use was 2.6% after one year of follow up, with no deaths, no evidence of an increased incidence of ectopic pregnancies, and only eight serious complications. If the same number of sterilisations had been performed surgically, 30 deaths and up to 1800 serious complications would have been expected.

If further studies can confirm the safety and efficacy of this simple, cheap procedure, it would have wide application throughout the world. It is particularly encouraging to find a new method that has been invented, developed and tested mainly by scientists and clinicians in developing countries. Of course, like all irreversible sterilisation procedures, it is open to abuse, so it is absolutely essential that women are required to give their fully informed consent beforehand. Perhaps if it was only available after payment of a small fee this would provide some protection against misuse. Maybe future research could improve the success rate of the procedure and find some simple way of determining in advance whether the fallopian tubes had indeed been successfully occluded.

5.2 Intra-uterine devices

These have proved particularly popular especially in China, but some of the earlier versions had relatively high contraceptive failure rates, and they all significantly increased the blood loss at menstruation. The Population Council in New York, in collaboration with the Finnish pharmaceutical company, Leiras, have now developed a hormone-releasing IUD, Levonova (Luukkainen, Lahtenmaki & Toivonen 1990). The stem of the device is surrounded by a silastic cylinder impregnated with the gestagen levonorgestrel, which is released into the uterine lumen at the rate of 20μg per day. This is not enough to interfere centrally with pituitary gonadotrophin release and ovulation, but the continuous progestational environment within the uterus drastically reduces the blood loss at menstruation, and the presence of a viscous cervical mucus plug significantly reduces the incidence of ascending uterine infections that result in pelvic inflammatory disease. The contraceptive failure rate of 0.1 per 100 woman-years of use is the lowest of any method other than surgical sterilisation. Although the device is relatively costly to produce, it is effective for at least seven years.

Since this device reduces the incidence of pelvic inflammatory disease (Toivonen,

Luukkainen & Allonen 1991) it might reduce the woman's susceptibility to HIV infection. It might also be the ideal contraceptive for the woman who is already HIV positive, since by reducing menstrual blood loss it would reduce her infectivity to her partner, and by maintaining a cervical mucus seal it would reduce her susceptibility to ascending opportunistic infections of the uterus which are a particular problem in women with AIDS.

5.3 Oral contraceptives

It is doubtful if we will see any major changes in the chemical formulation of oral contraceptive pills in the years to come. However, the use-effectiveness of oral contraceptive pills could be greatly improved by persuading all manufacturers to adopt a uniform method of packaging (for example, 21 pills and 7 clearly distinguishable placebo tablets), with uniform and simplified user instructions, and simple, clear recommendations about what to do if a pill is forgotten. The package inserts currently dwell at great length on the severe adverse side effects of the pill, which are very uncommon. These need to be balanced against the major proven health benefits, which include excellent contraceptive protection if taken according to instructions, and a halving in the risk of developing cancer of the ovary and cancer of the endometrium. Since the benefits of the oral contraceptive pill far outweigh the risks, the time has come to take it off prescription and make it freely available to all women.

There will always be a need for 'emergency contraception' for those who have had unprotected sexual intercourse, or for example in cases where a condom has ruptured during use. The Yuzpe regime of taking an increased dose of oral contraceptive pills immediately after the event is a very effective way of preventing pregnancy, although many women experience nausea and vomiting from this dosage regime. Since many women, and even some doctors, are unaware of this possibility of emergency post-coital contraception, or unable to obtain the medication when they need it, an appropriate package of pills and instructions should again be freely available to all women.

These simple modifications to the packaging and availability of existing oral contraceptive preparations would do much to lower the user failure rate of oral contraceptive pills, currently around 5% per 100 woman-years of use.

5.4 Condoms

Male latex condoms currently offer the best protection against STDs and HIV infection of any contraceptive, but unfortunately they have a rather high contraceptive failure rate. This is probably due more to user failure rather than method failure from condom rupture. However, latex does deteriorate if exposed to excessive heat, light or humidity, and is rapidly destroyed by oil-based lubricants, such as vaseline.

If we are to rely on condoms as the contraceptives of first choice for all young couples starting sexual activity, it may be advisable for the woman to take another form of contraception as well, such as the oral contraceptive pill. But unfortunately this will reduce the couple's motivation to use condoms for all acts of intercourse, undermining the original objective of preventing STD and HIV transmission.

Although condoms are popular contraceptives in some countries, such as Japan, where

45% of couples use them, they are very unpopular in many areas of the world where STDs and HIV infection are most prevalent, such as sub-Saharan Africa (Maudlin & Segal 1988). The reasons given for this dislike of condoms are usually loss of penile sensitivity and interference with the spontaneity of intercourse. And in many areas of the world, women are not in a position to insist that their partners use condoms.

Many of these objections could be overcome by a new range of plastic condoms that are currently under development in the USA and the UK. The great advantage of plastic condoms is that they are loose fitting, apart from the region of attachment at the base of the penis, and hence men find them much more 'sensational' to use. Furthermore, they do not deteriorate on storage, can be used with any type of lubricant, and are much stronger than latex condoms. They can also be re-used, and this would not only reduce costs but it would also ease the potential problem of non-biodegradable plastic condoms polluting the waterways, choking pit latrines and clogging sewage works. Plastic condoms could prove to be one of the most important new contraceptive developments and one of the most effective ways of containing the spread of STDs and HIV infection.

Also under development is a plastic female condom, which is like a small plastic bag placed in the vagina, and held open by an inner flexible ring that is pushed up to the cervix and a flexible outer ring around the opening that lies outside the lips of the vulva. In theory, the female condom gives the woman protection against STDs, HIV and pregnancy in cultures where she is unable to insist on male condom use. Early versions have suffered from a number of drawbacks; many women did not like using them, and there was a 56% dropout rate from one study. It was relatively easy for the penis to slip outside the condom, and there was a 15% contraceptive failure rate at the end of one year (Bounds, Guillebaud & Newman 1992). If female commercial sex workers, 'prostitutes', used them, they might be tempted not to insert a new one for each client, which would be disastrous. But if improvements in design and reduction in costs can overcome some of these drawbacks, female condoms would be a welcome addition to the list of contraceptives that also prevent the transmission of STDs and HIV.

5.5 Male sterilisation

Although vasectomy is a much safer and simpler operation to perform than tubal ligation, male chauvinism has perhaps ensured that vasectomy has never been as popular. Chinese doctors have developed a greatly simplified 'no scalpel' approach to vasectomy that can be performed under local anaesthesia in 5–10 minutes. A group of Thai doctors recently compared this new Chinese approach with the standard technique during a public vasectomy festival that is held in Bangkok each year on the King's birthday. A total of 1203 vasectomies were performed by 28 physicians on the one day. Using the Chinese technique, the doctors averaged 57 operations each, with a complication rate of 0.4%. Using the standard procedure, the number of operations per doctor fell to 33 and the complication rate increased to 3.1% (Nirapathpongporn, Huber & Krieger 1990). Thus the new technique is a considerable improvement and should be universally adopted. But maybe vasectomy will be eclipsed in the future by quinacrine-induced tubal occlusion in women, which is cheaper to perform and is not doctor-dependent.

5.6 Coitus interruptus and rhythm

These methods are of diminishing importance. Unfortunately, both have unacceptably high user failure rates, and neither of them offers any protection against the spread of STDs or HIV. These methods may also be particularly difficult for young people to use effectively. Young men may not yet have learned to recognise the premonitory signs of ejaculatory inevitability when the penis must be withdrawn from the vagina; premature ejaculation is also a particularly common occurrence in this age group. Young women usually have prolonged and irregular menstrual cycles during adolescence, and this makes the accurate prediction of ovulation particularly difficult.

Coitus interruptus is used predominantly by those men who are too ignorant, too poor, or too selfish to use anything else, and its use may decline as condoms become more available, affordable and acceptable.

If the rhythm method is used predominantly by those Roman Catholics who feel obliged to observe the dictates of *Humanae Vitae* (1968), reinforced by *Veritatis Splendor* (1993), perhaps they should think again, and use our new scientific understanding to inform their judgement. Covert ovulation seems to have been one of the key factors leading to our success as a species; it enabled us to use sex for social ends, and to live peaceably in large communities, something that would have been impossible if women came into oestrus. Hence it is going to be an uphill struggle to fight against Nature, and try to develop new scientific methods that predict the moment of ovulation. Pope Paul VI stated that 'the Church teaches that married people may take advantage of the natural cycles immanent in the reproductive system and use their marriage at precisely those times that are infertile, and in this way control birth'. Given that the Roman Catholic Church therefore accepts the need for birth control as a part of responsible parenthood, a doctrinal hair's breadth would seem to separate the approval of family planning if it prevents conception by avoiding intercourse at ovulation, from the condemnation of family planning as intrinsically evil if it prevents conception in any other way.

5.7 Injectables

We already have available a range of gestagen injections, like Depot Provera, and implants, like Norplant I, which inhibit ovulation and provide safe and effective long-term contraception. The disadvantage with the injections is that they have to be given every three months, and it may be extremely costly and inconvenient for a woman in a developing country to travel to a family planning clinic every three months for her repeat injection. In the future, longer-lasting implants may take the place of injections.

Norplant I implants, consisting of six silastic rods, which when placed under the skin of the forearm release 30–40µg of levonorgestrel daily, provide good contraceptive protection for 5 years, at the end of which time, or earlier if so desired, they must be removed. Norplant is relatively costly to insert and remove, and is principally used by those women who have completed childbearing, but do not yet wish to take the irrevocable step of sterilisation. The main drawback is that it produces irregular menstrual bleeding.

For the future, it would be useful to have biodegradable implants that did not have to be surgically removed at the end of their lifespan, and it would be advantageous in many cases to have a shorter duration of action, around two years, since this would make them suitable as a post-partum contraceptive, enabling women to space their births more than two years apart, thereby greatly increasing infant survival rates. Gestagen-only implants also have the advantage that they have no adverse effect of lactation. One such implant in early clinical trials is Organon's 'Implanon', which comes loaded in a pencil-type disposable inserter. The single biodegradable rod, about the size of a Norplant rod, contains a new, more potent gestagen, 3-ketodesogestrel.

Injections and implants have the advantage that contraception is entirely under the woman's control, and she does not have to remember to do anything. Alas, there is no evidence that they offer any protection against STDs or HIV.

5.8 Other methods

Dr Soledad Diaz will talk about breastfeeding, and Professor Talwar will discuss the new immunological approaches to contraception. Until we know more about the safety, efficacy and duration of effectiveness of these immunological methods, it is difficult to evaluate their potential usefulness in family planning programs. Unfortunately, they are the one form of contraception that may be compromised by HIV infection, since the virus progressively weakens the body's immune system.

Little attention has been paid to the development of immunological approaches directed against STDs and HIV infection, but this is an area of considerable promise. For example, it has recently been shown that IgA and IgM anti-HIV antibodies in the breastmilk of HIV positive mothers may protect the baby from HIV infection (Van de Perre *et al.* 1993). Whilst many researchers have been trying to develop vaccines against HIV that produce systemic immunity, a more feasible approach may be to try to stimulate mucosal immunity in the breast or the reproductive tract, since these locally secreted antibodies may prevent viral attachment. Since IgA and IgM antibodies in breastmilk are probably synthesised in the mammary gland from plasma cells derived from maternal Peyer's patches, it may be possible to stimulate maternal IgA and IgM secretion in breastmilk. If this reduced the postpartum transmission rate of HIV, 25–50% in Africa, many babies' lives would be saved—although they would live only to become AIDS orphans. Perhaps we might also find ways of increasing mucosal immunity to STDs and HIV within the male and female reproductive tracts.

5.9 Barrier methods

Conventional barrier methods like diaphragms and cervical caps have fallen from favour because of their unacceptably high contraceptive failure rates. The recent development of the Today sponge, which is impregnated with the spermicide nonoxynol-9, initially held out some promise, but then interest declined when it, too, was shown to have rather a high contraceptive failure rate. However, numerous studies have shown that nonoxynol-9 also has bactericidal and viricidal properties, and several clinical trials have demonstrated that the Today sponge, or other nonoxynol-9 formulations, when placed in the vagina, afford significant protection against gonorrhoea, chlamydia and HIV infection (Elias & Heise 1993). If used repeatedly however, high concentrations of nonoxynol-9 may cause significant vaginal irritation and actually increase HIV transmission, so such a method may not be useful for female commercial sex workers.

This serves to make an extremely important point. In searching for new forms of contraception that also protect against STDs and HIV, we may be making a mistake, since we automatically reject any methods that have a high contraceptive failure rate. Since we have very few methods of preventing STDs and HIV, yet many highly effective ways of preventing pregnancy, the priorities should be reversed. There is an urgent need to develop methods that women can use to protect themselves from STDs and HIV, and it is of less concern if these methods fail to protect against pregnancy.

An interesting recent development has been the discovery that during the luteal phase of the normal menstrual cycle, the uterine fluid contains high concentrations (6mM) of cholic acid. It has now been shown that sodium cholate exhibits strong spermicidal and antiviral activity; in particular, it inhibits the reverse transcriptase enzyme in HIV, and reduces the ability of HIV to infect human lymphocytes (Psychoyos, Creatsas, Hassan, Georgoulias & Gravanis 1993). A vaginal sponge, Protectaid, has been developed which is impregnated with 5g of gel containing 0.5% of sodium cholate, nonoxynol-9 and benzalkonium chloride. In a small clinical trial, there were no pregnancies and no adverse side effects in 20 women at the end of one year of use.

We already have at our disposal a number of spermicides that are also highly bactericidal and viricidal. They could be used precoitally by the woman as a vaginal lubricant, or at the time of coitus as a lubricant for the male or female condom, or they could be used postcoitally by either partner, when they might have no contraceptive effect, but still prevent STD and HIV transmission.

It is interesting to recall that in 1564 when Gabriel Fallopio first described the condom in his book 'De Morbo Gallico', he was using it not as a contraceptive, but as a protection against syphilis. Furthermore, his condom, made of linen and moistened with some medicament, was placed over the glans penis only *after* intercourse, and he claimed 100% success in preventing syphilis in 11,000 men.

We also need to remind ourselves of the success of 'chemical prophylaxis' campaigns used during the First World War in France, when any Allied troops having sexual intercourse with French girls had to submit to urethral lavage with either potassium permanganate or organic silver solutions, and cleansing the penis with mercuric bichloride or calomel. If this was done within three hours of intercourse, it was apparently very effective in preventing the man from becoming infected with syphilis or gonorrhoea. The fact that uncircumcised men appear to be at greater risk of acquiring HIV infection, and also other STDs, suggests that infected female vaginal secretions are trapped by the prepuce in the region of the urethral meatus, enabling the organisms to enter the penile urethra postcoitally where they set up an infection.

Perhaps we need to re-invent chemical prophylaxis, using more efficient and less toxic viricides and bactericides, which could be used as female vaginal douches and medicated fallopian nightcaps for men. Such an approach, coupled with the treatment of susceptible STD infections with antibiotics, might significantly reduce the spread of STDs and HIV.

5.10 Abortion
Although abortion is not regarded as a primary means of contraception, it is

nevertheless essential to have as a back-up facility in case of contraceptive failure.

For the 100,000 legal abortions performed each day, the method of choice in the first trimester of pregnancy is the Chinese vacuum aspiration technique. However, the recent development by Roussel-Uclaf of the orally active antigestagen mifepristone (RU486), which acts as a competitive antagonist of progesterone and therefore induces uterine contractions and fetal expulsion, means that we now have the possibility of transforming early abortion from a surgical procedure that has to be performed in a hospital to a medical procedure that can be carried out in the privacy of the woman's own home.

A large clinical trial of mifepristone in combination with a prostaglandin in France has proved the safety and efficacy of the procedure (Silvestre, Dubois, Renault, Rezvani, Baulieu & Ulmann 1990). The drug is also licensed for use as an early abortifacient in Britain and Sweden, and introductory trials are underway in China. It seems likely that an antigestagen in combination with a prostaglandin taken orally will become the method of choice for first trimester pregnancy terminations in the future. Mifepristone alone has also proved to be an extremely effective form of emergency post-coital contraception, with significantly fewer adverse side effects than the conventional Yuzpe oestrogen-gestagen regime (Glasier, Thong, Dewar, Mackie & Baird 1992).

Abortion is undoubtedly the most sensitive topic in the whole field of family planning. It is strongly condemned by the Roman Catholic Church, for example. Everybody would agree that it is far better to prevent pregnancies than to abort them, but the need for abortion will always be there since no contraceptive method is 100% effective. We owe it to the women of this world to see that they have access to the safest and most effective means of terminating an unwanted pregnancy. It is to be hoped that the rest of the world will soon follow the example set by France, Britain, Sweden and China, and make mifepristone available for first trimester abortion and post-coital contraception.

6. CONCLUSION

The future is one of hope, not of despair. Provided that the necessary financial support is forthcoming from governments, we have the ability to bring human population growth to a halt in the foreseeable future, using the contraceptives that we have already developed. We are also well on the way to developing even better contraceptives that will be cheaper and more effective. Family planning not only saves the lives of women and children, but also saves governments money in the long run.

The recent increase in the incidence of sexually transmitted diseases, which cause so much illness and may lead to lifelong sterility, is a problem that deserves immediate attention. The advent of a new, lethal sexually transmitted disease, HIV, gives an added sense of urgency to our endeavours. Already, there are a number of promising new leads.

For the future, we need to integrate family planning with maternal and child health, STD prevention and HIV prevention, and develop a coordinated approach to the solution of these problems. If good contraceptives are made freely available, family size will decrease and reproductive health can then become the normal expectation of all people.

REFERENCES

Bongaarts, J. 1991 The KAP-gap and the unmet need for contraception. *Pop. Dev. Rev.* **17**, 293–313.

Bounds, W., Guillebaud, J. & Newman, G.B. 1992 Female condom (Femidom): a clinical study of its use, effectiveness and patient acceptability. *Brit. J. Family Planning*, **18**, 36–41.

Elias, C.J. & Heise, L. 1993 The development of microbicides: a new method of HIV prevention for women. *The Population Council Programs Division* Working Papers No. 6, New York.

Glasier, A., Thong, K.J., Dewar, M., Mackie, M. & Baird, D.T. 1992 Mifepristone (RU486) compared with high dose estrogen and progestogen for emergency postcoital contraception. *New Engl. J. Med.*, **327**, 1041–1044.

Hieu, D.T., Tran, T.T., Tan, D.N., Nguyet, P.T., Than, P. & Vinh, D.Q. 1993 31,781 cases of non-surgical female sterilisation with quinacrine pellets in Vietnam. *Lancet*, **342**, 213–217.

Luukkainen, T., Lahtenmaki, P. & Toivonen, J. 1990 Levonorgestrel-releasing intrauterine device. *Ann. Med*, **22**, 85–90.

Maudlin, W.P. & Segal, S.J. 1988 Prevalence of contraceptive use: trends and issues. *Stud. Fam. Plan.*, **19**, 335–353.

Merson, M.H. 1993 The HIV/AIDS pandemic: global spread and global response. IX International Conference on AIDS, Berlin, June 1993 (in press).

Nirapathpongporn, A., Huber, D.H. & Krieger, J.N. 1990 No-scalpel vasectomy at the King's birthday festival. *Lancet*, **335**, 894–895.

Population Reports. 1991 Paying for family planning. Population Information Program. Baltimore, MD: The Johns Hopkins University, Series J, No. 39.

Population Reports. 1992 The reproduction revolution: new survey findings. Population Information Program. Baltimore, MD: The Johns Hopkins University, Series M, No. 11.

Psychoyos, A., Creatsas, G., Hassan, E., Georgoulias, V. & Gravanis, A. 1993 Spermicidal and antiviral properties of cholic acid : contraceptive efficacy of a new vaginal sponge (Protectaid^R) containing sodium cholate. *Human Reproduction*, **8**, 866–869.

Sadik, N. 1990 The state of the world population, 1990. United Nations Population Fund (UNFPA), New York.

Short, R.V. 1992 Breastfeeding, fertility and population growth. United Nations ACC/SCN Nutrition Policy Discussion Paper No. 11. Nutrition and Population Links. New York: UN Publication, 33–46.

Silvestre, L., Dubois, C., Renault, M., Rezvani, T., Baulieu, E-E. & Ulmann, A. 1990 Voluntary interruption of pregnancy with mifepristone (RU486) and a prostaglandin analogue: a large-scale French experience. *New Engl. J. Med.*, **322**, 645–648.

Toivonen, J., Luukkainen, T. & Allonen, H. 1991 Protective effect of intrauterine release of Levonorgestrel on pelvic infection: three year's comparative experience of Levonorgestrel- and Copper-releasing intrauterine devices. *Obstet. Gynecol.*, **77**, 261–264.

United Nations Department of International Economic and Social Affairs 1989: Levels and trends of contraceptive use as assessed in 1988. New York: UN, Sales No. E89, XII.

United Nations Department of International Economic and Social Affairs 1991a: Long-range world population projections. New York: UN, ST/ESA/SER.A/125.

United Nations Department of International Economic and Social Affairs 1991b: World contraceptive use data. New York: UN.

Van de Perre, T., Simonon, A., Hitinana, D-G., Dabis, F., Msellati, P., Mukamabano, B., Butera, J-B., Van Goethem, C., Karita, E. & Lehage, P. 1993 Infective and anti-infective properties of breastmilk from HIV-1-infected women. *Lancet*, **341**, 914–918.

Wasserheit, J.N. 1992 Interrelationships between human immunodeficiency virus infection and other sexually transmitted diseases. *Sex. Trans. Dis.*, **19**, 61–77.

Widdus, R., Meheus, A. & Short, R.V. 1990 The management of risk in sexually transmitted diseases. *Daedalus*, **199**, 177–191.

The World Bank. 1988 World Development Report 1988. Oxford, UK: Oxford University Press.

The World Bank. 1990 World Development Report 1990. Poverty. Oxford, UK: Oxford University Press.

The World Bank. 1991 World Development Report 1991. The challenge of development. Oxford, UK: Oxford University Press.

The World Bank. 1993 World Development Report 1993. Investing in health. Oxford, UK: Oxford University Press.

World Health Organization. 1987 Family health division: maternal mortality fact sheet. Geneva: WHO.

World Health Organization. 1987 Evaluation of the strategy for health for all by the year 2000. Vol. 1, global review. Geneva: WHO.

World Health Organization. 1990 AIDS prevention guidelines for MCH/FP programme managers. Geneva: WHO.

World Health Organization. 1992a Global programme on AIDS; a capsule summary. Geneva: WHO.

World Health Organization. 1992b Reproductive health: a key to a brighter future. Special Programme of Resarch, Development and Research Training in Human Reproduction, Biennial Report 1990–1991. Geneva: WHO.

Zipper, J., Stachetti, M. & Medels, M. 1970 Human fertility control by transvaginal application of quinacrine on the fallopian tube. *Fertil. Steril.*, **21**, 581–589.

Introduction to Session 5:
THE FUTURE
P.N. Tandon

The conference recognized that it was not prudent to rely on science and technology alone to solve the problems created by rapid population growth, wasteful resource consumption and poverty. Professor Sir Hermann Bondi and Professor Michael Chadwick discussed some societal and policy issues. It was emphasized that the political realm cannot be bypassed and economic instruments will still have their part to play.

Professor Gita Sen forcefully argued that although many of the past advances in research are illuminating, a much more consistent effort is needed to link research results and directions to the ongoing policy debate. It is not enough to improve the status of women but to empower them to build in their autonomy and self efficacy in reproductive decisions. There was a need to re-examine the ethical basis of population policies in relation to human rights in general and reproductive rights in particular.

Sir Crispin Tickell, in the concluding talk of the formal presentations, reminded the Summit that it would be sad—and wrong — for the voices raised at the conference to die on the wind. There should be continuing means by which world scientists make their views known to the decision makers at all levels, including the United Nations Population Fund.

5/1

The Role of Science and its Limitations
Sir Hermann Bondi

ABSTRACT

The decisions of individuals on desired family size are influenced by various factors: cultural, social and economic. The scientific argument that continued population growth is bound to lead to disaster will not directly have much effect in changing people's outlook. The importance of education, especially of girls, is stressed as one of the few means available to affect the choice of family size.

We humans have each a wide variety of wishes, desires, aspirations as well as fears and worries. Striving for the satisfaction of any one of them is likely to interfere severely with our ability to satisfy the others. We use our intelligence to mediate between our wishes and get what we regard as the optimal result. It is often necessary for this purpose to forecast the future effects of our proposed actions. Such forecasts, as we all know, have only a very limited probability to turn out to have been sound, but if we work collectively and test empirically all along the line, as we are accustomed to do in science, our forecasts have a much better chance to turn out to be reasonably right.

This conference has stressed that continued population growth is liable to lead to very serious damage to the environment due to the finiteness of the Earth, and that this deterioration of the environment is bound to have the most unhappy consequences for mankind. Although there used to be great optimism that human ingenuity and adaptability could overcome such difficulties, the environmental degradation that has already taken place has silenced most such voices. Personally, what impresses me most is the accelerating loss of top soil and of soil fertility, mainly arising from population growth and largely (but by no means wholly) occurring in the developing world.

I can easily imagine mankind surmounting the exhaustion of, say, molybdenum without any significant hardship. I have every confidence our species can adjust to a change of climate or a rise of sea level, albeit with great hardship for many. On the other hand, I cannot conceive of a tolerable future for humankind if too little top soil is available for food production. Although it could be argued that the sunlight falling on the oceans could be used for producing a great deal more of our food than the few percent so generated currently, I very much doubt that any large deficit could be covered in this manner soon enough.

All this is intended to underline what has been said here and to remove any lingering doubts that curbing and, indeed, halting population growth is a matter of the utmost importance and urgency. This conference has made clear to me the frightening momentum of the process. In a rapidly expanding population a large proportion is in the younger age groups. This implies that even if family sizes shrink immediately, such populations will yet increase to well above their present numbers. The longer before this shrinkage takes place, the more extreme the growth. Thus reductions in fertility are extremely urgent. Having or not having more children is inevitably an individual choice. Hitherto, far too many such personal choices have been made in a manner so as to generate the present population explosion. We all here believe that we know what these choices should be on average for the benefit of (or rather to avoid disaster for) humanity as a whole. Encouraging individuals to make choices for the good of the community as a whole is the stuff of politics guided by the insights of social science. In our field of natural science, we can point to the consequences of actions and we can, through contraceptives, allow certain choices to be made with less discomfort. Nevertheless, we can do little more than put information out to affect choices.

It is therefore necessary to go beyond natural science and examine what influences people's choices and affects them. I fully realise that I am straying far from my own field of competence, but I want to try here to convey to my colleagues what I have appreciated about the difficulties of the task and perhaps indicate the range of situations that needs to be thought about. I will also add a hint or two about how progress might be made.

To take an extreme case, in a society in which respect is accorded to a woman primarily for the number of children she bears and to a man for the number of children he begets, talk about global ill-effects of their actions or the provision of contraceptives is unlikely to have much effect. Fortunately, such societies are not common, although a small flavour of such attitudes is widespread.

The chief point I want to illustrate by this example is that people's outlook is formed by the values of their culture. Therefore, no one prescription can be universally valid. Next, I want to stress that the provision of contraceptives, although undoubtedly useful and widely appreciated, cannot be thought of as the panacea for population growth. First of all, people must want to have fewer children than it was customary to have in their societies and then family planning will assist them to put this choice into effect. Note that in western Europe, the demographic transition occurred largely before contraceptives became widely available.

It is therefore necessary first to investigate why in many of the rapidly growing populations so many births are desired. The starting point for making individuals appreciate the need for change must be that in most parts of the world the mortality of children has diminished greatly. Perhaps it has not yet entered fully into the consciousness of many that in order to have a certain number of their children grow to maturity, fewer births are now required than used to be the case. Thus, a double task emerges: every effort (clean water, vaccinations, availability of health care) should be made to reduce child mortality further, and it should be widely impressed on people how much the survival chances of children have, in fact, improved. Even so, we must be aware that there will remain a tendency for people not just to insure, but to overinsure against the loss of their issue in infancy.

However, how many surviving children are desired? This again must vary greatly between societies. Even wholly leaving out questions of habit and of prestige, it must be accepted that there are many situations where having a large family is a reasonable choice.In family based subsistence farming, the unit is uneconomically small in the quantity of labour available. A child adds to the labour force significantly from perhaps the age of five or six. The demands of the earlier years of the child constitute, therefore, a very rational investment for the parents to make, almost irrespective of the number of previous children. It can therefore scarcely be expected that people in such a situation will be impressed by global concerns to change their customary family size. On the other hand, if evidence of environmental deterioration (lack of firewood, scarcity of water, poorer soil fertility) is of concern to them, they might well appreciate that the future of their children is threatened by local population growth, and draw the consequences. Worry about the future is not confined to the educated. On the other hand, this very worry can also have the opposite effect: trying to insure against a hungry old age by having a large enough family for one's support.

Nevertheless, even when the economic arguments are wholly in favour of far smaller families than were previously the norm, values and attitudes will have to change to make people accept this desideratum. Thus, I am now thinking about a situation where individual advantage and communal need both call for a reduction in the large size of family which was the societal habit, but where it is difficult for customs and value judgements to keep pace with the changing needs.

It is said that the less sophisticated a society is, the more it resists change. This has good reasons: if a group makes a marginal but adequate living in precarious circumstances, even a single piece of unsuccessful experimentation can bring it to extinction.

However, I do not wish to sound too pessimistic. Societies have changed in their attitudes in the past and can do so again in the future. Those of us who live in western societies and, like me, are not young, have seen tremendous changes decade by decade not only in modes of living, but in attitudes and values. Why do some societies change fast (not necessarily always for the better) and others so slowly? I would suggest that education is the prime cause of making speedy change possible, and communication (travel, TV, films) is also very important. Education is, above all, the means of acquiring the competence to learn how others live and manage, and to weigh the advantages and disadvantages of different courses of action. Communication adds greatly to this ability. We all have the tendency to believe that our way of doing things is singularly appropriate and, if we do not see others acting differently and also successfully, we are unlikely to think seriously and reasonably dispassionately about alternatives to our current habits.

It is sometimes said that school has only a modest influence on one's way of thinking and that the influence of home and community is far stronger. This may or may not be the case (and no doubt this will be different in different societies), but the fact is that the school can be influenced from outside, which is far more difficult for family and community (although television can be quite effective there).

However, school has no influence on children who do not attend it, irrespective of whether non-attendance is due to lack of provision, or difficulty of getting there, or unwillingness of the home to spare the child from needed activities in the dwelling or in the fields. In all western countries, school was made obligatory in the 19th century, not in order to force unwilling children to school, but to compel parents to forego the labour of the child so it could attend school. So, from the point of view of this meeting, a most desirable development would be to spread schooling far and wide. Not only would an educated population more readily understand the message about the terrible problems that unrestrained population growth would create, they would also learn about rich countries they try to emulate in some ways and whose populations are steady due to limited family size. Nor should it be forgotten how much TV and films can contribute to the spread of this message.

It is comforting for the group here assembled to hear that education has such a powerful contribution to make to the stabilisation of world population. For not only do we all owe our presence here to the education we have received, we also know that spending the fruits of economic growth on enhancing educational provision is environmentally and socially preferable to any other use of them. Universal education would also change the economic balance for families. If much of the child's energy and time is taken up by education, it is a loss rather than a gain to the household to a far higher age than otherwise.

A special plea must be made for the education of girls. This is the core of fertility control. An educated woman has a very different position in society from an uneducated one. She has more to be selfconfident about than bearing children. Education gives mental independence and allows her to make informed choices on family size. She has also far more potential for attaining economic independence. Ideally, a longer education for girls would delay the onset of child-bearing, a change that would itself reduce the rate of population growth. Even quite a low level of education sharply enhances a mother's ability to take care of her child's health (thereby reducing the need to insure against the death of a child by having another) and her capacity to practise birth control. The education of girls may well prove to be the cardinal factor in stabilising population size.

The ethos and the values of a society are at the core of the population problem. As long as a large family is the chief way in which a poor couple can gain standing and prestige in their group, our message will not be received. However, the attitudes of societies can be changed. In my young days as a student, smoking was viewed as an almost essential social accomplishment, and my non-smoking as a somewhat deplorable oddity. Today, at least among the more educated population in my country, the few smokers are viewed as the odd ones out.

Yet we must not forget that there are also negative influences at work in many places, largely political in nature. In my young days, many a political leader called for a growing population, so that there would be more soldiers available to ensure the security of their own country and diminish that of their neighbours. This occurs in rather fewer places today, but the otherwise most welcome spread of democracy has also, in some locations, an unfortunate side-effect. These are districts (or regions or perhaps whole countries) where two somewhat hostile communities live side by side and most people cast their vote not for the candidate for election they regard as better, but for the one who belongs to their community. Of course, such a situation is democracy in name only, for the potential unseating of a government that has lost the confidence of the electorate is of its essence. If the relative size of the communities rather than approval by the voters determines the outcome of elections, then there is a strong temptation for one community to try to outbreed the other. Encouraging your group to be fertile is then a political ploy, and our message is unlikely to be heard above the din of the centrifugal political shouting.

What we are talking about in this meeting is ultimately an appeal to people to change their values and therefore their actions. We are indeed discussing the pressing need for people in the rapidly growing parts of the world to change their aspirations and thereby the most personal aspects of their lives. We should not be surprised that this is difficult. However, it is most encouraging that there are quite a number of countries who are managing their demographic transition with every sign of success. Although it will not be easy to make this change throughout many more regions, we are justified in hoping and expecting that the necessary changes will come about. After all, the global human population will never exceed the Earth's carrying capacity. What we can try to avoid is that this limitation takes place in a horrible manner. I trust that our message will help to ensure that it occurs in tolerable ways.

5/2

Visions of a Sustainable World:
Ethical Evaluations or Political Programmes?
M. J. Chadwick

ABSTRACT

Not only population size, but *per capita* resource demand determines the load which population exerts on the natural resource base and the environmental carrying capacity. Agricultural productivity, with allowances for the 'non-productive' requirements of land, is not *per se* a limiting factor, even at a total population in excess of 10 billion. Nevertheless, agricultural mismanagement and a high level of distributional inequity results in between 500 and 1000 million people operating at a level of poverty that represents, amongst other things, a condition of hunger. Ways out of the poverty trap require increased access to environmental goods and services by the poor but, because of the luxury levels of access by rich, developed countries, open access to resources is a cause of unsustainable development practices. Saving and sharing on a global scale, backed by an overall decrease in the use of renewable resources and the adoption of technologies that increase materials and energy intensity use, requires implementation. Political structures that have evolved to accept a shared sovereignty rather than narrow national interest are needed.

1. INTRODUCTION

It is impossible to address the issue of population in the global context without confronting the issues also of poverty and sustainable development. There is still a conviction amongst some that there is a simple causal relationship between too many people and any escape from the poverty trap. Furthermore, population pressure is perceived to result in such over-exploitation of environmental resources that they are irretrievably degraded, adding to concerns for the environmental health of the planet.

2. POPULATION, POVERTY AND ENVIRONMENT LINKAGES

Very few suppose that in poor countries the issue of poverty can be dealt with in the absence of economic growth. Economic growth will not ensure that the plight of the poor is addressed, and poverty alleviated, but it must be a major component of any action for dealing with poverty. However, it is possible to have economic growth but at the same time exploit forests to extinction, erode soils, pollute water courses and aquifers, bring wild-life to the point of extinction, severely overfish rivers, lakes and seas and overwork mineral reserves to a degree where mines must be abandoned. During this process, however, wealth is said to have increased and the natural resource depletion is registered by a measure of economic progress. Indeed, it is one of the ironies of the system that such is the selectivity in weighing the evidence that the poor may be implicated in such resource and environmental degradation. In spite of their modest *per capita* consumption, they are regarded as a major cause of environmental degradation rather than it being recognised that many are so relegated to the fragile and marginal ecosystems, by the rich and the powerful, that increased penury is the result rather than the cause of environmental degradation. Loss of entitlement to environmental resources (access) usually precedes and, thus, leads to degradation of the remaining accessible resources, leading to further impoverishment. The spiral of impoverishment and environmental degradation has begun (Figure 1). In the consideration of population, poverty and environment, effects are often mistaken for causes.

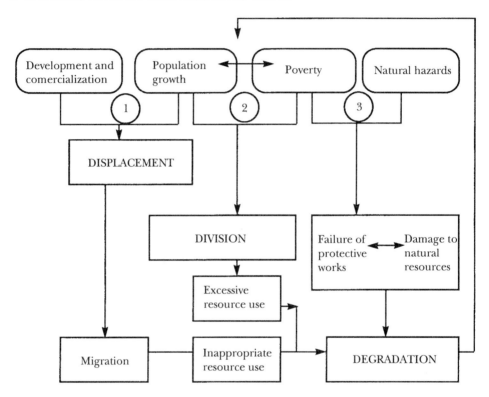

Figure 1. Impoverishment and degradation spirals (Kates & Haarmann 1992). (Reprinted with permission of the Helen Dwight Reid Educational Foundation from *Where the poor live: are the assumptions correct?* by R.W. Kates & V. Haarman, *Environment* **34**, 4–28. Copyright 1992 by Heldref Publications, 1319 18th Street, N.W., Washington, DC 20036–1802.)

2.1 Poverty alleviation and economic development

Economic growth is not a sufficient condition for alleviating poverty as the implementation processes can be very diverse. Measures to induce economic growth leading to the 'trickle down' or 'spread' effect is one income-enhancing process that is invoked, but the poor must have the capacity to respond and this includes access to productive resources and the acquisition of marketable skills (Vyas 1991). Another approach is for public investment to create income-earning opportunities for poor households. A third development mechanism is by the movement of prices in favour of the poor, particularly for goods they sell, including labour, and finally development opportunity instituted by direct income transfers. Sen (1993) draws attention to the success of the public employment approach (creation of income-earning opportunities) and the public ownership of stockpiles of food (pricing policy in favour of the poor).

2.2 The environment and economic development

Although there is an economic growth imperative associated with the relief of poverty in poor countries, there is also a recognition that the depletion of *natural* capital may severely restrict long-term economic development. This is because the resource base on which future growth is dependent is being, often needlessly, destroyed. The recognition that sustainable development requires a sustainable method of resource use and methods of sustaining environmental quality, needs to be more generally accepted and become a major policy goal.

3. SUSTAINABLE DEVELOPMENT

In recent years, there has been a general acceptance of the need for sustainable development. This concept has been espoused since the Brundtland Commission (WCED 1987) enunciated that, 'Sustainable development is development that meets the needs of future generations without compromising the ability of future generations to meet their own needs.' As an absolute objective this statement is laudable but it is necessary to accept that some resources are not, in any meaningful sense, renewable, all recycling systems are leaky and it is difficult to get any clear quantitative measure of the needs of future generations.

Operationally, little has been achieved on a global scale and problems surrounding sustainable development have been approached by giving action a local emphasis, by emphasising goals rather than the adoption of technologies to reduce resource loss, by resorting to a fortress approach of sovereignty over national resources, by focusing on very specific issues rather than the general, overall situation or by moralising about life styles rather than enunciating practical methods of reducing resource-wasteful practices. The approach has been scenario substantial but policy poor. It is difficult to sustain the argument that development that will contribute to satisfying the aspirations of less-developed countries must expand the access of the poor to resources, but that if non-renewable resource inputs are essential, then open access to environmental resources may be a key factor causing unsustainability (Pezzey 1992). Furthermore, studies suggest that intervention by governments in the form of resource conservation subsidies or depletion taxes will 'correct' open access and improve sustainability, but subsidies that encourage traditional forms of development will harm it (Pezzey 1992). Could it be that, however currently unfashionable this may be, the only practical way to overcome the 'open-access, sustainability constraining' linkage is to work towards a more equal, and for some more painful, distribution of resource use—and this based not on ideological grounds, but on sheer management and survival practicalities? In the absence of vision, survival! Nevertheless it might be instructive to follow this possibility and even at the same time address questions of allocation as well as questions of scale (Daly 1984).

4. POPULATION GROWTH: ALLOCATION AND SCALE

Writing nearly 200 years ago, it seems Malthus got it wrong: 'the power of population is indefinitely greater than the power in the earth to produce subsistence for man'. Malthus saw some populations doubling every 25 years in the early years of the industrial revolution in Europe, but he questioned whether food supplies could continually do the same. Malthus had little insight into the behaviour of populations and underestimated technological advances in food production.

4.1 Stages of population growth

It is now accepted that demographic growth takes place in a number of stages, collectively referred to as the *population cycle*. In countries that have passed through periods of technological and social change, it is possible to discern a pre-industrial, relatively *stable population size* stage where the high birth-rate is more or less equalled by a high death-rate, mainly due to a high infant mortality rate. As society progresses, the adoption of simple advances in personal and community hygiene and health care reduces deaths without affecting the birth-rate so that an *early expanding population* stage is evident. Many developing countries exhibit this stage of demographic growth at present. Subsequently, further more sophisticated advances in health care, in a society where income has markedly increased, mean death rates decline, but the availability and use of birth control means a *late expanding population* stage showing a much reduced birth rate increase is prevalent. Finally, a *low fluctuating population* stage is recognisable where the demands and aspirations for children in a much more affluent society represent a financial liability rather than an asset, as with earlier stages, and this causes careful regulation of family size. The four stages are correlated with a progression in *per capita* income from very low to relatively high levels. However, there is by no means a simple correlation between *per capita* income and many other human development indicators. For example, as Sen (1993) has pointed out, not all wealthy nations have greater life expectancies than poorer countries. Kerala has less than one-twelfth of the *per capita* GNP of South Africa or Brazil, but a higher life expectancy. As Sen (1993) points out, the fact that poor countries can achieve improvements in health care and life expectancy that rival those of far wealthier nations has far-reaching policy implications, not least for the allocation of development aid.

The perceived relationship between stages of the population cycle and *per capita* income in which the low fluctuating stage of population growth coincides with the increased level of affluence, has led many to assume that such levels of income can only be attained once low levels of population growth have been achieved. As with other stages in the population cycle, there is evidence to suggest it is the level of income that drives the rate of population growth rather than the reverse.

4.2 Population resource demands

Malthus also miscalculated on the future production capability of agricultural systems. Largely, he underestimated the power of technology to meet the power of population. The ability to take more land into agricultural production, the use of fertilisers, the increased ability to control disease and pests, and particularly the breeding of vastly improved varieties of crops (hybrid rice, slim-line maize and shorter-strawed wheat) and animals has meant that from 1950 to 1984 world grain harvests rose by 260% or yield improved on average by about 3% per annum. Other crop yields also showed a consistent improvement, as did meat and milk yields. World production of rice reached 257 million tonnes in 1965, but achieved 468 million tonnes by 1984.

4.3 Population supply limitations

Estimates of the physical constraints on food supply set limits at quite generous levels. Under agricultural conditions, for a wide range of agricultural crop species, it is possible to estimate generally applicable rates of photosynthesis. The total photosynthetic productivity of a geographic location depends on the sky conditions, latitude and date (least in winter, most in summer). Combining this with some reasonably well-founded assumptions concerning the leaf's scattering of light radiation, leaf photosynthesis rates, leaf area indices, leaf orientation and plant respiration rates, de Wit (1967) calculated the potential productivity of latitudinal bands of the earth's surface. Allowing for the proportion of production suitable for human consumption, an estimate was obtained also for the population it was possible to support from production *from* the land area on which production took place. Allowing 1 million kilocalories per year per person as food and 750 m² of surface area per person for non-productive purposes, de Wit (1967) calculated 146 billion people could be provided for. Allowing for meat production and for a larger provision of land for non-agricultural purposes (1500 m² per person), using the same methodology as de Wit (1967) it has been calculated that the 'carrying capacity' is reduced to 64 billion people, requiring 17% of the earth's surface as agricultural land (Table 1). Others (Vitousek *et al.* 1986 and Daily & Ehrlich 1992) have taken a different approach to this issue although many of the basic relationships displayed are conformable with those that emerge here. For a more sophisticated analysis, reference should be made to Shaw & Öberg (1994).

Estimates such as the one presented are indicative only. Land is utilised not only to grow food crops but for fibre production, industrial products, for fuel and for building materials. However, the estimates suggest that physical constraints to *production* will not begin to apply for some time to come in the population growth cycle. There is no reason to think that population has been or will be limited by the overall rate of food production *per se.*

Nevertheless, in recent years, the rate of increase of growth in crop yield levels has slowed. In Africa, although between 1977 and 1987 there was a 23% rise in food production, this represented an 8% *per capita* reduction. For several years recently, annual consumption has exceeded annual production and grain stocks have been depleted (WRI 1990). Norse *et al.* (1992) note however that it is mismanagement of the agricultural land presently in use that is the cause of this undermining of agricultural productivity. Others have noted that the slowing in the rise in agricultural productivity has appeared in the wake of a decade (1980–1990) that has included several of the hottest summers on record (Kennedy 1993). However, against this must be set the recorded 38% fall in real prices of basic foods over this previous decade (UNCTAD 1992).

The indication that it is not the physical limitation of supply by agricultural production

Table 1. *The potential productivity of latitudinal lands of the earth's terrestrial surface and their population carrying capacity (modified from de Wit 1967)*

latitude (degrees north)	land surface in ha ($\times 10^8$)	number of months above $10°C$	carbohydrate yield ha^{-1} yr^{-1} in kg ($\times 10^3$)	area* m^2 $person^{-1}$	population carrying capacity ($\times 10^9$)
70	8	1	12	3112	2.6
60	14	2	21	2438	5.8
50	16	6	59	1838	8.7
40	15	9	91	1720	8.7
30	17	11	113	1678	8.0
20	13	12	124	1662	5.1
10	10	12	124	1662	3.8
0	14	12	116	1672	6.2
−10	7	12	117	1670	4.4
−20	9	12	123	1662	5.5
−30	7	12	121	1666	4.4
−40	1	8	89	1726	0.6
−50	1	1	12	3166	0.3
total	132				64.1

*Estimate allows for carbohydrate and meat production (200g $person^{-1}$ day^{-1}) and 1500 m^2 $person^{-1}$ non-agricultural land.

systems for an expanding population but the management, policy and institutional insufficiencies that lead to estimates by the World Hunger Program, updated to 1990, that some 9% of the world's total population (477 million) are in a condition of energy deficiency for maintenance, and 20% (1053 million) in a state of energy deficiency for work. This point is reinforced by the analysis presented by Sen (1993) of famine and food supply. Famine often takes place where statistics give little evidence of decline in food supply. Sen (1993) quotes the 1973 famine in the Ethiopian province of Wollo where even though drought caused local impoverishment, food moved out of the famine-stricken region to more affluent areas! Conversely, severe droughts between 1972 and 1973 in Maharashtra, leading to a halving of annual yields, did not lead to widespread famine as public works programmes provided an income for displaced agricultural labourers who were then able to compete economically with others for the limited food available. This approach leads to a sharing of the total food supply more equitably. It underlines the *distributional* basis of poverty and famine and emphasises how they are rooted in economic and political failures rather than overall mass balance supply calculations. Problems arise from inequalities of distribution and, if open access to resources threatens sustainability, it is necessary to narrow the gap preferentially in favour of the poor.

Some seem intent upon reducing the whole question of population pressure, in the context of development and environmental issues, to a tyranny of numbers. In this context, it is quite evident that one plus one rarely equals two. Table 2 compares population numbers with a Country–Resource–Demand index for 18 countries. From the point of view of a simple population head-count, China, India, Indonesia and Brazil might be regarded as jeopardising the future of the Earth's resources, but using a resource demand index this risk is more fairly placed at the door of the USA, Japan, Germany, the UK, Canada and Russia. In the case of Indonesia, the USA exceeds its resource demand by a factor of 50. It is not difficult to see where the population control effort should be applied! Sweden as a country with a mere 8.6 million people exceeds the resource demand of Bangladesh (116.4 million) by some 15 times.

Table 2. *Population and country–resource–demand indices for 18 countries*

country	population	country	country–resource–demand index
China	1170.7	USA	5.51
India	862.7	Japan	3.20
USA	252.5	Germany	1.79
Indonesia	187.7	UK	0.93
Brazil	151.6	Canada	0.55
Russia	148.7	Russia	0.51
Japan	124.0	China	0.43
Bangladesh	116.4	Brazil	0.41
Nigeria	112.1	India	0.31
Germany	79.9	Switzerland	0.22
UK	57.6	Sweden	0.20
Canada	27.0	Indonesia	0.11
Sudan	25.9	Norway	0.10
Kenya	24.5	Kenya	0.09
Burkina Faso	9.2	Nigeria	0.03
Sweden	8.6	Bangladesh	0.02
Switzerland	6.8	Sudan	0.01
Norway	4.3	Burkina Faso	0

5. VISIONS

Some visions are apocalyptic, others are seen through a glass darkly; some are more mundane and postulate, as did Lester Thurow, a world with the productivity of the Swiss, the consumption patterns of the Chinese, the egalitarianism of the Swedes, and the social discipline of the Japanese (Meadows *et al.* 1992). One might also add, the directness of the Americans. My vision of the ten billion world embraces all these attributes and recognises firmly that no single feature holds the key to success or to failure. Success or failure of the future of such a world does not depend *solely* on reducing (or not) population growth rates, does not depend solely on 'technology to the rescue', or on free trade or rigid regulatory mechanisms. However, it does depend on recognising the interdependence of a range of factors and having at least some understanding of their functional linkages.

Shaw (1992) has indicated (Figure 2) how population, natural resource consumption and technology determine environmental well-being, but also how poverty and debt may alter relationships. Also included are the possible distortions (or corrections) brought about by management policies and the way in which national self-interest restricts developmental and environmentally positive flows and encourages negative ones. An overall analysis such as this, and others that emphasise a systems approach to sustainable development (Shaw and Öberg 1994), underline the necessity of a unified approach to any vision of human development and environmental protection and improvement. If this is grasped, then focus on a single issue will be seen only to skew perception of the way in which moves towards sustainable development must proceed.

Recognition of the multi-factor interdependency that will drive, or hinder, progress to sustainable development also suggests the necessity for establishing a political agenda—-the necessity to begin to move away from mere conceptualisation, from moralising, to targeted action, to a new approach to structural economic problems, to sharing sovereignty and moving away from narrow national self-interest. Local actions will play their part but a far more concerted approach is also needed: corrective action in one geographical region is deficient if it merely exacerbates counteractions in another. Fears of the 'water-bed' effect relate to free trade, open investment policies, national environmental regulatory actions, rigid sovereignty issues and even technology transfer. Certainly insistence on simple population regulation policies, unrelated to *per capita* resource use, will do little to address these issues, although there is no a *a priori* reason for thinking there are things that cannot be done with a global population of five billion that can with ten billion. However, playing the mere numbers game is not instructive.

In the visions of an effective interdependent, multi-factor political agenda, where should stress and emphasis be placed?

5.1 Renewable resources and consumption patterns

It is necessary to recognise in terms of renewable resources, particularly food, that overall production potential is not the limitation even for a 10 billion population. There is no guarantee that increased production would result in a more equitable distribution (or that with a smaller world population there would be a fairer distribution that would move towards eliminating poverty and hunger). Limited access to resources by a large number of the world's population is a major problem, and distributional inequalities need to be tackled by serious and coordinated initiatives. All demographic evidence suggests that rises in living standards precede, not follow, falls in population growth rates. Even small rises are effective triggers and need not be bought at the expense of massive natural resource demand. For example, it is not only dirigiste regimes in developing countries that can bring about checks in the population growth rate. The Indian State of Kerala has a high literacy rate, public commitment to health care and to

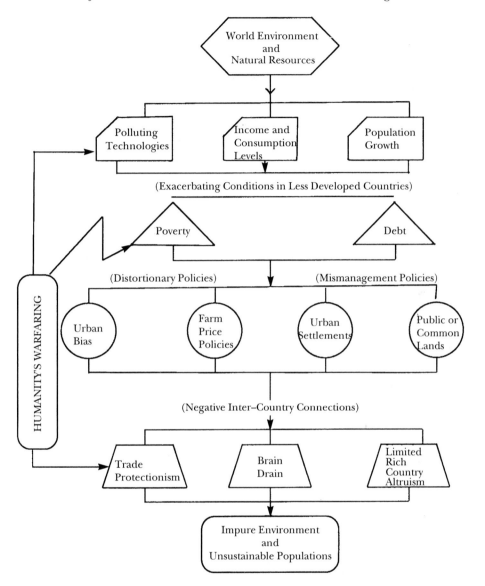

Figure 2. Causes of environmental degradation and unsustainable development (Shaw 1992). (Reprinted by permission of the publisher from *The impact of population growth on environment: the debate heats up* by R.P. Shaw, *Impact Assessment Review* **12**, 11–36. Copyright 1992 by Elsevier Science Publishing Co., Inc.)

improving the status of women. Life expectancy is above 70 years and the birth rate is showing signs of stabilising.

The fact that more access to natural resources is required to encourage development that will, in turn, encourage lower birth rates, but also may lead to increased environmental pressure, needs addressing. Ways of squaring this circle involve the need for action to reduce overall resource demand, but in a way that drastically re-distributes more equitably this more limited access to resources. That will need international coordination of effort, but eventually self-interest may lead to a readier acceptance of more equality in access to resources as resource consumption inequalities give rise to even greater pressures for migration to occur on a larger scale, and resulting civil strife escalates beyond anything yet experienced. Sharing and saving for survival may be one of the few options open to more privileged nations. Such a vision requires not only sharing resources, but also sharing sovereignty in order to reduce the overall scale of exploitation. Such a vision may seem naïve and lacking in realism at present, but it is based on a perception that 'we ain't seen nothing yet'!

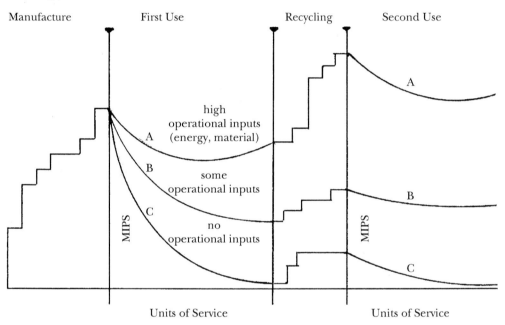

Figure 3. Possible changes of MIPS during use and recycling of goods (Schmidt-Bleek 1993).

5.2 Technological responses

Use of natural resources under present systems is accompanied by the generation of waste products that need to be disposed of in environmentally benign ways. Any vision of low but equitable *per capita* consumption patterns requires also a vision of the implementation of low (or no) waste technologies (Jackson 1993) and a vastly increased use of renewable resources (energy, food, forestry, fibre products) in conjunction with the acceptance of a recycling and materials intensity mode of operation for non-renewable materials. Schmidt-Bleek (1993) has argued that western country infrastructures, goods and services must be de-materialised by an average factor of 10. The material intensity (total material and energy throughput) of the entire cradle-to-grave life-cycle of a good has its environmental impact determined in terms of its MIPS (Material Intensity Per unit Service). A theoretical example is shown in Figure 3.

Such a vision would seek to encourage technological advances that embody a low MIPS for a large range of goods and services. This would need to be linked to labour-intensive technologies rather than output intensive ones. In the field of agricultural production, there is envisioned a considerable increase in the application of biotechnology over relatively short lead-times (Table 3) to encourage lower MIPS values.

Technological innovation and development will not automatically lead to more sustainable forms of development or even increased access to resources, goods and services by the population generally. Many technological advances have come about due to needs arising from conflicts and have been accompanied by social decline in a whole spectrum of communities. Other technological advances frequently result in the rich getting richer and the poor poorer—the opposite of the focus of vision shared here. Technological innovations should be judged and encouraged on the basis of their long-term promise rather than the advantage they confer on early users (Kennedy 1993).

5.3 Trade

Nations do not act in isolation. Most nations trade and, in a vision of shared sovereignty, will continue to do so. The way trade is conducted will affect the ability to achieve sustainable development. The idea that free trade is 'good for all', a sort of universal panacea, does not really bear detailed examination. As Daly (1992) comments, 'There may be good arguments for free trade but, in a world of capital mobility, comparative advantage cannot be one of them. The confident assertion that an open trading system will benefit all trading partners is utterly unfounded'. As von Moltke (1992) has pointed out 'Free trade is not unlike the free market: it requires rules to protect it from excesses implicit in its construction. The paradox is that without regulation there is no free trade, but excess regulation removes the discipline of competition'. Recently the whole issue of trade and sustainable development has been given more documented exposure and discussion (Runnals & Cosbey 1992).

The vision of a World Economic Community may not be everybody's Nirvana, but follows a certain logical progression from a Planet Earth–One World philosophy. A World Economic Community with regulated 'free' trade, development assistance to less developed 'regions', regulated equitably-based access to resources, sustainable development objectives, environmental protection agreements, technology focused on low-waste and recycling to give low materials intensity, and economic instruments to underpin this, is hardly a clarion call. Nevertheless, the degree of global economic interdependence today takes us some way along the trajectory. However, the 'community' aspect adds to the economic one: it predicates a political dimension. In *Preparing for the Twenty-First Century*, Kennedy (1993) quotes the opinion that, 'our achievements on the economic plane of life have outstripped our progress on the political plane'. The quotation goes on to remark, 'on the economic plane, the world has been organised into a single, all-embracing unit of activity. On the political plane, it has not only remained partitioned into sixty or seventy sovereign national States, but the national units have been growing smaller and more numerous and the national consciousness more acute' (*The Economist*). But Kennedy (1993) concludes, nevertheless, 'despite the size and complexity of the global challenges facing us, it is too simple and too soon to conclude gloomily nothing can be done'. The fragmentation and narrow nationalism will have to be reversed and a community of interest and shared determination encourage adaptation that will self-evidently give the conviction for a change in direction. Both vision *and* survival!

Table 3. *Summary of biotechnology applications in agriculture (Norse et al. 1992)*

crop applications		crop applications	
applications	time frame[1]	applications	time frame[1]
tissue culture		*transgenic crops* (cont.)	
rapid propagation	Near	cereals	
production of disease-free stock	Near	rice	Near
anther culture	Near	maize	Mid
embryo rescue	Near	wheat	Long
somaclonal variation	Near-Mid	fibre	
		cotton	Long
genetic mapping		oil seed	
RFDLs	Near	rapeseed	Near
		soyabean	Mid
diagnostics		tree crops	
monoclonals/polyclonals	Near	walnut	Near
nucleic acid probes	Near-Mid	poplar	Near
		coconut	Long
		cocoa	Long
use of microorganisms			
nitrogen fixation		animal applications	
legumes (select.of better N fixers)	Near-Long	applications	time frame[1]
cereals	Long		
plant growth promoter	Mid	in-vitro fertilization	Near
microbes (mycorrhiza)		embryo transfer	Near
biological control	Near-Long	new diagnostics	Near
post harvest food processing	Near-Mid	novel vaccines	Near
		novel hormones	
transgenic crops		BST	Near
horticulture/root crops		PST	Near
potato	Near	modification of rumen	Near
tomato	Near	microflora	
cassava	Near	use of RFLP for	Near
		genetic mapping	
		transgenics	Mid-Long

[1]Estimated time-frame for commercialization of products:

Near-term, 0–5 years; Mid-term, 5–10 years; Long-term, over 10 years

REFERENCES

Daily, G.C. & Ehrlich, P.R. 1992 Population, sustainability, and earth's carrying capacity. *Bioscience* **42**, 761–71.

Daly, H.E. 1984 Alternative strategies for integrating economies and ecology. In *Integration of economy and ecology - an outlook for the eighties* (ed. A-M. Jansson). Wallenberg Symposium, Stockholm.

Daly, H.E. 1992 Free trade, sustainable development and growth: some serious contradictions. *Independent Sectors Network '92.*

Jackson, T. (ed.) 1993 *Clean production strategies: developing preventive environmental management in the industrial economy.* Boca Raton: Lewis.

Kates, R.W. & Haarmann, V. 1992 Where the poor live: are the assumptions correct? *Environment* **34**, 4–28.

Kennedy, P. 1993 *Preparing for the twenty-first century.* London: Harper Collins.

Meadows, D.H., Meadows, D.L. & Randers, J. 1992 *Beyond the limits: global collapse or sustainable future?* London: Earthscan.

von Moltke, K. 1992 Free trade and mutual tariffs: a practical approach to sustainable development. *EcoDecision* **5**, 45.

Norse, D., James, C., Skinner, B.J. & Zhao, Q. 1992 Agriculture, land use and degradation. In *An agenda for environment and development into the 21st century* (ed. J.C.I. Doog, G.T. Goodman, T.W.M. la Rivière, J. Marton-Lefèvre, T. O'Riordan & F. Praderie). Cambridge University Press, pp. 79–89.

Pezzey, J. 1992 *Sustainable development concepts: an economic analysis.* Washington, DC: World Bank.

Runnalls, D. & Cosbey, A. 1992 *Trade and sustainable development: a survey of the issues and a new research agenda.* Winnipeg: IISD.

Schmidt-Bleck, F. 1993 MIPS – a universal ecological measure? *Fresenius Environmental Bulletin* **2**, pp. 306–311.

Sen, A. 1993 The economics of life and death. *Scient. Am.* May, 18–25.

Shaw, R.P. 1992 The impact of population growth on environment: the debate heats up. *Environmental Impact Assessment Review* **12**, 11–36.

Shaw, R.W. & Öberg, S. 1994 Sustainable development: applications of systems analysis. *Science of the Total Environment.* Amsterdam: Elsevier Science Publishers (in press).

UNCTAD 1992 *UNCTAD VIII, Analytical report by the UNCTAD secretariat to the conference.* New York: United Nations.

Vitousek, P.M., Ehrlich, P.R., Ehrlich, A.H. & Matson, P.A. 1986 Human appropriation of the products of photosynthesis. *Bioscience* **36**, 368–73.

Vyas, V. S. 1991 *Alleviation of rural poverty in the states: lessons of eighties.* Jaipur: IDS.

WCED 1987 *Our common future.* Oxford University Press.

de Wit, C.T. 1967 Photosynthesis: its relationship to overpopulation. In *Harvesting the sun* (ed. A. San Pietro, F.A. Greer & T.J. Army). New York: Academic Press.

WRI 1990 *World Resources 1990–91: a guide to the global environment.* New York: Oxford University Press.

5/3

Women's Empowerment and Human Rights: the Challenge to Policy
Gita Sen

ABSTRACT

Population policy is at a major crossroads. Earlier agreement regarding fundamental aspects of policy has been eroding steadily over the last decade. New actors and new voices have now entered the debate. The women's health movement has posed critical challenges to current policies. This paper argues from the perspective of the women's health movement that, if a genuine consensus is to reemerge, at least among those who believe in the value of birth control technologies, then there will have to be rethinking along five critical dimensions: the ethical basis of policy, its objectives, the strategies espoused, the programme methods, and the technologies upon which it relies.

1. AT THE CROSSROADS

Population policy is at a crossroads. The ambiguous results of policy and programme efforts over the last forty years, coupled with the emergence of multiple and conflicting voices in the global debate, have contributed to the erosion of public consensus. Concern, even agitation, about the possible consequences of continuing population growth has resurged in Northern Hemisphere countries during the late 1980s and the 1990s to the high levels of the 1960s, but the confidence of the earlier era on the appropriate ways to tackle the problem has given way to a multiplicity of views.

Five sets of forces, some overlapping, others contradictory, are engaged in the current debate about population policy. Ever since 1984, when the US government articulated what has come to be known as its Mexico City policy, there has been considerable concern within the international population policy establishment regarding both funding and political support. The Mexico City policy was rationalised *ex post* by the US administration on both scientific and ethical grounds. The National Academy of Sciences report of 1986 failed to find convincing empirical grounds for believing that population growth has negative economic and/or environmental effects (National Academy of Sciences 1986). Although this report was viewed by many as controversial, it provided grist to the mill of a US administration that was under strong pressure from conservative Christian fundamentalists opposing both abortion and contraception. Existing population programmes were criticised as violating the human rights of individuals—witness the furore regarding forced abortions in China during the Republican administrations of the 1980s. Regaining the high ground in terms of political support for family planning has become, therefore, a major concern for population organisations.

A second group engaged in the current population debate consists of environmentalists concerned about the implications of population growth for global environmental problems. Current concerns by environmentalists echo similar opinions held in the late

363

1960s and early 1970s, but now with considerably greater sophistication regarding environmental impacts.

Despite the similarities in the concerns of mainstream population and environmental organisations, the current polarisation between North and South on economic issues (such as debt, the terms of international trade, and resource transfer) has cast its shadow over earlier agreement on the serious nature of the population problem. In the context of global environmental negotiations, a number of Southern countries have taken the position that the North, with its excessive living standards, has no business to demand that the South devotes resources to population programmes, especially when faced with Northern unwillingness to seriously acknowledge or redress the paucity of resources for Southern development, or the inequities in global economic arrangements.

Also countering the voices of environmentalists and population organisations is the growing influence worldwide of fundamentalist religious forces opposed, in varying degrees, to contraception, abortion, sex education, and the newer reproductive technologies. The Vatican is an old and influential player in this camp, and one whose political acuity and sophistication in these matters was evident at the UN Conference on Environment and Development in 1992, and in the current preparations for the International Conference on Population and Development.

In sharp contrast to the views of religious fundamentalists are the positions taken by many women's health organisations and feminists who strongly favour access to safe birth control (contraception, abortion) for women of all classes and ages. However, women's groups [many of which are non-governmental organisations (NGOs) working with women] criticise existing population policies as being excessively driven by demographic targets rather than individual reproductive health needs. Family planning programmes in many countries are perceived as overly bureaucratic, insensitive to the concerns of women who are viewed as 'targets', and to the quality of the services they provide. Women's groups argue that current policies and programmes by their insensitivity have succeeded in alienating many women, potentially the best allies of good birth control and reproductive health services.

It should be clear from the above that neither proponents nor critics speak with one voice. The resulting public debate is, not surprisingly, complex, acrimonious, and sometimes difficult for those other than immediate protagonists to comprehend. Population organisations have been attempting, in this climate, to reshape consensus among some at least of the major actors. (It is clear that a full consensus among all the actors is impossible, given that some oppose all but 'natural' birth control methods on religious grounds.) The elements of this renegotiated position appear to be the following:

- agreement on the seriousness of population growth and its consequences if unchecked
- support for family planning as contributing to maternal and child health (equated to reproductive health)
- emphasis on the existence of a significant 'unmet need' for family planning services as revealed by national Demographic and Health Surveys (DHS), implying thereby that population programmes can be voluntaristic and need not resort to any form or degree of coercion

- a focus on education as the most important means of empowering women so as to increase their demand for family planning services.

I believe that elements of this approach are laudable and worth pursuing, in particular the commitment to voluntarism and to meeting individual needs, as well as its emphasis on educating women. However, I also believe it does not go far enough in shifting the ethical ground of population policies, and that it tends to narrow the meaning of reproductive health and, indeed, to obfuscate the issue by equating reproductive health with family planning. The approach disappoints in its refusal to address criticisms of the organisation and functioning of family planning programmes that have been cogently made not only by feminists but by a range of NGOs working on health care.

Meeting 'unmet need' is an attractive idea that elegantly distances family planning from any whiff of coercion, but the Demographic and Health Surveys that have been used to quantify the concept do little to ascertain the actual needs that women might have either for birth control or for other reproductive health services. Nor do they question whether the extension of the type of family planning services currently being provided would meet women's needs in quantity or kind. To equate the extent of women's stated desires not to have more children (according to the DHS surveys) with 'unmet need' for the type of services currently being provided through family planning is disingenuous. My point is not that all existing family planning programmes are bad, but that there has been serious and thoughtful criticism of many which warrants more careful attention.

Another source of disappointment with this attempt to refurbish the rationale for population policy is that, while it places a great deal of emphasis on female education, it continues to objectify and instrumentalise women for demographic purposes. There is little acknowledgement of the range of reproductive health problems women face, or of those needs that may be crucial to women's health but may be unrelated to fertility reduction. As with reproductive health and unmet need, empowering women becomes part of a language of obfuscation when little is done to ascertain women's needs from women themselves, and no attempt is made to reshape the organisation of programmes so as to involve women in design, decision-making, or evaluation.

The three catchwords of the above approach—unmet need, reproductive health, and women's empowerment—require careful content analysis of their meaning and implications for policies and programmes. If they continue to be used as loosely as they are at present, then there is a danger of quick erosion and disappointment with any agreement that might be patched together in the context of the ICPD. We need a deeper probing of the ethical issues, a willingness to examine and set right the problems as articulated by the largely female targets of current policies and programmes, and an acknowledgement that empowering women means a fundamental transformation in relations of power.

2. DIMENSIONS OF A NEW DIRECTION
Rebuilding agreement on population policies among those who are not opposed in principle to birth control technologies[1] requires, in my opinion, rethinking along five

dimensions: the ethical basis of policies, their objectives, the strategies employed to achieve those objectives, programme methods, and technologies.[2]

2.1 The ethical basis

Ethical discussions on population policy generally focus on whether there is a justification for some degree of coercion of individuals by the state. This is premised on the belief that the reproductive behaviour of individuals is likely to be antithetical to the public good or social welfare. Working from this premise, the role of policy is perceived to be to bring individual behaviour into line with the public good. It is worth noting that, with this as justification, states have devised policies not only to reduce population growth rates but also to increase them.[3]

While there has been some discussion of the ethics of incentives and disincentives and of more severe forms of coercion, certain fundamental questions remain largely unaddressed. Who defines the public interest, and can governments be trusted to do so impartially? (This problem of trust operates at both supra- and sub-national levels. Southern countries do not trust the intentions of Northern countries with regard to population, and many poor women and men in the South do not trust the government functionaries of family planning programmes.) What if there are few or no institutions or mechanisms for appeal or redressal of grievances? What are the potential biases when policies attempt to modify individual behaviour in societies where there are wide class and gender inequities? What if the pronatalist behaviour of individuals is driven by survival needs such as insurance against old age insecurity, the income from children's labour, women's need to protect themselves against childlessness or absence of sons in societies where these are negatively viewed? The answers to these questions may imply that the abstract presumption that it makes sense to modify individual behaviour in the presumed public interest might translate into ethically questionable programmes and practices.

Ironically, many attempts at behaviour modification in the population field do not seem to be terribly effective. Their principal result appears to be a violation of individual human rights, most often those of women. In Romania, the absence of contraceptives led to a significant rise not in birth rates, but in the number of illegal abortions. In India, the rigours of male sterilisation during the State of Emergency in the middle 1970s have made the family planning programme permanently too nervous, it seems, to promote vasectomies. While some forms of collective incentives such as those in Thailand may have been effective, private disincentives rarely seem to have the desired effect. Far better and more practical, it would seem, to create the social and developmental preconditions for people to need and want fewer children than to attempt to convince them against their own best judgement. Population policies must be voluntaristic and firmly grounded in the human rights of the individual and, in particular, the reproductive rights of women whose physical and emotional well-being is most at stake.

2.2 Policy objectives

The principal aims of policy-makers, concerned about the rate of population growth, have been largely to modify growth rates and to control the movements of people. Demographic objectives have been central. Health has not been the principal rationale, although limiting the number of births has been argued to be conducive to the health of children and women. This becomes clear when one looks more closely at programme goals which are generally stated in terms of birth rate targets (and related data such as couple protection rates and number of births averted), and not in terms of any direct measures of the health of either women or children. The welfare language being used increasingly in statements of population policy objectives[4] is rarely translated into concrete health goals. Where health goals have been explicitly integrated into population policies, for example, the Safe Motherhood initiative, or MCH (maternal and child health) programmes, they have been poorly funded (as in the case of the former), or focused on child health while largely ignoring the health of mothers.

The overemphasis on fertility in policy objectives distorts the ethical basis of programmes. If programmes are designed with fertility reduction in mind, they may exclude as irrelevant services vital to women's reproductive and sexual health (such as safe abortion services, testing and treatment of sexually transmitted diseases and reproductive tract infections), and aspects of the quality of services such as counselling and follow-up care, or services to those outside the reproductive age-groups. In addition, they will be evaluated not on the basis of whether they meet women's (or men's) reproductive health needs, but on their success in meeting fertility targets regardless of their health impacts. This can be seen more sharply by means of the following thought-experiment.

Suppose we knew that in region X women's ability to take fertility decisions is based on the following three general questions:

1. How do they assess the risks involved (and weigh potential gains and losses)?
2. Can they act on their assessment without family or community members hampering their ability to make decisions?
3. Are services available to support that action?

Now consider two different scenarios under which fertility might in fact decline in the region. In *scenario A*, the three conditions are met as follows. First, the potential costs of bearing children are increased through a set of disincentives reducing schooling and health services for higher parity children as well as restricting the household's access to the public distribution system that supplies essential consumption goods to low income groups; the potential benefits are also eroded through persistent and acute unemployment, and erosion of the asset base without opportunities for children to earn incomes through employment. Second, women's reproductive decision-making is enhanced as a result of male desertion, the rise of female-headed households, or increased nucleation of households under severe economic pressure. Third, birth control services are available through both private providers and an official family planning programme, but they include only sterilisation, long-acting hormonals, IUDs and some oral contraceptives, but not abortion services, or barrier methods that would also protect against STDs and HIV infection.

Scenario B presents a somewhat different picture. Here, the potential benefits from child labour are reduced through well-managed employment programmes and a public distribution system, while the need for the labour of girl children is reduced through better provision of safe water and domestic fuel. Second, women's autonomy to make reproductive and other decisions is enhanced through programmes focused on improving their asset base and access to money incomes; through the formation of women's groups for support and increasing knowledge and access; and through male education for involvement and responsibility. Third, a range of reproductive health services are provided including counselling and safe abortion services through local health facilities in whose evaluation women have a voice.

The two scenarios described above are not as extreme as they seem in cold print: scenario A is only too close to the truth in many countries. The birth rate may well fall equally under either scenario; there is little empirical reason to believe that the decline will be greater under one or the other. Indeed, if one examines the experience of countries which have had significant fertility declines during the last two decades, one encounters a bewildering range of conditions. It is clear which scenario is preferable from the perspective of women's health and well-being. But if policies are enunciated with largely demographic objectives, *then there is no reason to prefer scenario B over A*. This is a dilemma that population policy-makers find themselves confronting today. Furthermore, if the primary objective of policy is demographic, then secondary objectives such as health may well be sacrificed to the primary one under pretexts of financial stringency, institutional incapacity, or the overweening importance of demographic pressure. For all these reasons, I believe that policy objectives must be informed by their ethical base. If the ethical basis of population policy is voluntarism with support for the human rights of the individual and the reproductive rights of women, then the objective cannot be demographic. The aim of policy must be to enhance the sexual and reproductive health of people, women in particular.

2.3 Programme strategies

The chief programme strategy used by official population policies has been the family planning programme. In terms of their objective of fertility decline, family planning programmes have been judged both in terms of input indicators measuring the 'strength' of programmes (Mauldin & Ross 1991) and output indicators related to their impact on fertility. The latter have typically depended on proxies such as the contraceptive acceptance rate, continuation rate, prevalence rate, and couple years of protection. Jain and Bruce (forthcoming 1994) discuss these measures and propose an alternative that would be sensitive to the extent to which a family planning programme assists individuals to fulfil their reproductive intentions in a healthful manner. Measures of programme efficacy should be guided, they argue, by the extent to which a programme is client-centred. Quality of services would become central to such an efficacy measure (which would address both unwanted pregnancy and unnecessary morbidity). If programme evaluation measures were more sensitive to reproductive health, then programmes would themselves have to be modified in line with their performance according to those measures.

Transforming family planning programmes to meet the reproductive intentions of individuals can only be one part of a new strategy. A full range of sexual and reproductive health services should have three guiding principles: serving the underserved, providing missing services, and improving the quality of existing services. Typically, both the old and the young tend to get left out of services because they are perceived as being outside the childbearing ages. This perception is, of course, untrue for adolescents, but social taboos and cultural fears operate to keep young people out of many services as well as from meaningful sex education. Missing services include not only those such as safe abortion and STD treatment, which have already been mentioned, but also research into the causes and treatment of infertility (a serious problem in some regions of sub-Saharan Africa). Improving the quality of other services (such as the abortion services provided under the Medical Termination of Pregnancy Act in India) will depend in part on improvements in the system of primary care. Alternatively, they could be directly integrated into the provision of improved and reoriented family planning services.

Improving service provision is only one strategy, however. In the discussion of alternative scenarios in the previous sub-section, we saw that women's ability to make reproductive decisions depends not only on service availability, but also on their ability to act on an assessment of personal risks and benefits. Strategies to empower women therefore become crucial if the new policy objectives are to be fulfilled, but empowerment is in danger of becoming a fashionable but empty buzzword in the population debate. Rescuing it requires understanding that empowerment is fundamentally about altering the relations of power within which women are enmeshed, which constrain their options and autonomy, and adversely affect their health and wellbeing (Batliwala, forthcoming 1994).

I believe that a strategy shift to women's empowerment from the current narrow focus on women's education (generally acknowledged to be conducive to fertility decline) is needed. It would spell a positive resolution of the contradiction between an instrumental approach to women's education as a key to fertility decline and an approach based on a perception of women as legitimate social actors. While education can certainly help break down power relations, this is not automatic. Too many highly educated women with too little reproductive control would bear testimony to this. Exercising reproductive control means not only making decisions about bearing, timing and spacing children, but also being able to attend to other sexual and reproductive health needs, and taking part in decisions about sexuality itself.[5]

Women's empowerment involves altering power relations within the *home* between women and men, and between younger and older women; within the *community*, which generates and enforces a wide range of sanctions and practices affecting health (from son preference to female mutilation); *vis à vis* the *state*, whose functionaries and policy-makers ignore or downgrade women's concerns; and in relation to the *scientific community*, whose research and technology development determines the kind of contraceptive and other services that become available.

2.4 Programme methods

Programme methods flowing from these strategies will require the linking of reproductive health to strengthened primary and referral care, and improving public health infrastructure. This will be a far cry from current programme methods based on setting targets for fertility indicators and selecting human targets for programmes, incentives and disincentives to individuals and communities, and less coercive methods such as social marketing. Methods should also make a definitive break with past attempts to integrate family planning with maternal and child health care to the detriment of the latter. This paper is not the place for a detailed discussion of such attempts; they have been extensively critiqued by NGOs working in the primary health sector in countries such as India. Linking MCH with family planning has typically 'crowded' out health care especially when the same workers have been expected to provide both sets of services. The incentives or disincentives given to providers within the traditional family planning programme have tended to bias the limited time of the village level worker towards searching for and 'motivating' targets for female sterilisation.

Methods for women's empowerment range from income, employment, and credit access to informal education with consciousness and awareness building (Batliwala, forthcoming 1994). Whichever the method, group formation, building of solidarity through participatory processes, and strengthening the capacity of the poorest and most socially oppressed women appear to distinguish genuine empowerment from top-down poverty alleviation measures or welfare programmes.

Empowering women has another key component. There has been a tendency in some of the newer health programmes to shift the burden of health care increasingly on to women in the name of 'community participation'. In many third world countries, women's time and work are already under tremendous pressure both from the need to obtain cash incomes and to cope with the drudgery of providing water and fuel and coping with domestic tasks. There is much evidence of the consequences of such overwork and lack of adequate rest or leisure for women's health and nutritional status. Placing greater work burdens on women without easing the constraints imposed by the absence of the basic infrastructure for clean water, cooking fuel, fodder, or sanitation becomes a travesty of empowerment (Desai, forthcoming 1994). Over and over again, NGOs working with poor women have found that women prioritise income security and the provision of basic inputs for easing domestic drudgery, as well as basic public health infrastructure. Providing for these is key to empowering women.

2.5 Technologies

Probably the area of strongest dissatisfaction for the women's health movement is technology, both what is available and what is not available. It is also a bone of contention within the women's movement itself, with some sections holding the belief that much of the available reproductive technology (contraceptives as well as the newer reproductive technologies for fetal monitoring, infertility treatment, and genetic engineering) is dangerous and ought to be opposed. Other sections believe this is too broad-brush a picture, and that more nuance is needed which will allow for a distinction between harmful or ethically questionable technologies and beneficial ones.

Until very recently, the development of contraceptive technology has been guided by the criterion of efficacy coupled with reducing mortality risk, but with singularly little research on non-fatal side-effects or acceptability (Snow, forthcoming 1994). Mortality risk itself has been biomedically assessed, rather than as a product of both biomedical and social factors. The mortality risk from an IUD in a situation of endemic reproductive tract infection, anaemia, and poor health delivery is very different from mortality risk in their absence. Such context-specificity has generally been ignored or dismissed as a problem of service delivery and not of technology *per se.*

Women's health activists have attempted to argue in favour of user-controlled technology, but the very concept of user control is not technology-specific, but related to both the technology and the context within which it is being used. A technology that may enhance the user's autonomy in one situation might not in another. This depends upon the power relations dominant in a woman's life—those with husband, mother-in-law, male medical practitioners, or state functionaries. Rather than user control, some argue that it is more meaningful to talk in terms of the abuse-potential of a technology—-a concept that would integrate both the technical and social aspects.[6]

Whichever concept one uses, it is clear that far too little research funding and effort have been expended on barrier methods that would have few unknown long-term systemic effects, and on methods that would protect against sexually transmitted diseases.

Contraceptive testing has also come in for severe criticism; guidelines for clinical trials of new methods are often breached in field situations where women are poor, illiterate, or have little voice when faced with a prestigious and powerful medical research establishment. In some instances, testing stopped when there was suspicion that guidelines had been breached[7]; but, in most instances, tests go on. The remedy is greater voice for women's health advocates, activists and researchers in the setting of research priorities, the monitoring of trials, and the evaluation of technologies.

3. CONCLUSION

To summarise: I believe that for population policy to address the challenge of human rights and women's empowerment honestly, the following is required: grounding in an ethics of voluntarism, the human rights of individuals, and the reproductive rights of women; setting the objectives as the enhancement of the sexual and reproductive health of individuals; choice of strategies that will improve and enhance health and women's empowerment; adoption of methods that will link the provision of reproductive health services to strengthened primary health care and improved public health infrastructure, while promoting empowerment of women; and incorporation of women's health concerns in the development and testing of technologies.

Some movement along these directions can already be seen. For example, the Human Reproduction Programme of the WHO has started making attempts to involve women in technology development. However, powerful interests are also invested in the status quo. It would be all too easy for policy makers, international and national, to pay lip-service to catchy new phrases while avoiding the difficulties inherent in altering funding streams, or changing the content or management of programmes. Genuine change will require both conviction and courage. Can policy-makers meet the challenge?

NOTES

[1] Even so simple a clause as this is subject to caveats in the current charged atmosphere. First, some would argue that although they favour women's access to birth control, they oppose any notion of population policy; they believe that states have no business

interfering with or controlling birth rates or population movements. Second, a section of the women's movement strongly opposes the newer reproductive technologies (genetic engineering in particular) and tends to be ambiguous about other technologies. A third caveat is that population policy clearly is about larger issues than the focus of this paper; in particular, I do not address the complex issues around migration, but only focus on birth and death-related policies.

[2]   For a more detailed discussion of some of these, see Sen, German and Chen (1994).

[3]   Both Singapore, with its attempt to raise the birth rate of women with higher education, and Romania under Ceaucescu, are examples of the latter.

[4]   The Indian family planning programme was renamed the family welfare programme after the 1970s, but with relatively little substantive change towards welfare in the programme.

[5]   In much of the world, a woman is the last person to have a say in sexual access to her own body.

[6]   I first heard this term described by Judith Richter at a workshop on the politics of reproduction at the Harvard Center for Population and Development Studies in May 1993.

[7]   Brazilian trials of Norplant were halted after extensive mobilisation by the women's health movement.

REFERENCES

Batliwala, S. 1994 The meaning of women's empowerment: new concepts in action. In *Population Reconsidered: Health, Empowerment and Rights* (eds. G. Sen, A. Germain & L.C. Chen). Cambridge: Harvard University Press.

Desai, S. 1994 Women's burdens: easing the structural constraints. In *Population Reconsidered: Health, Empowerment and Rights* (eds. Sen, Germain & L.C. Chen). Cambridge: Harvard University Press.

Jain, A. & Bruce, J. 1994 Objectives and efficacy of family planning programs. In *Population Reconsidered: Health, Empowerment and Rights* (eds. Sen, Germain & L.C. Chen). Cambridge: Harvard University Press.

Mauldin, W. Parker & Ross, J. A. 1991 Family planning programs: efforts and results, 1982-89. *Stud. Fam. Planning* **22** (6), pp 350–367.

National Academy of Sciences 1986 *Population Growth and Economic Development: Policy Questions.* Washington, DC: National Academy Press.

Sen, G., Germain, A. & Chen, L.C. (eds.) 1994 *Population Reconsidered: Health, Empowerment and Rights.* Cambridge: Harvard University Press.

Snow, R. (forthcoming) 1994 Contraceptive clinical trials: untapped opportunities for reproductive health research. In *Power and Decision - The Social Control of Reproduction* (eds. G. Sen & R. Snow), Cambridge: Harvard University Press.

5/4

Where do we go from here?
Sir Crispin Tickell

At this conference, we have had an intellectual banquet. Thus nourished, we must look to the future. How do we get from where we are to where we want to be? What can be the role of the scientific community in future?

We have looked at population issues from many perspectives: demographic, biological, economic, social and environmental. Rightly so, as population issues range widely: from the mechanics of contraception through education and social welfare to what Dr Lindahl-Kiessling elegantly called "treading lightly on the biosphere". There have been more questions than answers. As has been brought out by several speakers, in particular Professor Cleland, our ignorance of causal relationships is still deep. Demography, like economics, contains a measure of necromancy. It would be nice to think that the solutions to some of our present problems could be drawn from past experience, but in this case the past is a poor guide to the future. Our current situation is unique.

It is in essence a direct and an indirect result of the industrial revolution some 250 years ago. New methods of exploiting resources, new techniques of production and new skills have served to generate untold wealth and well-being, albeit in uneven fashion and differently in different places. There are two associated slogans: one is the notion of *development*, as if all will eventually arrive at the same destination. It carries the implication that people move from an underdeveloped childhood through developing adolescence to developed adulthood. I believe this to be a profoundly misleading analogy. Equally misleading is the slogan of *economic growth*, or treadmill of economic expansion. Both terms urgently need redefinition if we are to look sensibly at our present world and realistically at the future one.

The industrial revolution has had negative as well as positive results. We have heard about many of them during this conference. Heavy strain has been placed on natural resources, whether renewable or non-renewable. The quality of the earth's land surface has been degraded in different ways. Here I recall the speech made by Dr Zhao Qiguo. Freshwater, the lifeblood of the planet, is in increasingly short supply, as eloquently explained by Professor Malin Falkenmark. We are changing the chemistry of the atmosphere: there is acidification downwind of industry; depletion of the ozone layer with its consequences for penetration of UV-B radiation; and there is the prospect of global warming involving substantial changes in patterns of weather and a rise in sea levels. Dr Norman Myers has demonstrated the effects on the diversity of life of which we are no more than a tiny part. A point to emphasize is that environmental change in all its complex synergies is often not gradual but subject to discontinuities as thresholds are reached, and new, sometimes unwelcome, equilibriums are established.

In all these processes, population increase is the prime engine of change. In looking to where we go from here, it is vital to distinguish how such change becomes manifest to peoples and governments alike. There are identifiable pressure points or markers. Here is a somewhat arbitrary selection of them:

- In poor countries, as populations get out of kilter with natural resources, there is the prospect of continuing poverty, and accompanying famine and disease. I thought Professor Dasgupta's remarks of particular significance in this respect.

- As a consequence of population pressure, we should expect a substantial increase in the number of refugees and migrants both within and between countries. The number of refugees on the official United Nations definition rose from around 2.5 million in 1976 to some 19 million in 1992. This figure does not include economic migrants and environmental refugees which could amount to somewhere between 10 and 20 million more. Here two reports are outstanding: that of the UNFPA on *The State of the World's Population 1993*, and that of the UNHCR *State of the World's Refugees 1993*. The subject is slippery and difficult to handle. The Climate Institute (of whose Board I am Chairman) is now working on a two-year programme to give further definition to the concept of environmental refugees, and to suggest what might be done about them.

- In industrial countries, population may be broadly static, or even in decline, but with constantly improving technology, especially in automation and robotics, there are growing problems of unemployment, especially among the unskilled. In many ways, the style of living in industrial countries, far from being a model to the rest of the world, is already visibly unsustainable for more than a small proportion of the human population.

- The problems of industrial and other countries are closely associated and cannot be separated. To take the example of refugees, all such tend to move from bad conditions to better ones. Thus the southern frontier of the United States and the Mediterranean coast of Europe already attract increasing numbers of migrants. In the case of the Mediterranean, an average mother on the southern shores has five children, and one on the northern shores one or two children. On the southern shores, aquifers are drying up and there is little prospect of their replenishment.

- All countries face structural problems. Are governments, especially democratic ones, equipped to cope? Can ordinary citizens, especially women, feel that they are fully participating in the life of their societies?

- Environmental change will accentuate problems and differences of health. Pathogens are more readily dispersed with rapid travel and crowding, and quickly adapt to changes in moisture and temperature. Already we are facing increasing bacterial and viral resistance to the drugs which have in the last fifty years so improved world health.

- Finally, there are many problems of equity: horizontal equity involves distribution of the world's goods from one country or community to another; and vertical equity means the need to care for the needs of future generations. Here, Professor Chadwick had some important things to say.

Some of these pressure points are more sensitive than others. It is important that they should be recognized for what they are, and that public and political awareness of them and their inter-connectedness should increase. Hence, the particular value of this

Conference, and that of the United Nations Conference on Population and Development at Cairo in September 1994. Obviously, an international approach, symbolized by agreement at the Rio conference on the Conventions on Climate Change and Biodiversity and Agenda 21 (with the consequent Commission on Sustainable Development) is indispensable.

Industrial countries now have special responsibility for making the Rio agreements work: in particular, those concerning the environment (where around 70% of current pollution comes from industrial countries); population issues (I endorse Dr Nafis Sadik's plea that the proportion of development aid given to family planning should rise from around 1.5% to 4%); refugees (the loose cannon of the future world economy); health (the need for more effective primary care and application of the right technology); and consumption of resources (which should be in such a fashion that substitutes can be found for non-renewable resources, and renewable resources can be made genuinely renewable).

I come now to the particular role of the scientific community. Obviously, science is needed as never before in understanding problems which are scientific as well as social and economic. How can scientific advice be best expressed, and scientific influence be best exerted? All governments and international organizations, including the UN agencies, have their own character, and some take better account of scientific factors than others. But none is exempt from such major external constraints as politics, religion or ideology.

Scientific academies likewise cover a wide spectrum. "Science" itself is differently interpreted in different places. Some academies exert major influence on their governments, parliaments and public opinion; some are concerned mostly with research; and some lack real resources and status. The present meeting of academies is the first of its kind since 1914, and is unique for its focus on a broad interdisciplinary subject. It is therefore distinct from conferences held by numerous other bodies, ranging from the International Union for the Scientific Study of Population to the International Planned Parenthood Federation to the International Council of Scientific Unions. Each occupies itself with aspects of our theme, and does so very well.

It seems to me that the world's Scientific Academies have today a unique opportunity if they are able to grasp it. Science in all its complexity and interdisciplinary range without ideological encumbrance could find a voice. It is also eagerly expected, as we have heard from Dr Nafis Sadik. It could make an important contribution to the United Nations Conference she is organizing at Cairo next year. Let me suggest a list of possible action points:

- First, those returning from this Conference should try to get its many messages across to their respective governments and public opinion. It may not be easy. There are problems of culture. In most of our countries, few politicians have much understanding of science and technology.
- Those returning should also try to identify the gaps as they have been exposed during this meeting, and initiate the appropriate research programmes.
- We must recognize that continuing cooperation and coordination are essential if our voice is to be heard. No-one wants a new bureaucracy, but some structure

however light is required.
- For this purpose, I suggest that a small standing body should be established, known perhaps as the Inter-Academy Panel. It would need an address, a telephone and a fax number. Our present hosts, the Indian National Science Academy, could take on this responsibility between now and the Cairo Conference. The Panel would consist of a few members, drawn from the major sponsoring academies.
- What would the Inter-Academy Panel do? It could first take responsibility for circulating the final documents of this conference, not only to the participants and other interested bodies, but also to the Secretary-General of the United Nations. It could make the necessary administrative arrangements for maintaining contact between the Academies. It could identify and, where possible, coordinate areas of research relevant to our present purposes. It could set up working parties which would advise Academy members, governments, UN agencies and public opinion on scientific problems. It could be a point of contact and reference not only for Academies, but also for governments, UN Agencies and other scientific bodies. It could give whatever help it could to the organization of the Cairo Conference, and help follow up whatever conclusions are then reached. Finally, it could be available to take on other subjects of global and interdisciplinary character as may seem desirable in the future.

Such an Inter-Academy Panel would be something new, and would have to feel its way along. It would be better to start small and build up later if necessary. There is a useful if inexact analogy with the Inter-Governmental Panel on Climate Change (IPCC), set up in 1988 and sponsored jointly by the World Meteorological Organization and the UN Environment Programme. The IPCC established three working groups: one to assess the science of the problem, one to examine environmental and socio-economic impacts, and one to formulate response strategies. The panel also established a special committee on the participation of developing countries. The first report of the IPCC, covering all aspects, was the basic document for the Second World Climate Conference in 1990 and, with its updates in 1992, has become a standard work of reference, widely used by policy makers as well as by scientists the world over. The IPCC's next major report will be in 1995.

Obviously, an Inter-Academy Panel would be different, but its independence of governments and its scientific character would give its work particular value. That indeed is the special virtue of this conference. I give warm thanks to all those who made it possible.

Population Summit of the World's Scientific Academies

*Let 1994 be remembered as the year when the people of the world
decided to act together for the benefit of future generations.*

Representatives of national academies of science from throughout the world met in
New Delhi, India from October 24–27, 1993, in a "Science Summit" on World Population.
The conference grew out of two earlier meetings, one of the Royal Society of London
and the United States National Academy of Sciences, and the other an international
conference organized by the Royal Swedish Academy of Sciences. Statements published
by both groups* expressed a sense of urgent concern about the expansion of the world's
population and concluded that if current predictions of population growth prove accurate
and patterns of human activity on the planet remain unchanged, science and technology
may not be able to prevent irreversible degradation of the natural environment and
continued poverty for much of the world.

The New Delhi conference, organized by a group of fifteen academies**, was convened
to explore in greater detail the complex and interrelated issues of population growth,
resource consumption, socioeconomic development, and environmental protection. We
believe it to be the first large-scale collaborative activity undertaken by the world's scientific
academies.

This statement, signed by representatives of sixty academies, reflects continued concern
about the intertwined problems of rapid population growth, wasteful resource
consumption, environmental degradation, and poverty. In keeping with the critical focus
of the conference, the statement deals primarily with population. The academies believe

---

* *Population Growth, Resource Consumption. and a Sustainable World,* a joint statement by the
officers of the Royal Society of London and the U.S. National Academy of Sciences,
1992; *Statement Issued by the International Conference on Population. Natural Resources and
Development,* organized by the Royal Swedish Academy of Sciences and the Swedish Council
for Planning and Coordination of Research, Stockholm, Sweden, 30 September – 3
October, 1991; See also: *An Agenda of Science for Environment and Development into the 21st
Century,* based on a conference convened by the International Council of Scientific Unions
in Vienna, Austria, in November 1991, Cambridge University Press, 1992; *World Scientists'
Warning to Humanity,* statement signed by 1600 scientists, Union of Concerned Scientists,
1992.

** African Academy of Sciences, Australian Academy of Science, Brazilian Academy of
Sciences, Chinese Academy of Sciences, Federation of Asian Scientific Academies and
Societies, Hungarian Academy of Sciences, Indian National Science Academy, Mexican
Academy of Sciences, Royal Netherlands Academy of Arts and Sciences, Pakistan Academy
of Sciences, The Royal Society of London, Royal Swedish Academy of Sciences, Russian
Academy of Sciences, Third World Academy of Sciences, National Academy of Sciences
of the United States of America.

that ultimate success in dealing with global social, economic, and environmental problems cannot be achieved without a stable world population. The goal should be to reach zero population growth within the lifetime of our children.

In anticipation of the approaching United Nations International Conference on Population and Development in 1994, we hope that this statement will reach the attention of governments and peoples of all countries; and contribute to further discourse and appropriate policy decisions on these complex but crucially important matters. The background for the statement is to be found in the published papers of the 1993 "Science Summit".

The Growing World Population

The world is in the midst of an unprecedented expansion of human numbers. It took hundreds of thousands of years for our species to reach a population level of 10 million, only 10,000 years ago. This number grew to 100 million people about 2,000 years ago and to 2.5 billion by 1950. Within less than the span of a single lifetime, it has more than doubled to 5.5 billion in 1993.

This accelerated population growth resulted from rapidly lowered death rates (particularly infant and child mortality rates), combined with sustained high birth rates. Success in reducing death rates is attributable to several factors: increases in food production and distribution, improvements in public health (water and sanitation) and in medical technology (vaccines and antibiotics), along with gains in education and standards of living within many developing nations.

Over the last 30 years, many regions of the world have also dramatically reduced birth rates. Some have already achieved family sizes small enough, if maintained, to result eventually in a halt to population growth. These successes have led to a slowing of the world's rate of population increase. The shift from high to low death and birth rates has been called the "demographic transition."

The rate at which the demographic transition progresses worldwide will determine the ultimate level of the human population. The lag between downward shifts of death and birth rates may be many decades or even several generations, and during these periods population growth will continue inexorably. We face the prospect of a further doubling of the population within the next half century. Most of this growth will take place in developing countries.

Consider three hypothetical scenarios* for the levels of human population in the century ahead:

Fertility declines within sixty years from the current rate of 3.3 to a global replacement average of 2.1 children per woman. The current population momentum would lead to at least 11 billion people before levelling off at the end of the 21st century.

Fertility reduces to an average of 1.7 children per woman early in the next century. Human population growth would peak a 7.8 billion persons in the middle of the 21st century and decline slowly thereafter.

---

* Population Reference Bureau, *The U.N. Long-Range Population Projections: What They Tell Us*, Washington, D.C., 1992.

Fertility declines to no lower than 2.5 children per woman. Global population would grow to 19 billion by the year 2100, and to 28 billion by 2150.

The actual outcome will have enormous implications for the human condition and for the natural environment on which all life depends.

Key Determinants of Population Growth

High fertility rates have historically been strongly correlated with poverty, high childhood mortality rates, low status and educational levels of women, deficiencies in reproductive health services, and inadequate availability and acceptance of contraceptives. Falling fertility rates and the demographic transition are generally associated with improved standards of living, such as increased per capita incomes, increased life expectancy, lowered infant mortality, increased adult literacy, and higher rates of female education and employment.

Even with improved economic conditions, nations, regions, and societies will experience different demographic patterns due to varying cultural influences. The value placed upon large families (especially among under-privileged rural populations in less developed countries who benefit least from the process of development), the assurance of security for the elderly, the ability of women to control reproduction, and the status and rights of women within families and within societies are significant cultural factors affecting family size and the demand for family planning services.

Even with a demand for family planning services, the adequate availability of and access to family planning and other reproductive health services are essential in facilitating slowing of the population growth rate. Also, access to education and the ability of women to determine their own economic security influence their reproductive decisions.

Population Growth, Resource Consumption, and the Environment

Throughout history, and especially during the twentieth century, environmental degradation has primarily been a product of our efforts to secure improved standards of food, clothing, shelter, comfort, and recreation for growing numbers of people. The magnitude of the threat to the ecosystem is linked to human population size and resource use per person. Resource use, waste production and environmental degradation are accelerated by population growth. They are further exacerbated by consumption habits, certain technological developments, and particular patterns of social organization and resource management.

As human numbers further increase, the potential for irreversible changes of far reaching magnitude also increases. Indicators of severe environmental stress include the growing loss of biodiversity, increasing greenhouse gas emissions, increasing deforestation worldwide, stratospheric ozone depletion, acid rain, loss of topsoil, and shortages of water, food, and fuel-wood in many parts of the world.

While both developed and developing countries have contributed to global environmental problems, developed countries with 85% of the gross world product and 23% of its population account for the largest part of mineral and fossil-fuel consumption, resulting in significant environmental impacts. With current technologies, present levels of consumption by the developed world are likely to lead to serious negative consequences for all countries. This is especially apparent with the increases in atmospheric carbon dioxide and trace gases that have accompanied industrialization, which have the potential for changing global climate and raising sea level.

In both rich and poor countries, local environmental problems arise from direct pollution from energy use and other industrial activities, inappropriate agricultural practices, population concentration, inadequate environmental management, and inattention to environmental goals. When current economic production has been the overriding priority and inadequate attention has been given to environmental protection, local environmental damage has led to serious negative impacts on health and major impediments to future economic growth. Restoring the environment, even where still possible, is far more expensive and time consuming than managing it wisely in the first place; even rich countries have difficulty in affording extensive environmental remediation efforts.

The relationships between human population, economic development, and the natural environment are complex. Examination of local and regional case studies reveals the influence and interaction of many variables. For example, environmental and economic impacts vary with population composition and distribution, and with rural-urban and international migrations. Furthermore, poverty and lack of economic opportunities stimulate faster population growth and increase incentives for environmental degradation by encouraging exploitation of marginal resources.

Both developed and developing countries face a great dilemma in reorienting their productive activities in the direction of a more harmonious interaction with nature. This challenge is accentuated by the uneven stages of development. If all people of the world consumed fossil fuels and other natural resources at the rate now characteristic of developed countries (and with current technologies), this would greatly intensify our already unsustainable demands on the biosphere. Yet development is a legitimate expectation of less developed and transitional countries.

The Earth is Finite

The growth of population over the last half century was for a time matched by similar world-wide increases in utilizable resources. However, in the last decade food production from both land and sea has declined relative to population growth. The area of agricultural land has shrunk, both through soil erosion and reduced possibilities of irrigation. The availability of water is already a constraint in some countries. These are warnings that the earth is finite, and that natural systems are being pushed ever closer to their limits.

Quality of Life and the Environment

Our common goal is improving the quality of life for all people, those living today and succeeding generations, ensuring their social, economic, and personal well-being with guarantees of fundamental human rights; and allowing them to live harmoniously with a protected environment. We believe that this goal can be achieved, provided we are willing to undertake the requisite social change. Given time, political will, and intelligent use of science and technology, human ingenuity can remove many constraints on improving human welfare worldwide, finding substitutes for wasteful practices, and protecting the natural environment.

But time is short and appropriate policy decisions are urgently needed. The ability of humanity to reap the benefits of its ingenuity depends on its skill in governance and management, and on strategies for dealing with problems such as widespread poverty, increased numbers of aged persons, inadequate health care and limited educational opportunities for large groups of people, limited capital for investment, environmental degradation in every region of the world, and unmet needs for family planning services in both developing and developed countries. In our judgement, humanity's ability to deal successfully with its social, economic, and environmental problems will require the achievement of zero population growth within the lifetime of our children.

Human Reproductive Health

The timing and spacing of pregnancies are important for the health of the mother, her children, and her family. Most maternal deaths are due to unsafe practices in terminating pregnancies, a lack of readily available services for high-risk pregnancies, and women having too many children or having them too early and too late in life.

Millions of people still do not have adequate access to family planning services and suitable contraceptives. Only about one-half of married women of reproductive age are currently practicing contraception. Yet as the director-general of UNICEF put it, "Family planning could bring more benefits to more people at less cost than any other single technology now available to the human race". Existing contraceptive methods could go far toward alleviating the unmet need if they were available and used in sufficient numbers, through a variety of channels of distribution, sensitively adapted to local needs.

But most contraceptives are for use by women, who consequently bear the risks to health. The development of contraceptives for male use continues to lag. Better contraceptives are needed for both men and women, but developing new contraceptive approaches is slow and financially unattractive to industry. Further work is needed on an ideal spectrum of contraceptive methods that are safe, efficacious, easy to use and deliver, reasonably priced, user-controlled and responsive, appropriate for special populations and age cohorts, reversible, and at least some of which protect against sexually transmitted diseases, including AIDS.

Reducing fertility rates, however, cannot be achieved merely by providing more contraceptives. The demand for these services has to be addressed. Even when family planning and other reproductive health services are widely available, the social and economic status of women affects individual decisions to use them. The ability of women to make decisions about family size is greatly affected by gender roles within society and in sexual relationships. Ensuring equal opportunity for women in all aspects of society is crucial.

Thus all reproductive health services must be implemented as a part of broader strategies to raise the quality of human life. They must include the following:

- efforts to reduce and eliminate gender-based inequalities. Women and men should have equal opportunities and responsibilities in sexual, social, and economic life.
- provision of convenient family planning and other reproductive health services

with a wide variety of safe contraceptive options, irrespective of an individual's ability to pay.

- encouragement of voluntary approaches to family planning and elimination of unsafe and coercive practices.
- development policies that address basic needs such as clean water, sanitation, broad primary health care measures and education; and that foster empowerment of the poor and women.

"The adoption of a smaller family norm, with consequent decline in total fertility, should not be viewed only in demographic terms. It means that people, and particularly women, are empowered and are taking control of their fertility and the planning of their lives; it means that children are born by choice, not by chance, and that births are better planned; and it means that families are able to invest relatively more in a smaller number of beloved children, trying to prepare them for a better future."*

Sustainability of the Natural World as Everyone's Responsibility

In addressing environmental problems, all countries face hard choices. This is particularly so when it is perceived that there are short-term tradeoffs between economic growth and environmental protection, and where there are limited financial resources. But the downside risks to the earth—our environmental life support system—over the next generation and beyond are too great to ignore. Current trends in environmental degradation from human activities combined with the unavoidable increase in global population will take us into unknown territory.

Other factors, such as inappropriate governmental policies, also contribute in nearly every case. Many environmental problems in both rich and poor countries appear to be the result of policies that are misguided even when viewed on short-term economic grounds. If a longer-term view is taken, environmental goals assume an even higher priority.

The prosperity and technology of the industrialized countries give them greater opportunities and greater responsibility for addressing environmental problems worldwide. Their resources make it easier to forestall and to ameliorate local environmental problems. Developed countries need to become more efficient in both resource use and environmental protection, and to encourage an ethic that eschews wasteful consumption. If prices, taxes, and regulatory policies include environmental costs, consumption habits will be influenced. The industrialized countries need to assist developing countries and communities with funding and expertise in combating both global and local environmental problems. Mobilizing "technology for environment" should be an integral part of this new ethic of sustainable development.

For all governments it is essential to incorporate environmental goals at the outset in legislation, economic planning, and priority setting; and to provide appropriate incentives for public and private institutions, communities, and individuals to operate in environmentally benign ways. Tradeoffs between environmental and economic goals

---

*Mahmoud F. Fathalla, "Family Planning and Reproductive Health: A Global Overview," invited paper presented at the 1993 Science Summit, Delhi, India, 26 October 1993.

can be reduced through wise policies. For dealing with global environmental problems, all countries of the world need to work collectively through treaties and conventions, as has occurred with such issues as global climate change and biodiversity, and to develop innovative financing mechanisms that facilitate environmental protection.

What Science and Technology can contribute toward enhancing the Human Prospect

As scientists cognizant of the history of scientific progress and aware of the potential of science for contributing to human welfare, it is our collective judgment that continuing population growth poses a great risk to humanity. Furthermore, it is not prudent to rely on science and technology alone to solve problems created by rapid population growth, wasteful resource consumption, and poverty.

The natural and social sciences are nevertheless crucial for developing new understanding so that governments and other institutions can act more effectively, and for developing new options for limiting population growth, protecting the natural environment, and improving the quality of human life.

Scientists, engineers, and health professionals should study and provide advice on:

- Cultural, social, economic, religious, educational, and political factors that affect reproductive behavior, family size, and successful family planning.
- Conditions for human development, including the impediments that result from economic inefficiencies; social inequalities; and ethnic, class, or gender biases.
- Global and local environmental change (affecting climate, biodiversity, soils, water, air), its causes (including the roles of poverty, population growth, economic growth, technology, national and international politics), and policies to mitigate its effects.
- Strategies and tools for improving all aspects of education and human resource development, with special attention to women.
- Improved family planning programs, contraceptive options for both sexes, and other reproductive health services, with special attention to needs of women; and improved general primary health care, especially maternal and child health care.
- Transitions to economies that provide increased human welfare with less consumption of energy and materials.
- Improved mechanisms for building indigenous capacity in the natural sciences, engineering, medicine, social sciences, and management in developing countries, including an increased capability of conducting integrated interdisciplinary assessments of societal issues.
- Technologies and strategies for sustainable development (agriculture, energy, resource use, pollution control, materials recycling, environmental management and protection).
- Networks, treaties, and conventions that protect the global commons.
- Strengthened world-wide exchanges of scientists in education, training, and research.

Action is needed now

Humanity is approaching a crisis point with respect to the interlocking issues of population, environment, and development. Scientists today have the opportunity and responsibility to mount a concerted effort to confront our human predicament. But science and technology can only provide tools and blueprints for action and social change. It is the governments and international decision-makers, including those meeting in Cairo next September at the United Nations International Conference on Population and Development, who hold the key to our future. We urge them to take incisive action now and to adopt an integrated policy on population and sustainable development on a global scale. With each year's delay the problems become more acute. Let 1994 be remembered as the year when the people of the world decided to act together for the benefit of future generations.

The Summit Statement has been endorsed by the following signatories:

Academy of Sciences of Albania
Australian Academy of Science
Austrian Academy of Sciences
Bangladesh Academy of Sciences
Academy of Sciences of Belarus
National Academy of Sciences of Bolivia
Brazilian Academy of Sciences
Bulgarian Academy of Sciences
Royal Society of Canada
Caribbean Academy of Sciences
Chinese Academy of Sciences
Columbian Academy of Exact, Physical, and Natural
    Sciences
Croatian Academy of Sciences and Arts
Cuban Academy of Sciences
Academy of Sciences of the Czech Republic
Royal Danish Academy of Sciences and Letters
Academy of Scientific Research and Technology,
    Egypt
Estonian Academy of Sciences
Federation of Asian Scientific Academies and
    Societies
Delegation of the Finnish Academies of Science
    and Letters
French Academy of Sciences
Conference of the German Academies of Sciences
Ghana Academy of Arts and Sciences
Academy of Athens, Greece
Hungarian Academy of Sciences
Indian National Science Academy
Iranian Academy of Sciences
Israel Academy of Sciences and Humanities
Kazakhstan National Academy of Sciences

Royal Scientific Society, Jordan
Kenya National Academy of Sciences
National Academy of Sciences, Republic of Korea
Latvian Academy of Sciences
Lithuanian Academy of Sciences
Macedonian Academy of Sciences and Arts
Malaysian Scientific Association
National Academy of Sciences, Mexico
Academy of Sciences of Moldova
Mongolian Academy of Sciences
Academy of the Kingdom of Morocco
Royal Nepal Academy of Science and Technology
Royal Netherlands Academy of Arts and Sciences
Nigerian Academy of Science
Norwegian Academy of Science and Letters
Pakistan Academy of Sciences
National Academy of Science and Technology,
    Philippines
Polish Academy of Sciences
Romanian Academy of Sciences
Russian Academy of Sciences
Slovak Academy of Sciences
Slovenian Academy of Sciences and Arts
Royal Swedish Academy of Sciences
Conference of the Swiss Scientific Academies
Third World Academy of Sciences
Uganda National Academy of Science and
    Technology
Ukrainian Academy of Sciences
Royal Society of London
National Academy of Sciences of the United States
    of America
National Academy of Physics, Mathematics, and
    Natural Sciences of Venezuela

Annex A.
Contribution of the Académie Des Sciences (Paris) to the Conference of the Science Academies on World Population

The Academy of Sciences of the Institut de France signs the Declaration submitted to the New Delhi Conference of the Academies of Sciences, for it approves its central message as well as many of its recommendations, and it joins fully in the alarm raised with all governments, all political, cultural and religious groupings in the world.

Such an appeal should encourage all the scientific and technical community to work effectively, by research, information and education, towards a better equilibrium, where the differences in the evolution of local populations could be reduced.

Considerations of the Pontifical Academy of Sciences on the occasion of the Population Summit

On the occasion of the Population Summit in New Delhi, the Pontifical Academy of Sciences, though participating only in the quality of observer, has been invited to present its considerations on the topic under discussion, object of study within the Academy for some time.

1. The world today faces a new, complex and in many ways worrisome situation, deriving from growth in population, increasing use of resources, deterioration of the environment and an ever greater imbalance between countries and segments of population. At the same time, scientific, technological and organizational progress is generating enormous possibilities for economic growth, which nevertheless tends to be concentrated in the most developed countries.

These problems are tightly intertwined. They can neither be examined nor resolved separately.

To highlight the complex interplay involved in population and development matters, the Pontifical Academy of Sciences organized a meeting in November 1991 entitled *Resources and Population.* This meeting noted the effective existence of the demographic problem and analysed its intrinsic connection with many other parameters, in particular those relating to resource availability and environment. The Pontifical Academy of Sciences is convinced that containment of birth rates is only one aspect of the complex array of problems to be addressed to ensure a sustainable development. These problems must be faced keeping in mind the differing circumstances in the various regions of the world.

2. Turning to the present situation and its predictable consequences over coming decades, the enormous disparities between countries, mortality rates – mostly infant – and rates of fertility and development are immediately apparent. On the one hand, the least developed countries (over 40 of which in particular are classified as at minimum development by the United Nations) face a very difficult future. On the other, there are the rich countries with very low fertility and rapidly ageing populations. Differentiated policies are required, with particular attention paid to the most disadvantaged classes in the first case and decisive support to critical family needs in the second. Among others, the phenomenon of the macroscopic growth of megalopolis calls for reflection. Megalopolis, above all in developing countries, brings a variety of problems which are proving difficult to overcome.

In the more distant future, the need for containment of birth rates emerges. This is required to prevent a further surge of irresolvable problems which are bound to occur if we turn our backs on our responsibility toward future generations. An example could be useful: no one can say with any reasonable degree of precision what the sustainable population of Africa might be, but certainly unlimited fertility cannot be maintained for long. Action to reduce the fertility rate, even if undertaken now, could only have an effect after 30–35 years.

But the pressing nature of the problem should not make us forget other needs, nor lead us into error in putting forward modes of intervention: applying methods which are not in accordance with the true nature of the human person actually leads to tragic consequences.

Demographic growth must therefore be approached with special attention, bearing in mind the multifold aspects of the life and nature of human beings, singularly and collectively. As Pope John Paul II underscored in his address on the occasion of the *Resources and Population* Meeting held at the Pontifical Academy of Sciences, 'Population growth has to be faced not only by the exercise of responsible parenthood which respects the divine law, but also by economic means which have a profound effect on social institutions. Particularly in the developing countries…it is necessary to eliminate the grave shortage of adequate structures for ensuring education, the spread of culture and professional training' (Pope John Paul II, Discourse to the Pontifical Academy of Sciences, 22 November 1991, n.6).

3. Analysis of economic growth rates shows that disparities between developed (or industrialised) and developing countries remain profound. Dramatic imbalances also emerge within developing countries. The situation appears, however, to be very different according to geographic area. Some parts of the South have begun to grow rapidly (for example in regions of Asia), whereas others (for example in regions of Africa) are regressing.

From these analyses (covering areas, sectors, problems, resources and needs), several positive elements emerge, making possible the hope and the conviction that – provided there is an adequate 'level of government' (above all centred on investment in human resources) – underdevelopment can be overcome, both in social and economic terms.

It is necessary that the governments and peoples of developed countries understand that it is in their primary interest, as well as in the intent of global solidarity, to ensure that development in developing countries takes place in the most complete way and as rapidly as possible. Within the least developed countries, progress towards equity and efficiency and, in general, toward economic democracy are equally necessary. Without this, in the pessimistic scenario of the permanence and exacerbation of economic and social imbalances between developing and developed countries, and within developing countries themselves, both social tension and unrest – and hence political–military disorder – as well as the pressure to emigrate, will become irresistible.

4. Humanity uses finite natural resources in quantities enormously greater than in the past in rich countries, to maintain a lifestyle based on consumption and wasteful expenditure; in poor countries, to support rapidly growing populations. Technologies for resource efficiency, or to substitute scarce resources, are already available – but only in industrialized countries. They thus are not utilized today by those most in need.

The environment is being threatened, if not damaged in an irreversible way, by human activity. This, for the first time, is producing quantities of pollutants comparable with, or superior to, those generated by natural phenomena, with the risk of distorting the balance of nature and climate.

Food production could still be improved to sustain the presently increasing population if crops and production technologies were properly matched to demand, but imbalances between the major regions of the world are accentuating, and shortage of water, degradation of soils and the negative consequences of intensive agriculture on the environment are creating constraints that are difficult to overcome.

In these conditions, it becomes imperative to find a feasible path for development. In other words, to find a path representing real progress in the human condition. A path that does not deny future generations the possibility of continuing to advance and does not undermine our very bases for survival. Moreover, it is important to find a path that respects the environment and natural resources, as well as economic, social and cultural conditions.

With regard to resources, we must consider not only natural basic resources, but even more those resources which can effectively be used by the application of human intelligence, spirit of initiative and labour.

5. We certainly must also question whether the economic, financial, demographic, politico-administrative, scientific and technological conditions that would allow people to find an acceptable lifestyle, without being constrained to live their whole lives in severe deprivation or to emigrate in mass, exist in developing countries, or whether they can be created in a reasonable time frame.

We also have to ask what commitment and what sacrifice technologically advanced societies are willing to accept to achieve at a global level an economy with more equal and more efficient distribution of resources. Consciousness of planetary solidarity is required, and only this will enable us to face the enormous problems, in part resulting from demographic growth, with any possibility of success.

6. Different education levels between and within peoples (for example, in developed countries, vis-a-vis foreign immigrants) risk becoming structural and also making permanent the stratification between rich and poor. This is also due to the fact that, today, more than ever, education represents a necessary strategic resource, both for the process of modernization and to allow the new technologies to be used, and not just developed.

The education and condition of women is particularly penalized today in most developing countries, in part due to complex cultural choices; this must be accorded top priority. It is required both as a matter of equity and as a condition to attain demographic restraint through responsible regulation of conception, lower infant mortality rates, better child care, higher participation in the work force. A new condition for the family and for women thus represents a fundamental element for greater human dignity, as well as for a more rapid process of development.

7. Medical progress has lowered infant mortality and lengthened life expectancies. Scientific and technological progress has brought about a real change in the conditions of life. But 'these new conditions must be met not only with scientific reasoning, but more importantly with recourse to all available intellectual and spiritual energies. People need to rediscover the moral significance of respecting limits; they must grow and mature in the sense of responsibility with regard to every aspect of life' (*ibid.*, n.6).

8. Also in terms of economics and of resource availability, the relationship between

developed and developing countries must be addressed with policies and government tools in many cases adapted to the global level (for example, the freeing of resources through controlled disarmament, foreign debt, North–South transfer). In other cases, a supranational intergovernmental approach is necessary for large geographical areas.

All this does not eliminate the need for developing countries themselves to constitute the root of their development. External aid alone cannot ensure development. International solidarity must always be associated with subsidiarity: what can be decided at a lower level should not be decided at a higher. This also touches the problem of the relationship between individual freedom and levels of government.

9. Particular attention must be paid to the time factor.

Until the middle of the last century, change in the world could be seen in terms of a slow and gradual evolution. Population, production, consumption of raw materials, energy and even culture may have varied rapidly from one country to another, but at the global level the variations were very slow.

In the 20th century, these transformations have accelerated at an increasingly faster pace. For the first time, the period of global change had become first shorter than the span of a human life, and then shorter than the interval between two generations. In a decade, more books have been produced than all those written in previous ages. The transmission of understanding from one generation to the next no longer constitutes the predominant part of knowledge.

On the other hand, the consequences of what we do today can make themselves felt for a very long time. The probability of damaging the environment in an irreversible way, changing the climate and provoking the disappearance of animal and plant species as an effect of human activity, has never been so high as it is today.

We must therefore take some action even though all the necessary information is not available and past experience is all we can depend upon. Not to act may have very grave consequences. The status quo, from being a condition of stability, is becoming a guarantee of instability, of profound, rapid and broadly unpredictable change.

10. To resolve these issues, we need to act quickly, in depth and on a scale that is without precedent. Effective action calls, however, for an effort in spiritual renewal, training one's conscience in the sense of responsibility, teaching moderation in consumption patterns and behaviour, seeking equilibrium between free choice and the common good, between the consensus of citizens and authority. 'It is the responsibility of the public authorities, within the limits of their legitimate competence, to issue directives which reconcile the containment of births and respect for the free and personal assumption of responsibility by individuals. A political programme which respects the nature of the human person can influence demographic developments, but it should be accompanied by a redistribution of economic resources among citizens. Otherwise such provisions can risk placing the heaviest burden on the poorest and weakest sectors of society, thus adding injustice to injustice' (*ibid.*, n.6).

Action at the right level of government (world, international, by great regions, national) must take as its basis solidarity, interdependence, subsidiarity, efficiency and equity. These express lines of behaviour from which all men and women of good will can, and must, draw their inspiration.

Statement by the African Academy of Sciences
at the Population Summit

The African Academy of Sciences has studied the draft statement intended to be issued at the Population Summit of the World Scientific Academies, and wishes to comment as follows:

1. Care must be taken to acknowledge that while current rates of population growth and even absolute rates of population sizes may and are a problem for particular countries, for Africa population remains an important resource for development without which the continent's natural resources will remain latent and unexplored. Human resource development must therefore form part of the population/resource issue. The forthcoming 1994 U.N. International conference on Population and Development must receive the message clearly.

2. Part of the complexity of the population issue is that there are wide variations both between and within regions and countries. Consequently, the strategic planning needs of each country and region could vary very dramatically. Therefore, defining population as a global problem without qualification obscures this dimension. There cannot, therefore, be one target for all countries at all times. An African agenda would be very different.

3. Population policy is not only about fertility regulation. Fertility is only one parameter that requires management. Policies relating to the entire health sector, migration and urbanization and socio-economic conditions (especially that of women) in a nation are important elements in an effective population policy.

4. For most African couples, marriage is not only for companionship but also, most importantly, for procreation. The statement completely ignores that for certain parts of Africa infertility is a major problem. Family planning should also be designed to look into the problems of infertility, so that couples who so desire may be able to procreate and meet their life desires.

5. To imply that family planning is the panacea for fertility regulation and even development is at least simplistic. An understanding of the social and cultural milieu of African societies is central to an analysis of the success or failure or the intrinsic value or otherwise of family planning programmes. In Africa, many of the so-called impediments to family planning have a rationality which require careful assessment.

6. Whether or not the Earth is finite will depend on the extent to which science and technology is able to transform the resources available for humanity. There is only one Earth – yes; but the potential for transforming it is not necessarily finite.

7. The international economic environment in which Africa's development policies and programmes are defined and executed is an important variable in the population debate. The contribution of the North to Africa's population predicament must be acknowledged in any suggestions as to how that situation is to be confronted.

8. The Summit statement should envision specific actions and collaborative strategies by the various Academies in the wake of the Cairo conference. A special panel on population and development could be set up by the Scientific Academies to develop and refine such actions and strategies.

Academies that submitted written comments on the draft Population Summit Statement prepared by the US National Academy of Sciences in conjunction with the Royal Swedish Academy of Science, the Indian National Science Academy and the Royal Society.

Australian Academy of Science
Austrian Academy of Sciences
Brazilian Academy of Sciences
Bangladesh Academy of Sciences
Bulgarian Academy of Sciences
Royal Society of Canada
Caribbean Academy of Sciences
Croatian Academy of Sciences and Arts
Academy of Sciences of The Czech Republic
Academy of Sciences of Estonia
French Académie des Sciences
Conference of the German Academies of Sciences
Ghana Academy of Arts and Sciences
Hungarian Academy of Sciences
The Israel Academy of Sciences and Humanities
Latvian Academy of Sciences
Malaysian Scientific Association
Academy of Sciences of Moldova
Academy of The Kingdom of Morocco
Royal Netherlands Academy of Arts and Sciences
Pakistan Academy of Sciences
Polish Academy of Sciences
Russian Academy of Sciences
Third World Academy of Sciences
Conference of the Swiss Scientific Academies
Royal Institute, Thailand
Uganda National Academy of Science and Technology

Index